SWITZERLAND 1978
(Including Liechtenstein)

FODOR'S MODERN GUIDES
Founded by Eugene Fodor

EDITORIAL STAFF

ROBERT C. FISHER
editor
RICHARD MOORE
executive editor, London
LESLIE BROWN
managing editor
DOROTHY FOSTER
research director

PRODUCTION STAFF

C.R. BLOODGOOD
director
EILEEN ROLPH
managing director, London

ADVERTISING STAFF

E.W. NEWSOM
director
SANDRA LANG
assistant director

FODOR'S
Switzerland 1978

(Including Liechtenstein)

Illustrated edition with map and city plans

Created by Eugene Fodor

MARGARET ZELLERS
Area Editor

ROBERT C. FISHER
Editor

LESLIE BROWN
Managing Editor

HODDER AND STOUGHTON

© 1978 FODOR'S MODERN GUIDES, INC.
ISBN-0-679-00280-4 (McKay edition)
ISBN 0-340-22434-7 (Hodder edition)

The following Fodor Travel Books are current in 1978:

AREA GUIDES:

AUSTRALIA, NEW ZEALAND
 & SOUTH PACIFIC
CANADA
CARIBBEAN, BAHAMAS
 AND BERMUDA
EUROPE
EUROPE ON A BUDGET

INDIA
JAPAN AND KOREA
MEXICO
SCANDINAVIA
SOUTH AMERICA
SOUTHEAST ASIA
SOVIET UNION

U.S.A. (1 vol.)

COUNTRY GUIDES:

AUSTRIA
BELGIUM AND
 LUXEMBOURG
CZECHOSLOVAKIA
EGYPT
FRANCE
GERMANY
GREAT BRITAIN
GREECE
HOLLAND
HUNGARY*

IRAN
IRELAND
ISRAEL
ITALY
MOROCCO
PORTUGAL
SPAIN
SWITZERLAND
TUNISIA*
TURKEY
YUGOSLAVIA

USA GUIDES:

FAR WEST*
HAWAII
MID-ATLANTIC*
MID-WEST*
NEW ENGLAND*

NEW YORK AND
 NEW JERSEY*
ROCKIES AND PLAINS*
SOUTH*
SOUTHWEST*

CITY GUIDES:

LONDON
VENICE*

PARIS
VIENNA

PEKING

LANGUAGE GUIDE:

EUROPE TALKING*

SPECIAL INTEREST GUIDES:

CRUISES EVERYWHERE
INDIAN AMERICA
OLD WEST*
OLD SOUTH*

ONLY-IN-AMERICA VACATIONS*
OUTDOORS AMERICA*
RAILWAYS OF THE WORLD
SEASIDE AMERICA*

LATEST ADDITIONS TO THE SERIES:

JORDAN AND THE HOLY LAND

BRAZIL

*Not available in Hodder and Stoughton editions.

MANUFACTURED IN THE UNITED STATES OF AMERICA

CONTENTS

CONTENTS

EDITORS' FOREWORD

Switzerland is the heart of the matter of Europe. Not only is it geographically right in the center, but its network of roads-with-tunnels, plus telephone, telegraph and postal services and the Swiss Federal Railways, are firm spokes to all of the continent. And its scenery is unmatched—with Alpine peaks, rolling fields, vast lakes with comfortable lakeboats an a southern canton (the Ticino) where palm trees line the lakefront and Italian traditions give a new look to the Switzerland you have been led to expect.

Switzerland is clean and efficient and, while prices may be high, you will get what you pay for. Setting a precedent now followed by several of its neighbors, Switzerland was the first to offer its Holiday Card, which you may purchase in 8-day, 15-day and one-month versions, for 1st- or 2nd-class travel. Since the national network of trains, postal buses, trams and lakeboats ties the entire mountainous mass together, you can go anywhere at whatever time you wish, at a fee you have already paid.

An innovation of recent seasons is the Swiss Travel Invention—a series of coupon books, color coded to the cost of the facilities included, so that you know, a⊙ the time you purchase your booklet, just exactly what your hotel room will cost, and what towns will give you tours, gifts, maps and extra services with the STI.

We mention both these gimmicks so that you see clearly that the Swiss have your best interests at heart. The goal of the effective and informative Swiss National Tourist Office is to open its country for travelers, to show them the best ways to tour on their own—whether their interests run to mountain climbing, learning to yodel, bicycling, studying languages, or just plain wandering around at will. The Swiss make it easy.

In a country that has four national languages, most travel routes are clearly identified by symbol. You'll have no problem getting around, and we urge you do do so with a minimum of baggage—mental and actual. The democratic Swiss have never made a fuss over finery. The less you carry with you in the way of luggage, the happier your travels will be.

This 1978 edition of Switzerland appears in our new format,

designed to put the information before you as clearly as possible. We've set the scene at the start, with special features on Swiss history, traditions, foods, and sports, including a special section on walking tours in the Valais, one of the southern cantons with some of the most challenging Alpine peaks.

Then we touch on highlights of the 22 cantons of Switzerland, the separate districts of the country that present so many different facets to visitors. We start at Geneva, that cosmopolitan, international city, and follow Lac Leman to the cantons of Neuchâtel, Fribourg and Jura before going to Basel, tucked in a border niche between France and Germany. The Rhineland leads us to Zurich and the places around the Zurichsee before we head into northeastern Switzerland. Bern and the Bernese Oberland, another of the country's rugged mountain regions, comes next, with Lucerne and central Switzerland, which are perhaps the most touristed parts of the country, and the place where Switzerland began. The unique cantons of Grisons, the Valais and the Ticino each have their own chapters—with highlights of these very different regions. Hotels and restaurants are mentioned for all the areas, but in this edition, for the first time, they are presented with the specific facts about travel at the end of the book. Some shops are also listed, and special features are included for the big hubs of Bern, Basel, Geneva, Lausanne, Lucerne and Zurich. The principality of Liechtenstein, a special fragment of Europe, is covered in a special chapter, with background, hotels, restaurants and touring suggestions.

* * *

This 1978 edition ushers in a new era for the Switzerland guide. John and Moira Hawkes, well-known British travel-writing and editing team, have worked tirelessly on the Swiss book for the past several years, sharing with you the expert knowledge they have of one of their favorite countries on the continent. With this edition, Margaret Zellers, well-known American travel journalist, whose book on Swiss Country Inns has led many travelers into the less known areas of Switzerland, is area editor. We continue to be indebted to the Hawkes for their background material, which is included in this edition, and to many with whom we have worked in the past—namely those in the London office of the Swiss National Tourist Office; the Pro Helvetica Foundation in Zurich through Dr. C. Doka; Dr. Werner Kämpfen, General Manager of the Swiss National Tourist Office in Zurich, and Mr. Fred Birmann, his press officer; Dr. Roy W. Hunziker, Assistant Secretary of the Press and Information Divison of the Swiss Political Department; Swissair personnel in New York, including Dr. Hugo Mayr and the public relations staff; Mr. Kenneth Westcott Jones for his feature on steam railways; and personnel in the Swiss National Tourist Office in New York, especially Mr. Bruno Baroni and Mr. Walter Bruderer.

*   *   *

Every effort has been made to have all information as current as humanly possible, but there are times when changes are made after we go to press or just after our visit to some small village. For that reason, errors are a part of any guide. We welcome your suggestions, comments and even criticisms, since it is only with a lot of help from friends and readers that a guide can pinpoint special places and those few trouble spots.

INTRODUCING SWITZERLAND

A Matter of Feeling at Home

by

HERBERT KUBLY

(Mr. Kubly, born in New Glarus, Wisconsin, is a hereditary citizen of Elm, Canton Glarus, Switzerland. He is best known for his book American in Italy, *which won the National Book Award, and his novel* The Whistling Zone. *He has written about Switzerland in his book* Switzerland (Life World Library), *in* Varieties of Love, *a selection of short stories, and in* At Large, *an autobiography.)*

Being a chauvinist Swiss, I write of Switzerland with a bias. But I am also an American who has traveled in many countries of the world and lived in a half-dozen, and I have become convinced of one fact—the country in which traveling Americans and Britons are most at home is Switzerland.

There are historical reasons why English and Americans find the Swiss, among all the peoples of the world, most like themselves. The primary one is successful communication. There is language, of course. Way back in 1872, the Swiss historian Jakob Burckhardt predicted that English would be the future world language. While

1

Switzerland is within itself a linguistic Babel, English is taught in the schools and most Swiss whom travelers meet at least speak it a little.

Beyond the language there are the broader and deeper recognitions of history, tradition and culture which exist between the Swiss and their English-speaking visitors. Britain and America are Protestant industrial countries whose ideology was born in Switzerland, in John Calvin's Protestant Vatican of Geneva. More than any other man, Calvin is the spiritual father of the modern era. His cardinal virtue of hard work, applied to European stores of capital, produced the industrial revolution. Calvinism, carried to Scotland by John Knox and from there into England and to North America by the *Mayflower* Pilgrims, formed the moral character of the New World.

The powerful flow of religious ideas carried from Geneva to Britain and to America is the source of a deep rapport between the three countries. The Swiss and Americans are traditionally middle-class peoples and the British are becoming so. All three live in increasingly welfare states, yet all are political conservatives who look on communism as the devil's workshop.

Politically large America and tiny Switzerland are curiously similar. Both are federal unions of states. In designing the American federation, Thomas Jefferson and the thirty-nine signers of the Constitution took as an example Greek historian Polybius' account of the Achaean Confederation, as well as the writings of Aristotle and Cicero. A binding sympathy between the United States and Switzerland was established in 1848, when, after a short "civil war" which lasted twenty-five days and cost one hundred twenty lives, the twenty-five Swiss states drew up a new federal constitution patterned after that of the United States. Although it provided a bicameral representation with checks and balances and declared the people sovereign, there are minor national differences in the two systems. Switzerland elects a president every year, and many citizens don't bother to remember the name of the incumbent. With their love of anonymity and distaste for status, the Swiss expect their president to pay the rent on his modest apartment and ride to work on the trolley.

The Discovery of Tourism

To the British, the Swiss are indebted for the discovery of tourism and the idea of turning the Alps into "export" revenue. Up to the eighteenth century, a few travelers gravitated around the gentle lakes of Neuchâtel and Biel, but the mountains were considered a formidable anathema. To the Swiss, struggling to wrest a living from the sterile slopes, they were a national catastrophe. A Genevese physicist, Horace Benedict de Saussure, spent twenty-seven years trying to climb Mt. Blanc, and when he finally made it, in 1787, wrote, "The instant in which I reached the highest point of the snow that crowns the peak, I stamped on it in rage rather than with a pleasurable sensation. . . . It seemed to me that I alone had survived the universe and that I was seeing its corpse spread out beneath my feet."

His words expressed the schizophrenia of love and hate for an enemy to be conquered which climbers have felt for mountains ever since. In Anglo-Saxon hearts, the Alps stirred a sublimated yearning for heights. British climbers rallied to the call, and by the late nineteenth century had climbed almost every Alpine peak. In Zermatt, the village at the foot of the Matterhorn, a small Anglican cemetery is filled with the remains of Englishmen who lost their lives on Switzerland's Olympus.

Having firmly established climbing as a craze, the British next popularized skiing. In 1894, Sir Arthur Conan Doyle published his account of a Swiss ski journey which sent hundreds of Britons swooping all over the slopes of Switzerland.

Americans and Europeans followed. Today, the Alps are mechanized, with more than 1,200 skilifts, aerial cableways and funicular railways, and, at several larger resorts, small airplanes and helicopters to fly crack skiers to snowy heights.

Recognizing a good thing, the practical Swiss were quick to respond to the invasion. As hoteliers, they have no peers; their luxurious hostelries are the aristocrats of the hotel world. In such pleasure-domes as the *Beau-Rivage* in Lausanne, the *Palace* or *Suvretta House* in St. Moritz, the *Bellevue-Palace* in Bern (with its transcending view of the Alps), or the *Grand* and *Palace* hotels at Bürgenstock on a belvedere above Lake Lucerne, life is sybaritic and unhurried. Generally, Swiss hotels are supreme in service and cuisine. Usually small, with fewer than one hundred beds, their atmosphere is that of a gracious and civilized home.

Taught by the British how to turn their scenery into gold, the Swiss have steadily and carefully built tourism up to a source of national revenue second only to that from capital earnings. In the country's delicate balance of trade the tourist industry covers approximately one-third of the gap between Switzerland's imports and exports. The French historian André Siegfried speaks of tourists depositing their riches in "the same way as the traditional inundations of the Nile fertilize the delta."

Switzerland's greatest advantage to tourists is its compactness. Within its 15,591 square miles are contained the most diversely beautiful landscapes of the world. In the single day that it takes to drive across the country, the visitor passes through a dozen different types of scenery and a half-dozen different climates. These can best be experienced in a new sport which the Swiss are developing with some success—ballooning over the Alps. A balloonist who rises somewhere near the 13,648-foot-high Jungfrau can, on a clear day, see the whole of Switzerland. The glaciers over which his balloon would probably drift are the apex of the European watershed, from which waters flow into all the great rivers of western Europe and its surrounding seas— by the Danube to the Black Sea, by the Po to the Adriatic and, within a few miles of one another, by the Rhine cascading toward the cold North Sea and the Rhône tumbling toward the warm Mediterranean. To the west, the balloonist sees the green slopes of the Jura and the glistening riviera around the Lake of Geneva; to the south, the silver-misted lakes of Lugano and Maggiore; to the east, the St. Gotthard massif with its serpentine-coiling road, and the forested cantons of Innerschweiz; and to the north, the city and lake of Zurich. Beyond the latter is the Rhine, flowing through hazy Lake of Constance toward Basel.

For the majority of more conventional and less adventuresome travelers, there are the Swiss Federal Railways. Railroading, which has fallen into disrepute in many countries of the world, continues to be one of the joys to be found in Switzerland. Swift, quiet trains cover 3,450 miles of electrified tracks, pass through 672 tunnels and over more than 5,000 bridges into every valley and crag of the country. Recognizing the value of such a system to tourists, the railroad offers several attractive types of reduced-rate tickets, including the new "go-anywhere," bargain-price Holiday Pass. For motorists, the Swiss are building a new superhighway network, and as long ago as 1964 opened the Grand St. Bernard auto-tunnel, the first of several wonderful tunnels which make Alpine crossings by road swift and easy in all weathers. Swissair's fleet of forty jetliners connects landlocked Switzerland with nearly sixty foreign countries and duplicates in comfort and service some of the luxury of Swiss hotels.

Cows, Cheese and Images

An inexplicable libel about Switzerland is that the food is dull and expensive. The truth is that Swiss cuisine, incorporating the best of French, Italian and German, is among the best in Europe, and although the cost to tourists, not only of food but also of hotels and transportation, has certainly risen in the last decade, it has done so less rapidly than in some other nations.

A happy dichotomy of Switzerland is that, although one of the most industrialized countries in Europe, it retains its image of a pastoral paradise. "Little herd boys," wrote Katherine Mansfield, "lie on their backs or their bellies, and their tiny white goats spring about on the mountain slopes. You meet tiny girls all alone with flocks of black sheep or herds of huge yellow cows." This rustic image has been challenged by Friedrich Dürrenmatt, who said, "The simpering milkmaid and the alphorn are about as valid national images as the gangster and gun-toting cowboy are in America." The playwright has forgotten that the cowboy is a very valid part of the American tradition and landscape, just as the herdsman and goat girl remain so in Switzerland. The rural idyll is kept alive by the Swiss themselves. No matter where a Swiss lives, he identifies himself with, and sentimentalizes, the canton where he was born, the fragment of land which his ancestors cultivated and which more than likely is still being cultivated by a brother or a cousin. He believes, as do Americans and Britons, that the welfare of man and nation is influenced not only by a world economy, but by the cycles of nature and fertility of the earth.

Katherine Mansfield's description is just as true today as it was when she wrote it almost half a century ago. Switzerland can be divided into four areas of approximately equal size: lakes and barren rock, forests, grazing pastures and cultivated land. Most of the pastures and fields are in areas of fairytale villages, prosperous farms with big brown barns, herds of fat cattle and, on the pine-covered Jura slopes, droves of horses. The sound of cowbells, ranging from treble tinkles to deep basso rumblings, is the same all over Switzerland. This dedication to land and cows is not romantic, but urgently expedient, for the more Switzerland can produce from its own meager soil, the less it is dependent upon imported food. As cows are one symbol of Switzerland, so its cheese is another. The 43,000 tons exported each year are a small item in the Swiss economy, yet Swiss cheese, even more famous than Swiss watches, remains the first product associated with the land. In its heart and soul, Switzerland has not broken with the land—therein lies its durability.

Like Americans and Britons, Swiss are materialists. "Jesus taught us that man cannot love God and Mammon both," said a prominent clergyman with a twinkle in his eyes. "But we Swiss prove Jesus wrong. We can." Allegiance to the golden calf was given theological sanction by John Calvin, who openly advocated the accumulation of riches. Money, he preached, is one of God's gifts to man; therefore, man must save money for God, and must account for every farthing. From such an ideology, western capitalism was born.

Downtown Saturday Nights

Soaring church spires form a heavenly lattice in the Swiss skies and visitors listening to the Saturday night curfew, when all the bells of a city are rung at once, will be convinced that the wrath of Calvin is still loose in the land. Not really—the Swiss are traditionalists and the bells are a link with history. In another sense, they might be considered a jubilant ringing-in of Saturday-night revels. Puritans need to kick over the traces now and then, and to hard-working Swiss, just as to hard-working Americans and Britons, Saturday night is a spree. If Calvin stalked through the streets of Geneva on Saturday night and Zwingli rampaged through Zurich, they would probably see Switzerland as a Babylon pepped up with considerable spice from "the cities of the plains." Zurich's entertainment quarter begins in narrow, winding Münstergasse, in the shadows of the twin spires of Zwingli's Grossmünster Cathedral. In Geneva's nightlife zone, on the slopes just beneath St. Peter's Cathedral (from which Calvin ordered women sent to jail for wearing their hair loose), strip-teasing is the most popular entertainment. Every village in the land has a Gasthaus, likely as not named the *Sonne,* where Puritan steam is let off on a Saturday night. The "orgy" is a necessary part of Swiss life—Basel's three-day-long carnival celebration is one of the most abandoned in Europe.

Such merrymaking would imply a presence of girls, of which there are many. When GI's in Germany discovered in the late 1940s that a lot more than chocolate and Emmental cheese was for sale across the border, Switzerland's reputation as a swinging fleshpot was established. There's no accurate check on the number of girls today, but every adult must register a profession for tax purposes and the favorite *Berufe* of the ladies in question are "hairdresser," "beautician," "masseuse" and "language teacher." (For years, the toast of the Zurich police department was a girl who listed her profession as "import-export.") It is the Swiss' tolerant attitude that everyone has a lot of business to mind, so the girls are left to prosper. The broad cultural horizons of Switzerland are beautifully illustrated by the apocryphal story of an English tourist who accosted a lovely young lady near the Zurich opera house and was told, "Not tonight—they're performing the *Missa Solemnis* of Beethoven."

It is one of the absurd clichés of our time that the Swiss are an uncultured race of hoteliers. On the contrary, they are one of the most enthusiastically culture-centered people in the world. The visitor is offered a Midas feast of art, theater and music. Because of the Swiss disdain of cultural snobbery, and because of Switzerland's literary identification, by language, with the schools of France and Germany, Swiss culture has never been properly comprehended by the world. Having no imperial court to rally creativity, Switzerland's culture is the culture of democracy, of popular participation. The galleries of Basel, Schaffhausen, Winterthur, Zurich, Bern and Geneva are bursting with paintings waiting to be discovered by tourists. The Swiss are compulsive collectors—without a doubt they own more art per capita than any other people—and many of the great private collections have recently been opened to the public.

The art for which the Swiss have a special affinity is music. Zurich has ten concert halls, fifty-three men's choruses and 560 music professors. The state-run opera house is famous for producing the works of contemporary composers, and draws singers from all over the world. (Among its stars, now permanent residents of Zurich, are the famous American man-and-wife team James McCracken and Sandra Warfield.) The *Schauspielhaus* premieres the dramas of Friedrich Dürrenmatt and Max Frisch, both Swiss, and presents a lively repertoire of contemporary American and English plays. The greatest pleasure of Swiss culture is its immediacy. From one's hotel in midtown Zurich or Geneva, one can walk within ten minutes to almost every theater, concert hall, art gallery and foreign-language cinema in town.

Home of Exiles

The Swiss graciousness, which makes foreigners feel at home, extends beyond tourism. Switzerland has traditionally offered asylum to the restless wanderers and politically persecuted of other lands. The first famous exile was Voltaire. Byron, the German poet Rainer Maria Rilke, James Joyce, Thomas Mann, Bertolt Brecht, Johannes Brahms, Richard Wagner, Igor Stravinsky and Paul Hindemith all lived and worked here. Exiled kings choose to live here, and lately a colony of American and British cinema stars is finding Switzerland a haven from devastating income taxes.

The human flow is reciprocal, as Swiss are peripatetic wanderers from their claustrophobic little country. In 1607, some Bernese helped the English settle Jamestown in Virginia. In the next century, several thousand Swiss settled in Pennsylvania and became known as

"Pennsylvania Dutch." One of them, Albert Gallatin, served Presidents Jefferson and Madison as Secretary of the Treasury and reduced the national debt by fifty percent. Swiss John Sutter settled in California and discovered the gold which triggered the Gold Rush in 1848. In our century hundreds of Swiss *au pair* girls go to Britain each year to live with families there, helping a little, and learning a lot of English. Also, many Swiss youths go to the United States to serve apprenticeships in American businesses.

Swiss are friendly with neighbors because it is the only way they know to keep life as pleasant and tranquil as possible. Historians sometimes point to Switzerland as a scale model for a future federation of nations, and today, former enemy countries are attempting to forge a peaceful Europe along the same principles of toleration and cooperation that have made strong nations of Switzerland's distrusting cantons and America's divergent states.

We don't have to be Swiss to be perfectly at home in Switzerland. While enjoying ourselves in the natural and easy compatibility which the Swiss offer, we may also gain, hopefully, some of their wisdom.

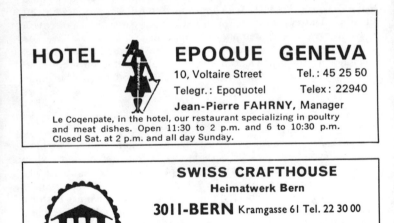

THE SWISS SCENE

THE MIRACULOUS SWISS LANDSCAPE

Plains, Peaks and Alpine Valleys

by

RENEE GRANDVOINET

On a map of Europe, Switzerland is the size of a postage stamp; on a map of the world, little more than a pinhead. A population of approximately six million and a half—half that of Greater London—is densely distributed in the fertile regions of the country: in Alpine and Jura foothills, along the broad Central Plateau, in remote valleys. A confederation of twenty-two sovereign states covering a total area of sixteen thousand square miles, 22.6 percent of which is composed of the High Alps, forest lands and barren rocks: a country that has no seaboard, virtually no natural resources except hydraulic power, and which, despite all this, is prosperous.

Approaching Switzerland by a land route from the south or northwest, one is eager to escape the flat monotony of the Plain of Lombardy, of central France, or even the green and orderly undulations of Burgundy and the Côte d'Or. Traveling north from the Riviera, however, one finds the steep escarpment of the Maritime Alps, which merge into the Mont Blanc range, south of Lake Geneva, rising over 250 miles to the Alpine heart of Europe.

Western Switzerland shares its Jura and Lake Geneva frontiers with France and incorporates the three French-speaking cantons—Vaud, Neuchâtel, and Geneva—and two bilingual cantons, Fribourg and Valais, which are also Catholic states. Even in Fribourg and Valais, French is predominant and the Swiss call this region "Suisse Romande," recognizing the Latin ascendancy of the populations here. Here lies the great basin of Lake Geneva, fed by the Rhône, which enters the lake after crossing the large alluvial plain between St. Maurice and Villeneuve.

The Swiss shore of Lake Geneva faces south and has a rich, agricultural hinterland, rising in the east to the lovely Pays d'Enhaut, in the foothills of the Fribourg Alps, and in the west to the Jorat, the wooded foothills of the bleak rolling Jura Mountains, with their long, narrow valleys. South of Lake Geneva, along the French coast, lie the impressive Savoy Alps, which incorporate Mont Blanc (Europe's highest peak, 15,777 feet, standing guard at the Franco-Italian frontier) and stretch from south of Geneva into the upper Rhône Valley. This towering mass forms the frontier between France, Switzerland, and Italy: the Valley of Chamonix, at the foot of Mont Blanc, leads northeast into the Rhône Valley, from which radiate the Great St. Bernard and the Simplon Passes.

The Rhône Valley is bounded on the south by the Valais (or Pennine) Alps, which include the great triangular peak of the Matterhorn (14,690 ft.), and Monte Rosa (15,210 ft.), the second-highest mountain in Europe.

From the Swiss shore of Lake Geneva, with the town of Lausanne as its central point, the Jorat provides the main access into the Central Plateau, a rich agricultural region of orchards and pasturelands running northeast and broadening in the north to include the Lakes of Constance and Zurich. In the Central Plateau, which is bounded on the west by the Jura Mountains, also lie the Lakes of Neuchâtel, Bienne, and Morat, and the cities of Fribourg and Bern, to the east of which, again, rise the Fribourg Alps and the Bernese Oberland. Central, eastern, and northern Switzerland have German-speaking populations.

Central Switzerland incorporates the classic Alpine scenery of Lucerne and its lake, known as the Vierwaldstättersee (Lake of the Four Forest Cantons), Lake Zug, and the more southerly Lakes of Thun and Brienz.

The most easterly of the Swiss cantons is the Grisons (in German, *Graubünden)*, which, like the canton of St. Gallen, shares a frontier with Austria. The Grisons and its beautiful Engadine district lie across two chains of the Alps, known as the Lepontine and Rhaetian Alps; it is also the home of Switzerland's fourth national language, Romansch. Leading south into Italy are the less well-known, dramatically beautiful, Alpine passes, the Splügen, San Bernardino, Maloja, and Bernina.

The Engadine (the valley of the Inn River) is accessible either from the north (from Zurich along Lakes Zurich and Walen; from the Lake Constance region up the Rhine); via Coire (Chur), Lenzerheide and the Julier Pass, or from the Central Alps via Andermatt on the St. Gotthard route (only during the summer season), over the Oberalp Pass through Disentis and Thusis and over the Julier Pass.

The lower Swiss Rhine is a very lovely region, extending from Lake Constance through Schaffhausen and Aargau to the canton and city of Basel, the great river port. Here there are lovely orchards, peaceful homesteads and small, medieval towns, whose architecture reveals German influence.

One canton only is Italian-speaking, the Ticino, somewhat isolated on the south of the St. Gotthard. As one crosses this great international pass and descends into the Valley of Bellinzona, scenery and atmosphere change miraculously. Here already is the vegetation and climate of the Italian lake district. Behind, to the north, lie the immense barriers of the Alps; southwards there are palm trees, flowering camellias, and sweet chestnut groves.

Travel in Switzerland offers an immense variety of natural scenery and atmosphere, ranging from the bleakness of polar landscapes to the sunny warmth of the Mediterranean. The Alps, romantic and beautiful as they are, are not the only high spots of a Swiss tour. Off the beaten track lie the rural charm of easterly Appenzell, the orchard lands of Lake Constance, the lovely rolling Jura. There are picturesque small cities such as Solothurn, with its indefinable elegance, legacy of the Swiss confederation of the French ambassadors who, for 150 years, had their official residence here. There are rich pastoral valleys, such as the Emmental, with its flaxen-haired, sturdy population and geranium-decked farmsteads. There are utterly rustic villages of clustering brown-roofed chalets in the rugged lateral valleys branching out from the upper Rhône Valley, Evolène or Hérens, for example; unbelievable nooks, such as the hamlet of Isérables, perched on a rocky crag and accessible only by a mule track or by an aerial cable cabin which swings perilously over a deep grove. Plain and mountain alternate with foothills and pastureland, Mediterranean warmth with glaciers at 14,000 feet above sea level.

THE SWISS WAY OF LIFE

Variations on a Harmonious Theme

With such diversity in the Swiss scene—four national languages, twenty-two Catholic and Protestant member states—it is astonishing that there should be a Swiss way of life. And yet there is one, which might perhaps be better defined as an outlook, an attitude to the outside world that has been shaped, not by history, but by economic and political necessity.

Switzerland is a very small country indeed. Nature here has been lavish only in the bestowal of beauty. Everything the Swiss possess they have had to work hard to obtain. The prosperity they enjoy is due to the foresight, orderly planning, business and political acumen of the federal and cantonal governments, of executives engaged in private enterprise, and also to the discipline and thrift of the nation.

Thoroughness. The struggle to win and maintain political and economic independence has undoubtedly colored the national character. The Swiss are cautious, extremely prudent in the acceptance of new theories, new methods, ideas, or commodities. Their ancestors could not afford to buy a pig in a poke and, at many turning points in Swiss history, a slight error of judgment might have spelled disaster.

The blend of German and Latin cultures has resulted everywhere in a love of orderliness and cleanliness, a keen appreciation of thoroughness. What the Swiss do, they do well. They may take a long time to decide on a course of action or an undertaking of any kind, but once the decision has been made, no detail is overlooked. Their new hospitals, such as Basel-Bürgerspital, Zurich-Triemli or Bern-Insel, or the surgical department of the Lausanne cantonal hospital, took a long time to build, but they are models of their kind. This trait is expressed even in the field of sport. Skiing, for example, was introduced from Scandinavia some sixty years ago and did not become really popular until a year or two before World War I. Now it is the national sport, and all enthusiasts are equipped with the finest possible kit, from boots to caps, all craftmade in Switzerland.

Love of quality. Closely linked to this characteristic is an appreciation of quality. There is no market in Switzerland for cheap and slovenly merchandise. Poor workmanship is generally considered a disgrace. In a typical Swiss home, even the most modest, you will find well-made—though not necessarily beautiful—furniture. Newlyweds with only a one-room apartment will spend the utmost on a handsome bedroom suite. Brides-to-be of all classes take pride in their trousseaus, cherish and embroider fine linens, even though it may strain their budget to do so. In central and eastern Switzerland, the general trend of taste is for all that is heavy and rather massive in line. In the western cantons, a certain Latin love of more refined elegance prevails. There is, nevertheless, everywhere, an intense love of fine craftsmanship and good quality.

It is hardly necessary to point out that this national trait has won for the Swiss a worldwide reputation for the production of high-quality goods. It is richly illustrated in their daily lives. Their stores, tearooms, restaurants, for example, are luxuriously appointed and furnished with handsome, craftmade equipment. Note the details in a city tearoom: chairs, tables, lamps, soft furnishings, all planned with careful art. One may not always appreciate the style, but there is nothing slovenly.

Craftsmanship. Thoroughness and love of quality have also directed the strict control of trades and skills. One cannot, in Switzerland, set up a shop or open a business at random. To be a hairdresser, an electrician, a plumber, a garageman, a stenographer, or what have you, one must produce a diploma of apprenticeship or a certificate of mastership. For this reason, craft work is of the highest order. Fine millinery, clothes, footwear, jewelry, lingerie, furniture are made and sold by professionally competent tradespeople. Mass-produced articles are, of course, available in the large stores but if they are of poor quality or bad workmanship, not many Swiss will buy them.

Practicality. The necessity for prudence has made the Swiss adopt a fairly materialistic or rather concrete outlook. Your typical Swiss does not daydream, or wander through life with his head in the clouds. He is put to work early and made to understand that "Life is earnest." School-leaving age is fifteen or sixteen and, after a three- or four-year term of apprenticeship, the young boy or girl goes into father's business (if there is one) or seeks to perfect his knowledge in his chosen trade. Safe government jobs are in great demand, for they mean security, a cosy home, and a pension. It is estimated that there is one civil servant (including officials of the state railroads, police, etc.) for every five people. Training for the professions is equally thorough, and Swiss universities set a high standard of scholarship.

Independence. Seven hundred years of democracy have given the Swiss nation a great love of freedom that, paradoxically, is contradicted by the extraordinary number of rules, regulations, and restrictions that overshadow the individual. Application forms, legal documents, statistics have grown and multiplied, since the war years especially, but the citizen does not pay undue attention to them. He is not really aware of the "Do not spit," "Do not walk on the grass," "Do not shout," "Do not" this and "Do not" that strewn across his daily path by order-loving officials. He proves his independence of spirit at the polls, in the cafés, where he grumbles freely, and by occasional sturdy refusals to comply with a municipal, cantonal, or federal order.

Diversity. It is often said, "There are no Swiss. There are Bernese, Genevans, and so on . . . in fact, twenty-two different nations, but no typical Swiss!"
  This is, to a certain extent, true. A Vaudois will fume at and criticize a Bernese. A Genevan will say of the people of Zurich that they are greedy, materialistic. The population of each canton supposedly has at least one outstanding "national" shortcoming. And yet, when it comes to the push, when a national emergency arises, there are no cantons, only Switzerland.

There are three official languages—German, French, and Italian—and a fourth "national" language, Romansch. Each language group has identical rights, and all official government communications must be in the three official tongues, so as not to favor one over another. You could, if you wished, speak only one language all your life if you were Swiss ... but, being a good democrat and as eager to protect the other language groups' rights as your own, you would probably learn at least one other tongue.

Unity. Despite their racial and linguistic differences, the people of Switzerland are one in their love of the soil. The Alps and their brown chalets, the quiet lakes and forests, have cast a spell over them, and maybe even helped to give unity to a strange medley of what might otherwise have been a very disunited people. Nevertheless, the cantons cleave to their independence, and there is frequently healthy disagreement by cantons and voters with the federal government in Bern. But in its militia Switzerland has found a remarkable smoother-over of difficulties; an infallible sponsor of enforced good fellowship. "My buddy in the army" may come from Geneva, Bern, Thurgau, or Solothurn; he may speak only broken French, German, or Italian, but four months of grueling military training at the age of twenty, and refresher courses every year after that, are most conducive to true human understanding among men.

Democracy. And perhaps, too, the Swiss militia system has served yet another purpose: the establishment of a true sense of democracy among the people. During the formative years, young men of every walk of life, of every class, are submitted to the same treatment, to the same pitiless commands. The effect is not forgotten in the course of years, because until the age of thirty-six there are the regular three-week terms of service and, thereafter, incorporation in the *Landwehr* and *Landsturm.* Young men who are unfit for the military must enlist in auxiliary services.

Atmosphere. The diversity of Switzerland is much a question of atmosphere. In the German-speaking cantons, in the large cities of Zurich, Bern, and Basel, one senses an earnest purposefulness, a certain rather unsmiling sternness. Life and the sustenance of life by hard work, the acquiring of security by money in the bank, are very real here. Swiss-German businessmen are efficient; they divide their time neatly and tidily into working days (and the office) and rest days (and the family).

It is significant that many German-Swiss girls of all but the top-bracket income classes are sent, immediately on leaving school, to serve as maids-of-all-work with families in French-speaking countries as well as in Britain. As they are often paid a mere pittance and work hard, life is far from easy. This is picturesquely called *manger de la vache enragée* ("eating humble pie") and is considered an excellent and cheap way of introducing girls to the cold realities of life and work; of giving them a practical illustration of the "Life is earnest" concept. Few French-Swiss girls are subjected to this system.

Parenthetically, it is appropriate to mention that this is far from being a one-way traffic. From Britain in particular there is a steady flow of girls going to work with Swiss families, to say nothing of with hotels, restaurants, and suchlike. Less appropriate here, but still worthy of mention, is the considerable number of young people of many nationalities—and especially from the United States—who go to Swiss universities and other educational establishments, sometimes for degree courses of several years, sometimes for summer courses of only a few weeks.

In the western cantons, in Geneva and Vaud especially, a strong Latin influence is prevalent. Life is taken more lightly; thrift is not so much the order of the day. The Germanic *Gründlichkeit* (thoroughness) prevails, but it is alleviated and made more joyful by a certain graciousness and a latent sense of *mañana*. "There are more days to come from behind the mountains," say Lausannites and Genevans. That does not mean to say that people work less hard. On the contrary, they work very hard indeed, but they also play hard. The entertainment trades—cinema, theaters, nightclubs, and so on—are prosperous in this region of Switzerland and patronized not only by visitors from abroad, but by the Swiss themselves.

To arrive in the Ticino, Switzerland's Italian-speaking and southernmost canton, from, say Zurich, is almost like entering another country. Here is a different climate and Mediterranean warmth. And south of the Gotthard massif the luxuriant vegetation at lower levels is obvious even to the most myopic traveler. The Ticinesi are different, too: hardworking like most Swiss, but largely of Lombard stock so that their mannerisms and appearance, as well as their language, are inescapable reminders of Italy.

With the coming of railways and good roads, and the growth of easy and rapid travel for all, especially over or through mountain barriers which had hitherto deterred all but the brave and hardy, the previous virtual isolation of many Swiss communities was brought to an end. Inhabitants began to move from one part of Switzerland to another, and intermarriage took place, so that many local traits and characteristics gradually became toned down or modified. Particularly noticeable was the movement of German-speaking Swiss across language borders to other parts of the country where they rapidly adapted themselves to life, and successfully established businesses.

Women and the Home

The Swiss home. There are many kinds of homes in Switzerland, rich and poor, plain and beautiful, farmsteads, apartments, houses in garden suburbs, but in the great majority of them there is an excellent housewife. Although, during World War II, she and her sisters remained inglorious on the home front while their menfolk stood guarding the frontiers, they accomplished miracles of skill in eking out meager rations; their untiring work contributed in no small measure to the solving of the national food problem.

The art of homemaking is the supreme seal of womanhood in Switzerland. Beautiful household linen, a fine kitchen, spotless cleanliness, and sleek tidiness are the Swiss woman's pride. Shining rows of bottled fruit and homemade jams testify to her skill.

Servants are rare and expensive in Switzerland. Even upper middle-class housewives are usually saddled with a fair burden of housework.

Swiss women only recently gained the right to vote but they are increasingly interested in politics although many still consider this to be essentially a masculine headache. Although women doctors, dentists and lawyers are excellent, until a few years ago the true career woman was virtually unknown in Switzerland. She had a hard time being taken seriously, society tending to feel that she was merely filling in time before marriage. She stood little chance of finding a niche in big business, committee work, or administration. These executive jobs were the preserves of men. But the situation is changing, and changing rapidly.

In the middle and lower income brackets there was a rather different attitude, most young wives adding to the family income by continuing work at least until the children arrive.

Hospitality. British and American visitors to Switzerland may be struck by the apparent lack of homely hospitality (although a number of Tourist Offices operate an excellent "Meet the Swiss" scheme designed specifically to enable foreigners to visit the Swiss in their homes). The reason for this is not very clear as the Swiss themselves are anything but an unfriendly people. It is probably due to the fact that here, as in many parts of the Continent, life is lived to a great extent in public. The Swiss, too, seem to experience a certain reserve or shyness towards strangers, due perhaps to the great emphasis laid on the family as a unit. Distant family connections are maintained to the nth degree, while relations with the outside world remain on a conventional footing.

Not many years ago it was the custom for Swiss men of forty and over to spend their Sunday afternoons playing cards in cafés with their buddies, possibly to be joined by their wives after tea. But in Switzerland, as elsewhere, times change customs. Nowadays, a growing number spend Sunday afternoons in front of the television set, or out in the family car.

Generosity. Despite their rather shy reticence and marked dislike of expressing deep emotion—a Swiss audience almost seems cold and sparing of rapturous applause—the Swiss are a most kindly people, secretly warmhearted. The nation as a whole feels a deep sense of gratitude for the peace it has enjoyed for over one hundred years and this thankfulness is shown by a great generosity towards the war-stricken populations of Europe. Children have been the special object of their attention. Thousands were brought into Switzerland in the few years immediately after the war. Placed in charge of foster parents for periods of three months, they blossomed into health and happiness. The love and care lavished on them, the parcels of warm clothing and toys they carried away with them at the end of their stay, testified to the sincerity of the welcome they received.

Towards the end of the war, the "Don Suisse" was instituted to provide, by voluntary, national subscription, material aid to war-stricken areas: trainloads of furniture, clothing, food, and hospital equipment were sent out of the country. A similar institution, "Caritas," was organized by the Catholic communities of Switzerland and still sends food and clothing to less fortunate people abroad.

Immediately after the collapse of the Mussolini government in 1944, thousands upon thousands of refugees came pouring over the southern border to escape Nazi persecutors. Old people and young children, men and women of military age who had reason to fear retaliation—the tide could not be held back. The rural population in the Ticino took matters into their own hands. Along the roads leading from the frontiers, they posted women and children with large baskets heaped with fruit, bread, and other food, shoes, and clothing. To the weary traveler, these gifts were given with a kindly word and a smile.

Some years later, the Swiss led in organizing relief for the flood of refugees that began streaming out of Hungary in the autumn of 1956 and out of Czechoslovakia in 1968. Not only did they spontaneously contribute clothing, medicine, and food, but the government welcomed many thousands of homeless families to Switzerland as permanent immigrants, finding them places to live, work to do, and new starts in life. Nor were the needs of the spirit forgotten in the flood of material assistance. Zurich's newspapers banded together to publish a newspaper in Hungarian for free distribution among the refugee camps in Austria.

. . . Next to Godliness. Relatively few Swiss are indecently wealthy, and there are even fewer of the much publicized "gnomes" who, with phone in hand, make fortunes out of buying and selling currencies they neither see nor own. Like every country Switzerland has its poor, but there are no slums—at least in the sense that a Briton or American understands the word. And, of course, the Swiss are exceptionally lucky in that no area of their country—not even Zurich, Basel and other industrial centers—lies more than half an hour from mountains, countryside, lake or river. Everywhere, within easy reach, are fields and forests.

True, in the cities heavy traffic fills the air with noise and fumes, but smoking factory chimneys are a rarity seen by few tourists anywhere in Switzerland. Cleanliness throughout the country, not least in the towns, is a matter in which the authorities and the people may have a subconscious pride, but certainly seem to accept as something no more than natural. Where else but in Switzerland would you see a post office official, armed with dusters and all the necessary materials, carefully cleaning and polishing a letter box in a busy city street? If cleanliness is next to godliness, Switzerland must be nearer to heaven than most.

But the country certainly has pollution problems. Concern about the condition of some lakes (where bathing has been strictly forbidden) and rivers has been such that strict anti-pollution laws came into effect in 1972. In a few years even the present offending lakes and rivers (and some are certainly offensive) will be as pure as the glaciers from which their waters come.

The salient traits described here vary in each language group, but there has been for centuries such an intermingling of the populations, so close to cooperation in matters national, political, and economic, that racial trends have been softened, modified, and influenced by the interplay. There is now quite definitely a Swiss outlook, a Swiss attitude to life, setting the nation apart in the international community.

A SYNOPSIS OF SWISS HISTORY

The Confederation That Works

Situated as it is at the crossroads of Europe's natural trans-Alpine routes, the territory we now know as Switzerland inevitably became the scene of much coming and going—tribal migrations, armies and, later, merchant caravans—even before the curtain went up on the European stage.

Prehistoric man of the Iron Age left traces of his passage at La Tène, the northeastern point of Lake Neuchâtel, where archeologists have found one of Europe's most important settlements of that period. At the dawn of recorded history Celtic tribes and especially the Helvetii migrated into the plateau lands, bounded on the west by the Jura mountains and on the east by the Alps, and wandered down into the Lake Geneva region. The Swiss of today, in poetry and in song and on solemn occasions, call their country Helvetia, symbolized by a lady of generous proportions. And, indeed, all official Federal documents bear the seal of the *Confoederatio Helvetica,* or Swiss Confederation.

The Romans, under Julius Caesar, interested in the conquest of

When creating comes to mind...
PIAGET

PIAGET at the world's finest jewellers

Gaul, put an end to the migrations of the Helvetii in 58 B.C. and, across the Great St. Bernard Pass, brought in the wake of their armies the culture and prosperity of their civilizations to territories of the conquered tribes and also to Rhaetia (now known as the Grisons). But the Romanization of Switzerland was at best patchy, and the Alemani, of German origin, infiltrated and settled in the northeastern part of what is present-day Switzerland, and in the central plateau. Meanwhile, the Burgundians established themselves west of the Sarine, the river which flows through Fribourg. A relatively peaceful people already converted to Christianity, the Burgundians in course of time were assimilated by the native population. Latin was the language at first spoken in the region but over the centuries various French dialects came to the fore, to be replaced in comparatively recent times by the French that is spoken there today. The ancient boundary between the Germanic Alemani and the French-speaking Burgundians varies little, in fact, from the language frontier which exists today.

In Rhaetia, where the Romans had gained a strong footing, the native population, firmly ensconced in their mountains, were able to resist assimilation by the invaders. Latin remained the language spoken there and so in the Grisons today many thousands speak Romansch, Switzerland's fourth national language and one which sprang from an old Rhaetian dialect. South of the Alps, the Italian-speaking territory now known as the Ticino, geographically part of Italy, remained untouched by these racial upheavals and for several centuries followed the destinies of Lombardy.

Aftermath of Empire

After the split-up of Charlemagne's colossal empire in the 9th century, the power of an insecure central government was broken: all over Europe, bailiffs, barons, lords, and overlords strove one against the other, eager to grasp power and wealth. West of the Jura, the house of Burgundy arose, to rule vast territories extending across the plateau to the shores of Lake Geneva. The Burgundian kings reigned wisely and well, introducing the cultivation of flax and the vine and many domestic crafts. Rudolf III of Burgundy made a gift of his lands to the Emperor of Germany and, at his death, in 1032, Conrad II formally took possession of his new territories and was crowned King of Burgundy at Payerne. Thus all the Alpine lands were incorporated in the German Empire.

Nevertheless, throughout this territory, far too vast for the wielding of a careful, centralized government, ducal families greedily continued to snatch what they could. During the 12th century, the Dukes of Zähringen owned most extensive estates reaching in a wide span from Lake Geneva to Lake Constance, and the populations under their sway strove in vain for freedom. However, modern Switzerland owes seven cities to the House of Zähringen: Fribourg, which was founded in 1178 by Duke Berthold IV, and Bern, founded in 1191, by Berthold V, who died childless in 1218, to mention but a couple.

A great opportunity was now to be had for the taking and one can imagine the eagerness with which the innumerable petty lords temporal of the dukedom—counts, barons, bailiffs—to say nothing of the lords spiritual—bishops and abbots—seized this great chance of dividing up the Zähringen estates.

The house of Savoy promptly invaded the north shore of that lake. Duke Peter extended his territories as far north as Gruyères and the Oberland. In the course of this victorious swoop, he also built many castles and fortresses, among them Chillon, with the aid of English military architects from the Plantagenet court of Henry III. Peter of Savoy died in 1268. He remains a brilliant and heroic figure and his clever policy firmly established his family on the road that was to lead to the throne of Italy in the 19th century.

One mighty opponent stood barring Savoy's way to a more complete victory: Rudolph IV of Habsburg, whose family had risen slowly to riches and power amid the disruption of medieval empires. History says that Rudolph was a generous, godly man. He was certainly astute and ambitious. From his family seat at Habsburg, in Aargau, he cleverly made his bid until, in 1273, he achieved the supreme success of being elected Emperor of Germany. It was then purely an honorary title, for the imperial authority had been undermined by warring nobles. Rudolph had no intention of remaining a mere figurehead, however. He set the imperial house in order, brought his lords and princes to heel and, by creating at least the illusion of peace, encouraged the commoners to work. Nor did he neglect his own interests, not the least of his acquisitions being the Duchy of Austria. At his death, in 1291, the House of Habsburg reigned supreme in Central Europe and the Alps.

Economic and human conditions were not so good, however, under the Habsburg domination and, in the central Alps, men were beginning to dream of freedom. The three clans of Uri, Schwyz, and Unterwald sent their magistrates to hold a secret conclave, according to legend at the famous field of Rütli, a meadow overlooking Lake Lucerne opposite Brunnen. The outcome of this meeting was a pact of mutual allegiance and assistance among the people of Uri, Schwyz, and Unterwald. A document was drawn up in Latin to which the three seals were set on the first of August, 1291. It is still reverently preserved in the archives of the canton of Schwyz, for it is the foundation stone of the Swiss confederation.

From that time on, the house of Habsburg played a losing game in the Alps. Its bailiffs and soldiers were harassed by guerrilla warfare and were the butt of such tricks as those attributed to the legendary William Tell. In 1315, Duke Leopold of Habsburg decided to put an end to all this, but, unfortunately for him, his fine army was defeated by the confederate army at Morgarten. After this victory, the three allies made their intentions public in the Pact of Brunnen.

The wave of revolt spread. Other territories and cities, subject to the Empire and the Habsburgs, unhesitatingly stepped out on the road of freedom. Lucerne joined the confederates in 1332, Zurich in 1351, Glarus and Zug in 1352, and, finally Bern in 1353.

Understandably enough, the house of Habsburg was not prepared to lose such vast territories without a fight. Leopold II organized a strong expeditionary force against the confederates, but was defeated at Sempach in 1386 and again, two years later, at Näfels. The Habsburgs had had their lesson and, in 1394, were ready to sign a twenty-year peace pact with their former vassals.

The Martial 15th Century

Meanwhile, the rest of the Alpine territories were split up into countless small vassal states. The house of Savoy still possessed the greater part of the Lake Geneva region, except for the city of Geneva, which was held in the benefice of a powerful bishopric.

The eight confederate states had tasted victory and liked it. In 1415, they set out to wrest from the Habsburgs the old imperial city of Aarau. A few years later, Thurgau also passed into their hands. The newly won lands were divided up among the victors and became vassal territories.

Neighboring populations continued to wrest their freedom from spiritual and temporal overlords. Schaffhausen asserted its rights as a free imperial city, Appenzell revoked the suzerainty of the Abbey of St. Gallen and the Grisons revolted against the feudal domination of the Bishopric of Coire.

The activities of the confederates had not escaped the notice of the wily old fox, the French king, Louis XI, whose great rival was Charles the Bold of Burgundy. To further his own ends, Louis negotiated a

perpetual peace pact between the Swiss and their old enemies the
Habsburgs. That took place in 1474 and the confederates were free
thereafter to expend their warlike energy in another direction. The
Habsburgs were in conflict with Burgundy in regard to the territories
of Alsace and Breisgau and it took little to persuade the confederates
that they should go to war on behalf of their new friend, Austria. So
began the Burgundian wars.

The first round went to the Swiss, who won the battle of Héricourt
in 1474 and followed up this victory with the invasion of Franche-
Comté. Two years later, Charles the Bold succeeded in mobilizing a
great army and marched against the Swiss. He was defeated, however,
at Grandson and at Morat.

In the flush of victory, the confederates invaded the territory of
Vaud (a fief of Savoy on the north of Lake Geneva) and then called
an international conference in Fribourg. Delegates from France,
Austria, Savoy, the Alsatian cities, and the confederate states decided
that Vaud should be returned to Savoy, that Bern should hold certain
communities in the Rhône Valley. Fribourg's status as a free and
independent city was recognized.

The Burgundian wars flickered out with the death of Charles the
Bold at the battle of Nancy in 1477. Thus France got rid of an
annoying rival and the Swiss won great military prestige.

Having tasted power, the confederates continued to pursue their
policy of territorial expansion. When, for example, Swiss merchants
complained that their cattle had been seized by agents of the Duke of
Milan, it was an excellent excuse for the occupation of Domodossola
and the Valle Leventina, south of the St. Gotthard. Uri and Obwald
retained a foothold in that region, despite peace treaties with Milan.
Thus other vassal states were added to the steadily increasing
territories of the eight Swiss states.

The allotment of war spoils is never conducive to harmony. Nor did
the confederates find it so. Strife arose between the three prosperous
cities of Bern, Zurich, and Lucerne and their poor relations, the rural
cantons of Uri, Schwyz, Unterwald, Zug, and Glarus. Dissension was
aggravated by the request of Fribourg and Solothurn to be admitted
also into the confederation.

By one of those rare strokes of good fortune that sometimes befall a
nation, the Swiss had in their midst a one-time farmer and political
leader who had become a venerable hermit and mystic, by name of
Nicholas of Flue. So in 1481 an emissary was dispatched posthaste to
the great man by the Council of Stans, where the cantons teetered on
the brink of civil war. His advice was earnestly sought, freely given

and wisely followed, the member states reinforcing their pact by a convention breathing brotherly love and promising mutual assistance against aggression or the revolt of minority populations. Fribourg and Solothurn were allowed to join the confederation.

The member states now numbered ten. Later, they were joined by Basel, Schaffhausen, and, in 1513, by Appenzell.

In 1500, the lingering dispute with Milan was aggravated when Uri, Schwyz, and Unterwald seized and held the fief of Bellinzona, south of the Alps. Nevertheless, to prove their goodwill, the confederates broke their alliance with France (whose King Louis XII had occupied the Duchy of Milan in 1499) and took up arms in favor of Milan. In 1512, the confederate army swept across the Alps into the plain of Lombardy and won victory after victory over the French armies. They graciously re-established Maximilian Sforza in his dukedom. For three years the Swiss remained invincible and the taste of power was sweet.

But the throne of France changed hands. The proud Francis I succeeded sickly Louis XII and set about regaining the lost kingdom of Italy. At Marignano, in 1515, 20,000 Swiss, with only a small force of artillery, came face to face with 60,000 French and Venetian troops armed with the most modern weapons. The defeat of the confederates was final and the following year they accepted and signed a pact of perpetual peace with France. Truth to say, the Swiss were treated rather well by a magnanimous victor: they were allowed to retain the territories they had won in battle, except the Valley of Ossola, and furthermore received a generous financial indemnity.

Renunciation of Empire and the Reformation

It is now, after the defeat of Marignano, that occurs one of the most astounding—and wisest—changes of policy in the history of any nation. The thirteen confederate states, realizing that the methods of warfare had changed by the introduction of modern artillery and that, with the limited means at their disposal, they could not hope to vie in the field with the great powers, renounced all thought of territorial expansion in Europe. Both the cities and the rural cantons settled down to achieve prosperity by commercial development and the arts of peace. True, this did not mean that all citizens within the confederation were free men: the sovereign cantons still held in fief many vassal communities and territories.

At this period, too, we find that the basic social structure of Switzerland began to grow and develop. Switzerland has no nobility, no aristocracy as understood elsewhere in Europe. The upper crust of Swiss society consists of old, and formerly rich and landed, patrician families, having their roots in both town and country. In the early days of the confederation such families provided military leaders and magistrates who actively pursued the federal interests and their own. In the 16th century, their descendants were sufficiently alive to the potentialities of trade and commerce to seek power and enrichment in this field.

For this reason, too, the thirteen cantons of the confederation, having but little to export and an energetic population to sustain, found a way of killing two birds with one stone by "exporting" their mercenary troops. For centuries to come, France, the German kings, and other European powers, great and small, were glad to avail themselves of the help of Swiss mercenaries in the fighting of their wars. These troops were commanded by their own officers and flew their own standards and were never assimilated into the armies amongst which they fought. The Swiss Guard of the Vatican is the last relic of this custom.

At home, also, for a certain period, men of the 16th century found ample opportunity to expend their energies in religious strife. The wave of reforms set going by Martin Luther and Ulrich Zwingli in the early years of the century led to the abolition of Catholic rites in Zurich in 1523. Bern listened to the inspired teaching of Berthold Haller; Basel to John Hausschein, known as Oecolampade. Geneva became the refuge and the fortress of the French Huguenots and their leader, William Farel, and his fanatical successor, John Calvin. By 1535, the power of the Bishop of Geneva had been entirely broken and the city became a sovereign republic.

These religious conflicts provided a glorious opportunity for the still territorially ambitious canton of Bern. Duke Charles VIII of Savoy, alarmed by the progress made by the Reformed Faith, commenced hostilities against Geneva. Bern came to the rescue and, at the same time, "peacefully" occupied, "liberated and annexed" Vaud, a fief of Savoy. The chief town of the district, Lausanne, remained the seat of the Bernese bailiff for two centuries.

Thus, gradually, the Swiss confederation was assuming the form and structure that we know today. Two religious faiths—the Catholic and the Protestant—were accepted by the thirteen member states, seven of whom remained faithful to the Church of Rome: Uri, Schwyz, Unterwald, Lucerne, Zug, Fribourg, and Solothurn.

Until the French Revolution, in 1789, Switzerland's story remained more or less uneventful, at least so far as the outside world was concerned. The confederation ably succeeded in remaining clear of the Thirty Years' War (1618-1648) and obtained official recognition by the great powers of its status as a sovereign, neutral state by the treaty of Westphalia.

Nevertheless, at home, the course of Swiss life did not run quite so smoothly. The ascendancy of the urban cantons—Bern, Zurich, Lucerne, and Basel—over the rural communities gained rapidly. Vassal states were treated with anything but brotherly leniency: heavy taxation, tolls, statute labor filled the coffers of the all-powerful cantons whose administrations and government had passed into the hands of a few patrician families. Revolts of the peasant populations against this oligarchy were sternly suppressed, as in the Peasant War of 1653. Almost a century later, in 1728, the heroic patriot of Vaud, Major Davel, was put to death by the Bernese for championing his country's liberties. Throughout the 18th century, Switzerland smoldered with sedition and revolt.

Despite this, Switzerland appeared to contemporary Europe as an idyllic state. The fashion for travel among the romantic Alps and along the no less romantic shores of Lake Geneva had been set by Jean-Jacques Rousseau, the Geneva-born literary giant of the pre-Revolution period. His novel *La Nouvelle Héloise,* with its setting in Montreux and Chillon, had taken Europe by storm. Replete with cosy though dilapidated farmsteads, rugged mountains, and glittering lakes, Swiss rural communities still gave a reflection of peace in a Europe already tossed on the surge of revolutionary ideas.

The French Revolution

Close neighbor to France, Switzerland could scarcely escape the influence of the French Revolution. In Basel, Geneva, Zurich, and elsewhere, subject communities rose against their masters. In January 1798, the people of Vaud stormed against their Bernese bailiffs and proclaimed their independence, christening their new state the Lemanic Republic. The cry of "liberty and equality" sounded throughout the confederation like a trumpet call.

This sudden dispersal of authority also served as an incentive for revolutionary France, whose armies invaded Switzerland in March 1798. First Vaud, then Bern, passed into their hands. The confederation of the thirteen cantons was doomed and in its place the French government established a tottering satellite state, the Helvetic Republic. The Republic of Geneva was annexed by France in the same year.

The artificial structure of the new republic was foredoomed to failure. It became the butt of conflicting interests and political factions. Finally, in 1803, Napoleon Bonaparte intervened and imposed his mediation, obtaining the restoration of a federal regime. Six states joined the new confederation: St. Gallen, Grisons, Aargau, Thurgau, Ticino, and Vaud. Legislative powers were vested in a federal diet presided over by a chief *Landammann,* who remained in office one year. Under his regime, Switzerland enjoyed ten years of peace.

Unfortunately, as Napoleon's power began to fade in 1812–1813, and despite the diet's declaration of neutrality, the Austrian army—160,000 strong—marched into Switzerland at Basel and Schaffhausen. In December 1813, the diet annulled Napoleon's act of mediation and freed the confederation from the tutelage of France.

Attempts were then made by Bern and Zurich to restore the old oligarchy, but the new sovereign cantons, such as Vaud and Aargau, found an unexpected champion in the person of Emperor Alexander I of Russia. Under his sternly liberal eye, the diet was forced to elaborate a new federal pact that was presented to and accepted by the powers, gathered together in godlike assembly, at Vienna, in 1815, their purpose being to reorganize Europe. Switzerland's 1815 constitution included three more member states: Valais, Neuchâtel, and Geneva. And so at last, after more than 500 years, Switzerland achieved its final shape and unity: a confederation of twenty-two sovereign states.

Nevertheless, all was not yet in order in the federal house. Conflicting interests were still at war and the political structure remained insecure until 1848, when, after a series of revolutionary movements and the religious *Sonderbund* civil war, a new constitution was drawn up and accepted by the twenty-two states. This constitution was further revised and completed in 1874. The bicameral system of government was established together with the rights of referendum and initiative.

The Swiss confederation is usually looked upon as an exceptionally "lucky" nation. Since the late 19th century, it has managed successfully to keep out of world wars and revolutions. Its people seem to sit securely upon an apparently impregnable Alpine stronghold and watch the world go by.

This is not quite the case, however. This immunity is the fruit of a wise policy, elaborated with keen foresight and strictly followed. The renunciation of all territorial expansion accepted by the confederation as a whole in 1515 involved the policy of neutrality, more and more clearly understood and applied as the centuries marched on.

Composed of a number of different racial groups, the Swiss confederation cannot afford to abandon this age-old policy, because in so
doing it would lay itself open to disruption. The necessity of having a
neutral state at the strategically vital crossroads of Alpine routes was
recognized by the great powers at the Congress of Vienna in 1815,
confirmed by the League of Nations, and again by the belligerents in
World War II. For this reason also, the confederation has wisely
refused to admit new member states, even though the populations of
the Gex district in France and of the Vorarlberg (Austria) have sought
this favor in recent years, the latter in 1920.

A LESSON IN DEMOCRACY

Greased Rifles and Referenda

The Swiss federal constitution as it stands today, although slowly evolved from the pact of 1291, was achieved in three stages during the 19th century. The 1815 federal pact—which received the blessing of the great powers at the Vienna Congress—made a new Switzerland emerge from the Napoleonic wars, but heralded a period of internal religious and political conflict. This pact was replaced in 1848 by the federal constitution, instituting a bicameral legislative body called the Federal Assembly and composed of a National Council and State Council. Executive powers were vested in the Federal Council and the Federal Tribunal served as the Supreme Court of Appeal. The cantons all conserved their own governments and undertook not to form alliances amongst themselves and to leave to the federal government the care of conducting negotiations with the outside world. Bern was selected as the federal capital.

The new regime proved acceptable to all the cantons; it had been elaborated with the cooperation of them all and was not submitted to the approval of the great powers. The Swiss confederation thus took its place among the nations as a wholly independent, sovereign state.

32

Nevertheless, as time went on, it was found that the 1848 constitution was in many respects insufficient; it was revised and augmented in 1874. The powers vested in the federal government were increased, especially as regarded the militia army. Compulsory, free schooling was to be introduced throughout the territory of the confederation, although the application of the law remained a cantonal matter. Two liberties were introduced: the rights of initiative and referendum. By the former, any male citizen, provided he can obtain the signature of 50,000 of his fellows, may propose the introduction of a new law to the federal assembly. Referendum means that 30,000 signatures suffice to force the federal government to submit any enactment to popular approval.

The structure of the Swiss federal constitution can be summarized as follows: a bicameral legislative body, the Federal Assembly, is composed of two houses: the National Council (corresponding to the U.S. House of Representatives), to which one deputy per 22,000 people is elected, and the States Council (equivalent to the U.S. Senate), in which sit two representatives of each canton. The executive body is the Federal Council, composed of seven members (elected for four years, but almost always re-elected), who rotate each year in the office of President of the Council.

Each canton is a republic, a sovereign state having its own government composed of an executive (State Council, Government Council, etc.) and a legislative (Cantonal Council, Great Council, etc.) branch. They have almost full control of cantonal affairs: education, public health, police, cantonal taxes, etc.

Federal and most cantonal elections are held every four years.

The civic-minded Swiss voter has quite a busy time. He is called to the polls frequently to voice his opinion (by ballot) on federal, cantonal, and municipal laws, policies, and enactments. Voting days are always set for weekends, to ensure that as many voters as possible will go to the polls. Nevertheless, in recent years, there has been a marked falling off in number of votes recorded, indicating a certain apathy among the population.

Outdoor Parliaments

Three cantons and two "half" cantons hold a popular open-air parliament once a year in spring. Every last Sunday in April and the first in May, voters of Glarus, Appenzell (Inner and Outer Rhodes) and Unterwald (Obwald and Nidwald) are convened to their *Landsgemeinde,* held in the main squares of the small capital towns of Stans, Sarnen, Trogen, or Hundwil (alternatively) and Glarus. Voters elect their magistrates for the coming year and vote "yes" or "no" by show of hands for any new cantonal legislation that may be put before them.

Appenzell A. Rh. can boast of having the largest *Landsgemeinde*— 10,000 to 12,000. They gather in the public square at Trogen or Hundwil, and the ceremony is opened by the arrival of the magistrates in office, headed by their chief, called the *Landammann*. They are preceded by a band of fifes and drums and take their stand on a central platform, from where they address the crowd. When the elections have been held and discussion on legislation is completed, the ceremony ends with a mutual exchange of vows. The *Landammann* takes an oath that he will be faithful to the people who have elected him and he is answered by an oath of allegiance from the electors: "And having understood fully that all that has been read to me this day, I shall hold to its truth, faithfully and without swerving. So do I desire, and may God help me."

A quaint ritual it is, in which religion and politics are closely intermingled: prayers, psalm-singing, and patriotic songs lend a solemn air to the ceremony. The men who are going to vote all carry a sword tucked into their Sunday suit, as a symbol of their rights and freedoms. Most remarkable to the onlooker is this crowd of black-clad men—Sunday suits are usually black, made of coarse serge and ill-fitting—with their clodhopper boots. Many of these rugged, weather-beaten faces are bearded, all are intense with concentration on the matter in hand.

The *Landsgemeinde* are ancient institutions, once common to all Swiss cantons, and date back to the 13th century. In the old days, they were convened whenever a nation-shaking decision had to be taken: in 1765, for example, the people of Schwyz were called 24 times to vote for this or that.

One important element in Swiss civic life is the commune. It is the town or village—in other words, the community—to which each family is bound by the accident of birth. Every Swiss, wherever he may live, remains legally attached to the commune of origin of his family, and his commune must help him in case of destitution. In the old times, burghership implied both obligations and advantages; today, there are few communes that still make gifts in kind to their burghers resident in their territory, gifts such as wood for the winter from the communal forests, cheese, butter, and so on.

By birth, the members of each family remain burgesses of the father's commune of origin. After marriage, a woman assumes the citizenship of her husband's commune. Citizenship of a commune can be obtained for the price of a donation to a designated charity, and this kind of "naturalization" is necessary often for men of other cantons or communes who wish to hold administrative posts in their town of residence. Aliens who wish to be naturalized Swiss must also donate to a charity in the commune.

Switzerland was late in giving to its women the vote and full civil rights. The women's suffrage movement started about 1898 but made slow progress, partly because of apathy and lack of interest in politics and civil affairs by the women themselves. There was even a modestly active "Women's League Against the Vote." But in 1971 Swiss women were given the federal vote and representation in the National and States Councils, Cantonal Parliaments and Courts.

The Swiss Army

The militia army of Switzerland is one of the most characteristic institutions of the country and unique of its kind.

Every able-bodied male citizen is a soldier. At the age of nineteen he is called for medical examination to be passed or refused for military service, which begins the following year. The initial period of training, the recruit school, is of 120 days, and a strenuous one. When the young soldier returns home, he takes his uniform and full kit with him, so as to be prepared in case of emergency and also for the subsequent three-week periods of "refresher courses" he will have to serve ten times until he is thirty-six. Men up to that age belong to the *Elite;* those of thirty-seven to forty-eight to the *Landwehr*. An NCO's duty ceases at fifty, an officer's at fifty-five. Recruits aiming for rank have to serve an extra 148 days for non-commissioned officer and a further like period for second lieutenant. Men exempted from military service can serve in auxiliary forces (air raid wardens, etc.), or have to pay an annual military tax. Fireman's service is also compulsory, including foreign male residents up to the age of forty-five, but you can get around it by paying the municipal fire tax.

In peacetime, when there is no General Headquarters, the highest authority of the militia army is an officer elected by the Federal Assembly. In times of emergency, that is to say, on the first day of general mobilization, the Federal Assembly appoints a supreme army chief. The Commander-in-Chief holds office until all danger of war or invasion is past.

This organization, which is purely a defense weapon, is highly efficient and speedy in its working. For example, the Swiss frontiers were entirely manned, every officer and soldier at his post, before the

British House of Commons had heard the announcement of the official declaration that World War II had begun. But the Swiss will tell you many hair-raising stories about their out-dated equipment and the shortage of essential military supplies, not least petrol.

And speaking of the Swiss army brings us to the question of Swiss neutrality, for the protection of which the military system has been devised. Neutrality is for Switzerland far more than a political line of conduct adopted to meet the contingencies of a decade or period: it is a fundamental necessity and a basic element of her national structure.

From early times, Switzerland has constituted herself the guardian of strategically important international routes, and the significance of this geographically imposed task was sanctioned by the Treaty of Westphalia in 1648, confirmed in 1815, when the Congress of Vienna explicitly announced its "formal and unconditional recognition of Switzerland's neutrality," in 1919 by the Treaty of Versailles and again in 1920, when the Council of the League of Nations admitted the "unique position" of Switzerland, "conditioned by a centuries-old tradition explicitly incorporated in international law." In 1939, also, the nations at war individually confirmed their recognition of this status.

The only nationalized utilities in Switzerland are the post office, telegraph and telephone and the main network of railroads (the Swiss Federal Railroads). Other utilities are private or municipal enterprises—gas works, streetcars, branch line railroads, and so on—but in some cases are subsidized by cantonal governments. Hydroelectric power plants are also owned by private companies under federal or cantonal grant. Freedom of trade and industry is one of the fundamental clauses of the federal constitution, and everything possible is done to encourage private enterprise.

PROSPERITY WITHOUT SMOKE

Buying Swiss Quality Products

The 19th-century slogan describing Switzerland as the "playground of Europe" seems to have created a general impression—further heightened by the intensified travel advertising of recent years—that Switzerland is the land where cowherds in quaint attire yodel eternally to bell-decked cows against a somewhat hazy Alpine background, from which chalet-like factories pour out a stream of watches, musicboxes, and chocolate, while a host of hotels accommodate the upper-crust of international society. How wrong this conception is can easily be proved by a few statistics. Only 17% of the population is occupied in agriculture and 3% in the catering trades, whereas 45% are factory and industrial workers.

The most important and characteristic feature of Switzerland's trade is that the staple industries are directed essentially towards export, because the domestic market is far too small to absorb their output. Switzerland must export in order to obtain even the essentials of life, for her natural resources are so restricted that even fodder, many foodstuffs, minerals, iron, and coal must be imported. As it is, the annual Swiss trade balance is always normally in the red, but the deficit is made good by a group of "invisible exports": banking and insurance, shipping and forwarding, the travel trades, dividends on capital invested abroad.

In the main, Switzerland has concentrated on industries that require as few raw materials as possible and a great deal of skilled labor to produce commodities of high value and small bulk. The exception to this is the heavy-engineering industry.

Travelers in Switzerland are astonished to find large industrial centers such as those in the neighborhood of Zurich (Winterthur, Baden, Oerlikon, Schlieren, Altstätten) or Basel (Olten) and towns like Bienne, St. Gallen, La Chaux-de-Fonds, Wohlen, which, though by no means large, are centers of important industrial regions, specializing in the production of this or that export commodity. British and American visitors, accustomed to all the gloom, smoke and smog of great factory cities, are sometimes astounded to find that they have traveled right through a Swiss industrial region without being aware of it, save for having noticed a few fairly large white buildings here and there. The cleanliness of Swiss factories is due to the fact that the industrial plant is electrically driven; there are few chimney stacks anywhere, save for chemicals, foundries, and smelting plants, and where they are necessary, they are, if possible, placed outside a city and appear as a mere speck against a background of fields and hills. They are more concentrated, it is true, around Basel and Zurich.

Watchmaking

This world-famous industry, which has developed slowly over the course of several centuries, is concentrated chiefly along the Jura frontier, from Geneva to Schaffhausen, but it has also spread to Solothurn and even to the Ticino.

The history of Swiss watchmaking is a series of trials, all of which have been overcome; but today it is confronted with a revolutionary technological development, the entry of electronics into the realm of mechanics, the production of watches called "solid state" (without any moving parts).

This has been a dramatic revolution because it has meant the elimination of jobs; while in 1970 there were nearly 90,000 watchmakers in Switzerland, working either in factories or at home, in the years to come there will be only 50,000, or fewer.

This change reduced watches to an almost entirely "functional" role, as mere timepieces, whereas previously they had belonged to the domain of jewelry, often as treasured gifts, with sentimental value.

By 1980 there will probably be three types of watches: mechanical watches; electronic watches with traditional faces and hands; and digital watches with either pushbutton-operated light-emitting diodes (LED) or permanent liquid-crystal display (LCD). In any case, it seems probable that by the end of the century there will be more electronic watches of one kind or another than mechanical watches.

For a long time it was feared that Switzerland would be more lastingly affected by this technological revolution than now appears to be the case. The Swiss waited a long time before accepting the challenge; but their patience and caution may actually have been strength and wisdom, for now that the novelty and gadget appeal of the new electronic watches has worn off, connoisseurs of fine watches are coming once again to prefer the traditional Swiss product for its striking beauty. Whether the movement is mechanical or quartz-operated but still uses the traditional face and hands, a fine Swiss watch is still, because of its excellence, the gift that everyone wants.

Equally, consumers are increasingly looking for quality, and they are willing to pay for it. The era of waste is finished. This development is particularly pleasing to Swiss watchmakers, for in their souls and consciences they are never happy when they have to produce cheap goods.

In other words, the Swiss watchmaking industry will tend more and more to specialize in the production of high quality watches that people will choose with affection, as gifts either to themselves or for someone else when they return home from their vacations.

Time on Your Hands

According to statistics, it is ten-to-one that you'll leave Switzerland with a new watch on your wrist. The choice is endless, and with increased competition from Japan and the U.S. with inexpensive watches, the range in Switzerland is also complete. You will be given a one-year guarantee (against faulty workmanship or materials) and parts will be available locally if your Swiss watch should need repair in the future. The Swiss Institute for Official Chronometers Tests has taken care of this by promoting standardization of parts, organizing a worldwide parts distribution system, and sponsoring an extensive repair education program.

Your Swiss retailer will address you in English and will be pleased to show you as many watches as you care to see. You will encounter no high-pressure sales tactics, and if you walk out of the store without buying, there will be no nasty remarks. The proliferation of stores in cities such as Zurich, Geneva, Montreux, Lausanne-Ouchy and all other tourist hubs encourages shopping for the watch you like best.

One thing to remember is that you can't go wrong buying a Swiss watch. Some are better than others, but all are good. (Cheap jeweled-lever watches and pin-lever or "drugstore" watches are of inferior quality, and you don't have to go to Switzerland to buy one.) Swiss watches fall into price and quality categories by trade names, much the same as automobiles.

In the Rolls Royce or Cadillac class are several brands whose reputations come from a long and noble tradition: Patek-Phillipe, Piaget, Audemars-Piguet, Vacheron-Constantin, and some whose fame is more recent and less widespread, such as Corum or Delaneau. Certain great trade names, familiar to everyone, Omega and Rolex in particular. have made Switzerland famous not only by their quality and styling but by the major importance which they give to their after-sales services.

On the next level are a large number of makes which deserve confidence and which are offered at roughly comparable price levels, although they generally try to serve the largest possible price range: Baume & Mercier, Bulova, Certina, Ebel, Eterna, Favre-Leuba, Girard-Perregaux, IWC International Watch, Jaeger Lecoultre, Longines, Milus, Rado, Tissot, Universal, Vulcain, Zenith and Zodiac.

There are a large number of other makes that are popular with the general public and with tourists coming from countries where they are firmly established: Camy, Cyma, Consul, Doxa, Enicar, Eska, Fortis, Invicta, Juvenia, Mido, Nivada, Oris, Roamer, Rodania, Rotary, Sandoz, Sicura, Technos, Universal, etc.

Of the many *Rolex* specialists watches, the waterproof, self-winding, GMT-Master tells clearly and simultaneously the time in any two time zones—invaluable for all world travelers as well as pilots, navigators and ships' captains; they were the inventors of the waterproof watch with their Oyster series in 1926.

Bucherer and Gübelin occupy a very special position in Switzerland itself because they sell, mainly in the major tourist cities, from their own retail shops.

And there are specialists such as Heuer and Breitling who produce universally known chronographs and sports recording devices.

Finally, there are certain manufacturers who have rapidly distinguished themselves in the new field of electronics by their spirit of innovation, such as Mondine Watch and, above all, Nepro.

Selecting Your Watch

The price you pay for a Swiss watch is determined by 1) the metal used in the case, 2) the special features offered (automatic, calendar, alarm, stopwatch, etc.), and 3) whether or not it is a chronometer. The last raises an important question of nomenclature. In Switzerland, a chronometer is a watch that has been tested and approved for accuracy by the independent, government-sponsored Swiss Institute for Official Chronometer Tests. With each you get a certificate stating the results of timing tests under conditions of extreme heat and cold and in a variety of positions. This is not to be confused with a chronograph, which is one of those complicated watches that tells you the phases of the moon and tides, the time in a dozen different cities, and has all sorts of stopwatch features, nor does it signify that *only* chronometers are accurate watches. A watch without a chronometer certificate may easily be just as accurate: no Swiss watch leaves a reputable factory without being carefully inspected.

Contrary to popular opinion, the number of jewels in a watch is not in itself or should not be a price determinant. A good watch, Swiss or otherwise, has no more jewels than it needs to reduce friction in pivotal parts. For uncomplicated watches this number varies from fifteen to seventeen. In special-feature watches the number may increase to thirty, but even in this case it is not the jewels (they are synthetic rubies, tougher than real ones, that cost the manufacturer a few cents each), but the workmanship that you pay for.

It is also good to know that automatic (self-winding) watches are not made solely for people who are too lazy or forgetful to wind every twenty-four hours, nor are waterproof watches manufactured under the assumption that people want to wear them in swimming or while taking a bath. The chief purpose of the self-winding mechanism is to keep the mainspring at a constant tension, thus ensuring greater accuracy. The waterproof watch, hermetically sealed, protects the delicate movement against dust and air, which tend to dry up lubricating oil. Remember to make a distinction between water-resistant and waterproof watches. If you feel like it, you can go swimming with your waterproof watch, whereas a water-resistant timepiece will give you only limited protection against water. One should also remember that the metal used in the case of a watch is rarely an indication of the quality of the movement. More often than not, within a given brand, a movement encased in stainless steel is identical to the one in solid gold. If not, the sales person will tell you, and you can rely upon his word.

In money terms, here are the approximate prices to keep in mind when shopping for a watch. For a utility watch, stainless steel, not waterproof or self-winding, without special features or chronometer rating, you should pay no more than 80 francs. Quality special-feature watches (self-winding, calendar, alarm, chronograph, etc.) in stainless steel start around 200 francs; the identical movements cased in gold plate cost 25 percent more, in solid gold 100 percent more. Name-brand watches with at least one special feature and a chronometer rating start at around 400 francs, correspondingly higher in gold-plate or solid-gold cases. The least expensive luxury watch made only in precious metals costs 1,200 francs.

In buying watches of a brandname that you have never heard of, it is best to ask and follow the advice of the sales person. Watch retailers in Switzerland do a tremendous business and they have no interest in unloading inferior merchandise. Shop around for the watch that appeals to you, not for price. Prices are strictly controlled and you'll pay exactly the same in one shop or region as another. There are no bargain prices. Above all don't buy a "Swiss" watch from a sidewalk peddler in any other country. It's either smuggled, in which case you have no written guarantee, or an out-and-out counterfeit.

The astonishing Jaeger-Le Coultre Atmos clock lives on air and is outstanding among the most notable creations of Swiss watchmaking. Its self-winding mechanism requires a temperature variation of only 2°F to provide it with forty-eight hours of power reserve.

An extraordinarily large assortment of artistic clocks, desk clocks with automatic dater, "world hour" clocks that show the time around the world, and traveling alarm clocks is on display in all specialty shops.

Machinery and Textiles

Engineering. Heavy-engineering products such as diesel and marine engines are made in Baden, Zurich, and its neighborhood. A great variety of special machinery for different trades is also made and textile machines are specialties that find excellent markets abroad. Precision engineering, in many cases closely allied to the watchmaking crafts, has developed into the making of machine tools and combined with a country's hydroelectric resources, given rise to a flourishing electrotechnical industry producing a great diversity of equipment ranging from highpowered turbines and transformers to the smallest of remote control and scientific apparatus. The heavy industries are concentrated in central and northern Switzerland.

Textiles. The textile industries are concentrated in central and eastern Switzerland, and several developed from domestic crafts.

Zurich is the center of a thriving silk-spinning and weaving trade that has specialized in the production of tie-silks. Ribbons are made in Basel. In both cities rayon manufacture is progressing.

Perhaps the most widely known of Swiss textile products are the embroideries, lovely eyelet fabrics, and organdies to which St. Gallen has lent its name, but which are also made both in the canton of Appenzell and in Thurgau. The industry is not entirely mechanized, and embroidery has remained a domestic craft in these regions. Fine lawns, grosgrain fabrics, cotton goods, and linen are spun and woven in St. Gallen, Glarus, the Zurich Oberland, at Langenthal, and in the Toggenburg district, where finishing trades also thrive, handling piecegoods sent, not only by Swiss manufacturers, but also from England, France, and elsewhere for special processing.

One particular branch of the textile trade has been centralized in Wohlen (Canton Aargau): the manufacture of millinery braids, a development of the old local domestic craft of weaving and plaiting fine straws. Wohlen is a great supplier of straw goods (synthetic and natural) to world fashion centers, especially Paris.

Chemicals. Basel is the center of the Swiss chemical industry, although factories and small pharmaceutical firms are to be found all over the country.

The main products of this activity are dyestuffs and industrial resins, pharmaceuticals and perfumes. A few heavy-chemical plants have been established at Basel, Zurzach, Monthey, Viège, Bex, Bodio, Vallorbe, Turgi, Mels, and Aarau, and aluminum is produced at Martigny, Neuhausen, and Chippis.

It is hardly necessary to mention chocolate, evaporated and dietetic milks, and cheese, the most popular of Swiss export products. Canning plants now absorb the surplus fruit and vegetables grown on the home market, and tobacco, quite a flourishing crop in some districts, is used for the domestic cigar and cigarette industry.

There are innumerable small factories all over the country producing quite well-known commodities ranging from typewriters to musical boxes, from glass and chinaware to sports equipment and toys.

Production must necessarily remain on a comparatively small scale, as compared with that of great industrial countries, and this factor has caused the Swiss to concentrate chiefly on the quality of good craftsmanship of high-priced goods and to avoid cheap mass-produced commodities.

Good Buys Around the Country

A rule of thumb on shopping in Swizerland is that—excluding Swiss products, which we shall discuss later—it is an excellent place to buy products of European countries you don't plan to visit. For example, German cameras and optical equipment are no more expensive than in Germany, and for several makes, notably *Zeiss,* the prices in Switzerland are even lower than in Germany. The *Alpa Reflex* is a first-rate Swiss-made camera and the *Bolex* movie cameras are as good as they come.

You can find an excellent selection of *Rosenthal* and *Arzberg* china, Danish silver and cutlery, British cashmeres, woolens, and sports equipment, Dutch *(Philips)* electrical appliances, and Scandinavian furs at moderate savings.

Shopping for gifts, you'll be on the lookout for items of a uniquely Swiss flavor. You can take care of the children (and have a great time yourself) by visiting any of the *Franz Carl Weber* toyshops; they are in Zurich, Geneva, Bern, Basel, Bienne, Lucerne, Lausanne, Lugano, and Locarno. For Swiss handicrafts, textiles, ceramics, and metal-works, be sure to visit one of the Swiss *Heimatwerk* shops, especially the two in Zurich and Bern. You may be absolutely certain of the quality and authenticity of merchandise offered in these attractive shops. No one will try to sell you anything, but few visitors leave these shops without buying.

Swiss winter sports equipment is of top quality. If you are coming for skiing, the best idea is to bring nothing and buy what you need here. Clothing styles tend to be conservative and prices high, but you can be sure of good quality. Equipment, though expensive, is first class, and good buys can be found at sales and on secondhand (in good repair) skis, boots and poles. If you're only going skiing (skating, tobogganing, etc.) for a short time, consider renting equipment.

Some of these countless shops are mentioned in the appropriate section of this book following hotel and restaurant listings for the city or area concerned.

CREATIVE SWITZERLAND

What Has She Given the World?

by

JAMES M. HATCH

(A free-lance writer and teacher, Mr. Hatch devotes all his energies to interpreting Europe, and especially Switzerland, to his readers in the United States.)

The visitor to Switzerland is generally so overwhelmed by Switzerland's natural beauty that it becomes difficult to focus on her artistic and cultural achievements—yet with time the problem only becomes more difficult. One almost understands Orson Welles' emotional outburst in the movie *The Third Man,* when he said, "The Italian Renaissance was full of crimes and excesses, and yet it gave us the greatest masterpieces of art.... Switzerland has lived in peace for three centuries, and what has she given us? The cuckoo clock...."

Though cuckoo clocks come from the Black Forest, Welles' improvised remarks seem an accurate index of the popular misunderstandings about Swiss art and culture. There is no Leonardo or Michelangelo in Swiss art, but, in the 20th century alone, there are Giacometti, Le Corbusier and Klee. The last, although not a Swiss citizen, was educated in Bern and lived there for many years. It is not a question of names alone (a situation made more difficult by many Swiss artists becoming expatriates), but rather a question of a whole country with a high cultural achievement, frequently denigrated by the unknowing.

Switzerland, after all, is a small country with a small population—a little over six million. Yet she has given to the world major talents in every field of culture. Individually and collectively, Switzerland's achievement is high.

André Gide once remarked in his *Journals,* "I am constantly reminded as I walk through Zurich how much more conducive to art is sensuality than sentimentality. Really, I am quite at sea here; I feel more alien to these people, and they to me, than I would among Zulus or Caribbeans." For the Swiss artist, the same feeling seems to prevail. Perhaps because of the bourgeois character of the nation, or perhaps because things are too stable to be interesting at home for the artist, many Swiss talents have chosen to live and work elsewhere. Le Corbusier (C. E. Jeanneret), though born at La Chaux-de-Fonds and educated in Switzerland, claimed himself as French, and Giacometti, from the Grissons, also became a resident of Paris. In the 18th century, Madame de Staël, and her friend Benjamin Constant, author of *Adolphe,* seemed more French than Swiss.

There are, of course, strong contradictions to this frequent pattern. C. F. Ramuz, perhaps the best-known modern Swiss writer, stayed at home, and Hans Erni, one of the most versatile and prolific of modern artists, is proudly Swiss. Despite the exceptions, however, the problem of assessing Swiss cultural achievements has been made difficult by the significant number of expatriate talents.

Where Music Reigns

Music, rather than the visual or literary arts, ranks highest with the Swiss themselves. Almost every major town or city boasts a fine musical group—such as the internationally known Orchestre de la Suisse-Romande. Concerts and musical festivals are frequent throughout the year, and of universally high quality. The visitor should check with local tourist offices for special information—tickets are generally easy to obtain. In conducting, composing, and perform-ing, the Swiss have distinguished themselves. Arthur Honegger is perhaps the best-known of modern Swiss composers, but Rolf Liebermann and Frank Martin are also internationally known. The sopranos Lisa della Casa and Maria Stader, both Swiss, are familiar to concert audiences everywhere.

Opera has received a big boost in Switzerland at Geneva's Grand-Théâtre, beautifully rebuilt after the interior was gutted by a fire some years back, caused by a too realistic rehearsal of *Valkyrie*. It was as its Director that Herbert Graf (who died in 1973) went to the Grand-Théâtre after more than twenty years as the New York Metropolitan's Stage Director. In Geneva he established his own permanent company, formed around a nucleus of young and talented American singers. Zurich has always had a fine opera season, and opera festivals are popular in various cities during the year. In ballet, the Swiss have been less fortunate, except possibly at Basel—most ballet treats are provided by visiting foreign companies.

In literature, the Swiss have produced authors of merit, but because there are at least five national literatures—Latin, German, French, Italian, and Romansch—it becomes difficult to talk about a "Swiss" literature. To outsiders, Wyss' *Swiss Family Robinson* and Johanna Spyri's *Heidi* would probably come to mind first, but these books have seldom been thought very highly of at home. The most famous early Swiss chronicle, the *Chronicon Helveticum,* documents the story of the legendary William Tell. Written in the late 16th century by Giles (Aegidius) Tschudi, a leading Glarus magistrate, it inspired Schiller's play *Wilhelm Tell* and Walter Scott's translation, *The Ballad of Sempach.* Zwingli, in Zurich, added to early Swiss literature, though he, too, wrote mostly in Latin.

Unlike the French, who had a brilliant 16th century on which to base a literary upsurge, the Swiss-French writers have been somewhat without inspiration. Perhaps because of this, the Swiss delight in claiming Madame de Staël and Benjamin Constant as their own: there is, surprisingly, some foundation to the claim. But they can certainly claim without contradiction Albrecht von Haller (who wrote *The Alps)* and Solomon Gessner (author of *The Idylls)* as genuine Swiss contributors to 18th-century literature. In the 19th century, Amiel, in his journals, revealed himself a brilliant, if erratic, genius. And in more recent times it is C. F. Ramuz, who died in 1947, with whom the claims must rest for French-language literature. Among German-language writers, C. F. Meyer and Gottfried Keller are singled out in the 19th century; more recently, Carl Spitteler, who won one of the first Nobel Prizes in Literature, is considered by many to be the finest poet of his time in the German language. Hermann Hesse, though German-born, became a Swiss resident and eventually a naturalized citizen. He celebrated the Ticino in many of his late writings, won the Nobel Prize in 1946, and is buried in Gentilino, near Lugano. The playwrights and authors Friedrich Dürrenmatt and Max Frisch testify to the vitality of German-language literature in our own time. The Italian-language writers, though small in number, have produced Francesco Chiesa, a poet and novelist who taught for many years at the university of Bologna and was one of the more important critics in the Italian language. He died recently at the ripe old age of 102. The Romansch tradition, though it has been vital, is primarily of interest to scholars.

The Arts

Caesar in his *Gallic Wars* speaks frequently of the Helvetii and relics of Roman times abound in various regional museums. Many fine Roman sculptures are preserved in the former Roman theater at Avenches. Known to the Romans as Aventicum, the city was an important link in the empire—it was here, in 1939, that the highly prized gold bust of Marcus Aurelius, now in Lausanne's Musée des Beaux Arts, was found.

The Swiss achievements of the Dark Ages in art primarily survive in the priceless illuminated manuscripts in the baroque library of the abbey of St. Gallen. The Romanesque tradition is shown strongly in small churches and chapels throughout Ticino, Thun, Vaud, and Schaffhausen, as well as in the cathedrals of Basel, Zurich and Geneva.

In the 15th and 16th centuries, art was dominated by Conrad Wirtz and Hans Holbein, both German immigrants. Wirtz's Gothic altarpiece, originally created for the Geneva Cathedral in 1444, is now on display in the Geneva Museum of Art and History, while the museums of Basel and Geneva have many Holbein masterpieces.

One of the curiosities of Swiss art history is the almost complete lack of influence of either the Italian or French Renaissance. Swiss Protestantism of the late 16th century damned to fiery hells the Renaissance sensuality; her artists therefore avoided foreign influences. Were it not for the abbey of St. Gallen, Einsiedeln, and a few monastic churches, there would be little of baroque art to see in the country. The lack of a natural evolution from late Gothic style to the modern style left Swiss artists in limbo—and only recently have they began to recover. The English championed the art of the 18th-century mystical painter Johann Fuseli, and many admire the works of Ferdinand Hodler of Bern, a brillian genius who died in 1918. Despite these two eccentric talents, from the Renaissance to the present, the Swiss have had little artistic influence on the world.

Now, however, things have changed for the better. Giacometti (whose sculpture is seen in Zurich's Kunsthaus) and Paul Klee have taken their places in the history of modern art. Hans Erni, who was given a brilliantly displayed retrospective exhibition in the Cantonal Museum in Schaffhausen in 1966, is the ranking Swiss artist of the present; he has shown himself to be a brilliant, if perhaps too facile, draftsman, painter, print maker and designer. Other contemporary artists of great talent are the versatile Max Bill, painter, sculptor, architect, industrial designer and typographer, and Felice Filippini, the Ticino painter and writer, who since 1945 has been a director of the Swiss-Italian radio station as well.

Hans Erni's fascination with poster design, shown previously by Hodler and Cuno Amiet, is indicative of the overall standard of Swiss graphic design. Streets in every community are immeasurably brightened by colorful posters of great integrity; publication of such magazines as *Du* and *L'Oeil* also testifies to the richness of Swiss graphics. In art publishing, the Swiss name of Skira has become synonomous with excellence. Skira is but one first—thoughout the country the aesthetic standards of printing and publishing are equally high.

Of architects, Le Corbusier is best known, but by no means the only name of note. Pascal Häusermann, whose egg-shaped houses have drawn much attention, is but one of many young architects who are winning popularity with their distinctive style. Through history, Swiss architects have been known for their excellence. In the 16th century, several Ticino architects achieved fame in Italy—Carlo Maderno, the architect of the portico of St. Peter's, Rome; Francesco Borromini, architect of Rome's Palazzo Barberini; and Baltazar Longhena, architect of Santa Maria della Salute in Venice. Along with the architects, one should mark the work of Othmar Ammann, the engineer who designed New York's George Washington Bridge.

The art museums and private collections of Switzerland are second to none. Though few great artists through the ages are Swiss, one should never fear that the museums might be filled with third-rate art—the Kunsthaus in Zurich alone would be the envy of any country, but Basel and Geneva have outstanding museums as well, and the cantonal museums have fine collections, particularly of folk art and early artifacts. Special shows of foreign artists are frequent, like the gigantic Chagall retrospective of 1967 in Zurich. (Information on these exhibitions can be obtained from national and local tourist offices.)

Switzerland has three great, privately assembled art collections: the Müller at Solothurn (which is not shown to the public), the Reinhart Collection at Winterthur, and that of the late Baron Heinrich von

Thyssen, in the Villa Favorita, outside Lugano. The Reinhart Collection was donated to the government in 1970, but is shown at the former home of Oskar Reinhart, on a hill overlooking Wintherthur, about 20 minutes by train from Zurich. The von Thyssen collection is one of the finest private collections in Europe and is open to the public on weekends from April to October.

Education

In psychology, while not forgetting the Bleulers (father and son), Hermann Rorschach and Jean Piaget, the achievements of Carl Jung pushed him to the forefront of 20th-century thinkers. Though Jung declined to be Freud's appointed successor and was hesitant to let the Jung Institute grow up around him in Zurich, his fame is richly deserved. Other thinkers of note in modern Switzerland appear in the field of theology—Karl Barth and Emil Brunner among Protestants, and Hans Küng among Roman Catholics.

The universities of Switzerland contribute highly to her cultural life. The University of Basel, founded in 1460 by Pope Pius II, is the principal center of learning. Here, Erasmus taught, as did Vesalius, the 16th-century medical authority, the Bernoullis, the mathematician Euler, Jakob Burckhardt, and Frederick Nietzsche. Zurich's university, particularly the medical school, has a high reputation, but has recently been overshadowed by the Federal Institute of Technology (next door), which has produced more Nobel Prize winners than any other scientific school in the world.

Both the university and the Federal Institute of Technology at Lausanne are notable, as is the architecturally adventurous University of St. Gallen. Bern's law school is celebrated, and Fribourg's university is one of the world's leading Catholic institutions. There are also good universities at Neuchâtel and Geneva, the latter well-known for international affairs and political science. Private secondary schools in Switzerland have an international reputation—most are found in the French-speaking area of the country. With such outstanding institutions, it is little wonder that some 30 percent of all Switzerland's students, at both university and secondary level, are foreigners.

Foreigners living and working in Switzerland account for more than 20 percent of the population, a matter of growing national concern. Many work with the countless international organizations located in the country, but a large and growing number are employed in the less attractive jobs such as in hotels, on building sites and so on; in short, immigrant labor on a large scale.

Foreign artists, however, have lived and worked in Switzerland to great advantage—a curious situation, considering the plight felt by many native artists. Richard Wagner wrote *Die Meistersinger, Siegfried,* and *Götterdämmerung* while living near Lucerne from 1866 to 1873, and earlier completed *Tristan und Isolde* and *Parsifal* in Zurich. Gibbon wrote his *Decline and Fall* in Lausanne; Rilke lived and worked in the Valais and is buried in Raron; Nietzsche taught in Basel and Einstein in Zurich and Mary Shelley wrote *Frankenstein* (as a joke) in a cottage by Lake Geneva. The list continues indefinitely: Lord Byron, Thomas Mann, Goethe, Ruskin, Mark Twain, George Sand, James Joyce, and F. Scott Fitzgerald all found Switzerland a source of inspiration, or, perhaps more accurately, a quiet haven in which to work.

The Swiss at Leisure

The Swiss film industry has at last built up a national reputation, especially in French-speaking Switzerland, and to a lesser extent an international one. There is no lack of Swiss talent as the box offices showed with Maria and Maximilian Schell.

Swiss radio and television are largely non-commercial, but because there are three different networks—one for each language—efforts in this field are somewhat dissipated.

Movie and theater attendance are high, with most theaters municipally subsidized. The dramatic fare offered is usually of classical repertory, but new life blood is coming into the Swiss theater—particularly as the impact of traveling foreign troupes is felt in the larger cities. Low-brow humor is popular in nightclubs in Zurich but one really needs a strong command of the Swiss-German dialect to appreciate it.

Book sales are high in Switzerland, but the newspaper is the most popular reading matter. The quality of Swiss journalism is unparalleled—the *Neue Zürcher Zeitung,* regarded by many as one of the world's best newspapers, is a good index. The paper is published daily. An extraordinary amount of newsprint is devoted to editorials, art and literary criticism, political analysis, technical news—and very little to comics and the standard pap familiar to many foreign readers.

At home the Swiss are conservative, and great joiners, clubs of all sorts providing an excuse primarily to go out and drink with the boys. Perhaps as a response to this, the good wives, normally homebodies, have banded together to form the *Frauenverein,* an antidrink league.

Despite the ultramodern appearance of most cities, Switzerland is still largely a nation of tiny rural communities—consequently, the folk arts flourish. All the traditional yodeling and alphorn-blowing survive, and with great popularity, but in the cities, these customs are seldom authentic. In the less traveled areas of the country, one can still find folk festivals staged for their intrinsic merit, rather than for the tourists. Rural culture is best seen in the weaving, woodcarving, ceramics and metal work—arts encouraged by the cantonal governments. Every canton has a shop where the native crafts are available, and though the goods are not inexpensive, they are of high quality, with profits going to the craftsmen themselves.

FOOD AND DRINK

Cuisine? . . . Kochkunst? . . . Cucina?

Swiss cooking, like the patchwork that is Switzerland, is a medley drawn from several countries. It has borrowed from the French *cuisine,* the German *Kochkunst,* and the Italian *Cucina.* Gastronomic pleasures are appreciated by the Swiss, and their home cooking has been brought to a fine art by the housewives without the aid of tinned or packaged foods.

However, the traveler in Switzerland is more concerned with the art of the professional chef, and in many reputed restaurants and hotels he will catch glimpses of highhatted *maîtres queux,* master cooks commanding a bevy of skilled helpers. Innumerable inns and small restaurants all over the country do a thriving trade with Swiss and local patrons, who know that here—or there—one can enjoy a specialty dish. Many popular regional dishes relished for centuries in farmstead kitchens now appear on the best menus.

Originally devised in Vaud, Valais, or Geneva—no one quite knows which, for all three of these cantons claim priority—*fondue* is the dish that set the fashion for dunking when it was introduced to the United States at the Swiss Pavilion at the 1939-40 New York World Fair. It is a concoction of cheese, mainly Emmentaler and Gruyère, melted and skilfully mixed with a soupçon of garlic, a teaspoonful of flour, white wine, and a little Kirsch *(eau de vie* made from cherries). The richly aromatic whole is brought to the table in the pipkin and placed on a flame in the center of the table. Guests armed with long-handled forks spear small squares of bread which are thrust in turn into the steaming dish.

The eating of fondue is a fine art. Each guest who fails to withdraw his morsel of bread from the pipkin is called upon to offer a bottle of wine to the company.

Guests are warned never, *never,* to drink water or beer with or after fondue. White wine, Kirsch, tea, or coffee are suitable beverages. The season for fondue begins in early September and continues merrily until summer.

Cheese and Other Specialties

It is understandable that, in a country famed for its dairy produce, cheese is an important food item. A great variety of cheeses are made in Switzerland, ranging from the widely exported *Gruyère* and *Emmentaler* to the less known Jura delicacy *Tête de Moine,* which must be scraped from its sugarcone-shaped cake. *Vacherin* is a fine cream cheese, made in Jura and Alpine pastures during the summer and stored by the cowherds in round boxes made of tree bark; it is ripe in late November and adorns the Christmas and New Year table. The Valais produces the slightly insipid, rather hard and very delicate *Bagnes* and *Conches,* also made in Alpine pastures and used for *raclette.* The Ticino favors the locally made *Piora* and *Muggio* or, for grating, *Sbrinz* (rather like Parmesan). *Schabzieger,* made with herbs, is a Glarus specialty.

Among the cheese dishes popular in Switzerland, the Valais *raclette* runs a good second to fondue. It is not served at just any restaurant, for its making requires an open fire to which a half cake of Conches or Bagnes is exposed; as it softens, it is scraped directly onto your plate, to be eaten with potatoes boiled in their skins, pickled spring onions, and gherkins.

Salées au fromage, or cheese cakes, are eaten all the year round and can be bought in most bakers' shops. Nevertheless, their yearly climax of popularity is at the Lausanne Swiss Comptoir, the national autumn trade and agricultural fair. Big brother to the *Salée* is the *Gâteau au fromage.* Then, too, there is the *Croûte au fromage,* the Swiss version of the Welsh rarebit.

Elegance
in time...

Φ

BAUME & MERCIER
GENEVE
1830

On sale at the leading
watchmakers' and jewellers'.

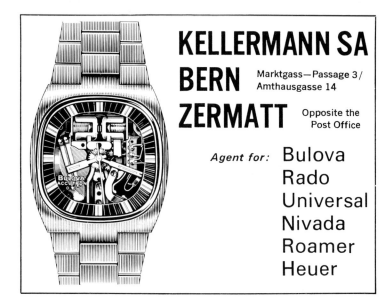

Kässuppe, or cheese soup, is a specialty of central Switzerland, served in Lucerne, Zug, and neighboring cantons.

In the western lake district of Switzerland (Lakes Geneva, Neuchâtel, Beinne, Morat) delicious fish specialties are served in summer, when fresh-water fishermen can ply their trade to their heart's content. *Friture de perchettes* (fried fillets of small lake perch) are served piping hot in butter. With a glass of local white wine and a romantic view at hand, what better end to a warm summer's day can a gourmet wish? Pike *(brochet),* grayling *(ombre),* char *(ombre chevalier),* and trout also appear on western Swiss menus. *Blue Lake trout* (from the hatcheries at Blausee on the Spiez-Kandersteg route) are a great delicacy.

Croûtes aux morilles (delicious little mushrooms served on toast) are much prized when in season as a lunch or supper dish. And Fribourg cooks are specialists in the making of mushroom sauces.

Country-cured pork meats abound in this region and weekly markets are replete with sausages of all kinds: *saucisse au chou* and *au foie, saucisson, boutefas,* neighboring with smoked hams and pork chops. Served with boiled leeks or French beans, they make a most appetizing dish. Genevans are partial to *pieds de porc au madère* (pig's trotters with Madeira sauce). *Choucroute garnie* (sauerkraut with boiled ham and Vienna sausages) also agreeably replenishes the inner man.

A Valais and Grisons specialty in great demand is *viande séchée* or *bundnerfleisch* (dried beef or pork). The meat is not cured, but dried in airy barns where the air is crisp and dry. Cut wafer-thin, with some pickled spring onions and gherkins it makes a delectable, if somewhat expensive, hors d'oeuvre.

In Bern you will find *Bernerplatte* listed on the menu; it is a Rabelaisian dish of sauerkraut or French beans "garnished," that is to say piled high, with broiled ham, pork chops, Vienna sausage, smoked sausages, and other delicacies. *Röschti* is the German Swiss form of fried potatoes, excellent when served with small squares of fried bacon and always served with *geschnetzlets,* (thin slices of veal in cream sauce). *Mistkratzerli* is a dish much favored in the Rhine cantons—young roast cock fresh from the farmyard served with baked potatoes.

St. Gallen has *Schüblig,* a special type of veal sausage; Zurich its *Zürchertopf* (macaroni, minced meat, tomato sauce, oven-baked en casserole), *Geschnetzeltes* (minced veal with thick cream sauce) and *Leberspiessli* (liver skewered and fried). Basel is partial to *Klöpfer,* a particularly succulent cervelat sausage.

In these regions, too, you will find delicious lake and river fish: trout, pike, red mullet, ferra (a type of Central European salmon).

Lucerne has a specialty called *Kugelipastete,* a *vol-au-vent* served with *Luzerner Allerlei,* a vegetable and mushroom salad.

Pork meat in sausage form has a variety of names, each locality having a special recipe for its making: *Knackerli* and *Pantli* (Appenzell), *Mostmöckli,* and *Kalberwurst* (the latter being made of calf's liver). The Grisons boasts of its *Salsiz* (small salami), *Beinwurst, Engadiner Wurst,* and *Leberwurst,* as well as the previously mentioned *bundnerfleisch.*

Pâtisserie—all those temptingly displayed little cakes seen in tearooms and bakeries throughout Switzerland—is not a western Swiss specialty. But in the region under review, you will find *petits pains de Rolle* (sugar buns); the *cuchéole* of Fribourg (large sweetened bread loaves made with eggs); *merveilles,* crisp, sweet wafers, fried in oil and served on high days and holidays; *gâteau au nillon,* a rather stodgy salted cake made from *greubons,* the dialect word for the residue of melted lard; *bricelets,* a square, wafflelike, sweet wafer; *tresse,* fine white bread in plaited form.

Cakes and sweetmeats are equally varied in this part of the world. *Leckerli* are Basel specialties that have found favor all over Switzerland; they are a sort of spiced honey cake, flat and oblong in shape, with a thin coating of sugar icing on top. In Bern, they are sold with a white sugar bear for decoration. *Fastnachtküchli* are a sort of *merveille* eaten in Zurich at Mardi Gras festivities. *Gugelhopf* are large, high bunlike cakes with a hollowed center, useful for stuffing with whipped cream. *Schaffhauserzungen,* which as the name implies are made in Schaffhausen, are cream-filled cakes; *Fladen* and *Krapfen* are rich fruitcakes made with pears, nuts, and almond paste. *Birnbrot* is a less interesting fruitcake made chiefly of dried pears.

In the Ticino, much has been borrowed from Italian cooking. Here menus list *ravioli al pomodoro* (ravioli with tomato sauce), *risotto con funghi* (which means "with mushrooms"), *fritto misto alla ticinese* (mixed grill), *polenta. Coppa* and *zampone* are Ticino sausages and *busecca* is a soup made from tripe, while *zuppa del paese* is a thick, vegetable broth. Snails—*lumachi*—are served with a walnut paste and *panettone* is a plain fruit cake, shaped rather like the northern *Gugelhopf,* an importation from Lombardy.

Wines

The Swiss, especially the populations of the west and south, are great drinkers of wine, which is for them what beer is to an

Englishman or an *espresso* to an Italian. That is to say, when two Swiss buddies get together for a friendly drink, they order three *decis* (deciliters) of open wine. White wine is appreciated as an appetizer in preference to a cocktail or vermouth. Travelers in Switzerland soon learn to value the advantage of being able to drink, at any café or wayside inn, at any hour of the day, a glass of these excellent vintages.

Much of the vine stock cultivated in Switzerland is the Chasselas, imported from Burgundy. In Canton Valais, Rhineland stock, especially the green Sylvaner, has been imported, together with the famous Black Pinot from Burgundy. Ticino wines are produced mostly from Nostrano, Americano or Isabelle and a little Bordeaux stock. It is said that the Romans first introduced the vine into Switzerland. At all events, in the 10th century, Good Queen Bertha of Burgundy encouraged her vassals in the Lake Geneva region to carry on this husbandry.

Vaud wines are divided into two major groups: Lavaux (Dézaley, Espesses, Rivaz, St. Saphorin, etc.), and La Côte (Féchy, Luins, Bégnins, etc.). A third, smaller group is the Vaud Chablis wines, produced in the Alpine foothills from Montreux to Aigle. A fourth wine-producing region in the Canton is at the southern end of Lake Neuchâtel (Bonvillars, Vully, Concise).

Valais has a dry climate and long, hot summers, ideal for the cultivation of vines. Fendant is a popular white wine and Dôle the most popular red. Specialty wines of delicious bouquet are also produced: Johannisberg (similar to Rhine wine), Riesling, Hermitage, Malvoisie (a sweet dessert wine).

Neuchâtel produces light, sparkling vintages, usually sold under the name of their canton of origin. A Neuchâtel wine is said to be "excellent" when a star forms in the glass after it has been poured.

Ticino is a great producer of wine, but until recent years the vintages here have been of inferior quality. Modern methods of viniculture and the introduction of new stock have brought forth smooth, fruity white wines (Nebbiolo, Bonarda, Freisa, Merlot) and the rich red Nostrano. Genuine pure Nostrano is, unfortunately, available only in small quantities. It is hard to find anywhere, unless you know some Swiss gourmets.

Central Switzerland has Herrliberg, Meilen, Erlenbach, and Limmat. Schaffhausen boasts of its Blaurock, Hallauer and Käferstein; the Grisons of the light red Maienfelder, Fläscher and Zizerser.

INVISIBLE SWITZERLAND

The Largest Country in the World

by

GEORGE MIKES

(Mr. Mikes, the Hungarian-born author of How to be an Alien, How to Scrape Skies, *etc., etc., is never happier than when given a chance to aim a few barbs at a contented group of people. The Swiss appear to be a perfect target, so here he tries to put them in their place by putting them on—or taking them off, the term depending on whether your slanguage is American or British.)*

One of the best-guarded secrets of the Swiss is that there are really no such people. There are no Swiss. The outside world may be misled by superficial external appearances; the Swiss themselves—for reasons of policy and diplomacy, and also because it would be too complicated to explain all this to dense foreigners—refrain from pricking the legend and behave as though they existed. But they do not. As I have said, there are no such people, a fact I shall soon explain.

Moreover, on looking at the map, you might easily jump to the conclusion that the United States is a larger country than Switzerland. Wrong again. It is much smaller. This is one of the reasons why you

58

can speak of "Americans" but you cannot really speak of "the Swiss." In the United States, quite a lot of people, whether from the Wild West (Oregon) or the Wild East (New York), from the deep South (Georgia) or the deep North (Michigan), are prepared to call themselves "Americans." [1] There is a legend (which plenty of songs and poems try to keep alive) that America does something peculiar to your soul. Well, it certainly does; but it does not transform a Central European bank-clerk, an African witch-doctor, a Syrian bookmaker, a Japanese wrestler, a Sicilian tourist-guide, and a Scandinavian sailor, in no time, into that instantly recognizable, wonderful and unique paragon of humanity, the *Homo Americanus,* as they are so fond of maintaining.

The Swiss know better. It is not only that the Swiss French will have nothing to do with the Swiss Germans, while neither of them will have anything to do with the Swiss Italians—life is never quite as simple as that. But ask a man of Lausanne what he thinks of the people of Geneva; ask the same man of Lausanne if he likes the people of Bern; ask a man of Basel if he would like to be taken for a man from Zurich; ask a man of Chur, in eastern Switzerland, if he feels himself nearer to the man in the moon or to a man from St. Gallen. As to the last, there is a saying that there are three qualifications any Bishop of Chur must possess: 1) he must be a Roman Catholic; 2) he must be a consecrated priest; and 3) he must be a native of Chur or, at least, of the Canton of Graubünden. But, people like to add, the first two requirements might be dispensed with.

How To Thoroughly Hate Your Neighbor

I once knew a charming old gentleman, a prominent manufacturer in one of the three original cantons, who had classified all his compatriots very precisely. He would never employ a man from Appenzell (forty-three miles northeast from his village), because people from Appenzell are "impertinent and mean"; people coming from about twenty-five miles south of Appenzell, the people of the Grisons or Graubünden, while quite different, were not much better, because though they were certainly capable, they were utterly unreliable; people from about thirteen miles to the north of Appenzell, the people of St. Gallen, were quite different again, in fact

---

1. *Scholarly Footnote:* There are, of course, no such people as "the British," either. A man is either an Englishman or a Scotsman, or a Welshman or an Irishman; only newly naturalized people would describe themselves as British; and the Americans, of course, talk of "the British".

people from another planet, and were of no use at all, either, because they were lazy; people of Bern were too slow-witted and people from Lucerne too weak and irremediably spoiled by the tourists. In short, no people were any good at all, except those from his immediate neighborhood. Moreover, they were all rotters anyway, and not to be touched with a barge pole. When his son (who was also his general manager) married, he moved out of the paternal home and went to live with his wife in Zug, about twelve miles away (but in another canton), from whence he drove daily to his job in his father's factory. After eighteen months, his father managed not only to quarrel with him but also to drive him out of his job. The son is convinced that the real reason for this break was his father's deep and unalterable conviction that the "people of Zug are petty and calculating."

This ethnic variety, these irreconcilable differences between the people of Appenzell and those of Schwyz (divided from each other infinitely by forty-three miles), between the people of Zug and those of Winterthur, make Switzerland one of the biggest countries in the world. This mutual dislike, contempt and healthy detestation of one another is the firm foundation of Swiss democracy and neutrality. "Love thy neighbor," says the Christian teaching—and a profound and noble teaching it certainly is. But loving Christians fought each other for thirty years in a devastating and cruel war in the seventeenth century and, indeed, during long centuries before and ever since. No—you cannot love someone if you simply detest him. Ask any man of Basel if he could possibly love a man of Zurich, ask a man of Olten if he could possibly love a man of Aarau. You cannot love him, but you can *tolerate* him. And love if not sincere is hypocrisy; *tolerance* is the shining democratic virtue. For people of Basel to tolerate the people of Zurich as neighbors is incredible self-discipline; for the people of Uri to live in peaceful co-existence with that impertinent and mean lot at Appenzell is a great and admirable achievement; for the people of Lausanne to restrain themselves and start no wars of revenge against the Bernese, who once invaded and subjugated them, is the pinnacle of civilized self-control.

I knew a lady in Schaffhausen, the watchmakers' town, whose son married a girl from Winterthur, about fifteen miles away. She was heartbroken, of course, and explained to me in confidence that she was making a great effort to treat her daughter-in-law "as if she were one of us," although she knew very well that "these mixed marriages never work." She, too, regarded herself as a paragon of self-sacrifice and almost superhuman self-control.

And that is the whole point. The human soul needs to get rid of a certain amount of hatred and nastiness just as an internal combustion engine must get rid of a certain amount of poisonous gas. The Swiss get rid of these gases by despising each other so intensely that they have no energy to spare for hating the rest of humanity. Look at Germany, to mention only one example: since her unification, she has plunged the world into two world wars. It seems to be clear that the original unification of Germany was bad luck for humanity. And humanity hardly knows how lucky it is that there is no hope and not the faintest chance whatsoever of bringing about the unification of Switzerland.

Disgusting Old-fashioned Virtues

The Swiss are hard-working people, and this devotion to work is one of their most repulsive virtues. Altogether it is the virtues of the Swiss which I find a bit hard to bear. Coming from England, I regard work as some sort of nuisance you must pretend to be engaged in between cups of tea. But the Swiss take work seriously: start early, finish late; and they are even proud of it! They are paid for it handsomely (more handsomely than the English), and their old-fashioned idea is that they ought to play fair. The employer is not simply the chap you organize strikes against: he must pay, to be sure, and pay a lot, but he must also receive value for his money. This attitude is, of course, quite outmoded in the second half of the twentieth century.

Another Swiss virtue that tends to drive me slightly crazy is their kindness and politeness. (I am speaking now of German Switzerland only.) Whatever is going on—in an office, in a shop, in a restaurant, in all fields of private life—they keep on saying *Bitte schön* almost endlessly, to which you are supposed to reply *Danke schön*. Should you stop this exchange of *Bitte schön-Danke schön* before twenty-two rounds are up (and with a few exclamations of *Ja gerne* thrown in), you are regarded as an uncivilized barbarian. I have seen people drop with exhaustion, their last words before passing out completely being a few whispered *Danke schöns* or *Bitte schöns*.

You also have to say *Grütsi* to all and sundry all the time. This is a typical Swiss greeting, and you cannot say it often enough. You do not really say it, you sing it. When you meet several people, you say, *Grütsi mitenander . . .* " or something like that; it sounds like a whole operatic aria from the mouth of any true-born Swiss. In wild mountain passes, everyone you meet will sing *Grütsi* to you. You sing

Grütsi to them and exchange, if you have any manners at all, a few
Danke schöns and *Bitte schöns*. You'll be quite hoarse by the time you
part. Once, near Interlaken, I was walking alone in the mountains of
the Bernese Oberland when I saw a solitary cow coming towards me.
She stopped. I stepped out of her way, but she did not move. She went
on looking at me with her sad brown eyes. There we were, the cow
and I—neither of us would move. I was nonplussed. At last, after two
or three minutes, I said, *Grütsi*. She nodded to me with approval and
walked on.[2]

Honi Soit Qui Mal y Pense

The honesty of the Swiss is not easy to bear, either. I do not insist
on being diddled as one can be diddled fifty times a day in Venice or
Naples—I can do without that reasonably well. I do not mind if in
restaurants I know that there is no need to check up on bills because it
is unlikely that the waitress has added the date to the total. But there
comes a point where you feel that honesty has gone a little too far:
when everybody's honesty is always in his buttonhole. Too much
shining honesty tends to blind you a little. A year or two ago, my wife
and I went into a shop that had a number of electric irons displayed in
the window, to see if we could leave a few things to be cleaned and
ironed. It turned out, however, that the shop was not a cleaner's, but a
place where they sold electric irons. "Sorry," we said, and turned to
leave. The lady behind the counter, unwilling to see us disappointed,
offered to lend us an iron for a day or two. My wife accepted gladly:
how much did we pay for it? "Oh nothing," the lady said, there was
no charge. My wife then offered to leave a deposit, which the lady
refused. My wife then wanted to leave our name and address at least—
upon which I dragged her out of the shop and fled. I realized that the
shopkeeper was getting suspicious and had started looking at us as if
we were habitual criminals: the *ideas* we had! The fact that we were
offering deposits and trying to leave our name and address clearly
proved that we were the kind of people to whom the *possibility* had
occurred that the electric iron might not be returned, might be stolen.
This was suspicious indeed. I took to my heels because I was afraid
that she might call the police.

But cleanliness is the most terrifying and off-putting of all Swiss
virtues. I personally am not enamored of cleanliness. It is a Germanic

---

2. *Scholarly Footnote:* I have not translated any of these polite expressions. If a cow doesn't need an
interpreter, why should you? (This, by the way, is my last scholarly footnote.)

virtue, and I am all for a little Latin dirt. Not too much of it (one can go too far), but a little surely lends color to life. But when you go on making jokes for years about the Swiss dry-cleaning their roads between villages and then, one day, you actually see a vast electric Hoover vacuum-cleaner sweeping the open road, you say to yourself that this mania for spotlessness has got out of hand. When you realize that a roadsweeper and a dustman are actually cleaner in Switzerland than many a waiter in certain other countries, you start longing for just a little dirt here and there.

The problem has, however, its glorious side, too. The Swiss have, in fact, solved the perennial question which has troubled philosophers throughout the centuries: What is the aim of life? The answer the Swiss give to this question is simple, original and convincing: The aim of life is to make your door-handle shine!

From Alcoholic Soups to Sacred Sausages

I am no drunkard, but I love Swiss soups. No one who has tasted a variety of Swiss soups will be astonished by this statement, because he will know that the Swiss love putting Kirsch, a kind of cherry brandy, in everything they eat, particularly their soups. Many good people get roaring drunk on Swiss soups before they know what has hit them. And in a popular Swiss winter resort I once saw a patriotic Englishman get to his feet, raise his soup plate and call out in a loud voice, "Ladies and Gentlemen: the Queen."

In Switzerland, many of the girls are as beautiful and many of the men as lanky, sporty types as are to be seen anywhere in the world; but you can see as many fat people, too, as in the most sedentary countries of Europe. Quite a few Swiss are worried about their obesity and devote much ingenuity to finding reasons for it. They will give you a great many scientific answers, but only a few of them will hit on the very unscientific explanation: they eat too much. A slice of apple tart in Switzerland is a foot round, a portion of cheese reminds you of the cheese-counter in the average English grocer's, and they eat piles of whipped cream. They are always darting off to their excellent *confiseries* on the slightest provocation and their purpose in going there is not to abstain from sweet, sugary, and creamy things. A worried Swiss lady once told me, "I don't know why I am still gaining weight. . . . Honestly, I eat only half the amount of whipped cream I used to. . . ."

Swiss restaurants, too, make universal use of a shrewd trick to entice you into an early grave through overfeeding. They have a cunning habit of serving only *half* of your portion at once. You fail to notice this because half a portion in Switzerland looks like a whole portion anywhere else. So you eat your share (with some difficulty, because even half is more than enough), and then along comes the waitress, all smiles, and dishes out the other half. If you are as weak a character as I am, you eat that, too.

Swiss food, on the whole, is good and healthy, but, I think, the Swiss cuisine cannot compete with the finesse of the French. I am, however, one of the greatest living connoisseurs of sausages, which I regard as one of the supreme creations of the human race. Now the Austrians and the Bavarians are no mean sausage-makers by any standards, but the Swiss excel them all, by virtue of a giant sausage called the *schüblig*. What Shakespeare is among writers, the *schüblig* is among sausages. A nation which gave the *schüblig* to undeserving humanity is a nation of giants, and must be forgiven anything, including its winter sports; and including its impudence in being a tiny people which yet sets a shining example to the whole world on how to behave normally; how to live graciously; how to act sensibly in a mad world; and how to hate your friends and neighbors, and how to be able to love humanity—which, if you come to think of it, deserves neither their love nor their *schüblig*.

PARADISE FOR SPORTSMEN

Always in Season

by

PETER UBERSAX

(The author of this chapter is a Swiss journalist who roamed up and down Europe before returning home to become sports correspondent for the United Press.)

Switzerland is a land of sports. You can watch or take part in almost any sport that strikes your fancy; that is, unless you are a surfboard enthusiast. The country of the Alps and lakes has its peculiar national sports such as Swiss-style wrestling *(Schwingen)*, the regular Sunday morning shooting, gymnastics, and *Hornuss,* a game American visitors have baptized "Alpine baseball."

If you like to sit back and watch international sporting events, Switzerland has more than its share to offer. Automobile Grand Prix racing has been forbidden, but there are still some thrilling uphill events and rallies. The grueling Tour de Suisse cycle race will make you wonder what happened to the leg muscles you once had. In addition, there are the usual sporting events such as international tennis, golf and ice hockey tournaments as well as soccer, sailing, swimming, and skating championships. If you want a thrill, you can watch or participate in skijoring (with horse, jeep, or airplane), mountain automobile races, Alpine fishing, horse-races on frozen lakes, curling, and tobogganing. But above all: Switzerland is the land of skiing and mountaineering.

Skiing Regions

The three best-known regions of Switzerland for Alpine skiing are the Valais, the Grisons, and the Bernese Oberland. The last area is bounded on the north by the lakes of Thun and Brienz and to the south by the Bietschhorn, Finsteraarhorn, Oberaarhorn, and Breithorn mountains, the southern slopes of which descend into the Rhône Valley. As soon as new snow has settled and the danger of avalanches has gone, peaks such as the Eiger, Mönch, Jungfrau, Schreckhorn, and Wetterhorn can be reached by experienced skiers. The inner part of this mountainous region, with peaks averaging between 7,800 and 10,500 feet, offers countless opportunities to the skiing enthusiast. The Swiss Alpine Club has established dozens of huts, one of which has over sixty berths, and access to the area is made easy by the Interlaken–Lauterbrunnen–Kleine Scheidegg–Jungfraujoch mountain railway. If you are an experienced skier, you can combine skiing with a visit to some of the most beautiful mountain country in the world.

The second main region for all-year high Alpine skiing is the southern Valais, limited to the north by the Rhône and to the south by the Italian border, and such peaks as the Grand Combin, Mont Collon, the Matterhorn, and Monte Rosa. Recently "La Haute Route" (The High Route) between Martigny, on the Rhône River, and Zermatt, has become famous as one of the most beautiful skiing-climbing itineraries in the entire chain of Alps. One can race over the middle part of "La Haute Route" in twenty-four hours, as do Swiss army patrols, or one can take it easy and spend days or even weeks climbing peaks and skiing through the tens-of-miles-long valleys. There, too, huts such as the *Val-des-Dix,* the *Britannia, Cabane Bertol,* and *Hörnli* offer the possibility of establishing mountain headquarters or spending a night or two between two legs of a trip through this strange region where three entirely different languages are spoken— the old German dialect, French, with the rolling accent of the Valais, and Italian, which, although only spoken along the border region, influences the pronunciation and syntax of the entire area.

The third region where the ski enthusiast can enjoy his sport, whether it be January or August, is in the Grisons. In the area around the Albula Pass, flanked by the Piz d'Err and the Piz Kesh, skiers can establish their headquarters in any one of a number of huts, and they will find the scenery magnificent.

Ski Schools

Just about every Swiss ski resort has its ski school (SSS). It is a good idea to have a few days instruction at the outset of a visit whether you are a piste basher or a bunny, both to get your legs in trim, and to familiarize yourself with the local runs. It is also a top way of meeting people. You can sign on for half a day, a day or a week and all instructors speak at least ski-English.

For a beginner it is an absolute necessity. Skiing can be either agony or bliss and a good teacher can make all the difference. Here are a few things to look for in ski schools: the class should not exceed ten people; the instructor should rotate members so that all have a chance to ski in the best position directly behind him; he should watch all pupils individually rather than expect the class to admire him sailing down the mountain, leaving them to their own devices.

If you are wondering about resorts and ski schools, set your mind at rest. The only problem is one of elimination. Full information can be obtained from the Swiss National Tourist Office in New York, London or Zurich. Our map shows several resorts that have ski schools.

The equipment you use will also determine the agony and the ecstasy. The safest bet is to get neither the most expensive racing gear nor the cheap stuff. But, for a beginner, the safest thing is to buy the best you can afford. Rental equipment in Switzerland is of high quality and will do if you only ski a week or so every few years. If you go every year and enjoy it, you will want your own. Metal-edged skis come in plastic, metal or a combination, the latter is probably best for all-purpose skiing. Skis should be as long as you are tall, but shorter for beginners. Safety bindings come in two varieties: step-in and plate. They should have heel and toe release and should be adjusted to your boots and weight at the ski shop. Poles can be of light metal or plastic and should be about waist high. Boots are of prime importance and you will have to strike a fine balance between a too-comfortable boot which gives no support and a vice-like killer that cuts off circulation. There are several styles (a back-opening one is popular in America) but essentially what to look for is a hinged, clip-binding, hard plastic outer boot, with a flo-fit inner boot that reaches about two inches above your ankle and needs only one pair of socks. Be sure to check that you can stand flat on your skis when wearing your boots; if you don't, you'll need wedging.

Anything goes where clothing is concerned, but it had better be waterproof, especially if you are a beginner. Alpine skiing weather is usually sunny and mild, so don't lumber yourself with parkas and sweaters. Underwear is of fundamental importance. Silk or thermal longjohns are best, on the theory that it's more important to keep body heat in than cold out. Sunglasses and sun lotion vital, too. Mountain sun can burn you badly.

The longest of the popular ski runs in Switzerland is the one from the Weissfluhjoch, near Davos, to Küblis, ten miles away and 5,400 feet lower than the starting point. While participants in the Parsenn Derby cover this stretch in less than a quarter of an hour, the average skier may expect to spend an hour or more making the descent. But if you are seeking speed, the fastest of the standard Swiss runs is the Windspillen stretch, near Gstaad, where the experts average over fifty miles per hour. Another extraordinary run is the one from Gornergrat to Zermatt, where contestants in the races cover slightly over five and a half miles in about eight minutes.

Switzerland's Best Ski Runs

The tastes of skiing fans usually differ, and it is difficult to find any two who have the same opinion as to the best ski run in Switzerland. A pool, however, was recently held among the experts, and these dozen or so runs were selected as the best and fastest.

Resort	Starting point of run (Altitude in feet)
Davos (5,100)	Weissfluhjoh (9,300)
Zermatt (5,300)	Furrggjoch (11,000)
Wengen (4,200)	Lauberhorn (8,100)
Grindelwald (3,400)	Männlichen (7,300)
Mürren (5,400)	Schilthorn (9,750)
St. Moritz (6,000)	Corvatsch (11,000)
Arosa (6,000)	Weisshorn (8,700)
Klosters (4,000)	Weissfluhjoch (9,300)
Gstaad (3,400)	Wasserngrat (7,000)

Resort	Starting point of run
Engelberg (3,300)	Kleintitlis (9,900)
Flims (3,800)	Cassonsgrat (8,800)
Verbier (4,900)	Mont Gelée (9,900)
Meiringen (1,950)	Plan Platten (5,900)

The experienced skier who would like to engage in a new sport will find some thrilling variations to enjoy. Skijoring is a kind of motorized, dry-land, water skiing (if that doesn't sound too Irish!) and for the real pro there are kites and helicopters to provide the motive force. Hang-gliding on skis is an amazing experience. Ski-bobbing (a tricycle on skis) is also fun, but all these are merely frills on the simple basic pleasure of a good clear run through superb scenery.

If you have climbed the Matterhorn and dashed down the Weissfluh ski run and still feel that you have not completed your quota of thrills, buy a crash helmet and go tobogganing.

One of the best toboggan runs in the world is the St. Moritz Cresta Run, a steep 1,327-yard-long ice channel through which you flash on a four-inch-high, 35–50-inch-long, and 20-inch-wide steel sled called a "skeleton." You lie on your stomach, head to the front, and steer with steel hooks attached to your shoes. It looks easy—try it!

The record time from the top is a mere fifty-five seconds. Speeds of over 80 miles per hour cause little astonishment, but if I were in your toboggan, I would hold the speed to a mere 50 miles per hour. That's fast enough to keep you from becoming bored. The eight hairpin turns, which have been given the promising names of Stable Junction, Church Leap, Battle Dore, Shuttle Cock, Stream Corner, Bullpetts Corner, Scylla, and Charybdis, are guaranteed to keep you from worrying about your income tax, but the thought of inheritance taxes may flit through your mind from time to time.

Today, the high-class St. Moritz Tobogganing Club counts several hundred members. Its books have carried such famous names as those of Charlie Chaplin, Douglas Fairbanks and Jan Kiepura, and even now the payment of a modest membership fee will put your name on the club rolls along with such well-known persons as Lord Brabazon of Tara, Henri Martineau, Jr., Ralph Harbour, Carl Nater-Cartier, and Count Theo Rossi di Montelera. It does not cost much to risk your neck in such expensive surroundings. Non-members may rent "skeletons" for only a few francs a day.

For those who do not care to slide around corners at 50 miles per hour, it is also a spectator sport. There are various contests during the

winter season, the best known being the Curzon Cup, and the Grand
National. There are bobsleigh runs at St. Moritz, Davos, Mürren,
Gstaad, Klosters, Engelberg, Crans, and several other resorts.

Curling and Skating

Once you have sufficiently frayed your nerves on the toboggan or
ski runs, you might try relaxing with the Scots' game of curling. To the
uninitiated, a curling party from afar looks like a group of elderly
ladies and gentlemen pushing metal hot water bottles over the ice. As
a matter of fact, you do not have to be elderly to enjoy the game, but
the rest of the description is not unjust. As the rules of curling are long
and involved, we will not go into them at this time. Suffice it to say
that curling is a team game. Each team has four players, each of
whom has two hot water bottles, or, to use the parlance of the game,
"stones." The players push their "stones," which are 40-pound granite
blocks with metal handles, toward the center of the target area (the
"tea" or the "dolly"). "Stones" barring the direct line to the "tea" can
be avoided by "in-handling" or "out-handling" one's own "stone,"
but once the "stone" has been tipped, it glides over the ice in a curved
rather than a straight line. The team whose "stones" are nearest the
"tea" at the end of 9, 11, or 13 "heads" is the winner. (You are
probably thoroughly confused by this time; but console yourself with
the thought that if you play the game someone will probably repeat
the rules to you.)

Incidentally, curling is highly recommended for married couples. A
rule prohibits players from talking to each other. They may only
address their words of endearment, or whatever other sentiments they
may have, to the "stone"—from which there will be only a stony
silence.

While we are on the subject of rinks, don't forget ice skating is
popular in Switzerland. There are good skating rinks at all of the
winter resorts, but according to the Swiss, at least those who do not
own rinks in other areas, Davos has one of the best speed-skating
rinks in the world. It is a center for speed and figure-skating as well as
ice hockey. There are also good rinks in most of the cities, and you
seldom have to go far to reach a lake.

Each season there is a large number of international hockey
matches, and tourists with a minimum of experience will be welcomed
by the local hockey clubs at the various resorts. Skates can be hired in
all of the resorts for up to two and a half francs per day, and skating
lessons cost between five and ten francs an hour.

Golf, Tennis, Riding, Cycling

Switzerland has a reputation for being the home of winter sports, but for those persons visiting the Helvetic Confederation during the summer months there are innumerable forms of recreation. During the June to December golf season there are numerous tournaments on the magnificent courses situated in Alpine surroundings. In the better clubs there are hefty greens fees but you can watch the International Open Championship of Switzerland for little or nothing.

Like golf, tennis is a popular sport in Switzerland, and the visitor will find suitable courts in all of the major tourist areas. If he is the guest of one of the hotels that have their own courts, and a great many do, his problems will be solved, but other tourists may play at a local club for a small fee.

If you like tennis best when observing a match from the stands, over thirty open tournaments are held in Switzerland each year. The most important is the International Championship of Switzerland, which holds the stage annually in June or July. Star players from all parts of the globe take part, and many of them stay to compete in the matches at Villars, St. Moritz, and Gstaad.

Other events attracting participants from abroad are the International Horse Shows at St. Gall (annually) and Lucerne or Geneva (every other year). There is horse racing in spring and autumn in a dozen towns, while Davos and Arosa have horse shows or races on snow in the late winter.

Tourists who are willing to content themselves with a dip in one of the lakes will be able to relax in the bright summer sun for the price of a bus or tram ticket. Of course, there are artificially heated pools in many of the resorts as well as some of the big cities, but if you insist on the lake, the swimming season, even in the low country, is limited to the period between June and September. Water skiing is popular on most larger lakes and fees quite reasonable.

For the cost of a few francs (about five francs an hour) you can combine swimming with sailing. Sailboats can usually be hired on all the big lakes, and a sailing school exists at Gunten, on the Lake of Thun. Here you can learn all the best techniques while living in picturesque Alpine surroundings. Licenses can be obtained in some cantons easily, not so easily in others, and you must have one to take a boat out (or else hire a sailor to accompany you).

Cycling is a sport that attracts many of the younger tourists. It provides plenty of exercise, and at the same time it is an economical way of touring the country. In rural Switzerland half of the population seems to move on two wheels. If you do your traveling on a bicycle, you are certain to get a better view of the country and to get closer to the people than you would whizzing along in an automobile or a train. But, if you feel a bit short of wind and leg muscle, cycling is also a spectator sport. Amongst the Swiss people the annual *Tour de Suisse* is the most popular single sporting event of the year. In eight days, professional bicycle racers from all parts of Europe cover about a thousand miles of grueling mountain and valley roads, and at every stage of the race the route is lined with rows of eager spectators waiting a chance to cheer their favorite as he pedals past. There are several other road races as well as the track seasons at the Zurich and Basel Velodromes and occasional track events at Lausanne.

Automobile uphill racing has become very popular since Grand Prix Racing on road circuits was forbidden for safety reasons. The Geneva Automobile Rally in spring and heats for the motorcycle cross-country World and European Championships are other annual motoring events. The uphill races draw big crowds. The drivers, starting at regular intervals, cover anywhere from one to fifteen miles, climbing sharp grades. A fine driving technique rather than horse-power usually decides these contests on the narrow, winding roads.

Hunting and Fishing

Hunting and fishing, however, present a problem. The Swiss hunting laws are extremely rigid, and the tourist arriving for a short sojourn has little or no chance of bagging a hunting permit, let alone any game. Licenses are obtainable for those who have the time to fight their way through the red tape, but it would be easier to settle for a day's fishing. You can obtain a card, which will permit you to fish, from the local authorities in most towns, and with that in hand, the angler may try his hand casting, trolling, or pulling them in with a net. Some of the lake trout are said to run as much as 20 pounds, but if you prefer casting in a river or a stream, the many icy torrents that rush down out of the Alpine highlands should furnish you with a wide choice of locations.

CLIMBING IN A CIVILIZED WILDERNESS

BY

FRED JACOBSON

(This section has been contributed by Fred Jacobson, whose affair with the Swiss Alps started with a 10-day holiday while at Yale University. His interest in climbing and skiing led to the realization of a childhood dream that summer: his first climb of the Matterhorn. Since that time he has juggled his New York business career and a love of the Alps, turning his own enthusiasm into a professional summer job, leading small groups of people on walking and hiking tours of the Alps.)

The Alps have a striking beauty, with savage and sharply defined rock and snow peaks. These features are highlighted even more dramatically when viewed from a valley which provides hayfields, Alpine flowers, chalets and cows in the foreground. To be sure, there are far larger glaciers in the world (such as in ice-bound Alaska, for example), and yet consider the 16-mile-long Aletsch Glacier in the center of an area just twice the size of New Jersey! From Brig in the Rhone Valley, with the assistance of a postal bus and then a cable car, one may easily view the glacier's impressive snout from Belalp. Or, from Fiesch in the Upper Rhone Valley (also known as the Goms), one can take a cable car to the summit of the Eggishorn, which provides a striking view of the entire glacier, right to its source at the Jungfraujoch, between the Jungfrau and the Monch.

To me, the Alps are the greatest of the many wonders of Switzerland. I've climbed on three continents, and while the Andes and the Himalayas offer spectacular scenery, to find such grandeur with such ease and at such close proximity, one must go to Switzerland. Switzerland is small, little more than half the size of the state of Maine, and nothing is very far from the beaten paths. The Swiss have been living at the feet of their highest mountains for at least five centuries. Even today, few areas look like pure resorts; they are mountain villages that have adapted with the times. The Swiss have been catering to mountain climbers for more than a hundred years. Cog railroads and cable cars go to the middle heights, well-defined paths to the very foot of the climb, and comfortable huts are ready at appropriate spots to host climbers before they undertake the most difficult ascents.

Since civilization is so close to the high peaks, there is less emphasis on camping and more time and energy for climbing. It almost seems as though climbers are less competitive here than in some other parts of the world, although the last parties laboring up to a hut may get pretty competitive when word filters down that there are a limited number of mattresses left for that evening!

One of the main reasons why things work so well in the Swiss Alps is an organization known as the Swiss Alpine Club. Founded in 1863, the Club today has some 60,000 male members, Swiss and foreign. It is organized into sections, Monte Rosa being one of the oldest, dating back to 1865, the year that Edward Wymper first scaled the Matterhorn. British climbers, members of their own Alpine Club, were a contributing factor to the formation of the Swiss group. Today, there are 96 sections, each with its own members from a geographically small area where it is easy for members to meet regularly and know each other. The Club teaches mountaineering to neophytes, conducts advanced courses for leaders, promotes safety through rescue courses, and publishes an excellent quarterly journal devoted to climbing (around the world as well as in the Alps) in addition to a more businesslike monthly bulletin. Most important is maintenance of the hut system, providing accommodations for thousands of climbers at the feet of their intended peaks.

There are hundreds of climbing huts scattered throughout the Swiss Alps, some privately owned and some run by local and academic climbing clubs, but the great preponderance are run by regional sections of the Club, offering reduced rates for Club members. The more popular huts have a guardian to supervise the kitchen, cook and supervise the hygiene, and smooth operations of the hut. These men are entrepreneurs, running the huts for profit. Since many of the huts are above the permanent snow line, many of these hut wardens are former guides, past their prime, but still anxious to spend their days among their beloved peaks. The ambience is special. One meets climbers from all nations—not only Europeans, but also Asians and North and South Americans. Thanks to an honor system which is respected by all, these huts are never locked. One of my most pleasant memories is of an evening spent in the Tasch Hut in late September. My guide, Rony Inderbinen, and I were alone in the hut, cooked a leisurely dinner over the wood fire, watched a perfect sunset in solitude, and had the entire sleeping area to ourselves. The climb of the Feekopf and Allalinhorn the next day was almost an anticlimax! While some of the higher huts and the bivouacs (ruder shelters) require some climbing competence, the vast majority of the huts lie at the end of signposted, well-marked walking paths.

While there is interesting climbing in all of Switzerland, the major ranges include the Pennine Alps in the south central canton of Valais, the central range of the Bernese Oberland, the easterly ranges of the Engadine and, to a lesser extent, the Bergell, which abuts on the Italian border. The highest peaks are in the Valais, particularly that portion south of the Rhone. The Oberland is characterized by its great snowfields and the three longest glaciers in the Alps. The Engadine is noted for its wider and gentler valleys, with the peaks rising dramatically from the valley floors. The magic circle in the Alps is 4,000 meters, or somewhat over 13,000 feet. There are eight in the Oberland, topped by the 4,273-meter Finsteraarhorn. The most famous peaks of this range are the Jungfrau and the Eiger (which is actually slightly below the 4,000 level). the Engadine has a single 4,000-meter peak, Pin Bernina. The Valais contains no less than 37 of the giants, crowned by the 4,634-meter Monte Rosa (whose summit is shared with Italy) and the highest peak entirely in Switzerland, the Dom (4,545 meters). Although topped by no less than five of its immediate neighbors, by far the most famous peak of the range—and perhaps the world's most photographed mountain—is the Matterhorn. The last of the 4,000-meter peaks to be climbed (in 1865), it vindictively claimed the lives of four of its seven conquerors during their descent and has had a tremendous reputation ever since. No mountain lover should fail to see this incredible peak. After twenty years, I still spend hours gazing at its unforgettable form!

The key Alpine centers in these ranges would include Pontresina in the Engadine, Grindelwald in the Oberland, Zermatt and Saas Fee in the German-speaking part of the Valais, and Zinal and Arolla in the French-speaking parts. Such smaller villages as Murren, Kandersteg, Lauterbrunnen, Sils Maria, Grimentz, Fiesch, Orsieres, Champex, Adelboden, Lenk, Wiler and Les Hauderes all offer excellent mountain ambience, a wide selection of hikes and climbs and numerous competent Swiss mountain guides.

The tradition of the Swiss guide goes back more than a hundred years, and it is a highly professional and proud tradition. Each guide must pass several years of intensive examinations. He must be more than just a good climber. He must know about rescue and first aid; he must know how to climb with equal ease on ice and snow as well as rock. He must understand meteorological conditions as they will affect mountain weather, and be able to diagnose snow conditions as they are affected by prevailing weather conditions. Most of them have learned their trade from their fathers or an uncle and are guides because that is what they want to be more than anything else. I have climbed with Swiss guides for two decades and have had generally excellent results. Besides their skill in route finding and the safety they afford the less skilled amateur, they are also filled with tales of the mountains and high mountain adventures. Their safety record is nothing short of spectacular. For example, almost every year the Matterhorn claims 10–20 lives. And yet, there have been no fatal accidents involving Zermatt guides in thirty years on the Matterhorn—a record involving thousands of ascents, often with inexperienced climbers. While many will want to climb on their own, for those who are less skilled, or less adventuresome, the Swiss guides offer a delightful alternative in approaching the heights.

In several of the leading centers, groups of guides have banded together to open climbing schools. While less personalized than the one-on-one guide-and-client relationship, the schools offer excellent instruction, usually at far lower rates (normal guides' tariffs are regulated by the cantons). In addition to the actual instruction, most of these schools also offer high mountain ascents or even high touring weeks in the principal ranges. Perhaps the oldest and best-known school has been the one at Rosenlaui (not far from Grindelwald) run by Arnold Glatthard. More recently, schools have begun at Fiesch in the Goms, La Fouly above Martigny, and Leysin near Lake Geneva. The Bergsteigerschule in Pontresina offers not only individual instruction but a large variety of high touring weeks, as does its counterpart in Fiesch. Areas such as Zermatt and Zinal are now starting to organize instructional weeks, although they are not as yet on a season-long basis. For further information on climbing schools and Swiss guides, contact the Swiss National Tourist Office, 608 Fifth Avenue, New York, N.Y. 10020.

Trails and Paths

For those whose tastes don't run as far as roped climbing, but who would like to do more than stroll through the woods, there are hiking trails and mountain paths to suit all tastes, including places where fixed ropes and ladders serve where otherwise ropes would be required. One can cross glaciers, hike to most of the climbing huts, even climb 11,500-foot peaks, without the necessity of ropes. It took me many years to realize the eminent wisdom of the Swiss trail-marking system. All signs give times in hours *(stunden)*, rather than distances, between points. Whom did they have in mind when they determined these times? Olympic athletes? Out-of-shape hackers? Or something in between? In fact, it really doesn't matter. Once you are able to relate your own pace to the times given on the signposts, this relationship should be constant throughout. (A notable exception is the crossing of the Aletsch Glacier from Belalp to Rieder Alp. Suggested time was about half of actual time for a group that generally does better than the recommended times.) Instead of a sign which says "4.8 miles," with no mention of the kind of terrain to be encountered, these suggested times take into consideration not only the distances but the ups and downs you will face. To help the hiker, there are high-quality topographical maps which are on scales of 1:200,000, 1:50,000, or even as detailed as 1:25,000. These are part of the Carte National series and are an excellent aid to the mountain lover, not only for the hike or climb itself, but also as a means of identifying the beautiful surrounding peaks. There are extensive guidebooks (in French and German) to the key climbing areas, and the Alpine Club Guide Series (published in London but available in major Alpine centers in Switzerland) is an excellent alternative for those who are not fluent in French or German. For the hiker, it is most helpful to have a command of one of these two languages or to be hiking with someone who does, since there is a truly outstanding series of *guides pedestres,* or *Wanderbuchen,* put out by the Berne firm of Kummerly and Frey. These excellent volumes include historic details of the region and comments on the flora and fauna, architecture and inhabitants, as well as all the necessary details on the walks (distances, hours, altitude differences, possible side trips, villages along the route, possibilities of refreshment and lodging). For those who lack the necessary linguistic fluency, the best thing I've seen in English is William Reifsnyder's *Footloose in the Swiss Alps,* a Sierra Club Totebook. Some of the finest mountain adventures I have had were along the Swiss trails which connect one valley with another, often over high (10,000–11,000-feet) passes, with strenuous walks in remote areas, yet well within the limits of an accomplished mountain walker. I particularly remember one clear September when I left from St. Niklaus in the Zermatt Valley and wandered in solitude for a week, always heading west. I visited such small villages as Gruben in the Turtmannthal, St. Luc, Chandolin, Zinal and Grimentz in the Val d'Anniviers, La Forclaz, Evolene, Les Hauderes and Arolla in the Val d'Herens. The scenery was incomparable, the autumn foliage unforgettable, the absence of crowds a welcome delight, and the hospitality of the mountain people unfailingly warm well beyond the needs of commercial necessity. I don't have to be 100 miles from the nearest civilization to enjoy the mountains. The character of the Alpine villages and the people who labor in the shadows of the high peaks add immeasurably to my enjoyment of the mountain environment.

An interesting variation on hiking and climbing the mountains is to cross them on skis. With the help of animal skins attached to the bottoms of the skis to prevent slipping during climbing, and with adjustable bindings which permit the heel to come up while climbing but fasten it securely to the ski during the descent, one is able to climb beautiful peaks and passes, enjoying downhill runs of many miles as a reward. While ski-mountaineering is practiced throughout the Swiss Alps, perhaps the most celebrated adventure is the crossing from Saas Fee through Italy to Chamonix in France, known to aficionados as the "High Route." I had the good fortune to complete this trip back in 1969, and I returned in 1974 for further ski-touring adventures. Strength (you carry packs of 25–35 pounds) and endurance (some days you are on the trail for 8–10 hours, many of them spent in climbing uphill) count for more than advanced parallel technique. The trip is best between mid-April and mid-May, the period during which the snow has become reasonably consolidated and avalanche danger is at justifiable levels, while there is still enough snow to ski most of the way down into the remote valleys which lie along the route. To see some of the quaint tourist-free villages, with flowers blooming at the edge of the snow, is an unforgettable experience. From the point of view of civilization, I find delight in getting to know some of the other skiers, drawn to the mountains as I am, in talking with the villagers, in listening to the hut guardians who have encyclopedic information about the snow conditions, the conditions of the glaciers (which vary greatly from year to year) and climbing in general. I would recommend that all but the most experienced ski mountaineers undertake the "High Route" with the help of a Swiss Guide. There are guides in both Saas Fee and Zermatt who will hire out for the trip at a cost of about $60 per day, plus expenses. If two or three amateurs band together for the trip, the cost is reasonable, out of all proportion to the enjoyment. For those whose budgets do not permit the luxury of a private guide, there are organized groups. Gottlieb Perren and Alfons Franzen are two of several Zermatt guides who do this. Allow two weeks for the trip. It can be done in half the time, but to be in a hurry is to defeat the purpose. Spend a couple of days getting acclimatized; it's a lot harder to ski uphill. And bring plenty of sunscreen. It took me several weeks to recover from the oversight!

Naturally, when embarking on hiking, climbing and ski-touring expeditions, things can go wrong. It is comforting to know that Switzerland is the home of the International Red Cross and is highly sophisticated in mountain rescue. Guides are well-trained and respond to emergency calls, and the St. Bernards' effectiveness in avalanche rescues is legendary. In recent years the helicopter has revolutionized mountain rescue. (Some critics of the choppers say that they have made rescues so much simpler that climbers take unnecessary chances. Air Zermatt is the leader in this field. Rescues are expensive, but it is possible to take out insurance, at a nominal cost, to cover the cost of air evacuation.

You'll learn to expect this habit of "thinking of everything" in Switzerland. Whether you're a cable-car rider, a gentle walker, an athletic hiker, a climber or a ski mountaineer, the Swiss make it easy and very safe to put yourself in the picture!

THE FACE OF SWITZERLAND

GENEVA

Our hotel group offers their guests a varied scale of
rates and accommodation.

Hotel Bristol

1st class ★★★★ New

Phone: (022) 32.44.00   Telex: 23.739 HBL

Cable BRISTOL

10, Rue du Mont-Blanc

Near the lake, central station and air terminal.
Sound proofed rooms with bath, phone, radio and television.
"Deluxe" suites. Bar and restaurant.

Single Sw. Frs. 100/120
Double Sw. Frs. 130/180
Suites Sw. Frs. 220/450

Hotel de Berne

Commercial ★★★ Modern

Phone: (022) 31.60.00   Telex: 22.764

Cable BERNOTEL

26, Rue de Berne

First class hotel. Near the central station and air terminal
Rooms with bath, phone, radio and television. Bar and restaurant

Single Sw. Frs. 60/70
Double Sw. Frs. 90/110

Hotel Eden

★★★ 1st class

Phone: (022) 32.65.40   Telex: 23.962

Cable EDENHOTEL

135, Rue de Lausanne

First class hotel. Near the United Nations Building and
International Labour Office. 70 beds. Restaurant and bar.

Single without bath   Sw. Frs. 40/45
Single with bath   Sw. Frs. 55/65
Double without bath Sw. Frs. 55/70
Double with bath   Sw. Frs. 80/100

General Manager: G. de Mercurio

GENEVA

Cosmopolitan Corner of the Lake

by

JOHN and MOIRA HAWKES

(Mr. and Mrs. Hawkes, the noted travel-writing and editing team, leave their British home base behind as often as possible to visit Switzerland, for many years the subject of one volume in their remarkable and concise series, Holiday Factbooks. *They have also written most of the chapters following this one.)*

The motorist who enters Switzerland from Lyon and the southwest, or from Grenoble and the south, rolls smoothly into Geneva through Chancy or St. Julien. If he comes via the impressive Mont Blanc tunnel, he will cross the frontier in the French town of Annemasse. By air, the traveler to Geneva is deposited at the city's pride—the ultramodern airport of Cointrin. But whatever the approach, sooner or later he is confronted by the vast reaches of the Lake of Geneva, dramatized for centuries in prose and poetry.

The third largest city in Switzerland, with a population of 175,000, Geneva faces northeast, spreading out comfortably around the lower end of the lake. With all the room it wants for broad avenues and formal gardens, it makes a dignified setting for the outflowing waters of the River Rhône on its rush from Alpine glaciers to the warmth of the Mediterranean.

Although modern in aspect, Geneva is an ancient city, whose story fades back into a shadowy past. The crest of the hill on which the Cathedral of St. Peter now stands offered an excellent strategic position, first for primitive tribes; next for the Romans, who stayed there for 500 years (until A.D. 443); and then for the early Burgundians and their later kings. In the first part of the 5th century, Geneva became a bishopric, and by the end of the 11th century, its prince-bishops had developed a see both rich and powerful. But they had to fight hard to defend it against the territorially greedy house of Savoy. Their conflicts fill the pages of 12th- to 14th-century history. In the meantime, the merchant classes were gradually gaining in wealth and power, building up their independence by freeing themselves whenever possible from the feudal lordship of the bishops.

This prosperity was given a boost at the beginning of the 15th century by a close commercial alliance between Geneva and the cloth-manufacturing town of Fribourg, about 100 miles to the northeast. Fribourg textiles found a ready market at Geneva's fairs, the medieval city's greatest source of trade and revenue. But in 1462, Louis XI of France and his nephew, the Duke of Savoy, put a stop to that by forbidding French merchants to attend the fairs, at the same time cunningly switching the dates of the Lyon fairs to coincide with those at Geneva, steps which virtually brought an end to the city's prosperity.

Commercially almost ruined, torn by internal strife and threatened continually by the increasingly aggressive new Duke of Savoy, Geneva at last appealed for aid to the Swiss Confederation. The Swiss army intervened with typical Swiss efficiency, and in 1530, the Duke of Savoy signed a treaty by which, in effect, he agreed to trouble the city no longer. Geneva then concluded an alliance with the cantons of Fribourg and Bern and, almost for the first time, felt master in its own house.

Reformation and Prosperity

But from Bern, hand in hand with freedom from outside domination, came William Farel, a fervent disciple of Zurich's great reformer, Zwingli, bringing with him all the restrictive zeal of the

Reformation. By 1536, the city had enthusiastically switched from Catholicism to the Protestant faith, said goodbye to the last of the Catholic prince-bishops, and was already under the influence of John Calvin, a French refugee who came to visit Farel and stayed to eclipse him.

Calvin turned Geneva from a gay city into one where theaters were closed, entertainment frowned upon, dancing forbidden, and food and drink regarded only as necessities of life to be taken without indulgence or enjoyment. Banquets, the wearing of jewels and all forms of finery were forbidden by the Sumptuary Laws. But despite all this, Geneva owes much to Calvin, for he also made it a citadel of French learning, the academy he founded being today's university. And he did much to restore Geneva's commercial prosperity.

All this time, the Duke of Savoy was still coveting Geneva and hoping to restore Catholicism. On the night of December 11th-12th, 1602, he made a surprise attack on the city, in an operation known as the Escalade (because his men attempted to scale the walls with ladders). They were ignominiously defeated, an event commemorated to this date every year since by the Festival of the Escalade, with processions, balls and general jollification. And if you are there, you will hear Psalm 124 still sung in the cathedral as it was on the morning after the victory. ("Our soul is escaped even as a bird out of the snare of the fowler: the snare is broken, and we are delivered.")

Although many left the city to escape the austerity and bigotry of Calvinism, far more English, French and Italian refugees came in, giving Geneva a taste of the cosmopolitan atmosphere she has today and bringing with them new crafts and trades as well as a keen sense of business. Since the 16th century, Geneva has been one of Europe's leading watchmaking and jewelry centers, and the Reformation (which left citizens few leisure activities and little on which to spend their money) allowed for concentration on work and an accumulation of wealth. The city also became one of the main intellectual centers of Europe, but it was steadily getting less democratic, the government passing into the hands of a few wealthy aristocrats.

All this received a severe check in 1798, when this rich but melancholy city was annexed by the France of the Revolution, to become the capital of the French Department of Léman, which it remained until 1814, after the fall of Napoleon. The following year, Geneva was admitted to the Swiss Confederation as a canton in its own right, since when it has followed the general destinies of Switzerland.

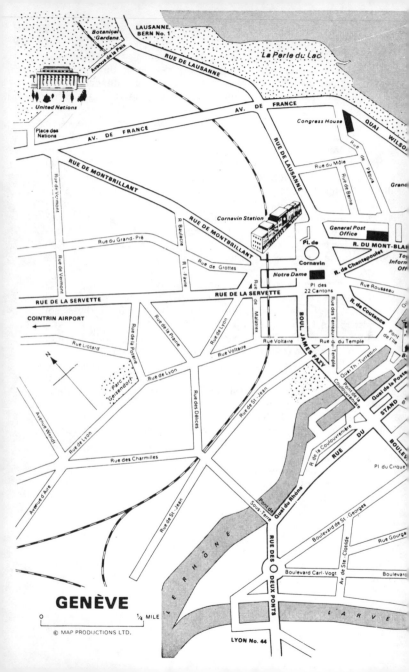

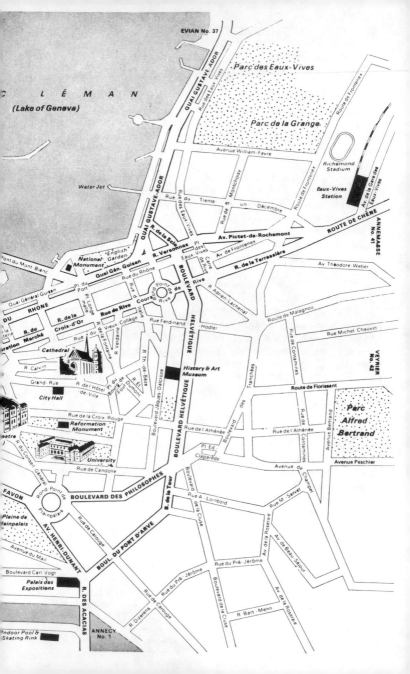

Exploring Geneva

You can see a considerable part of Geneva's attractions in a single walk by starting off along the broad Rue du Mont-Blanc from the railroad station to the lake. Here you will be rewarded with a lovely view which, if you are lucky with the weather, includes a distant glimpse of Mont-Blanc. It's visible from Geneva about one day out of three. You will probably see Geneva's trademark, the Jet d'Eau, rising like a gigantic plume from a jetty thrusting out into the lake. On a sunny day, this towering stream of water (which reaches over 400 feet) can be seen for miles. Weather permitting, it plays daily from May to September.

A right turn takes you along the Quai des Bergues, beside the Rhône, which leaves the lake at this point. Beneath the water alongside the opposite bank is a four-story, electronically controlled car-park capable of taking 1,500 cars. In the center of the river is Rousseau Island, with a statue of the Geneva-born French philosopher, Jean-Jacques Rousseau, surrounded by tall poplars. Just beyond, you will pass the Pont de la Machine. There, the new crystal-clear Rhône, its waters having lost the mud they carried when entering the eastern end of the lake, tumbles in a tumult of foam over the dam which regulates the level of the lake. By crossing the river at the next bridge, the Pont de l'Isle, you will pass the Tour de l'Isle, a one-time prison dating from the epoch of the Bishopric, and now almost swallowed up by more modern buildings on either side.

This brings you to the Place Bel-Air, in the center of the banking and business district. If you cross the Place, you can follow the Rue de la Corraterie to the Place Neuve, which is the site of the Grand Théâtre, the Rath Art Gallery and the Conservatory of Music. Just ahead of you is the entrance to a park, and on your left, bordering the square, a high wall, part of the ancient ramparts, above which is a row of fine old buildings. Enter the park, which contains the university, and keep to your left.

Almost immediately, at the foot of the ramparts, you will come to Geneva's most famous monument, the international memorial to the Reformation. Built between 1909 and 1917, the Reformation Monument, as it is generally known, is a gigantic 300-foot-long wall, impressive in its simplicity and clean lines as well as its sheer size. It is worth sitting down facing the wall on the terrace steps, made of Mont-Blanc granite, for this remarkable monument is full of interest. The central feature is a group of fifteen-foot statues of the four great leaders of the Reformation—Bèze, Calvin, Farel and John Knox.

Down the wall, on either side of the central group, are smaller statues (a mere nine feet tall) of other personalities, including Oliver Cromwell. And between the smaller figures are bas reliefs and inscriptions which tell the story of important happenings connected with the Reformation. Carved in the wall to the right of Cromwell, you'll see the presentation by the Houses of Parliament of the Bill of Rights to King William II in 1689, and above it, in English, the Bill's main features—the essence of democracy. To the left of Cromwell is a bas relief of the Pilgrim Fathers praying on the *Mayflower* before signing the Mayflower Compact. And left again, another bas relief shows John Knox preaching with obvious passion in St. Giles Cathedral, Edinburgh.

St. Peter's and City Hall

When you have absorbed the fascination of this unique monument, you can leave the park by the gate just beyond it. If you turn left into Rue St. Léger, pass under an ivy-hung bridge and climb up the winding street, you'll come to the charming Place Bourg-de-Four. This dreamy little Place was once the crossroads of important routes going to southern France via Annecy and Lyon, to Italy, to the Chablais, and elsewhere; before that it served as a Roman Forum and as a cattle and wheat market. If, in the Place, you turn right down Rue des Chaudronniers you'll find, not far away on the left, Calvin's College, sponsored by the stern reformer himself in 1559, and now the Cantonal Grammar (High) School for boys. Straight on down Chaudronniers it's only a short walk to the splendid Art and History Museum and the Baur Collection, while on the left, looking like a part of Moscow's Red Square, are the golden, onion-shaped cupolas of the Russian Church.

But it may be wiser to save this side trip for another time. So, in Place Bourg-de-Four turn left along any of the narrow streets, ramps, and staircases leading up to St. Peter's, whose stubby stone towers and green spire will be your guide, and pay a visit to this fine, historic cathedral. You can climb the north tower to see the city and lake spread out below you. Opposite, the City Hall, dating from the 16th century but restored and enlarged in later years, houses the famous Alabama Hall, in which two internationally important events have taken place. It was here that on August 22nd, 1864, the Geneva Convention was signed by sixteen countries, laying the foundation of the International Red Cross. Eight years later, in 1872, a court of arbitration was convened in this same room to settle the *Alabama* dispute between Great Britain and the United States, easing the latter's unhappiness over British support to Confederate ships during the Civil War.

The winding, cobbled streets leading from the cathedral to the modern city are picturesque and pleasing. Rue Calvin has a number of 18th-century *hôtels,* or town residences of noble families, No. 11 being built on the site of Calvin's house. In Rue du Puits-Saint-Pierre, No. 6 is a 12th-century building. The Grand Rue is the oldest street in Geneva, No. 11 having once been the residence of French ambassadors to the city before it joined the Confederation. The Rue Hôtel-de-Ville, once the headquarters of Italian religious refugees, is lined by 17th-century dwellings built with the typical craftsmanship of their former owners.

At the bottom of the hill, below the cathedral, lies Geneva's main shopping district along Quai Général Guisan, Rue du Rhône (the Café du Nord at No. 31 is said to have been one of Lenin's favorite spots), Rue du Croix d'Or and Rue du Marché, where superb shops, fashionable boutiques and the dazzling window displays of jewelers are an irresistible magnet for even the most budget-conscious tourist. But don't neglect the side streets, where the prices are often noticeably lower. Lovers of antiques will also find it worthwhile, if expensive, to stroll along the narrow streets which tumble down from the old quarter which we have just visited; these offer a fine assortment of antique shops. The district also abounds in art galleries, sometimes minute.

Despite growing competition from other countries, Geneva is still the world's watch-selling center. All the leading Swiss makers have offices or headquarters here. But much of the city's life also revolves around the European headquarters of the United Nations, the International Labor Office, and a host of other international agencies. So there is a final visit to be made in Geneva which is more or less a "must"—a trip to the buildings of the United Nations (once the home of the League of Nations) in the Ariana Park.

LAUSANNE

Sober Capital of Léman

The story of Lausanne, two-thirds of the way along the north shore of Lake Léman, is possibly less illustrious than that of Geneva, although just as ancient. Traces of prehistoric man have been found in and around the city, and when Julius Caesar arrived at the end of the first century B.C., he found settlements of lake dwellers and a primitive stronghold. The Romans established a military camp and relay point by the lake at Vidy, on the western fringe of present-day Lausanne (or "Lousonna," as they called it). The place was an important junction of routes into Gaul and over the Great St. Bernard Pass into Italy. Four centuries later, the Alemanni, a German tribe, burned the township, and its citizens took refuge at another smaller settlement already established a bit higher up the hill. To this refuge came Bishop Maire (or Marius) fleeing from his burnt-out see of Aventicum (now the town of Avenches), near the eastern shore of Lake Neuchâtel. A church was built and trade begun, merchants climbing with their pack mules to the developing town on the hill.

In the 12th century, Italian, Flemish and French architects, with the encouragement of Pope Innocent IV, set about building a cathedral. By 1275, the beautiful Burgundian Gothic edifice—today considered one of the finest medieval churches in Switzerland—was ready for consecration. Another Pope, Gregory X, came expressly to perform the ceremony. To mark the occasion, the ubiquitous Rudolph of Habsburg brought his wife, eight children, seven cardinals, five archbishops, seventeen bishops, four dukes, fifteen counts, and a multitude of lesser lords, spiritual and temporal, for the Pope was to make it a double event by crowning him Emperor of Germany and the Holy Roman Empire.

With such a flying start, Lausanne's Cathedral of Notre Dame could not fail to become a pilgrimage center—and so it did. Merchants, traders and innkeepers thrived, their houses spreading down the hillside and into the two rocky valleys surrounding the crag on which the cathedral stood. The bishops, in their palace-fortress, waxed powerful and wealthy, building themselves a summer island-castle at Ouchy, the growing town's lake port and fishing village. Although the House of Savoy owned most of the neighboring territory, Lausanne itself was ruled firmly by the bishops.

Towards the end of the 15th century, tension between the citizens of Lausanne and the all-powerful bishop mounted, with the result that in 1525, to assert its right of franchise, the city council concluded a treaty of "fellow burghership" with the powerful cantons of Bern and Fribourg. Bern proved a fickle friend, however. Eleven years later, in the summer of 1536, she declared war on Savoy and invaded the Pays de Vaud, the region around Lausanne which was a vassal territory of Savoy. Pretending that Sebastian of Montfaucon, Bishop of Lausanne, was a partisan of Savoy, Bern also marched into his city, where the invading army was greeted as a liberator. But Bern promptly treated both Vaud and Lausanne as occupied territory, putting a bailiff in the bishop's castle and reducing the power of the city fathers to zero. That August, the city council felt compelled to renounce Catholicism and accept the reformed faith. Catholic churches were ransacked and the cathedral's treasures sent to fill Bernese coffers.

Meanwhile, despite the stern eyes of the Bernese, social life in 18th-century Lausanne was particularly brilliant. The élite of the district offered warm-hearted hospitality to the cream of European society and intellect. From many countries, aristocrats and literary celebrities, such as the historian Edward Gibbon, the Duke of Württemberg and Voltaire, were drawn to Lausanne and caught up in a social whirl of parties, amateur theatricals, whist and gay little picnics. But revolt seethed behind this brilliant façade. It was in January, 1798, that this erupted; the liberal party, led by Fréderic César de la Harpe, proclaimed the independence of the Vaud and threw out the dismayed Bernese. Years of bickering followed, until, in 1803, Napoleon Bonaparte introduced the Act of Mediation. Among other things, this document, which for the first time in history used the word "Switzerland" as the name of the whole country, created the independent Canton of Vaud, making Lausanne its capital.

The Modern City

As a prosperous market town, renowned as a center of culture, and with a romantic attraction for English travelers and residents, Lausanne began to take itself seriously towards the end of the 19th century. Construction of roads, avenues and bridges went on apace, and the city gradually took on its present aspect. Lausanne today is as nearly picturesque as a modern, bustling city can be. Rising in tiers from the lakeside at Ouchy (1,200 feet above sea level) to 2,000 feet, it is ideally situated on three hills. Two small rivers used to flow through gorges between the hills, but they are now entirely covered over and the valleys spanned by several handsome bridges carrying the flow of modern traffic high over the streets and houses beneath.

In the last fifteen or twenty years, this civic-minded community has become the business center of western Switzerland and has adopted the proud title of "capital city of the Léman region." Its prosperous agricultural hinterland and the expanding industrial towns of the canton, such as Yverdon, Cossonay and Sainte-Croix, must channel their trade through Lausanne, which not only lies on major international rail routes but is also an important national railroad junction.

Although Lausanne is often called "the city of kings" because it has become the home of so much royalty, crowned, ex- or retired, the general tone of the town is set by the hard-headed, humorous peasant stock from which even some of the "best" families have sprung. Moreover, many of the leading business families have descended from 17th-century French Huguenots. There has never been an oligarchy in Lausanne, as in Fribourg, Geneva or Neuchâtel. As a result, less stress is laid here on the quality of the family tree. In Lausanne society, an old farmstead or vinegrower's vault almost equals a castle as a family seat.

Exploring Lausanne

Lausanne, a splendid excursion center and long popular with tourists, is a cosmopolitan city; one with an air of youthful vitality, stimulated by the great number of young people who attend its famous university and many educational establishments. Since 1945, with quite inexhaustible vigor, the city has been enjoying a building spree.Old houses and whole quarters have been pulled down to make way for shining new blocks of offices and apartments. Garden suburbs are expanding to meet the housing shortage caused by the growth of new industries on the fringes of the city.

Architectural exuberance has given Lausanne a rather lopsided air. A hillside skyscraper (seventeen stories on one side and fifteen on the other) contrasts brutally with the beautiful proportions of the cathedral rising in majesty on the crest of its hill. Atmospheric, although possibly unhygienic, alleys and narrow streets have been ruthlessly demolished, but the old *cité* clustered around Notre Dame is being painstakingly and attractively restored and refurbished.

Most of Lausanne's sightseeing and shops are within a radius of 600 yards from the Place St.-François, the hub of the city and a traffic maelstrom. North of the Place and close to the cathedral of Notre Dame, a fine example of Burgundian Gothic (carefully restored since the vandalism of Reformation days), is the 15th-century castle of St. Maire, formerly the bishop's palace, and the university (Palais de Rumine), with its fine musuems. To the left, on the way from the Place to the cathedral, is the charming 17th-century City Hall, its clock tower looking down onto the bustling, colorful market in the Place de la Palud. To the west of St. François, beyond the terminal of the funicular (which goes all the way down to Ouchy), are the 19th-century Law Courts. To the east, in the Park of Mon Repos, is the more modern, but handsome, Federal Palace of Justice, Switzerland's Supreme Court of Appeal, as well as the Olympic Museum.

But almost any walk around the hilly streets, steep alleys and stairways is rewarding for it will take you past a succession of charming and quaint old buildings and incongruous, often impressive, new ones. And you will get a hundred different views of the lake across rooftops, between buildings or from the gardens. (But remember: in Lausanne it is "Lac Léman"—none of that silly "Lake Geneva" nonsense!) Perhaps the two finest views in Lausanne are from the Park of Montriond, a short walk from the station down Avenue W. Fraisse, and from Le Signal (2,100 feet), a justly famed viewpoint about three-quarters of a mile north of the cathedral.

For those who enjoy walking, there are innumerable day and half-day trips to be made in the wooded hills of Jorat, about 2,700 feet high, above the city. A little lower, at Sauvabelin, just beyond Le Signal, there is a fine park, a charming little lake and a restaurant.

And down by the waterside is Ouchy, with its long, elegant, tree-lined promenades offering splendid views of lake and mountains; with its colorful gardens and gamut of hotels (including fashionable ones in the super-deluxe class). Ouchy is Lausanne's port, although far from a conventional one. True, it's quite a busy spot, but its activity is mainly with the smart white steamers; more call here than at any other place on the lake. So it makes a fine starting point for excursions as well as being an attractive international resort.

THE LAKE GENEVA COUNTRY

Vevey, Montreux and Other Delights

One of Lake Geneva's joys is that when you travel along the northern, or Swiss, side the road never strays far from the shore and provides an unending succession of lovely views of the lake, mountains and vine-clad hillsides. But if you are in a hurry and take instead the modern motorway which now goes all the way from Geneva to Villeneuve and beyond, the other drivers, rather than the views, will claim your attention.

From Geneva to Rolle, the shore road is bordered by fine parklands and estates strikingly reminiscent of the English countryside, a likeness which is more than mere coincidence. In the late 18th century, the sons of wealthy Genevan and Vaud families often became tutors in prosperous English families. They returned with money in the bank and new ideas, planning their estates and gardens in the style they had admired in England.

At Coppet, eight miles from Geneva, is the lovely old château where the dynamic Madame de Staël spent many years in exile. She was the daughter of Suzanne Curchod, whose father was a Vaud parson. Suzanne had been jilted by the youthful Edward Gibbon in 1756 and, on the rebound, did very well for herself by accepting the hand of Jacques Necker, a Genevan banker who later became financial adviser to Louis XVI. Far-sighted Necker bought the mansion at Coppet as a retreat, and he was glad to take refuge there when the French Revolution broke out. At the château, Madame de Staël established an intellectual court, whose literary salons were attended by giants of the early romantic period: Byron, Benjamin Constant, Sismondi, August Schlegel, the faithless Edward Gibbon, and others. The château, still kept as it was in Madame's time, may be visited every day except Monday.

Nyon, some five miles from Coppet, was founded by Julius Caesar in about 45 B.C. as a camp for war veterans. The castle was built by Louis, first Baron of Vaud, and taken over by the Bernese in 1570 as residence for their bailiffs. Today, it houses the municipal offices and a museum noted for its collection of Nyon china. In the 17th and 18th centuries, Nyon was the center of a flourishing chinaware craft; its flowersprigged tea-sets, vases and bowls were in great demand and today are still sought by collectors. Nyon motifs are now used by Swiss manufacturers and for hand-painted craftwork. Clinging to a hillside, Nyon is an attractive little market town. If you leave the road to visit the town center, on the way up you'll find one good view from the gardens and another from the castle. Down by the shore, with its delightful promenade, the Lake Léman museum features models of the lake's boats through the ages.

If you have time, some three miles beyond Rolle, a pleasant, small town with the most inevitable castle—this time on the water's edge—it is worth turning left at Allaman to visit Aubonne, for much of the latter village has remained practically unchanged since the 16th century. The 12th-century castle was bought in 1670 by the eccentric J. B. Tavernier, a great French traveler who visited the courts of Persia and Turkey and wrote entertaining accounts of his journeys.

Morges, about eight miles from Rolle, is a peaceful little lake port, popular among sailing enthusiasts. It, too, has a castle, in this instance built by the Duke of Savoy in about 1286 as a defense against the bishop-princes of Lausanne. The great Polish pianist and statesman Ignace Paderewski spent the last years of his life on his beautiful estate at nearby Tolochenaz, where he attracted a brilliant international group of musicians. He left Morges in 1940 on his last trip to the United States. You'll see a statue of him at the eastern end of the town. Nowadays, Audrey Hepburn has a home at Tolochenaz.

La Côte

The district between Coppet and Morges is known as La Côte, the sunny slopes providing excellent conditions for vine-growing. La Côte vintages are light, white wines, mostly consumed on the home market. About four miles before the city of Lausanne, you'll come to St. Sulpice, where, from May onwards, the owners of countless weekend houses move in for the summer enjoyment of Lake Geneva. St. Sulpice is also the proud possessor of the best preserved 11th-century Romanesque church in Switzerland, a charming little building. It was built by monks of the famous Cluny Abbey in Burgundy. Three original apses remain, although the nave has disappeared. The short bell tower is built of small stone blocks that were probably brought from the ruined Roman township at nearby Vidy. The adjoining priory was converted into a private residence during the 16th century.

On the eastern side of Lausanne is the Lavaux, a remarkably beautiful region of vineyards, rising up the hillside along the fifteen miles between Pully, on the outskirts of Lausanne, and Montreux. Brown-roofed stone villages in the Savoy style, old defense towers and small baronial castles stud the green and brown landscape. The vineyards, enclosed within low stone walls, slope so steeply that all the work there has to be done by hand. Insecticides, fungicides, manures, and even soil washed down by summer storms are carried in baskets and containers strapped to men's backs. No wonder harvest in mid-October is a period for rejoicing! The grapes, picked by cheerful-looking girls and women, are carried down by the men to the nearest road, emptied into vats and taken by horse or tractor to the nearest press. Some Lavaux vintages are excellent and in great demand, but unfortunately, the yield is small.

At Cully, about five miles east of Lausanne, the motorist has a choice of roads just before entering the village. Straight on will take you along the main coastal road to Vevey. If, instead, you fork right, you will eventually come to the beautiful Corniche Road leading to Chexbres, a spick-and-span summer resort some two thousand feet above sea level. Winding high above the lake through delightful, narrow-streeted villages among steeply sloping vineyards, the Corniche Road offers a succession of fabulous views across the lake. But this magnificent detour is best savored in early summer or autumn, when traffic is light, for the road is often narrow, and parking places few. From Chexbres, the Corniche Road winds down through the Dézaley (vineyards owned by the city of Lausanne which produce a light white wine) to rejoin the lake highway just before it enters Vevey.

Vevey to Montreux

Vevey needs no introduction to globetrotters. Together with neighboring Montreux, it has been a resort popular with the British since the early 19th century. Facing the lofty Dent d'Oche peak across the lake, its romantic outlook exercises a great attraction. It's also the center of an important wine producing region which, four or five times a century, celebrates the fact with a prodigious, world famous 'Fête des Vignerons' (vine growers).

On the heights above Vevey and Montreux lie several delightfully quiet summer or winter resorts accessible by road or rail: Les Pléiades, Les Avants, Mont Pèlerin and Blonay. Between Bloany and Chamby, a three-mile scenic journey, enthusiasts can travel on summer weekends in a train hauled by lovingly restored, fifty-year-old, steam locomotives. The neighboring mountain slopes and valleys, particularly at Les Avants, are famous for the wonderful spring display of wild narcissi and daffodils, usually in bloom from about mid-May to mid-June.

At the eastern end of Vevey's lakeside promenade is La Tour de Peilz, named after a castle built here in 1280 by Peter of Savoy. Booklovers will remember that the Vevey/La Tour de Peilz/Montreux region is the setting for Jean-Jacques Rousseau's *La Nouvelle Héloise,* the 18th-century bestseller which took Europe by storm and, incidentally, did much to make Swiss travel fashionable.

Exploring Montreux

Montreux, one of Europe's most beautifully situated resorts and the most popular in the Lake Geneva region, is a French-style Edwardian town, much modernized, that caters almost exclusively to foreign visitors. It enjoys a remarkably mild climate thanks to mountains which protect it from cold north and east winds. Mulberries, magnolias and palm trees grow in its lush, well-tended gardens. Yet, despite the sheltering mountains, Montreux has a fine, open situation, looking across the vast expanse of the lake, or eastwards up the wide Rhône valley, to a magnificent background of snow-capped peaks.

On the main Simplon railway line, Montreux is also the terminus of several mountain railways, not least the scenically splendid M.O.B., whose comfortable little trains will take you on a winding journey among the mountains of the Bernese Oberland to Saanenmöser, Gstaad, Zweisimmen, and the Simmen valley.

While at Montreux, a trip by mountain railroad (the trains leave from the main station) to the Rochers de Naye is imperative. There, from November to May, skiers enjoy, at 6,700 feet above sea level, both the magnificent snowfields and the splendid view over Lake Geneva, the Savoy and the Swiss Alps.

Another lovely trip from Montreux is the drive to Glion and Caux, both also accessible by train. At the top of the winding road is a memorable view, and the vast "Mountain House" (Caux), former Palace Hotel and now the international conference center of the Moral Rearmament movement.

The famous castle of Chillon lies about one and one-half miles from Montreux. Forming an island, although only a few yards from the shore and in strange contrast to the wide modern highway and the overhead cables of the electric railway that pass close by, the romantic-looking castle keeps stern watch over the lake, reflected in intense blue-green water.

As it stands today, Chillon was built under the direction of Duke Peter of Savoy in the 13th century with, it is said, the help of military architects from Plantaganet England. During its long period as a state prison, among the many unfortunate guests in the castle's dungeon was at least one famous prisoner, François Bonivard. As Prior of St. Victor in Geneva, he had supported the Reformation, an act which infuriated the Catholic Duke of Savoy. To ponder on the error of his ways Bonivard was sent to Chillon, where he spent six gloomy years, much of the time chained to a pillar in the dungeon, before being released by the Bernese in 1536. Up to the 17th century, Chillon was the scene of many trials for such things as sorcery, the wretched victims coming to a gruesome end in the castle courtyard.

When he was in Clarens, on the other side of Montreux, in 1816, the poet Byron visited Chillon. He learned of Bonivard's incarceration and wrote his famous poem, "The Prisoner of Chillon." If you visit the castle, usually open from mid-morning to late afternoon or early evening, you will see that Byron, like a true tourist, carved his name on a pillar in Bonivard's dungeon. You will also be able to see the great hall and torture chamber, and a fine collection of medieval furnishings and decorations.

Beyond Chillon, the road curves round the end of the lake to the small town of Villeneuve, guarding the estuary of the River Rhône and the long narrow plain which lies beyond. Until 1940, most of this area was considered unsuitable for agriculture. It was covered with reeds and horsegrass and was swampy, but wartime food problems provided the spur to drastic action. Drainage and irrigation were undertaken on a large scale by private enterprise and vast areas of land were reclaimed. At Vouvray, about five miles from Villeneuve, there is a fine model farm, established during World War II by one of Switzerland's leading pharmaceutical companies to secure farm produce for its thousands of workers. If you drive on up the valley, you will see more evidence of how ingeniously nature can be harnessed to the needs of man.

Return to Geneva

At Villeneuve, your tour of the Swiss playground along Lake Geneva is almost ended, but if you wish, you can return to Geneva along the southern (French) shore. About four miles from Villeneuve, the road crosses the Rhône, here a muddy river which discolors the water where it enters the lake. A right turn soon after the bridge will bring you quickly to the lakeside village of St. Gingolph, half Swiss, half French.

The first large township in France is the popular resort and spa of Evian-les-Bains, which the Swiss often visit, crossing the lake on one of the busy little steamers to spend an afternoon shopping or, more likely, an evening trying their luck at the casino. Thonon, about six miles beyond Evian, is not only an important agricultural center, but like Evian, another popular lakeside resort and spa. At Sciez, some six miles beyond Thonon, you can either go straight along the direct main road to Geneva or turn right for the more interesting secondary road along the lake through the little resort of Yvoire, crossing the frontier to re-enter Switzerland at Hermance, nine miles from Geneva.

There are several interesting side-trips from the road along the northern shore of Lake Geneva. The first is from Nyon, where the northwestern exit from the town will bring you to Highway 90. This rises steeply into the Jura, winding and twisting up to St. Cergue (3,400 feet), a winter and summer sports resort noted for its bracing climate and outstanding views.

From St. Cergue, a secondary road cuts away to the northeast, passing through Bassins and St. George, and then over the Marchairuz Pass to Le Brassus, a watchmaking center in the Vaud Jura. The countryside here is rather bleak, the bare rolling hilltops windswept and bitterly cold in winter.

In a cleft of the straight valley of Joux, so typical of Jura scenery, lies the Lake of Joux. You can drive along either shore, for both roads converge at Le Pont, a bustling, popular rendezvous on fine weekends, at the far end of the lake. The road then climbs over the

Mollendruz Pass (3,500 feet). Halfway down the other side, there is a magnificent panoramic view of Lake Geneva, with Lausanne in the foreground. From L'Isle, a village at the bottom, you can return to Nyon through Apples, Aubonne and Rolle.

Another pleasant little sidetrip—one you can complete in an afternoon—leads northwards from Lausanne or Morges, both roads joining up at the village of Cossonay. A few miles beyond Cossonay is La Sarraz, whose castle, on a rocky promontory, was originally built in the 11th century by the Burgundian kings. Reconstructed in the 13th century, it was destroyed by the Confederates in 1475 and once again rebuilt. Its last owner, Henri de Mandrot, gave the Castle of La Sarraz to the Canton of Vaud in 1920. Today, it is a national monument, containing a museum with a fine collection of furniture.

If you fork left at Croy, about four miles from La Sarraz on the Vallorbe road, you will quickly come to the charming old Jura village of Romainmotier, noted for its Romanesque church, dating from the 11th century. Returning through Croy, it is a mere five miles to Orbe, once the Roman town of Urba. Quaint, rather than beautiful, Orbe was later an important focal point in Charlemagne's Europe. According to the legend it was at Urba that the cruel Queen Brunhilda of Burgundy held court in the 9th century and that Charlemagne's sons met to divide their father's estates.

Roman Ruins

At Boscéaz, about two kilometers from Orbe along the road to Yverdon, are the ruins of several Roman villas from the 1st and 2nd centuries. Apart from Zofingen, near Olten, this is the only place in Switzerland where Roman mosaics can be viewed on their original sites. From here, you can either return via La Sarraz or go on to Yverdon and back via Echallens.

Any of the roads, too, which lead up into the hills and valleys behind Vevey or Montreux are worth exploring. In only a few minutes they will bring you to splendid views and, in the late spring or early summer, to fields of wild flowers, all designed to send film speeding through your camera.

Quite different but equally lovely views can be seen from the fleet of smart, white paddle-steamers, diesel motor boats and even a 45-m.p.h. hydrofoil, which ply busily around and across the lake, calling frequently at all the towns and many of the lakeside villages.

THE SWISS JURA,

NEUCHATEL AND FRIBOURG

Where "East Ist Ost" and "West Est Ouest"

Although the subtitle of this chapter is roughly correct, you will find there is no sharply defined geographical boundary with "German" Switzerland on one side and "French" on the other. However, for the sake of convenience, if you draw a line from Montreux to Fribourg, extending it to Neuchâtel, then up through Biel (Bienne) and due north to Delémont, you can say fairly confidently that the country is mainly French-speaking to the west and German-speaking to the east. The western half of the upper valley of the Rhône is also predominantly French-speaking but differs in character from the Jura and is described in a later chapter.

It is well to keep in mind that there exists a shaded area on either side of the "language frontier," where French and German influences are rather delicately balanced. Along the imaginary line it is not unusual to hear towns referred to by either their French or German names: Bienne = Biel; Morat = Murten; Neuchâtel = Neuenburg; Soleure = Solothurn. And your "thank you" may well be answered cheerfully by a bilingual *"Merci vielmal."*

Exploring the Jura and Fribourg

The southern section of this region is dominated by the city of Fribourg; in the northern part, the influence of Neuchâtel is more strongly felt.

Fribourg's Unique Role

Between the rich pasturelands of the Swiss plateau and the Alpine foothills, Fribourg has an air of happy satisfaction. And well it may have, because for centuries it has been both a prosperous city and one of considerable importance in the Catholic world. Fribourg was founded about 1178, when Berthold of Zähringen decided that the rocky cliffs of the twisting Sarine River exactly met his idea of security. The House of Zähringen died out in 1218, and Fribourg then passed first into the hands of the counts of Kyburg and next to Count Habsburg-Laufenburg, who sold it a few years later to his cousin, Rudolph of Habsburg. In the first half of the 15th century, the city saw many battles between Bern on the one side and Savoy on the other, receiving little help in the process from the Habsburgs, who had other fish to fry. Eventually, in 1452, Fribourg came under Savoy's "protection."

Throughout this span of years, however, the city had won many rights and liberties and extended its territory, absorbing the estates of neighboring feudal lords. The Burgundian Wars, in which Fribourg supported the confederate states, brought further spoils in the form of more estates and parishes. In 1481, thanks to the intervention of Nicholas of Flüe, Fribourg was admitted to the Confederation as a sovereign canton. Thereafter, skillful purchases brought Fribourg still more estates and parishes while, externally, its history merged with that of the Confederation. Citizens stubbornly resisted the onslaught of the Reformation, making their state a stronghold of Catholicism, further strengthened by the foundation of the Catholic College of St. Michael in 1584 and, three centuries later, of Switzerland's only bilingual Catholic state university.

Six centuries of peace were broken when, overnight on March 1st, 1798, French troops suddenly occupied the city, and the influence of the French Revolution ended the power of the patrician oligarchy in whose hands the city's administration had lain for nearly two centuries. In 1814, with the loosening of France's grip on Switzerland, a patrician, or aristocratic, government was restored in Fribourg, only to be replaced once again in 1830 by a democratic regime.

The city of Fribourg, although having all the prosperity of an important agricultural center, is not essentially ambitious or pushing. It has preserved much of its medieval charm, but is at the same time an up-to-date place, particularly in the new quarter around the main station. From here you can go down the Rue de Romont and Rue de Lausanne towards the cathedral, and to the old town, with its lovely Gothic houses clinging to the clifftop and spilling down to the river-eroded valley.

A "must" for sightseers is the Cathedral of St. Nicholas, dating from the 13th century. It has all the magnificence of a house of prayer, and its organ is famous throughout the world. The Church and Convent of the Cordeliers is an 18th-century building on the site of an earlier edifice. Its treasures include a 16th-century triptych on the high altar by the anonymous "Nelkenmeisters" (two artists who signed their works only with a red and white carnation), a carved wood triptych believed to be Alsatian, a notable side altar, and a 16th-century retable by the Fribourg artist, Hans Fries. The Church of the Augustines possesses a magnificent 17th-century altar by Peter Spring, the sculptor-monk. The ultramodern university buildings, a surprising contrast to the atmosphere of the old town, are spaciously laid out in the new quarter.

Architecturally, Fribourg is a delight. The ancient patrician houses in the old quarter around the cathedral are treasured and well-preserved. The city hall has all the pristine glory of its 16th-century origin, and picturesque fountains in the Bernese style add a note of rural humor to winding streets. Fribourg is a city of memorable views; from the Zähringen viaduct, you can look down to the River Sarine far below, with the ancient covered wooden bridge of Bern, and the high-arched Gotteron bridge beyond; and from the Gotteron bridge itself, from the Chapelle de Lorette, or the Milieu or St. Jean bridges, you can get splendid views of the town.

Wednesday and Saturday are market days, and the farmers and their wives may wear national dress: for the men, this means a white, short-sleeved shirt under a linen jacket, and a skull cap of embroidered velvet or straw; for women, a dainty blouse under a sleeveless cotton dress, tight-waisted, with full ankle-length skirt ornamented by a colorful apron, the whole set off with a draped neck square and a wide-brimmed straw hat. This is weekday dress; Sunday costumes are more ornate, with long sleeves and elaborate, lace-trimmed hats.

Fribourg to Gruyères

The canton of Fribourg is bilingual because it straddles the language frontier. But as two-thirds of its inhabitants speak French and only one-third German, it may be considered French. The canton's lush pasturelands, particularly around Gruyères, are rich in milk and cream yielded by plump little Fribourg cows, black and white like the cantonal coat of arms. Gruyère cheese, home-cured hams, bacon and sausage, *Vacherin* (a delicious creamy cheese made in Alpine pastures during the summer and preserved for winter in cherrywood boxes)—these are all products of Fribourg's agricultural hinterland.

In all Europe, few more picturesque villages than Gruyères can be found. If you go there from Fribourg by train (you must change at Bulle for the final ten-minute ride to Gruyères), or the long way round by car, you will pass through Romont, enjoying along the route the rich and prosperous countryside studded with farms.

As you go, note the architecture of the homesteads. You will find it different from the modified Bernese style of Vaud's rural buildings and different again from that of Bern, which you will soon be entering. Fribourg farmsteads are composed of two units: the stone-built living quarters, to which are attached, under the same roof, the wooden barns and stables. The eaves are wide and peaked, and shelter from the cold is provided by a lean-to on the windward side. Over the stables hang rows of medals won at cattle shows.

Romont is a delightful, sleepy Fribourg township, looking from its walls onto cool meadowlands. The modern highway bypasses it at the foot of the old ramparts, but it is worthwhile climbing into this 13th-century town (composed of two broad streets), to enjoy the magnificent view from the castle terrace.

To the castle built by Peter II of Savoy, the government of Fribourg added a new wing in 1581. Today it houses the administration of the district of Glane. The 13th-century ramparts completely surround the town and form a belvedere from which the whole range of the Alps from Mont Blanc to the Bernese Oberland may be viewed. A 12th-century Cistercian convent and a 17th-century Capuchin monastery blend with the ancient houses and inns of the township.

You will find Gruyères enchanting if you are here when bus tours are *not*. . It stands high on a rocky crag, its medieval houses and single main street cozy within its ramparts. It is a perfect specimen of the medieval stronghold, and was once capital of the idyllic Alpine estates of the counts of Gruyères, vassal lords of the Kingdom of Burgundy. Symbolically, their crest bears the crane (French: *grue*); there were nineteen counts who, from the year 1080 until 1554, fought, went to the Crusades, and lorded it over their serfs. Michael of Gruyères, the last of them, was a lover of luxury and spent lavishly. Fribourg and

Bern did not mind his extravagances, for when at last he fled from his creditors, these two powerful cantons divided up his estates between them. Fribourg and Bernese bailiffs succeeded each other in the old castle until, in 1848, it was bought by a wealthy Genevan family whose members were patrons of the arts. One of their guests was Corot, who painted several panels in his hosts' drawing room.

The one real street in Gruyères is lined with Renaissance houses in perfect condition; their late Gothic façades are 15th- to 17th-century. From the ramparts and the castle terrace, the view extends to Broc, the place where Peter-Cailler-Kohler chocolate is made. Beyond is the artificial Lake of Gruyères, built to feed new hydroelectric power plants. In Gruyères there's a cheese dairy open to visitors.

A few miles southeast of Gruyères is one of Switzerland's newest resorts, Moléson-Village. From there, you can go by aerial cableway to Plan Francey (4,900 ft.) and thence to Mount Moléson (6,600 ft.), or to Vudella (5,400 ft.). Moléson-Village offers several ski lifts, miles of marked ski-runs, and no less than four mountain restaurants seating a total of a thousand persons. There's a postal bus service between Moléson-Village and Bulle.

Gruyères to Château d'Oex

From Gruyères it is a twenty-five minute train ride to Montbovon, where you change trains for the quarter-hour trip which follows the glorious Sarine River to Château d'Oex (pronounced *shat-oh-day*), the gateway to the Pays d'Enhaut ("the upper land"), one of the most scenic regions of southwestern Switzerland. Château d'Oex is a growing winter sports and summer resort. Within a few miles, there are nearly a couple of dozen assorted ski lifts and cableways, the latter going up to La Montagnette (5,600 ft.). If you are interested in peasant handicrafts, a visit to the local museum will be worthwhile but, on a clear day, let nothing interfere with an hour's postal bus ride to the Col des Mosses. This will be one of the most unforgettable experiences of your visit to Switzerland. You will see the entire panorama of the Alpine chain, extending into France and Italy, and any questions in your mind as to why this region is called the "Pays d'Enhaut" will disappear forever.

An alternative excursion from Fribourg is north to the lovely lakeside town of Murten (or Morat), a half-hour by train. This bilingual township belongs to Canton Fribourg; its name is emblazoned on Swiss history, for it was here that in 1476 Charles the Bold met his second defeat at the hands of the Confederation army.

Murten and Avenches

Murten has retained all its medieval charm. The modern highway enters and leaves the old part of the town through the 13th-century gates. The houses and shops lining the broad main street (Hauptgasse) look at the busy traffic from under the deep, vaulted arcades. Founded by the dukes of Zähringen in the 12th century, Murten became an Imperial city in the 13th, only to pass into the hands of Savoy, whose dukes built the imposing castle and ramparts. Its diminutive namesake lake is fed by the River Broye and its outflow goes into Lake Neuchâtel.

It is a pleasant fifteen-minute drive southwestwards, at first along the lakeside, to Avenches, the old Celtic capital of the Helvetians. Later, as Aventicum, it became an important Roman city of 40,000 (about twenty times its present population), until the Alamanni destroyed it in the third century. You can still see the remains of a Roman amphitheater where 12,000 bloodthirsty spectators watched what they called "the games." The collection of Roman antiquities at the museum is noteworthy although the famous bust of Marcus Aurelius, unearthed in Avenches a few years ago, has been moved to Lausanne.

A bare twenty minutes on the smooth-running electrified Swiss Federal Railways mainline, or an eight-mile drive along the Lausanne road, will take you to Payerne. Here you should visit the 11th-century, carefully restored Romanesque abbey church, one of the finest you will see anywhere, before returning to Fribourg, a half-hour's journey.

Neuchâtel

The story of Neuchâtel really begins in 1011, for in that year it is first mentioned in a deed of gift made by King Rudolph III of Burgundy to his wife Irmengarde. The township was then probably little more than a fortified village. In 1034, two years after the death of Rudolph, Neuchâtel was given by the German Emperor Conrad II in fief to a local lord whose descendants, using the title "count," greatly developed their domains, encouraging both agriculture and industry. Three centuries later, the original direct line of the house died out. Thereafter, Neuchâtel came under the rule of several dynasties until 1707, when it passed to Frederic I, Prussia's first king. But although in theory a Prussian principality, this made little difference to the life of the people because their sovereign left them to manage their own affairs. Neuchâtel retained its French culture, and the 18th century saw the rise of a new and lucrative craft—watchmaking.

From 1806, Napoleon inevitably loomed into the picture, and for the next eight years Neuchâtel was held by his Chief of Staff, Maréchal Berthier.

In 1815, Neuchâtel became a member of the Swiss Confederation, and a very odd member, too. With the fall of Napoleon, it had reverted to the King of Prussia, and was, therefore, the only nonrepublican canton in a republican confederation. Its loyalties were therefore not only to its prince, the King of Prussia, Frederic-Guillaume III, but also to the Federal Parliament in Bern, who were not wholly on speaking terms! The events which shook the great European powers in the beginning of 1848 allowed the people of Neuchâtel to become a republic without bloodshed. Eventually, in 1857, the king formally acknowledged Neuchâtel's independence.

Throughout the 18th century, watchmaking progressed rapidly from a home craft to the status of an industry, and a number of allied trades sprang up, absorbing the canton's labor. During the present century, watchmaking has become increasingly scientific, and the city of Neuchâtel has helped manufacturers by placing an observatory and an Institute for Horological Research at their service. Astronomical observations, research on metals, and improved manufacturing methods have carried watchmaking one step further, from an industry to a science. Not everyone in this region is a watchmaker, of course. There are also farmers and vintners along the sunny shore of the lake, but scientific horology is the main source of the canton's, and the city's, income and prosperity.

Exploring Neuchâtel

Neuchâtel is a prosperous, but not very large, city. With a population of some 37,000, it has an air of almost tangible dignity. In the lower part of the town, bordering the placid lake, broad avenues are lined with imposing butter-colored buildings of sandstone, the whole effect being one of unruffled but compact grandeur. The old quarters of the city lie around the castle and Collegiate Church on the hillside. The influence of Prussia has not even left a scratch on its culture and way of life, and it is the citizen's proud boast—and one with some substance—that they speak "the best French in Switzerland." This is one reason why so many boarding and finishing schools have been established here and why Neuchâtel has won fame as an educational center. The academy, now a university of note, was founded in 1838.

Located at the foot of the Jura, flanked by vineyards and facing southeast, Neuchâtel is a belvedere from which can be viewed, across the lake and central plateau, the whole crowded range of the middle Alps, from the majestic mass of Mont-Blanc to the Bernese Oberland. Climb to the main station of Neuchâtel on a clear day, and the bristling array of serried peaks stands clearly revealed.

Sightseeing in Neuchâtel should include the Collegiate Church (Collégiale), a handsome Romanesque and Gothic structure dating from the 12th century, around which are grouped the castle (mainly 15th and 16th centuries), ramparts, cloisters and a shady terrace. The influence of French architectural styles predominates in the city. In the Rue des Moulins, for example, are two perfect specimens of the Louis XIII period; there is a fine Louis XIV house in the Market Square (Place des Halles), notable for its turreted 16th-century Maison des Halles. The Renaissance has left its mark at the Croix du Marché, while in the City Hall Square (Place de l'Hôtel de Ville) the 18th century prevails. There are several fine patrician houses, such as the mansion of Du Peyrou, the friend, protector and publisher of Jean-Jacques Rousseau. But almost anywhere in the old town you will find picturesque buildings. When tired of walking, one can relax in the shade of the trees lining Neuchâtel's lively, lengthy quays while looking across the water to the distant Alps.

The Jura

Behind Lake Geneva, and straddling the French frontier from near the city of Geneva itself almost all the way to Basel, lie the Jura mountains, a considerable range although one very different in character from the Alps on the other side of the lake. By Alpine standards the mountains of the Jura are relatively low, almost puny. Few peaks exceed 5,000 feet. It is a region of pine forests, lush pastureland, and deeply cleft, often craggy valleys where farmsteaders lived in relative isolation until the advent of railroads and the automobile. Nevertheless, in winter some parts of the Jura can be very cold. La Brévine, a windswept hamlet between Le Locle and Les Verrières on the Franco-Swiss frontier, is sometimes called the Swiss Siberia. Winter temperatures there drop as low as 15 to 25 degrees below zero Fahrenheit. And the Jura has a number of thriving winter sports resorts although most are comparatively small and have local rather than international appeal.

Surprisingly it is a region which is relatively uncluttered with tourists. Travelers usually by-pass the Jura, being attracted by more famous, romantic or better publicized places.

Strangely, too, it has a number of pockets of industry. Occasionally, without warning and in the middle of nowhere, one comes to a large, white factory—probably bearing a world-famous name. If you look at your watch face you may well see the same name, for watchmaking—one of Switzerland's most important industries—has long been one of the principal occupations of the region.

The Jura is divided into several well-defined districts; Franches-Montagnes, with its chief town, Saignelégier; the French-speaking Bernese Jura, including St.-Imier, Delémont, Porrentruy, and the Ajoie area, where a strong secessionist movement is developing as the inhabitants want to establish a canton of their own; and the Neuchâtel Jura, with the great watchmaking centers of La Chaux-de-Fonds and Le Locle.

To La Chaux-de-Fonds and Ste.-Croix

From Neuchâtel, take the main highway north to Valangin, where the beautiful mountain road known as the Vue des Alpes begins. As the highway rises, the view extends over Lake Neuchâtel towards the Savoy Alps and into the Bernese Oberland.

La Chaux-de-Fonds, which lies in a hollow, is not a picturesque town. Its straight, broad streets and avenues lie stiffly at right angles, bordered by prosaic stone houses. It has all been built in recent years, for the old town was destroyed by fire at the turn of the last century. But recently an ultramodern industrial and residential section has sprung up among the pastures and meadows on its western outskirts. As you pass through La Chaux-de-Fonds, you will see the many factories, large and small, which make internationally famous watches and their components. There's a remarkable, underground museum with over 3,000 timepieces. Here you turn off southwest to Le Locle.

At Le Locle, another important watchmaking center, it's worth going on a couple of miles to Col des Roches and then through the tunnel, for at the other end the horizon opens up suddenly onto France, revealing the magnificent site of the River Doubs, with its high cliffs, little lake, and waterfall. Next, backtrack to Le Locle, turn right, and continue among pine-clad hills and meadows to Les Petits-Ponts. There, another right turn will take you to Fleurier along the Val de Travers; the winding gorges of this valley are extremely picturesque. Beyond Fleurier you climb up to Ste. Croix, where, from the pine-covered ridge above the village (which, incidentally, makes music boxes) there's a splendid view. If you're a glutton for views, turn left here to Les Rasses—it's only about two miles—for another fine one. From Ste.-Croix you drive down towards Yverdon and then return along the lake shore to Neuchâtel.

To Moutier and Delémont

From Neuchâtel, take the Vue des Alpes route to La Chaux-de-Fonds and bear northeast (right) along the pretty valley of St. Imier, a small watchmaking center at the foot of Mont Soleil (4,200 ft.) and facing Mont Chasseral (5,300 ft.), the Jura's highest mountain. St. Imier is a modern township, but not blatantly so, and legend has it that it was founded by a holy hermit from Burgundy. A trip by funicular up Mont Soleil is worthwhile, especially if you have time to spend a night there to see the sunrise the following morning. On winter Sundays, Mont Soleil is a favorite haunt for skiers from Basel.

From St. Imier, it is twenty-five miles to medieval Moutier, which produces a special cheese curiously named *Tête de Moine* (Monk's Head), the only reminder of the once renowned monastery of Bellelay. At Moutier, you turn north to Delémont, the chief town of the Bernese Jura, located in a wide picturesque valley. It has an ancient story and is first mentioned in history in A.D. 727. In the 11th century, Delémont was annexed by the bishop-princes of Basel, who often used it as a summer residence. At the beginning of the 18th century, they built a castle for this purpose, but they had left things too late, for in 1793 the town was seized by France and later, in 1815, given to Bern under the Treaty of Vienna. Visitors will find that even today Delémont retains an 18th-century charm.

The thirty-five-mile round trip from Delémont northwest to Porrentruy and back is a beautiful run along part of the Corniche du Jura. This is one of the finest routes in the region, rising to 2,800 feet at the summit just before you get to the national Les Rangiers monument, which commemorates Swiss mobilization in World War I. If you have time for a side-trip, take the secondary road on the left just beyond Les Rangiers. In about four miles, you'll come to the charming and ancient fortified townlet of St. Ursanne, where, despite all the watches made in the region, time has apparently stood still for centuries. At the far end of the narrow bridge, there's a picturesque view of the old houses lining the side of the River Doubs. Porrentruy, at 1,400 feet, has about 8,500 inhabitants and is the chief center of the Ajoie district. Its splendid castle, above the town, was yet another residence of the bishop-princes of Basel, and it can boast several fine 18th-century buildings. Like many of the Jura towns, Porrentruy has an excellent watchmaking school where for generations skilled craftsmen have been trained, but it is also a popular summer holiday center, thanks to the lovely surrounding countryside and the excellent food in the district. Year round, it organizes special horseback riding holidays, trekking from village to village in the region. At the local airfield, you can learn to fly or glide, and if you aspire to be a balloonist you can make a trip over the Jura with an expert pilot.

Saignelégier to Bienne

From St. Ursanne, which we mention above, a delightful, picturesque drive takes you along the secondary road, often steep and winding, which leads southwest into the Franches-Montagnes, among forests, meadows and hills, and past the villages of Soubey and Les Enfers, to Saignelégier.

Saignelégier is the center of a horse-breeding area and, on the second weekend in August, the scene of a fascinating horse show and market with races that attract large crowds. The Franches-Montagnes horse is used chiefly for military purposes and agriculture.

The district has typical Jura scenery: rolling hills, long valleys and ridges, and pine-capped hummocks, but grazing lands are mostly poor. Peat is obtained in certain areas and the roots of the yellow gentian are used for making a powerful liqueur, said to have medicinal properties.

From Saignelégier continue to Le Noirmont, a typical Jura village, to La Chaux-de-Fonds, and so down again to Neuchâtel.

At Neuchâtel the vineyards begin. Their wines, chiefly white, are light, somewhat sparkling, and have a distinct bouquet. They are bottled before the second fermentation begins, so have a rather high carbonic acid content. These wines are exported, as well as consumed on the home market.

Four miles southwest of Neuchâtel, just off the main road to the right, and well worth a visit, is the medieval village of Colombier, approached through a massive stone gateway beside the impressive, 16th-century castle.

The lakeside village of Grandson (Vaud) is about sixteen miles farther on. It is said that a member of the Grandson family accompanied William of Normandy (better known as the Conqueror) to England in 1066, where he founded the English barony of Grandison. Otto I of Grandson took part in the Crusades, and one of his descendants, so legend has it, was a troubador whose poems were praised by Chaucer. When the Burgundian wars broke out in the late 15th century, Grandson castle, much rebuilt in the 13th and 15th centuries, was in the hands of Charles of Burgundy. In 1475, the Swiss won it by siege, but early the next year, their garrison was surprised by Duke Charles; 418 of their men were captured and hanged from the apple trees in the castle orchard. A few days later, the Swiss returned to Grandson and, after inflicting a crushing defeat on the Burgundians, retaliated by stringing their prisoners from the same apple trees. After being used for three centuries as a residence by the Bernese bailiffs, the castle was bought in 1875 by the de Blonay family, which restored it.

Three miles beyond Grandson is Yverdon, a busy market and industrial town, as well as a spa, at the southern end of Lake Neuchâtel and on the estuary of the River Orbe. Yverdon has a claim to interest because it was here that the famous Swiss educator John Henry Pestalozzi (born in 1746) opened an experimental school in the castle. His enterprise attracted reformers from Germany and England (one of his visitors was the poet Southey.) The castle, in its present form built by Peter II of Savoy in the middle of the 13th century, has been restored and modernized. In front of Yverdon's town hall, notable for its Louis XV façade, is a monument to commemorate Pestalozzi. From Yverdon you can return to Neuchâtel by the other side of the lake, the road passing alongside the mini-lake of Morat (Murtensee). On the way, you will pass the ancient, lakeside townlet of Estavayer, almost every corner of which has some special charm of its own, not least of which is the well-kept, moated castle.

Only about seven miles from Lake Neuchâtel is Lake Bienne (Lac de Bienne or Bielersee), its smaller but sprightly neighbor. Projecting from the southern shore, like a long thin finger pointing to the city of Bienne at the other end of the lake, is the extraordinary St. Peter's Isle. On the island's lumpy wooded headland you will find an old monastery, now a small hotel, where Jean-Jacques Rousseau stayed for a time in 1765.

Bienne (or Biel) itself is a busy industrial and commercial city, which also has a tourist eye-opener—the well-preserved and restored "old town." This can best be seen by walking from the busy junction of the Rue du Canal and Rue de Nidau up Rue du Bourg, past the fine Gothic town hall with its 17th-century fountain, and taking one of the streets on the right to the famous "Ring," a medieval architectural gem. The focal point of ancient Bienne, the "Ring" is a picturesque little square with a 15th-century church, arcaded houses and, in the center, a fountain. Almost adjacent to the "Ring" is the High Street (Obergasse), again with lovely old arcaded buildings and, of course, the inevitable fountain.

Today (need you guess?), watchmaking is one of Bienne's main industries, but at the same time, the town has much to entertain the tourist, from theater to water sports, and it's a good excursion center with boat trips down the lake or up the River Aare to Solothurn. Both French and German are spoken with equal ease and, indeed, are often mixed together in conversation. Such is the language frontier of Switzerland.

THE CITY OF BASEL

Gateway to Switzerland

Basel (population 210,000), astride the Rhine, sheltered in the north by the French Vosges and the German Black Forest, and to the south by the northeastern end of the Swiss Jura, is the center of Europe's road and rail network and, despite being over 500 miles from the North Sea, a major inland port. Switzerland's northern gateway, through which countless travelers pass, is a lively city which has many rewards for those who stay a few days to savor its culture and interest.

Six bridges span the great river as it turns majestically northwards, dividing the city into two parts: Gross-Basel (Greater Basel), the city's commercial, cultural and intellectual center, looks down from the upper, or western, bank to Klein-Basel (Little Basel), the industrial section across the Rhine. Gross-Baslers are spared the trouble of expressing their feelings on the subject for, on a building near their end of the central bridge, a facsimile of the famous *Lällenkönig* king's head in the History Museum stares fiercely across the water, sticking out its tongue at the Klein-Baslers.

Basel has a proud history. Near the present city, there had long been a primitive town, when Munatius Plancus, a Roman general and friend of Julius Caesar, arrived in 44 B.C. True to type, the Romans quickly realized its strategic and commercial importance and developed a town of some note called Augusta Raurica, near Augst, about six miles upstream from today's city center. In the 3rd century A.D., invading Alamanni completely destroyed Augusta Raurica, but the remains, including an 8,000-seat amphitheater, carefully excavated and partly reconstructed, can still be seen. Meanwhile, another Roman, the Emperor Valentinian, had moved into the site of the present city. The castle of Basilea was built, from which Basel takes its name. Shortly afterwards, the city became a bishop's see, its bishop-princes in the succeeding centuries gaining immense spiritual and temporal power. In 1226, the first stone bridge to cross the Rhine between Constance and the North Sea was constructed at Basel, by that time a city of trade and transit.

In 1471 the Basel merchant fairs were instituted, attracting the beautiful products of medieval craftsmanship. Ideally situated as a receiving and distributing center for goods, Basel lay open to the cross-currents of thought as well, and became a mart, not only of merchandise, but of ideas. Its university, the oldest in Switzerland, is said to have been founded in 1460 by Aeneas Silvius Piccolomini, who later became Pope Pius II. Early Renaissance and Reformation thinkers brought a great deal of inspiration to this crossroads city. Paracelsus, the great physician and alchemist, and many painters (Konrad Witz, Urs Graf, Niklaus Manuel Deutsch, Tobias Stimmer and Hans Holbein the Younger) lived and worked here. Crafts and skills prospered, as Basel was carried forward on the crest of booming Renaissance trade.

In 1501, the wealthy city joined the confederate states of Switzerland. Nearly thirty years later, it formally adopted the teachings of the Reformation, subsequently becoming one of the leading cities of the movement in Switzerland. This event spelled the end of the restrictive powers of the bishop-princes of Basel, who retired to live in the country.

Holbein's city is one of Europe's greatest inland river ports. Gigantic Rhine barges and steamers come in laden with fuels, foodstuffs and minerals, returning to Antwerp, Hamburg and Rotterdam with Swiss chemical products and heavy manufactured goods. From 1940 to 1945, the busy wharves and docks fell into silence; the great warehouses with their bold white cross on red ground—the Swiss national emblem—warned belligerents and their aircraft that here lay neutral territory.

Basel is, above all, a city of trade and industry, and its name is known throughout the world as a center of international banking and insurance. It is the headquarters of Switzerland's international forwarding and shipping trades as well as the center of the country's chemical industries, including pharmaceuticals, perfumes, dyestuffs and inorganic chemicals.

The Prosperous Baslers

Not surprisingly, there is an air of prosperity about Basel, of a prosperity founded not on a generation or two of wealth, but on centuries of successful enterprise. The tradition of earlier merchant fairs was revived in 1917, when the city was selected as the seat of the nation's most important trade event, the Swiss Industries Fair, held annually in early April. During World War II, the Basel Fair was practically the only one of its kind in Europe, a circumstance which gave it great impetus and attracted buyers from all countries.

The many beautiful houses lying outside the city's inner ring testify to the wealth of the community. It is commonly said that more than half of Switzerland's millionaires (and there are quite a number) are Baslers. But this wealth is discreetly and soberly used and is never blatant. Country mansions have square, solid, unpretentious façades; there is no ostentatious display of jewels and mink, no cigar-chewing in chauffeur-driven limousines. The Baslers enjoy their prosperity quietly, almost shyly, in the privacy of their own homes.

Basel is a city with an atmosphere wholly its own, in which elements of quaint medievalism and bustling modernity are unexpectedly mingled. Baslers are gay, as their uproarious carnival every February can witness. Perhaps they have something in common with their neighbors across the frontier, the inhabitants of Alsace and southern Germany—a certain rustic joviality and wit, and an appreciation of boisterous fun.

Exploring Basel

To capture something of the atmosphere of Basel, one should sit at a terrace café beside the Rhine or stroll along the tree-lined Rheinweg, a pleasant riverside esplanade backed by old houses pressed one against the other. Either way, one looks across the fast flowing water of this great river as it sweeps through the heart of the city. You'll sense a tang of the sea about this Swiss city for, although most of the river's traffic stops at the docks a mile or so downstream,

Regional costumes are still used on grand occasions throughout Switzerland.

Fountains and flowers are the features in most village squares, as in Oberstammheim, near Zurich.

If you long for quiet roads, try this one at Les Brenets in the Neuenburger Jura.

The architecture may be hard to place, but the camellias say Ticino (Caviano, to be precise).

you'll probably see some gigantic barges chugging past laboriously, perhaps to or from Rotterdam, 500 miles away. You'll notice the odd little gondola-like ferryboats, attached to a high wire, silently crossing from shore to shore with no power other than the river current itself. Silhouetting the skyline is Basel's cathedral, and behind and around it splendid old buildings and fine modern ones, a maze of quaint old lanes and busy streets, the old merging imperceptibly with the new.

The cathedral (or Münster), with its viewpoint terrace on a hillock overlooking the Rhine, has all the charm of Rhenish architecture. Of dark red sandstone, it was consecrated at the beginning of the 11th century. Three hundred years later, it was almost completely destroyed by an earthquake and then rebuilt to its present Romanesque-Gothic style. Inside you will find the 14th-century tomb of Queen Anne, wife of Rudolph of Habsburg, near that of Erasmus of Rotterdam. In front of the cathedral is the Münsterplatz, an exquisite square known throughout Europe for the perfection of its proportions. From here a pleasant walk is down Augustinergasse past the Natural History Museum (worth a visit only if you are interested in zoology, mineralogy, entomology or in relics of the prehistoric lake-dwellers) to the Martinsgasse. On the way to the 13th-century Martinskirche, Basel's oldest church, you will pass two magnificent baroque residences on either side of the street. Known as the Blue House and the White House, both have splendid wrought-iron gates and are considered to be outstanding examples of patrician Basel homes.

Now, go back to the Münsterplatz and take the picturesque Rittergasse as far as it goes, turning left to the Wettstein Bridge, where there is a marvelous panorama of the city on both sides of the Rhine. Retrace your steps once more and just beyond the Rittergasse junction, in St. Alben-Graben, you'll see the huge Kunstmuseum (Fine Arts Museum). One of the best in Europe, it features great works by Flemish, German and Basel late-medieval and early-Renaissance painters. Here you'll find the world's largest collection of Holbein paintings. Hans Holbein the Younger, probably the most realistic northern painter of his time, came to Basel in 1515 at the age of eighteen. The city's wealthy burghers and guilds were generous to him as they were to his contemporaries, Deutsch, Graf and Stimmer. Virtually all the great masters are well represented and the museum's long galleries are star-studded with famous pictures, from medieval Cranach and Grünewald to Rothko and today's exponents of minimal art. The impressionists are marvelously covered and so are the Swiss painters Klee, Böcklin and Hodler.

To see most of the remainder of the places of interest in Gross-

Basel, it is best to begin from the central railway station. If you feel in the mood to spend half a day at one of Europe's most delightful zoos, turn left as you leave the station, walk until you see the viaduct crossing the Birsig River, and follow the signs to the entrance. You can have an excellent lunch, by the way, indoors or on the terrace of the zoo restaurant.

Picture Gallery and Barefoot Square

From the zoo, follow the Birsig River and then along Steinen-torstrasse to the Steinenberg, in which street you will find the Kunsthalle, or Picture Gallery. Whether or not you stop for a visit will depend upon your interest in what is being shown at the time. Close to the Kunsthalle is the Stadttheater and on the opposite side of the road, beside the bustling Barfüsserplatz (Barefoot Square), there is the municipal casino with its elegant restaurant and concert hall. The old Franciscan church in Barfüsserplatz houses the Historical Museum.

A few paces farther on, Freiestrasse, Basel's fashionable shopping street, leads to the busy market square, dominated by the colorful 16th-century town hall. It's worth going into the cool, quiet courtyard. If you sit down on one of the benches, you will see the red walls of the courtyard are covered with interesting, if somewhat crude murals, with three inscriptions—one being "Freiheit ist über Silber und Gold" (Freedom is above silver and gold).

Just beyond the Town Hall is the fish market, where there is a Gothic fountain. From here, by climbing up narrow medieval streets, you arrive at St. Peter's Square and the New University, where the scholarly traditions of Erasmus, Paracelsus, the Bernoullis, Euler, the mathematician, and Burckhardt, the historian of the Renaissance, are still felt. In the immediate vicinity are the university library (over a million volumes) and the twin-towered 14th-century Spalen Gate.

Basel's busy port on the downstream side of the city warrants a visit. There, from the viewing platform on the tall red silo (reached by elevator), you can get a fine panorama of the port area, the city and the surrounding countryside—France, Germany and Switzerland. Not far from the silo is a prominent pylon on a jetty marking the point where the three frontiers join. All city tour buses stop there. Walk round it and in half a dozen steps you'll have been in three countries—without a passport.

SWITZERLAND'S RHINELAND

Upstream to Lake Constance

Basel is the gateway to what is often called "Switzerland's Rhineland," a beautiful region lying along the river (and mostly to the south of it) between Basel and Lake Constance. The river is only navigable to Rheinfelden, to which point, in the summer months, there are pleasant riverboat excursions. The departure point in Basel is near the *Three Kings Hotel* (journey time about two hours). A more accurate title would be "Switzerland's Northern Rhineland," for the river goes far beyond the lake. Lake Constance is to the Rhine what Lake Geneva is to the Rhône—a vast, intermediate reservoir, a natural regulator of waterflow. At the eastern end of Lake Constance, the Rhine changes character abruptly, turns southwards, past Austria and Liechtenstein, and then continues southwest to its sources high in the Gotthard mountains. But this southern section of the river we'll meet in later chapters.

Switzerland's Rhineland (we'll stick to that name) takes in the cantons of Aargau, Zurich, and Thurgau, all on the southern bank of the river, and the surprising enclave of canton Schaffhausen on the northerly shore. It's a region of easily seen contrast: along the river are the delightful medieval towns of Laufenburg, Schaffhausen and Stein-am-Rhein, and the impressive Rhine Falls, Europe's biggest waterfall, which forms an effective navigational barrier. Above the falls, by the reed-covered banks of canton Thurgau, are pleasant little resorts and villages.

To the south of the river is a highly prosperous agricultural countryside, favored by fertile soil and a mild climate, as well as some important pockets of thriving industry, several spas and a sprinkling of castles.

Exploring Switzerland's Rhineland

To see both of the Swiss Rhineland's faces—the river itself and the country lying to the south—only two trips are necessary. One takes you in a broad sweep south of the river; the other follows the Rhine and leaves you in the Lake Constance area, ready for further explorations.

The first trip goes to the Canton Aargau, and then back through Solothurn and the Baselbiet (Basel-Land) to Basel. If you drive to Brugg—about thirty-two miles east of Basel—you'll be in what is known as Rübliland ("the carrot country"). This is one of the most fertile parts of Switzerland, 95 percent of the land being under cultivation. Most of its best-known products are agricultural: the canned foods and jams of Lenzburg come from these parts, and the straw products of Freiamt, but also, a little disconcertingly, the cement of Wildegg. On the way to Brugg, before the road climbs over the Bözberg, the lowest pass of the Jura (underneath which the railway burrows in a mile-long tunnel), you'll go through the Fricktal and the little town of Frick, a paradise in spring, when cherry trees are in blossom.

Brugg is a charming old town not far from the point where the Reuss, Lucerne's river, and the Limmat, coming from Zurich, flow into the Aare, the river of Bern. Many old castles bear witness to the importance of this part of the country in olden times. Habsburg, Brunegg, Wildegg, Aurenstein, Lenzburg, Bibenstein and Wildenstein castles are all within a dozen or so miles south of Brugg. Six miles east of Brugg is Baden, a long-established spa known even to the Romans; not far away are the ruins of Roman Vindonissa, including a large amphitheater. Today, Baden is also a major center of the Swiss electrical industry. Bad Schinznach, a smaller spa (but, like Baden, renowned for its sulphur springs), is barely three miles south of Brugg, and boasts a golf course. Nearby is the little village of Birr, where Pestalozzi is buried.

If you drive five miles southeast from Lenzburg, with its 11th-century castle, turn left and keep to Highway 1 at the intersection, you'll soon come to Wohlen, a small town noted for its straw-work, and, a little farther on, to the picturesque old townlet of Bremgarten, with a delightful 11th-century covered bridge over the Reuss. Had you turned right at the intersection, about six or seven miles' driving along secondary roads would have brought you to Lake Hallwil, with an 11th-century castle on an island at its northern end. From nearby Boniswil, picturesque roads lead south through Reinach and Menziken, the tobacco-processing centers of the Aargau, to Beromünster, where the Swiss German-language radio station is located. The fine old Collegiate church here certainly rates a visit.

Doubling back (northwards) through Reinach, you will shortly reach Aarau, the capital of Canton Aargau. Famous throughout Switzerland for the bells it casts, it also manufactures electric light bulbs and high-quality telescopes. There is a fine view of the city and its splendid old houses from the bridge over the River Aare.

Follow the Aare upstream (south), and you come to Schönenwerd, its past mirrored in its beautiful 12th-century church, and its present in a world-famous factory—the Bally shoe plant. Still on the river is Olten, an important railroad center, a favored setting for conventions, and consequently well-provided with hotels and restaurants. Its modern bridge and up-to-date business section are of today, but walk across the wooden bridge into the narrow streets of the old town, and you will think yourself in some small and ancient village.

Three miles south of Olten, just off our route, lies historic Aarburg, with its castle dating from the 11th century. We turn southwest, however, through Hägendorf, with its Devil's Gorge, Oensingen, with its castle, and the rock redoubt of Neu-Bechburg, to Solothurn (Soleure), capital of the canton of the same name. We have now left the Aargau, although not the river Aare.

To Solothurn and Liestal

Solothurn, with its rich cathedral, holds the record with Trier (Treves) in Germany for being the oldest Roman settlement north of the Alps. The city's fortifications, different sections dating from successive periods of Solothurn's long history, are of great interest. More recently, elegant homes with lovely gardens have contributed to the special charm of the town.

The Aare continues southwest, now through flat country planted with fruit trees, now between hills, and under aged covered bridges, but we leave it just beyond Solothurn, turning northwest along a secondary road for our journey back to Basel, through the Baselbiet. By a steep and narrow road we cross the Weissenstein, with its splendid Alpine views, then turn east at Gänsbrunnen and head for Balsthal, near which are the impressive ruins of Neu-Falkenstein castle.

At Balsthal we have a choice. Northeast, through the hill-country of the Baselbiet, takes us first to Langenbruck, a holiday paradise in both winter and summer, next up a valley to Waldenburg, a watch-manufacturing town, then close to the spa of Bad Bubendorf, and finally to Liestal. This is the region's chief town, and its main attractions are St. Martin's church, in the center; the late Gothic city hall; the Upper Gate; and the little back streets which give Liestal its character. From here, it is only ten miles back to Basel.

The other route, less direct, is more interesting. From Balsthal you head north to Mümliswil and the Passwang Pass, which reaches an altitude of 3,280 feet and provides some fine views. Passing through the Lüssel valley and Erschwil, you come to Laufen, upstream from Basel on the Birs River. Laufen, a city with a glorious past and still enclosed within its ancient walls, is the chief community of the Birs Valley, which winds northeast through Aesch towards Basel. The important castle of Angenstein, as well as several other castles and the cloister of Marianstein, lie in the Aesch area. Passing through Dornach, with the fantastic Goetheanum, world headquarters of the Rudolph Steiner Anthroposophical Society, and then through Arlesheim, with its fine 17th-century baroque Collegiate Church, we cross the Münchenstein bridge and find ourselves in Basel again.

Upstream Along the Rhine

Whether you travel by rail or road, the trip eastward from Basel along the Rhine follows the same route. The first sizable town you pass through is Rheinfelden, whose ancient walls and towers (or what is left of them) have been carefully preserved and restored. Once a border post of the Holy Roman Empire, Rheinfelden was besieged a number of times during the Thirty Years' War, and several battles were fought in the vicinity. Today, Rheinfelden, which looks across the river towards the Black Forest, is a well-known spa, noted for its brine baths and mild climate. The upper gate and the storks' nest tower are worth seeing, as are the Höllenhaken (Hell's Corner)

Rapids, the salt works, and the bathing establishment some distance outside the town.

Beyond Rheinfelden, our road continues due east, while the river makes a huge semi-circle northwards, rejoining us once more near the village of Stein (not to be confused with Stein-am-Rhein, nearer to Lake Constance). At Stein, connected by a narrow covered bridge with German Säckingen across the river (the town of Scheffel's poem "The Trumpeter of Säckingen"), the road forks. To the right, going over the Bözberg to Brugg, is the road we took on our previous tour. But this time we follow the river, here teeming with salmon, and pass the hydroelectric generating station, to reach Laufenburg, a small town of much charm, clustered about a late Gothic church and the ruins of a Habsburg castle. There is a fine old city gate and several of the characteristic Swiss fountains.

Koblenz marks the spot where the Aare somewhat fussily joins the Rhine. But, unlike its big German namesake two hundred miles north, where the Moselle flows into the Rhine, Swiss Koblenz is a mere village. Just beyond is the small but up-and-coming resort and spa of Zurzach, where the tomb of St. Verona lies in the Gothic church. At Kaiserstuhl, eight miles farther, there is an old watchtower, a pretty little baroque church, and Zur Linden (or Au Tilleul; in English, "Limetrees"), a small château dating from the late 18th century. Half a dozen castles, once the pride of Bavarian nobility, now brood emptily on the northern bank of the Rhine, giving it a fairytale atmosphere.

At Eglisau, source of a well-known brand of mineral water, both road and railway to Schaffhausen go over the Rhine, and shortly afterwards cross a narrow strip of German territory. Frontier formalities have been reduced to a minimum, so the trip out of Switzerland into Germany and on into Switzerland once again causes little delay.

Neuhausen and the Falls

On the northern bank of the Rhine, Neuhausen and Schaffhausen, with a combined population of over 40,000, are for all practical purposes the same town, the former being the industrial section. Neuhausen's factories, which make among other things arms, railroad cars and aluminum products, derive at least part of their power from the famous Rhine falls on the southern fringe of the town. Probably the most impressive waterfall in central Europe, it is easy to understand how it inspired an enthusiastic description by John

Ruskin. Just above the falls the river is nearly 500 feet wide and it then plunges down 80 feet in three giant leaps, the flow of water sometimes reaching the rate of nearly 1,100 tons per second. In the huge rock basin below it seethes and roars angrily.

Probably the best view of the falls is from the grounds of Laufen Castle, almost directly above them on the southern shore. In the castle itself, there is a collection of Swiss carvings worth half an hour of the visitor's time. A path leads down from the castle to a small tunnel in the rock, against which the water booms heavily, and on to Känzeli, a wooden platform beside the falls. Descending again, you enter through a massive doorway to the Fishcetz, another platform overhanging the cascade. You'll need a raincoat here, for the spray is quite heavy. Alternatively, from the center of Schaffhausen a fifteen-minute trolley bus ride will take you to Neuhausen. There, a walk of a couple of hundred yards down a steep lane will bring you to a fine viewpoint on the northern side of the falls. Nearby there's a good restaurant, and a picturesque little Fischerstube, or fisherman's museum, where souvenirs of great salmon catches of the river are to be seen.

The falls are best viewed early on a sunny morning, when the rainbows are all around, or at sunset. On moonlit nights, the effects are exquisite, and often, in summer, the falls are illuminated to provide an eerie and quite different aspect.

Schaffhausen

Schaffhausen, capital of the northernmost canton of Switzerland, is an easy train ride or drive from Zurich. England's William Cox writes, with characteristic British modesty: "Here, every person has the mien of content and satisfaction. The cleanliness of the homes and the people is peculiarly striking, and I can trace in all their manners, behaviour and dress some strong outlines that distinguish this happy people from neighboring nations. Perhaps it may be prejudice, but I am the more pleased because their first appearance reminds me of my own countrymen, and I could think for a moment that I am in England." It is certainly true that the people of Schaffhausen are far less inhibited and more easy-going than most Swiss. The reason they give is that they are not surrounded by mountains, which are said to have the tendency to make the Alp dweller introspective and silent. Another reason may be the fine red wines produced by the region!

A city of about 36,000 inhabitants, Schaffhausen has preserved, like most towns in this area, a medieval aspect. From the early Middle

Ages, it was an important depot for river cargoes, as these had to be loaded and unloaded there because of the natural barrier created by the waterfall and rapids. The name Schaffhausen is probably derived from the "skiffhouses" ranged along the river bank. Rising picturesquely from the water's edge, Schaffhausen, with its numerous oriel windows and fountains, has an air of antiquity, so that it is sometimes called the Swiss Nuremberg.

Schaffhausen is dominated by the 16th-century Munot Castle, perched on a hilltop seemingly made for the purpose. A covered passage links this formidable fortress to the rest of the town, and there is a fine view from its massive tower. In some of the winding streets of the older sections of the town, there are some interesting frescoed houses, notably the Haus Zum Ritter in the Vordergasse, with its 16th-century frescoes by Tobias Stimmer. The Münster, a Romanesque basilica dating from the 11th century, is, however, the chief architectural feature of Schaffhausen. In a small courtyard of the cloisters stands a famous old bell (cast in 1468) that inspired Schiller to write his *Lied von der Glocke*. The adjacent monastery of All Hallows (zu Allerheiligen) has been transformed into a national museum, one of the most important in Switzerland.

En Route to Constance

From Schaffhausen, many visitors prefer to go on by river steamer to Constance and Kreuzlingen, a scenically splendid trip taking about four hours. There are boats two or three times a day, depending on the season. The train and highway both follow the same route and, of course, take less time.

Leaving Schaffhausen, the steamer passes the old convent of Paradies on the starboard side. It is said that, nearby the Austrian army under Archduke Charles crossed the Rhine in 1799. Farther on near Diessenhofen, is the scene of another historic crossing—that of the French army in 1800, before the battle of Hohenlinden, celebrated in Campbell's poem "On the Linden, When the Sun Was Low." The scenery along the river banks changes continually: forests and vineyards, trim little medieval villages, stern old fortified castles. Diessenhofen, called Gunodorum by the Romans, has a lovely old clock tower and some houses dating from the 16th and 17th centuries.

Stein-am-Rhein, where the river starts to widen out into the lower parts of Lake Constance, is one of the most picturesque medieval towns in Switzerland. Near the northern shore is the old hilltop castle of Hohenklingen, approached by a steep road. From the battlements, you can get a superb view of the river, the lake beyond, and the surrounding countryside, as well as the little gem of the town below. Lining the streets of Stein-am-Rhein, particularly the high street (Hauptgasse) and the town hall square (Rathausplatz), is an unrivaled collection of quaint houses rich in oriel windows and elaborate frescoes. The town hall has a museum of arms and stained glass, much from the 16th and 17th centuries, which is well worth a visit.

The 15th-century Sonne, distinguished by a medieval golden emblem of the sun, provides delightful surroundings in which to enjoy a good dinner or simply a glass of white Steiner or red Rheinhalder wine, both native to the region. Immediately below is a fountain with a statue of a Swiss mercenary leaning on his pike, surrounded by beds of flowers. All the houses opposite are adorned by their owners' coats of arms painted in bright colors.

A short distance up the river, past the last bridge over the Rhine before Lake Constance, is the Benedictine monastery of St. George, built in 1005 and well-preserved. A curious old monument with a lovely cloister, it also has a small museum open to the public and featuring some fine examples of woodwork and old paintings. As the river widens into the Untersee—the southwestern branch of Lake Constance—the boat passes the Isle of Werd, on which you can see the beautiful old chapel of St. Othmar. Opposite lie the village of Eschenz, the castles of Freudenfels and Liebenfels, and the one-time monastery of Oehningen. On the Swiss side, at the foot of a chain of hills, picturesque villages succeed one another. Between Mammern and Steckborn, in a small bay, is the little summer resort of Glarisegg, located in the middle of a large natural park. One of Switzerland's best-known private schools is in Glarisegg, housed in the old château. Steckborn is dominated by the imposing Turmhof Castle, built in 1342, and has some fine old houses, including the Baronenhaus and the Gerichtshaus.

In the middle of the Untersee is the German island of Reichenau, two miles long and a mile wide. Charles the Fat, great-grandson of Charlemagne, was buried there. The island has three small villages—Mittelzell, Unterzell and Oberzell—and there is an interesting Roman-esque basilica at Niederzell. On the Swiss side of the lake, and behind the village of Mannenbach (nearly opposite Reichenau), is the castle of Arenenberg. There, from 1818, Hortense de Beauharnais, formerly Queen of Holland, lived with her son, who was later to become Emperor Napoleon III. After the fall of the Empire, Empress Eugénie stayed there for some time before giving it to the canton of Thurgau in 1906. Nowadays, it is a museum containing numerous souvenirs of the Second Empire. Nearby are two additional châteaux with

Napoleonic memories. In Salenstein, which was at one time the traditional residence of the Abbot of Reichenau and which dates from the 12th century, the Duchess of Dino, a companion of Hortense de Beauharnais, went to live in 1817. Eugensberg Castle was built four years later by Eugène de Beauharnais, the son of the Empress Joséphine, born before she became the famous wife of Napoleon I.

Not far beyond Ermatingen, the Untersee quickly narrows to become, at Gottlieben, a riverlike channel which, on the other side of the German city of Constance, joins the main body of the lake. The Dominican monastery at Gottlieben is where the Protestant reformers John Huss and Jerome of Prague were imprisoned in the 15th century by order of the Emperor Sigismund and Pope John XXII. Pope John was himself confined in the same castle a few years later.

Constance

The German city of Constance (population about 55,000), with its Swiss suburb of Kreuzlingen, dominates the straits. It is on the Swiss side of the lake, but in 1805 was ceded to Baden by the Treaty of Pressburg. In Roman days, it was known as Constantia, and its name in German now is Konstanz. As a focal point for many of the routes crossing the main Alpine passes into Italy, it achieved early significance as a trading center, and has had a long and turbulent history. Together with the Gottlieben monastery, it is alive with memories of John Huss, burnt at the stake in 1415 by order of the Council of Constance. His house in the Hussenstrasse bears his effigy, and in the cathedral, visitors can see the spot on which he stood when the sentence was delivered. Kneeling before his accusers, he cried, "Lord Jesus, forgive my enemies." Those who revere his memory say that the stone on which he knelt always remains dry, even when those around it are damp. Protestantism having gained the upper hand only temporarily in the 16th century, Constance is now mainly Catholic.

The Münster, or cathedral, of Constance, was founded in 1052, but did not begin to assume its present form until the start of the 15th century. The Gothic tower at the west end was erected in 1850. From the platforms around the openwork spire, there is a magnificent view of the town, the lake, the valley of the Rhine and the Austrian mountains. The oak doors of the chief entrance are decorated with reliefs by Simon Haider, dating from 1470 and representing scenes in the life of Christ. The nave is supported by sixteen monolithic pillars, and the choir stalls are handsomely carved. The cathedral contains the tomb of Robert Hallam, Bishop of Salisbury, and in the ancient crypt, there is a representation in stone of the Holy Sepulcher.

Other points of interest in Constance include the Konzilgebäude, where the Council of Constance held its sittings; the Renaissance town hall (Rathaus), with historical frescoes on its façade; the Rosgarten Museum, notable for its prehistoric Roman and medieval collections; and the monument to Count Zeppelin, whose famous airships were built near Friedrichshafen on the other side of the lake. In the market square stands the house in front of which the Emperor Sigismund gave Frederick of Nuremberg the "March" of Brandenburg in 1417. And another old house, inscribed with the words "Curia Pacis," is said to be where peace was signed between Barbarossa and the Lombardy city-states in 1183. Outside the town is the Field of Bruhl, where John Huss was burned at the stake in 1415 and Jerome of Prague a year later. The spot is marked by a rough monument of stones.

Constance is a good center for excursions, with steamer services to many of the towns and resorts around Lake Constance itself and on Uberlingensee, its northwestern branch. You can get steamers in the adjacent Swiss town of Kreuzlingen for excursions to the Untersee and down the Rhine to Schaffhausen.

If it were not for the frontier stations in the connecting streets, it would be difficult to know where the German city of Constance ends and Swiss Kreuzlingen begins. There is no difficulty in walking from one to the other, but a valid passport is necessary (although, in some cases, an identity card is accepted). Kreuzlingen, much smaller than Constance, has a picturesque old quarter. In what was formerly an Augustine priory, founded in the 10th century by Bishop Conrad of Constance, there is now a teachers' training college. The original building was destroyed during the Thirty Years' War and the present structure built shortly afterwards. In the chapel a magnificent piece of woodcarving, the Passion of Kreuzlingen, contains many hundreds of separate sculptured figures, all being the work of one anonymous Tyrolean craftsman. Also on view is an embroidered vest, adorned with pearls, presented to a local dignitary by the medieval antipope Pope John XXIII when he came to Constance in 1414.

Lake Constance

Called the *Bodensee* in German, Lake Constance is about forty miles long and, in places, nearly ten miles wide, being second in size only to Lake Geneva. Since it is not protected by lofty mountains, it is turbulent in stormy weather and even on fine days is apt to be hazy. Thus it has a gloomy, brooding aspect, in contrast to the jewel-like quality of other Swiss lakes, but many visitors find that this makes it more romantic. Certainly it abounds in lore of a more lurid type than is usual in Switzerland—tales of smuggling and fleeing refugees, rather than poetry and William Tell. One of these stories relates that after the war, a group of smart contraband runners was found to be operating a submarine in its waters in connection with a highly profitable but illicit trade between Germany and Switzerland. The local geography favors this sort of thing, for down the middle of Lake Constance are the boundaries of three countries—Switzerland, Austria and Germany. There is excellent fishing in the lake for either trout or *Felchen,* and it is frequented by some seventy species of birds. In the distance can be seen the Appenzell Alps—which include the majestic, snow-clad Säntis—and the Vorarlberg Alps.

The German island of Mainau, the former home of the Grand Duke of Baden and also the residence of Prince Lennart Bernadotte, nephew of the lake King Gustav VI Adolf of Sweden, is about four miles north of Constance. Connected to the mainland by a bridge, it can be reached from Constance either through a wood or by lake steamer. It has a remarkable garden of subtropical vegetation, reminiscent of the most beautiful Italian gardens, for the climate of Lake Constance is exceptionally mild.

On the opposite shore of Lake Constance, again in Germany, is the town of Friedrichshafen, a pleasant town with a population of around 40,000, a castle that was formerly the summer home of the Kings of Württemberg, and a notable exhibition of Zeppelin mementoes in the municipal museum. Farther along the lake, still on the German side, is the splendidly situated little island town of Lindau with some 25,000 inhabitants. Approached by rail over a causeway or by road over a long bridge, Lindau was once a powerful fortress, an Imperial city and, in ancient times, the site of a Roman fortification. Its town hall, although much restored in 1887, dates from the 15th century.

Back to Switzerland

After our brief excursion to some of the German parts of the lake, let us return once more to Switzerland, at Kreuzlingen. From here, as we proceed southeast along the shore of the lake, we come first to Bottighofen, and then to Münsterlingen, which has a former Benedictine convent, founded in the 10th century although rebuilt in the 18th. It is now a hospital for the canton of Thurgau. A little beyond it, on a hill overlooking the lake, is the pretty village of Altnau, then in rapid succession, Güttingen, Kesswil, Uttwil and, finally, Romanshorn. The last one is a small industrial town and an important ferry port for Friedrichshafen, but also a surprisingly pleasant place with fine views of the mountains of Switzerland and Austria.

Halfway to Rorschach, the town and resort of Arbon (known to the Romans as Arbor Felix) lies on a little promontory jutting out into the lake and surrounded by lovely meadows and orchards. It was a Celtic town before the Romans came in the year 60 B.C. and built military fortifications. There is a medieval château, which became public property and is open to visitors, and right near this legacy from the past is an ultra-modern bus and lorry factory and machine shop operated by Saurer Co. The St. Gallus church, with its fine stained-glass windows, and St. Martin's Church are both worth seeing. The latter is late Gothic and has an interesting collection of relics dating from the days of the Romans.

Rorschach

Rorschach, with 13,000 inhabitants, is the largest port on the Swiss side of the lake. It is on a small, well-protected bay at the foot of the Rorschach Berg, a beautiful 2,900-foot mountain covered with orchards, pine forests and little meadows. Rorschach carries on a thriving trade with Germany, and the imposing Kornhaus, built by the convent of St. Gallen in 1746, indicates what was for generations the nature of that trade. The building is in baroque style and has an interesting little folklore museum. The village church (1667) is also baroque. Near the town is the Dornier factory and Altenrhein, a small airport capable of accommodating both land-based planes and seaplanes.

One can make a number of scenic excursions from the town of Rorschach. On the surrounding hills, there are several old castles, and a good road leads to the ancient abbey of Mariaberg, built by the abbots of St. Gallen and now used as a school. Nearby is St. Anna Castle, long inhabited by the lords of Rorschach and restored during the early part of the last century. Although it is not open to visitors, the Duke of Parma's château of Wartegg, formerly the summer residence of the Prince of Hohenzollern, is worth seeing from outside, and the ascent of the Rossbüchel, 3,150 feet, is rewarded with an excellent view of the Rätikon and Vorarlberg mountains.

There are two railroad stations in Rorschach, the main station and another smaller one, by the port in the town center, from which the cogwheel trains climb up to Heiden. Only three and one-half miles long, the train's route ascends through lovely orchards, past old castles and over a number of viaducts, disclosing beautiful views of the valleys, mountains and the upper Rhine. Heiden itself (2,600 feet) is situated on a sunlit terrace surrounded by meadows and nicely wooded hills. The village was almost entirely destroyed by fire in 1838 and was rebuilt to a uniform pattern (but in traditional style), so that it has a neat charm. It is a well-known health resort, with carbonic acid and brine baths, electrotherapy, massage and other treatments. It also has a famous Kursaal with frequent concerts. Henri Dunant, founder of the Red Cross, spent many years working in the local hospital.

Another interesting trip from Rorschach is to St. Margrethen, where, in 1900, the Swiss and Austrian governments undertook important engineering works to regulate the Rhine's flow. Two long cuts were made, one at St. Margrethen, and another, a little farther south, between Altstätten and Diepoldsau. These enable the river to flow straight into Lake Constance instead of winding around the countryside to join the lake at Altenrhein.

From Rorschach, the end of this tour, both rail and road lead on to Zurich, via St. Gallen, or through Bad Ragaz to the Grisons.

THE CITY OF ZURICH AND ITS LAKE

Industrial Prosperity and Elegance, Too

To most people who have never been there, Zurich is thought of as the industrial heart of Switzerland, its Pittsburgh or Manchester. Thus, when on holiday, travelers tend to concentrate on Lucerne or Bern, giving Zurich the go-by. This is a mistake, for they would find Zurich a jewel set among rolling green hills, with one end of the long, crescent-shaped Lake of Zurich nosing inquisitively into the center of the town like a shimmering blue eel. The largest city in Switzerland (it has a population of about 410,000), Zurich is built around the northern tip of the lake and on the flanks of the surrounding wooded hills. Through its heart run the swift but shallow Limmat River and the smaller Sihl River, which rises in the nearby Sihl Lake and wanders down the western shore of Lake Zurich to join the Limmat in the center of the town. There are factories (most of them in the industrial suburbs north of Zurich), but there is no smoke; moreover, there are no slums. The industries run on electricity, and the buildings in which they are housed look more like sanatoria or colleges than factories. And Swiss workers don't live in drab streets or dirty houses, but in pretty little villas with flowers around the door, or in

134

ultramodern apartment blocks. They can afford to, because they are among the highest-paid workers in Europe.

Zurich is a Protestant city. Besides the Wasserkirche, overlooked by the Grossmünster—a church said to have been founded by Charlemagne—stands the statue of Ulrich Zwingli. As pastor in the Grossmünster he first preached the Reformation there on New Year's Day, 1519, and continued to do so with such effect that four years later almost to the day, after a great public debate, the city formally associated itself with the new faith. Until his death in battle in 1531 at the village of Kappel some fourteen miles south of Zurich, Zwingli defied the Pope and much of the Swiss Confederation in his fierce championship of the Reformation.

One has only to look at the bronze replica of his face to realize that this man took a stern view of life. It is as if the disapproving regard his statue directs towards Bellevue-Platz (which happens to be the amusement center of the city) were meant to burn continually into the consciousness of every citizen, a constant reminder of the pitfalls of the pleasures of the flesh and of idleness.

The good citizens of Zurich work hard, go to church and avoid self-indulgence. Are they then Puritans? Perhaps. But if so, a lot of good old Christian virtues, all too rare in the world today, go along with their Puritanism. They are scrupulously honest, fastidiously clean, and noted for their generosity and kindness.

The very Puritanism of the Zurichers has its engaging side. Although they live their own lives according to their lights, permitting themselves no foolishness, they don't expect other people to follow their example, and are, in fact, anxious to prove to others that they are broad-minded. Visitors to Zurich are constantly being assured that the blue-laws don't apply to them, and this is done in an apologetic tone of voice that implies, "Please bear with us. We can't help it if we don't know how to play." In fact, they *do* know how to play. The Schauspielhaus (Playhouse), for example, handsomely supported by Zurich's upper crust, puts on all kinds of daring, avant-garde plays, and people go to them and applaud like mad.

But nightlife is moderate here, although a number of cafés, restaurants and dance-spots stay open until two in the morning. Zurich, with its surrounding lakes, woods and hills, and the nearby mountains, entices the majority of the inhabitants to spend their leisure in outdoor activities—and exercise during the day is incompatible with very late hours at night. However, there is plenty of entertainment on offer for those who want it (see under *Practical Information.*)

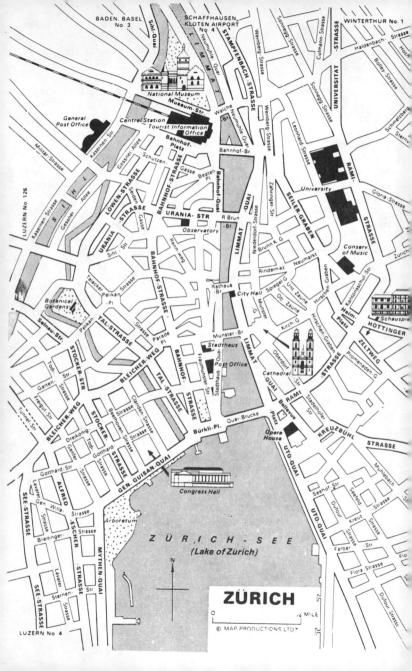

Once, back in the Middle Ages, the women of Zurich saved the city from conquest by the Austrians. The Zurich army had fought valiantly on the approaches, but had been beaten and were falling back to within the city gates. The women donned armor, took up spears and swords, and marched to the Lindenhof, a small hill in the center of the town, in full battle array. The Austrians, seeing them from a distance, thought they had to do battle with a second Zurich army as tough as the first, and discreetly withdrew. A fountain and small statue on top of the hill commemorate this event, and today the women of Zurich continue this tradition of service, an example being their influential women's club, the Frauenverein, which devotes itself indefatigably to social activities of all kinds.

A Bit of History

Zurich can trace its history as far back as any other Swiss city, and has some ancient buildings and monuments to prove it, but for the most part the city is ultramodern. Visitors often have the impression that they are seeing some sort of exhibition of the "bright new world of tomorrow" when they walk through the spick-and-span streets of downtown Zurich, but not all buildings are modern. Where possible Zurich architects have retained the fine exterior lines laid down by the craftsmen of former generations, while converting the interiors to the gleaming Swiss efficiency of today. You'll see, particularly in the old part of the city around Lindenhof-Platz, that they've done an excellent job in harmonizing the new with the old.

As long ago as 3000 B.C., there were human habitations on the site of what is now Zurich. During the Stone Age, according to the best authorities, and towards the end of the Bronze Age, 1000 B.C., a dwelling existed on Lindenhof Hill. Certainly, during the Roman occupation (which started in the middle of the 1st century A.D.) a fort and a customs station were built on the Lindenhof, then known by the Latin name Turicum—not very different from the city's name today. In the 5th century, the Alamanni ousted the Romans. Charlemagne did much for Zurich in the 8th century and was probably responsible for founding what is now the Grossmünster. His grandson, Ludwig the German, founded the original Fraumünster, on the opposite bank of the Limmat, in 853, installing his daughter, Hildegarde, as abbess.

Zurich became one of the Imperial cities of the German Empire in 1218, and joined the Swiss Confederation in 1351. In the 16th century, after the initial turmoil of the Reformation, the city started an era of great cultural activity and economic growth. The French Revolution brought a period of decline and confusion, but afterwards Zurich quickly got back into stride to become, as it is today, one of Europe's most important and prosperous commercial and industrial cities.

It is also a major cultural and educational center. The University of Zurich and the Federal Institute of Technology are famous. The city was the birthplace of Johann Pestalozzi, the great Swiss educator, and the poets C. F. Meyer and Gottfried Keller. More recently, Zurich has become a mecca for students in the field of psychological studies through the establishment of the C. G. Jung Institute for training and research work in analytical psychology.

Many famous people have lived and worked in Zurich, including Lenin, who used to study at the Sozialarchiv. James Joyce, who is buried at Zurich's Fluntern church, wrote part of *Ulysses* in the city. Wagner composed much of *Tristan und Isolde* there, and it is also where Thornton Wilder wrote *Our Town*.

Exploring Zurich

Arriving at Zurich's Hauptbahnhof, which is both the main station and city air terminal, you don't have to go far to start your sightseeing. Inside the station is the tourist office, and on the north side the Swiss National Museum.

At the other (south) side is Bahnhofplatz, hub of the city transport system. Once a moderately elegant square, it is now a conglomeration of shudderingly drab shelters for bus and tram passengers. You can avoid this eyesore by taking the escalator which burrows down to "Shop-Ville," a vast, brilliantly lit mini-town of excellent shops beneath Bahnhofplatz itself. Up the other side, with drab old Bahnhofplatz behind you, is fashionable Bahnhofstrasse, which leads all the way to Bürkli-Platz on the shore of Lake Zurich. Bordered by lime trees, sophisticated shops and opulent offices, most of Bahnhofstrasse is now a huge sidewalk free of all traffic except for the Holy Cows—as some Zurich citizens call their trams. Towards the end, on the right, is Parade-Platz, around which are clustered some of Europe's biggest banking houses and "gnomeries." On either side of Bürkli-Platz—a busy traffic junction—are attractive quays with lawns, flower beds and trees which encircle the end of the lake. To the right is the Kongresshaus, accommodating over 8,000 people in its halls, concert hall and restaurants. Facing the lake, too, are the offices of big insurance companies, a reminder of Zurich's importance in the insurance world.

The right-hand, or western, shore of Lake Zurich, including the suburbs of Enge, Wollishofen and Kilchberg, is a smart residential district. Each year, on December 6, Wollishofen puts on a rather eerie Christmas Parade. The young people dress up in white nightshirts and carry illuminated tiaras. Accompanied by Santa Claus, they march through the streets of this suburb of Zurich, tooting horns and clanging cowbells in an effort to exorcise the Spirit of Winter. It never works—winter always comes anyway—but they go on trying. The custom is believed to date from the pre-Christian era. Between Enge and Wollishofen is the lakeshore Strandbad, or public lido.

On the left shore of the lake stretches the long tree-shaded Utoquai, a lovely promenade where all of fashionable Zurich likes to stroll on Sunday afternoons. It is lined with boat harbors and bathing establishments. Farther down, on Seefeld-Quai, are more fine mansions and public gardens.

For leisurely sightseeing with some unorthodox views, try the regular May to September motor-launch service from the Central Station up the Limmat River and to the lake.

Where to Find the Action

From Bürkli-Platz a bridge crosses the river Limmat where it leaves the lake. At the far end is Bellevue-Platz, the entertainment center of the city with a host of cinemas, nightclubs, cabarets, restaurants and cafés clustered around it. Due to the 2 a.m. closing hours, it is well to start early if you wish to take in any of these places. Many are found along the Limmatquai, past the Grossmünster; others are in the narrow, winding streets of this section of the city. The aspect of the place is somewhat sinister at night because of the narrow streets, but that's just an illusion—there's nothing very dangerous or exciting to be found in the way of night life in Zurich.

The Limmatquai is lined with old guildhalls, including the Rüden, Saffran, Schmiden, Schneidern and Zimmerleuten, all with interesting façades. You'll find some good restaurants in these guildhalls, and elsewhere in the neighborhood, too.

The Grossmünster cathedral, towering above the Limmatquai, is dedicated to the saints Felix, Regula and Exuperantius, who converted the inhabitants of "Turicum" to Christianity in the 3rd century. Legend has it that they were beheaded by the town's governor, named Decius, after having been scourged, plunged into boiling oil, and forced to drink molten lead, in an effort to induce them to deny their faith. These intrepid saints not only underwent these ordeals without flinching, but after the headsman's axe had fallen they still had strength enough to pick up their heads and walk to a nearby hilltop where they lay down to eternal rest in graves they dug themselves! The Great Seal of Zurich shows them carrying their heads jauntily under their arms. The 12th-century Romanesque cathedral has two 15th-century Gothic towers, one bearing a statue of Charlemagne. Crossing the Münsterbrücke (cathedral bridge), we come to the Münsterhof, a charming old square notable for the Waag and Meise guildhalls and the Fraumünster.

Although founded around 853, the Fraumünster's present structure dates back only to the 13th century. The remains of the original cloisters have been incorporated in the adjacent Stadthaus. Just to the north of the Fraumünster is the old parish church of Zurich, the Peterskirche, part of which dates from the 13th century. It has a massive tower surmounted by a large, golden-faced clock. All around this church is another maze of narrow, winding streets leading up to Lindenhof-Platz, site of the old Roman fortress and statue of the Women of Zurich, who saved their city from the Austrians. It is the most picturesque quarter of the town and also has many fine restaurants.

Crossing the river again, via the Rathausbrücke, the visitor comes to the old town hall, a fine building dating from the 17th century. It is now the seat of the city and cantonal parliaments. The old council chamber contains a splendid porcelain stove, presented to Zurich by the people of Winterthur when the town hall was built, and an elaborate tapestry. In another room is the Peace of Zurich, the document by which Austria ceded Lombardy to the house of Savoy in 1859.

Zurich from Above

If you now follow the Limmatquai down to the end, only about four hundred yards, you will come to the terminus of a curious old cable railway that, setting off through the back of an apartment house, leads up to Leonhardstrasse, near the twin campuses of the University of Zurich and the Federal Institute of Technology. From the latter, there is a fine view of the city.

Some clear day during your stay in Zurich, you should go to the little Selnau railroad station on the Sihl River and take the twenty-five-minute ride to Uetliberg, 2,800 feet up, on the heights above the city. It costs a few francs, round trip, to reach this point, from which you have a magnificent view over the lake to the snow-clad peaks beyond. In case the bracing air makes you hungry, a pleasant restaurant is installed on a terrace where you can drink in the view while eating. Or bring your own lunch: there are plenty of picnic spots here.

From the same station, you can get a train along the valley of the Sihl to Gontenbach, with its deer park and zoo, to Sihlwald with its forest house, or Sihlbrugg, where there are beautiful walks.

On the northeastern fringe of Zurich, about three-quarters of a mile from the railway station, is Zurichberg, a 2,000-foot-high series of hills which can easily be reached by cable car or by tram. There, apart from the fine views and equally fine walks, you'll find the zoo, a large model railway, small golf course, a swimming pool with artificial waves and an ice rink in winter.

Excursions Down the Lake

One of the many excellent excursions from the city takes the visitor on a pleasant steamboat voyage down the Lake of Zurich to the historic town of Rapperswil. It is an easy four-hour trip—the boat leaves from the landing stage at the end of the Bahnhofstrasse in Zurich. The lake is about twenty-four miles long and some three miles wide at the broadest part. Although other Swiss lakes, such as that of Lucerne, offer more grandiose scenery, none can present such a succession of charming views. The banks rise in gentle slopes, in the midst of which are numerous pretty villas and thriving villages, and on the east side are lofty wooded hills, with the snow-clad Alps forming a striking background.

Each town along the lake has its own character, and the entire area is rich in charm, even for a country as well-stocked in this commodity as Switzerland. Most of the tourists making use of the excursion steamers on the Lake of Zurich are Swiss, which in itself is a fair recommendation to foreign visitors to become acquainted with a district which, in recent years, has become one of the most attractive "suburbias" to be found anywhere.

The first stopping place of interest after leaving Zurich is Meilen, an idyllic little town with a 15th-century church. It was here, in the winter of 1853, when the lake was unusually low, that ethnologists discovered the traces of prehistoric lacustrian settlements that provided graphic evidence of the fact that there were human dwellings in the area as long ago as 3,000 years before Christ. Arrows, tools, bones of tame animals and other evidence of this long-ago civilization were discovered and can now be seen in Zurich's Swiss National Museum. The exact site where the traces were found is now covered with water, but other evidence of pile-dwellings can be found several miles from Meilen at Wetzikon, where a former lake has become a peat moor.

Another town along the lake is Stäfa, once with a noted silk industry but now engaged in making wine. Here Goethe stayed for a time in the year 1797 and wrote his play *Jery and Bately,* inspired by the Swiss scenery. Nearly opposite is the little island of Ufenau, which has a ruined church and the grave of Ulrich Von Hutten, a friend of Luther's, who had fled to Zurich from his persecutors to seek the protection of Zwingli.

Rapperswil is seen long before the steamer reaches its snug little harbor, since it stands on a knoll above the lake, its monastery and venerable castle outlined against the sky. The castle was built in 1229, and in the 14th century it became a Habsburg stronghold. It was in this castle that a group of conspirators met in 1350 to plot the Massacre of Zurich, the first of a series of feuds with the city at the other end of the lake. From 1870 until just before World War II, the castle became the repository for the national relics of Poland, during that country's long fight for freedom. The Rapperswil town hall has a carved Gothic portal and, inside, a colossal old wrought-iron stove. The monastery, built by the Capuchins, is fairly recent, but its tall spire adds to the quaintness of the little town, which has many fine old houses and a distinctly medieval appearance.

NORTHEASTERN SWITZERLAND

St. Gallen, Appenzell and Glarus

Northeastern Switzerland is rich in variety, rich in tradition—and just plain rich! Yet despite its prosperity, evident throughout the region, it retains an air of other-worldliness. Everywhere you see past and present interwoven: houses, new as well as old, with frescoes and carved-wood balconies, or turrets, roofs and entire walls of wood shingles—so delicate that, when weathered, they look like fur. Old customs are as alive today as they were centuries ago. Yet St. Gallen's textile industry leads in technical development, and some of her new public buildings achieve dizzy heights (or depths, if you see it that way) of modernity. Because tourists have been slow to appreciate northeastern Switzerland's widely differing attractions, it has kept its personality intact, unharried by tourism with a capital "T." Consequently its prices are often lower than in some more famous parts of Switzerland.

The region lies to the east of Zurich and roughly comprises the cantons of Glarus, St. Gallen and—cocooned within the latter—Appenzell. Northeastern Switzerland has many faces ranging all the way from snowcapped 8,200-foot Mt. Säntis to the shores of Lake Constance. Its many mutations include the rolling hills of Appenzell; a host of lakes, from ten-mile-long Walensee to little mountain gems like Seealpsee; the vast Rhine valley plain and a mountain valley for every mood. To the east, the Rhine separates Switzerland from the little principality of Liechtenstein, and from Austria with the mountains of Vorarlberg and the charm of Bregenzerwald within easy reach.

Towns range from St. Gallen, a textile center of international importance, but also delightful for tourists, to spas such as Bad Ragaz, and scores of summer and winter resorts. Some smaller towns, notably Appenzell, played a big part in forming the Swiss Confederation. In several the picturesque "Landsgemeinde," or open-air parliament, is still in being.

Medium-grade hotels include the 140-bed *Lattman,* the 110-bed *Badhotel Tamina,* and the 100-bed *Sandi.*

Restaurant: *Hotel Wartenstein* (M), high above resort. Views of Rhine valley and mountains.

Exploring the Northeast

St. Gallen, largest city in the northeast, is among Switzerland's most interesting for tourists, and the center of one of the loveliest Swiss regions. From it you can easily explore a string of delightful resorts along Lake Constance; the rugged, snowy mountains in the Säntis range, rising to 8,200 feet; and the Appenzell country with its curious folklore customs.

Barely an hour and a half from Zurich by electric train, St. Gallen is a modern little metropolis of 79,000 inhabitants, and an important textile city that also zealously maintains its fine heritage of medieval culture. The city's origins date back to 612, when the Irish missionary Gallus laid the foundations of an abbey that was to become a major cultural center of medieval Europe. The abbey itself was largely destroyed during the Reformation, but in its magnificent rococo library (rebuilt in the 18th century), containing over 100,000 volumes, visitors can see illuminated manuscripts of over a thousand years ago.

The valley town of St. Gallen, which grew up in a semicircle around the abbey walls, owed allegiance to the abbot until the early 15th century, when, by making an alliance with the farmers of Appenzell, the citizens gained political freedom. Religious freedom followed a century later, when the humanist Vadian—whose statue stands in the market place—brought the Reformation to the region. As a Protestant town St. Gallen then formed an independent miniature state surrounded by monastic territory. This lasted until the French Revolution, when the present canton was founded and the monasteries secularized. The abbot's former residence is now the seat of government and the local parliament.

The splendid twin-towered baroque Kathedrale, built in 1756, is the town's most imposing building; its superbly restored interior fairly scintillates with light and color. On the northern side of the cathedral lies the old quarter where ancient houses are rich in oriel windows and frescoes. By way of contrast it is worth visiting the new Municipal Theater and University; both are almost stark in their simplicity, but conceived with great imagination. St. Gallen's long connection with textiles is traced in the fascinating *Gewerbemuseum* (embroidery museum) in Vadianstrasse. There you can see lace and embroidery made in St. Gallen from the 16th century to the present day. The collection includes many pieces worn by famous European courtiers as well as some really stunning examples of modern techniques. St. Gallen's citizens love parks and gardens and have many, including the Peter and Paul Deer Park, where you can see ibex, chamois, stags, marmots, deer, wild boars, and also enjoy wonderful views extending from Lake Constance to the Säntis mountains.

About seventeen miles west of St. Gallen is Wil, a beautiful 700-year-old town, once part of the estates of the Abbey of St. Gall. The massive 15th-century residence of the Bishop-Princes, the Hof zu Wil, still dominates the old Hofplatz but now houses the local museum. From the terrace of St. Nicolas church you may see the Vorarlberg, Säntis, Churfirsten and Glärnisch Alps.

A fine half-day excursion by road from St. Gallen is about twenty miles southwards to Schwägalp for the cable car which takes you to within a few feet of the summit of 8,200-ft. Mt. Säntis. Weather permitting, you'll have incredible views not only of the Swiss Alps, but also far beyond the frontiers. There is a restaurant and small hotel near the summit.

Appenzell

Another delightful trip from St. Gallen is to Appenzell, in its namesake canton. A narrow-gauge railway takes you in about half an hour via the mountain village resorts of Teufen and Gais. Appenzell canton had until recent times almost no communications with the surrounding provinces, and so has retained many of its ancient customs. It is one of three cantons (including Glarus and Unterwalden) where the Landsgemeinde is still held. This is an open-air town-meeting where each male citizen votes personally on all the laws by which he is governed, and says "yes" or "no" to the budget and tax proposals of his administrators. It is one of the few survivals of direct (as opposed to representative) democracy. Each man of Appenzell takes pride in carrying his sword, the symbol of his right to vote, to these assemblies—although he may well have an umbrella tucked beneath his arm! The women dress in their beautifully embroidered regional costumes.

The assembly takes place on the last Sunday in April in the towns of Appenzell (every year), Hundwil (years with odd numbers) and Trogen (years with even numbers). Trogen is also the home of *Kinderdorf Pestalozzi,* a group of houses in which more than 200 orphans from many European countries are educated together in an effort to bridge differences of language, religion and outlook.

The Appenzell countryside is rich, being covered with fruit trees and meadows; the per capita wealth here is the highest in Switzerland. Dairying is the major industry. In the spring, when the herds are driven up to the mountain pastures, picturesque festivals are held, and in the fall, when they come down to the valleys again the cow with the greatest milk-yield during the year is fêted and decked with flowers. Hand embroidery is also a specialty of the Appenzell, and few tourists leave without buying some. But don't imagine that you'll get any fantastic bargains, as the peasant women are not the least bit simple when prices are concerned! In the town of Appenzell itself, the old town hall, dating from 1561, with its folklore museum, is worth seeing. A delightful side trip can be made up the Schwende Valley, by railway or road, to the resort of Wasserauen. From here, it is only a short walk to the Seealpsee, one of the loveliest mountain lakes in Switzerland. From Wasserauen, you can also take a cable car to Ebenalp (5,400 ft.), another splendid viewing point.

You can return to St. Gallen from Appenzell by a different route, slightly longer, via the winter sports and summer resort of Urnäsch, and Herisau, capital of the subcanton of Appenzell/Outer Rhoden.

Resorts and Spas

A popular resort area in the northeast region is the Toggenburg Valley, which runs in a great curve between Mt. Säntis and the

Walensee. In the fine Alpine surroundings of the Upper Toggenburg, beside the River Thur, are the neighboring resorts of Wildhaus, Unterwasser and Alt-St. Johann, skiing centers in the winter and starting points for excursions in the Churfirsten and Alpstein ranges in summer. Wildhaus is the birthplace of Swiss reformer Ulrich Zwingli, whose house can still be visited. Lower down the valley, also on the River Thur, are the adjacent resorts of Nesslau and Neu-St. Johann. A secondary road leads eastwards from the latter, through the spa and winter sports resort of Rietbad, to Schwägalp, the point where we joined the cable car to Mt. Säntis on our previous excursion from St. Gallen.

The southern slopes of the Churfirsten mountains, across which there are no roads, drop steeply to become the northern shores of the lake of Walensee, a deep, ten-mile-long gash in the mountains. Quiet little Weesen, at the western end, is a resort noted for its mild climate; four miles away, above the northern shore, there is the winter sports center of Amden. Along the southern shore, a spectacular new road, cut into the mountainside and passing through several tunnels, leads to a number of tiny resorts and the lakeside village of Unterterzen. This is the lower terminal for the cable railway, which goes up to Tannenbodenalp and the Flumserberge health resort and winter sports area, a picturesque region of forest- and meadow-covered mountain slopes which look across the end of Walensee to the Churfirsten mountains. You can also reach it by steep roads that wind upwards from Flums, a small town in the valley that runs from the east end of Walensee to. the Rhine, near Bad Ragaz. At Tannenbodenalp, you can go on one of the world's longest cableways. Over a distance of nearly two miles, a procession of little four-seater cabins climbs steadily up to Maschgenkamm (6,630 ft).

Bad Ragaz, with its beautiful golf course, is a well-kept, well-run and long-established resort in a quiet setting among mountains beside the Rhine; one with excellent hotels from deluxe down and a splendid, modern spa establishment. But thanks to the cablecar up to Pardiel (5,350 feet) and the connecting chairlift to Laufboden (7,300 feet) Bad Ragaz is a winter sports resort as well. From Pardiel, and more particularly from Laufboden, there are outstanding views. In summer Laufboden is the starting point for the "five lakes excursion," a walk taking in five beautiful mountain lakes. In complete contrast, the famous walk (you can now go by minibus part of the way) up the Tamina Gorge will give you a dramatic taste of a journey to the center of the earth. Deep down in the gorge a narrow path winds along under overhanging rock sides. In places they touch to form a natural bridge. It's best in May or June when the snows are melting and water roars down the gorge in a tumbling, tempestuous torrent. At the end of the path is the hot spring from which over a million gallons of healing waters a day come up, at over 90°F, to be piped down to the spa at Bad Ragaz. The healing properties of the waters were known many centuries ago. Then, it is said, luckless patients were lowered into the waters by a rope from the top of the chasm! In yet further contrast, a trip of about eight miles northwards from Bad Ragaz will bring you into the pocket principality of Liechtenstein.

Glarus

Before we leave northeastern Switzerland, let us return to Walensee and its eastern end. To the south is the tiny canton of Glarus, almost a land in itself (and a secluded one too, with its deep valleys and high mountain barrier), which includes Mt. Tödi (11,900 ft.) on its southern boundary. Shortly after you leave Walensee, you will join the River Linth, which cuts southwards through the canton. Surprisingly, scattered along the deep valley are prosperous little industrial towns, much concerned with textiles and electrical appliances. But this is not characteristic of the canton, for the Linth Valley is outstandingly beautiful. In the little world of its own, the canton of Glarus has not only industry but also Alpine pastures, snow-capped peaks, lovely mountain lakes ranging from diminutive Ober-See to the larger but equally picturesque Klöntaler-See, as well as figs, vineyards, chamois, marmots and a noticeable air of seclusion.

All this is within a radius of a dozen or so miles from Glarus, the cantonal capital, itself no farther from Walensee. Glarus is a small industrial town—one which had to be almost entirely rebuilt after a disastrous fire in 1861. There, in the disproportionately large Zaunplatz, with the twin spires of the nearby church spearing upwards against a backdrop of mountains, the citizens gather each year on the first Sunday in May. For this is the day of the Landsgemeinde, the open-air parliament.

Finally, a look at Winterthur, northeast Switzerland's second largest city; easily the biggest, of course, is Zurich. With a population of about 90,000, Winterthur is an industrial center that traces its origins back to 294 A.D. During the Middle Ages it was a craft center until it fell under the yoke of Zurich. A Heimatmuseum chronicles the city's development with furniture, paintings, manuscripts, old toys, and everyday articles. Two art collections, the Oskar Reinhart Foundation and the Public Art Gallery, provide a survey of Swiss, German, and

Austrian painting since the 18th century. The town's 330-year-old symphony orchestra is one of the best in Switzerland. Contrasting with the modern industrial plants are four historic castles on surrounding hills, most notable among them the Kyburg, for several centuries seat of the counts of the same name who played a prominent role in Swiss history.

BERN

Arcades, Bears and Fountains

Bern, the seat of government of the Swiss Confederation, ascribes an exact date to its foundation—1191. It also possesses a legend of how it came about, and how the city got its name. According to one version, Berthold V, Duke of Zähringen, had decided to build a city on the bend of the River Aare where Bern stands today. He was hunting in the forest, which at that time stretched on both sides of the river, and told his followers that the new city would be named after the first animal he killed. It happened to be a bear. Coincidence it may be, but the name of Bern differs only slightly from the German word for bear, and to this day a bear is the principal feature on the city's coat of arms.

It does not matter much whether or not the legend is true, but the rise of Bern can definitely be ascribed to the Zähringen family (although in 1191 there was already a fortified position here—an outpost of the free imperial city of Nydegg). As for the name, modern philologists smile at the bear story, and some attribute it to a local deformation of the name of an Italian city from which some early

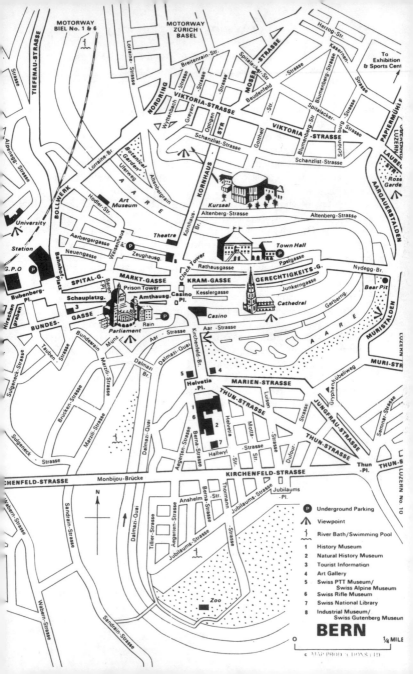

BERN

Legend:

- **P** Underground Parking
- **⚠** Viewpoint
- **≈** River Bath/Swimming Pool
- 1 History Museum
- 2 Natural History Museum
- 3 Tourist Information
- 4 Art Gallery
- 5 Swiss PTT Museum/ Swiss Alpine Museum
- 6 Swiss Rifle Museum
- 7 Swiss National Library
- 8 Industrial Museum/ Swiss Gutenberg Museum

0 ¼ MILE

c MAP PRODUCTIONS LTD

settlers in this region are supposed to have come—Verona. Since B and V are interchangeable in some languages, Bern, it is argued, is simply Verona with a Swiss accent. Be that as it may, on Sundays the children of Bern, uninterested in semantics, still carry carrots to give to the occupants of the Bear Pit beside the Nydegg Bridge, whose antics no doubt, you'll find amusing to watch.

In 1353, Bern became the eighth "state" to join the Confederacy started by the original three cantons of Uri, Schwyz and Unterwalden in 1291. Almost immediately, the hard-headed merchants and patricians of this prosperous city began to establish the supremacy over their colleagues that was to result in Bern becoming the center of government of the nation. A major disaster struck the city in 1405, when most of its houses, built chiefly of wood, were destroyed in a great fire. The city was rebuilt with sandstone from municipally owned quarries, a fact which accounts for the pleasing unity of Bern's appearance today. (This unity is little disturbed by the baroque and rococo overlay of the 17th and 18th centuries.) The additions of the 19th century are not at all out of tune with what had been built before, as you can see in the avenues and stately mansions of the "diplomatic quarter," where the legations of the countries represented at Bern have grouped themselves (Elfenstrasse, Thunstrasse, Marienstrasse and the other spacious streets around the Helvetiaplatz).

Bern has many buildings that are modern, some fantastically so, such as the city's enormous glass railway station, but these buildings, although certainly not always eyesores, are restricted to a few clearly defined areas. Elsewhere, indeed over virtually the whole of the old city, there are strict laws which say, in effect, that anything can be done to the inside of a building but the outer appearance must remain unchanged. The result is a city which has all the character and charm of an age past but is nonetheless as up-to-date as today.

Lively in Its Fashion

Some say that Bern is lacking in highlights, gaiety and fun, and that they find it dull and drab. But if they do they have missed its true personality. For one of the greatest charms of Bern is that although it has more of interest and entertainment than many similar cities, these are provided not so much for tourists as for its own worthy citizens. It has life and preoccupations of its own, features which the perceptive visitor will find to be a relief after the stereotyped amusements of many other places.

Bern is primarily a patrician city, the product of long-established families, of conservative tradition, conscious of responsibility. It is a city devoted to the serious pursuit of government—not of politics; the Swiss have come near to eliminating politics, in the unsavory sense of the word, from government. Bern has always been staunchly Swiss, firmly enough grounded in its own traditions to have escaped the cosmopolitan influence of the international society that customarily rules in capital cities. Diplomacy in Bern is a sober matter, not a by-product of dances and dinner parties. Bern is in a sense bourgeois, but it displays the best qualities of the bourgeois temperament, surrounding itself with solid enjoyments, heartily satisfying food and unostentatious comfort.

Never gay? How then do you account for the frolicsome fountains that are the trademark of Bern? For the animated markets? For the centuries-old popular festival, the Zibelemärit (Onion Market) held on the fourth Monday of November? Bern *can* be gay, but its gaiety is never raucous.

Exploring Bern

It is not difficult to cover the principal attractions of Bern in a comparatively short time, since the geography of the city has compressed its sights into a restricted area, albeit a hilly one. The old town is perched on a high rock that juts into a loop of the River Aare. Most of what the visitor wants is contained within this loop, and the few places outside it lie just on the far side of the bridges.

As you stroll through the streets of the capital, three architectural features will almost certainly impress you—arcades, fountains and towers. The arcades, which roof the sidewalks of so many of Bern's streets, are one of the city's chief characteristics. These *Lauben*, as they are called, are a welcome asset in the main shopping streets. With their low, vaulted roofs, they extend to the edge of the pavement, where they are supported on sturdy 15th-century pillars. Under their protection, comfortable window shopping is possible even in the worst weather. You will find most of the four miles of them in the old town, on the Spitalgasse, Marktgasse, Kramgasse, Gerechtigkeitsgasse, Junkerngasse, Münstergasse and Rathausgasse.

The brilliantly colored and skilfully carved fountains, their bases surrounded by flowers, are for the most part the work of Hans Gieng, and were set up between 1539 and 1546. Witty and joyful, they provide light relief from the often severe structure of the medieval houses that form their background. The Fountain of Justice might seem less than original with its figure of the blindfolded goddess, with her sword and scales, perched on a high column, until you glance at the severed heads that lie at the base—not only those of the emperor, the sultan and the Pope, but even, striking nearer home, of the mayor of Bern! The Ogre Fountain bears a giant enjoying a meal of small children. Then there are the Bagpiper, the Messenger, Moses, the Zähringer Fountain (with its harnessed bear and its cubs feasting on a bunch of grapes), Samson (overcoming a lion), and many others, some of them sculptured references to historical events. You will pass most of these in the walk outlined below.

A Bern Walk

Start on busy Bahnhofplatz in front of the Schweizerhof hotel, facing the mirror-like glass walls of Bern's futuristic railway station. To your left, and at the end of Spitalgasse, is the Church of the Holy Ghost, finished in 1729 and now plainly uncomfortable amid the modernity and bustle of the seventies. If you now walk down Spitalgasse you will quickly come to samples of Bern's fountains and towers. The Bagpiper Fountain stands in the middle of the street with the Prison Tower (Käfigturm), a city gate in the 13th and 14th centuries, beyond it. Straight down Marktgasse and past the Anna Seiler and Marksman Fountains, you'll come to Kornhausplatz on the left and its Ogre Fountain (an ogre munching an apparently tasty child). To your right is Theaterplatz, and in front of you Bern's colorful showpiece and trademark: the Clock Tower (Zeitglocken Turm).

Originally built as a city gate in 1191, but much restored and rebuilt since then, the "Zytgloggeturm", as it is called in the local dialect, has been providing hourly entertainment since 1530 when the astronomical clock and various mechanically operated puppet figures in a pulpit-like structure beside it were installed on the eastern side. Here the hour is not merely struck (by a knight in golden armor at the top of the tower), it is performed—and performed by a large and varied cast of characters.

To see the show it is best to take up position at the corner of Kramgasse and Hotelgasse at least five minutes before the hour. You won't be the only one there. For photographers, the best time in summer is 10 or 11 a.m. At two or three minutes to the hour, heralded by a jester nodding his head and ringing two small bells, the puppet show begins. From a small arch on the left of the "pulpit" a couple of musically inclined bears emerge, a drummer and a piper, heading a procession of a horseman with a sword, a proud bear wearing a crown, and lesser bears, each carrying a gun, sword or spear. When the procession comes to an end a metal cockerel on the left crows and flaps his wings in delight, after which our golden armored knight at the top of the tower hammers out the hour, while Father Time on a throne in the middle of the pulpit beats time with a sceptre in one hand and an hour glass in the other.

From the Clock Tower our route continues down Kramgasse. It's a lovely old street with many guildhouses, the inevitable arcades and, needless to say, a couple more fountains, the Zähringer and the Samson. At the next intersection it is best to make a brief diversion and turn left down a short, narrow lane. This will bring you to Rathausplatz and Bern's Town Hall (Rathaus).

Originally built in the 15th century after the great fire which destroyed most of Bern, the Rathaus is a pleasingly simple building in the late Gothic style. The markets once occupied the ground floor, and city business was conducted above. But today, after several restorations, it has become the center of both city and cantonal government, the council chamber being a really charming old room. In the courtyard is a lovely fountain which, although modern, shows a distinct affinity with the medieval ones outside. The Rathausplatz in front of the Town Hall is a beautiful little medieval square with delightful dimensions and lines. It contains the Venner (Ensign) Fountain.

Bern's Bears

If you now leave the Rathausplatz, return down the lane and turn left at the intersection you will walk down Gerechtigkeitsgasse and past the Justice Fountain. A left turn at the bottom will take you steeply down Nydegg Stalden, through one of the oldest parts of the city, past the fountain depicting a 16th-century messenger with his delightful little bear companion, and on to the 15th-century Untertor Bridge over the river Aare. From here it is a short, steep climb to the far end of the high Nydegg Bridge which will later take us back over the river. However, if you are feeling energetic it's well worth while crossing the road and then either climbing up the little path to the left, turning right at the top, or walking up Alter Aargauerstalden, and then turning left. Both will bring you to the entrance (free) of the splendidly arranged and kept Rose Gardens. Allow a little time here, not only to enjoy the 200 varieties of roses, and the fine plants and shrubs, but also the best panoramic view there is of the city of Bern, tightly squeezed in the bend of the river. On a hot summer day, too, you'll find it difficult to resist a rest in the cool shade of the trees before returning to the Nydegg Bridge where, at the end on the left, you'll find the famous, but surprisingly drab, bear pits. Here, Bern's mascots, alive and not made of metal or stone as on the Clock Tower or fountains, will put up a fine bit of clowning if you dangle a carrot above their heads.

Leaving the bears we now cross the Nydegg Bridge and at the far end turn left up Junkerngasse, a street notable for the façades of its fine old houses. At the top you come to the pride of Bern—the magnificent Gothic cathedral. Started in 1421 by master mason Matthias Ensinger on a site formerly occupied by an older church, it was planned on lines so spacious that half the population of Bern could worship in it at one time. Its construction went on for centuries. Even the Reformation, which converted it from a Catholic to a Protestant church, did not prevent work being continued. Daniel Heinz of Basel directed this for twenty five years (from 1573 to 1598) completing the nave and the tower. The finishing touch, the tip of the 300-foot-high steeple, was not added until 1893.

The cathedral has two outstandingly fine features, one on the outside and one inside. Outside is the main portal, with a magnificent sculptured representation of the Last Judgement (1458) whose 234 carved figures may distract attention from the admirable statues of the Wise and Foolish Virgins. This work was completed immediately before the Reformation, but fortunately escaped destruction by the iconoclasts who emptied the pedestals of the side portals.

Inside the church, while the elaborately carved pews and choir stalls are worth attention, the real attraction is the stained glass. Possibly the best are the 15th-century windows of the choir, but Bern has not been content to rest with the heritage of the past. Many fine windows have been added in recent years, like that of the Dance of Death which, though modern in execution, is old in design, for it was made from a sketch by Niklaus Manuel Deutsch, Bern's artist-statesman-warrior of the 16th century. Before leaving the cathedral, walk across to the terrace at the back where, from the walls, there is a splendid view down on to the river.

If you now walk from the cathedral up Herrengasse or Münstergasse you'll quickly come to the Casinoplatz, and the Casino, center of entertainment with a concert hall (frequent concerts), restaurants, banqueting rooms, and dancing. Most Swiss cities have a building called the Casino or the Kursaal, but Bern has both. The latter lies on the other side of the river to the north and is devoted to rather lighter entertainment than the Casino. It also has a gaming room where *boule* is played to a five franc limit. The Casino, however, stands at the northern end of the Kirchenfeldbrücke. If we turned left now and crossed the bridge we would come into Helvetiaplatz, a square surrounded by museums. Beyond is the fine residential quarter of Kirchenfeld, with the zoo farther away at a point where the capricious river Aare describes another loop.

This is part of the city which had better be explored another time. So instead of going over the bridge, cross Casinoplatz, turn left down Münzgraben and then right along the terrace behind the Houses of Parliament. Here there's another fine view across the river and, in good weather, to the distant Alps. A diagram at the bridge end of the parapet will help you pick out the principal peaks. You can walk round the end of the Parliament building into Bundesplatz, and then into the traffic-free Bärenplatz with its Tuesday and Saturday morning markets, and lively cafés and restaurants. At the far end of Bärenplatz is Spitalgasse down which we started this walk. The tourist office publishes a free leaflet which illustrates a walk broadly on the lines we've followed.

This walk should give you an idea of what is most notable in Bern. But there are other areas to explore if time permits. To the south of the city you can go by funicular up the Gurten Kulm and enjoy not only a fine view of Bern but also a famous one of the Alps to the south with Jungfrau in the middle. The return fare from anywhere in Bern to Gurtem Kulm is about 4.50 francs. And there is another excellent view of the city from the fine park behind the railway station.

Beyond the park is the university with its famous law and medical schools. The students sometimes add a touch of gaiety to the city's streets, but as a rule they find their fun in their own *Stämme,* the fraternity meeting places. The north side of the river offers not only the Kursaal, already mentioned, but also the nearby botanical gardens.

Finally, if you exhaust the attractions of the city itself, you will find it an excellent headquarters from which to make excursions to other parts of Switzerland. It is an important rail and road junction, and round-trips to many of the country's tourist centers can be made from it within one day. Zermatt or Jungfraujoch can be comfortably visited on day excursions, and a two-hour radius includes a dozen of the country's most-visited localities.

THE BERNESE OBERLAND

Aristocrat of Alpine Scenery

The Bernese Oberland covers an area of some 1,800 square miles. It comprises nine valleys, the lovely lakes of Thun and Brienz, and a number of lakelets in the heart of the mountains, such as Bachalp-See (7,400 ft.), just below the summit of Faulhorn, and Oschinen Lake, above Kandersteg and one of the most beautiful of Switzerland's mountain lakes. And, of course, there are the mountains, lots of them, with a beauty and grandeur which have to be seen to be believed.

The Bernese Oberland was discovered as soon as traveling itself, as an independent art or pastime, began. Jean-Jacques Rousseau was one of the first who praised the beauties of these wild mountains, and in the early 19th century, fashionable Paris society started to visit the Interlaken district. Madame de Staël, Necker, and La Rochefoucauld were among those who came. During the 19th century, the district had many French and English royal visitors, and in 1816, Byron stayed on the Wengernalp. Other poets and authors who came to the Bernese Oberland and worked here were Goethe, Shelley, Thackeray, Ruskin, Matthew Arnold and Longfellow. Mark Twain wrote some of his works at Thun. The Bernese Oberland was also popular with the great musicians—Brahms, Mendelssohn and Weber spent much time here. And some respected painters—Lory, Koenig and Wocher—painted well-known canvases in the area.

The inhabitants of the Bernese Oberland are mainly German, or rather Schwyzerdütsch-speaking Swiss. Decent, hardworking, modest and friendly, they are mostly peasants, craftsmen or hotelkeepers. Foreign visitors are extremely important to them, but the Swiss do not sponge on tourists, preferring instead to do their utmost to please their guests so that they will want to return.

The wide variety in altitude creates a great diversity of scenery. Around the Lake of Thun you will see fig trees, vineyards and even southern vegetation; in two hours' time you will reach the region of Alpine plants, and after another hour and a half you are in the land of eternal snow and ice. On an early July morning, you may bathe comfortably in Lake Thun, and in the afternoon ski on the slopes of Jungfrau. You may sunbathe at Brienz or walk among the southern plants at Gunten in the morning and be among snowy peaks with glacier lakes and floating ice-blocks four hours later.

Even the two neighboring lakes, Thun and Brienz, vary greatly in character. The former has a mild climate and a relatively open situation, although the hills rise steeply along the northern shore. It is surrounded by fertile land, flowers, orchards, vineyards and fig trees, the whole sprinkled with centuries-old villages, castles and manors. But the Lake of Brienz, on the other hand, is encircled by wild mountain ranges, rocky cliffs and dark forests; when traveling around it, you keep hearing the thunder of waterfalls. Lake Thun is much the larger; thirteen miles long and about two miles wide. The Lake of Brienz is eight and one-half miles long and one and one-half miles wide.

However fascinated you are by the natural beauty of the district, do keep an eye on the little towns and villages you pass, for in architectural charm the Bernese Oberland is almost unsurpassed. Whether you travel by bus, car or train, you will see enchanting houses with terraces and graceful little towers, their gardens bursting with color.

Hasli and Zitterli

On Sundays you often see women and children in local costume. But the thick-boned bodices are not very comfortable and have mostly been replaced by modern clothes, except in the more remote villages. The Swiss Society for the Preservation of Historic Sites, however, is concerning itself more and more with conserving national dress, and its branches organize festivals and pageants to encourage the wearing of these picturesque costumes.

The men's traditional dress has almost entirely disappeared—although some cowherds still wear it in a few almost unapproachable villages. Many women, however, still have their *Hasli*—white for Sundays, blue for weekdays. The white *Hasli* is a chemise with starched sleeves. With it, they wear blue or purple stockings and a heavy wool, ankle-length skirt that fastens in front. The many ribbons add color to the women's appearance. Their headgear, a small black cap perched on the head, is called *Zitterli*. But the costume varies a great deal in the Bernese Oberland. For example, the Emmental girls—from the country of the immortal cheese—wear black knitted mittens in summer and long gloves in winter, usually with a bracelet over one glove.

The world-famous Swiss woodcarving industry originated at Brienz in the last century. A man named Fischer started carving pipes of horn and later of maple. Soon he applied his knowledge to carving napkin-rings, boxes, egg-cups and cigarette holders and eventually experimented with figures—first trying William Tell, of course. Gradually he gained a following, and his neat artistic work caught the eyes of merchants. Fischer's whim became a vast industry. Some years ago they started on cabinetwork, and today you can buy many carved wood objects from simple bazaar products to large and impressive pieces of furniture. These latter may not be particularly comfortable, modern or easily cleaned, but are pleasing to the eye and original. At Frutigen, matches and matchboxes are manufactured. Curiously enough, one of the well-known industries of the Bernese Oberland is ivory carving from imported walrus and elephant tusks.

Lacemaking is one of the oldest industries of the Oberland, and handweaving is still practiced on a small scale. The handmade torchon lace of the Lauterbrunnen valley is well-known and justly admired. First-rate fancy leather articles are manufactured by a firm in Spiez, and the artistic and lovely pottery made at Steffisburg is gaining popularity.

Apart from the craftsmen and the hotel-keepers, the inhabitants of the Bernese Oberland, as mentioned at the beginning of this chapter, are mostly peasants. If you are traveling by car, you have to stop every now and then to let the cows pass, and wherever you go you hear the tinkle of the bells hung around their necks. Even in the elegant streets of Interlaken—that world-famous sophisticated holiday resort—you meet the homecoming cows every evening.

Exploring the Bernese Oberland

Astride the River Aare where it leaves Lake Thun, Thun is a picturesque medieval town of some 32,000 inhabitants. It is dominated by the four-turreted Zähringen Castle, which with the church and the town hall forms a coherent photogenic group approached by steep streets and flights of stairs. Down on the lakeside is another castle, called Schadau, built in the English style. Thun, although a town with many modern buildings and elegant villas, has managed to retain much of its medieval charm and character, so much so that if you wander around aimlessly—the best way—you will probably imagine yourself walking into the Middle Ages.

The town is an excellent center for a number of fascinating walks. Within pleasant walking distance are the heights of Goldiwil, Heiligenschwendi and the Grusisberg. A morning's gentle walk will take you to several small resorts round the end of the lake, or to the bird sanctuary at Einigen. If you are a glutton for exercise (although you don't need to be a mountaineer), you can make the pleasantly tiring climb up Stockhorn (7,100 ft.). Alternatively, if walking doesn't appeal, there are good boat services from Thun, bus services around the lake, and trains along the southern shore.

Between Thun and Interlaken, on the northern shore of Lake Thun, there is a string of interesting villages, all of them fairly well-known resorts. During the season, these resorts are filled to capacity, but, being smaller and less worldly places than either Interlaken or Thun, they are quieter and, of course, less expensive. Hilterfingen, the nearest resort to Thun, has a yachting school and, like adjacent Oberhofen, is notable for its gardens and lush vegetation. Oberhofen, on a lovely bay, has a picturesque 12th-century castle on the waterside. Next comes Gunten, a water-skiing center, which is also well-known for its rich southern vegetation and very mild climate. From here, one can take a bus to the hillside resort of Sigriswil. A little bit farther on is Merligen, lakeside resort at the entrance to the Justis Valley, where, every September, cheese produced during the summer is gathered together for solemn division between dairymen and cattle-owners of the district at the ceremony known as the *Käseteilet*. Just beyond, at the shore terminal of Beatenbucht, you can take the funicular up to Beatenberg (3,800 ft.) and then a chairlift on to Niederhorn (6,300 ft), both being winter sports and summer resorts with remarkable views. Farther on still is the entrance to the illuminated Beatus caves.

Spiez

If, from Thun, we travel along the southern shore of the lake in the direction of Interlaken, the first locality of note that we touch is the small town and popular holiday resort of Spiez. Here you breathe the air of ancient poetry and can still hear the songs of troubadours. It was Rudolph II, King of Burgundy, who built the present castle of Spiez, then called "The Golden Hall of Wendelsee." Afterwards it belonged to the Strättliger family, one of whom, Heinrich, was a great troubadour. Poets and troubadours, even in the 13th century, were in a habit of becoming penniless, and Heinrich von Strättliger was forced to sell his castle. It was bought by a nobleman called Bubenberg and later acquired by the von Erlach family, to whom it belonged from 1516 to 1875. Now it is the property of a public foundation. Appropriately, concerts and open-air theatrical performances are periodically held there.

Leaving Spiez, we pass through some villages that are less known and less popular with visitors than the resorts on the opposite shore. They include the small sailing resort of Faulensee (behind which, at 2,800 ft., is the small winter sports and summer resort of Aeschi), Leissigen and Dárligen.

Interlaken

Gateway to the Bernese Oberland, for generations Interlaken had one purpose only, to attract summer tourists. Out of season most of its great hotels, tearooms and bars then closed down. But nowadays more and more are open year-round as winter sports enthusiasts begin to realize the wealth of superb facilities so readily accessible.

Interlaken, as its name implies, it situated "between the lakes"— Lakes Thun and Brienz. On a strip of flat, grassy land bisected by the river Aare, it is surrounded by a superb mountain panorama. The west and east sections of the town are connected by the Höheweg, the central esplanade lined with trees, formal gardens, hotels and souvenir shops. A quaint touch is given by the fiacres as they clip-clop alongside modern motor coaches, but it's a nostalgic touch, too, for they are among the few remaining relics of 19th-century and Edwardian Interlaken. The older hotels have been pulled down or modernized, and new ones have arisen such as the skyscraper *Metropole* with its breathtaking views from the upper floors.

Halfway along Höheweg, on the north side and almost hidden behind shops, is Interlaken's Casino, standing in beautiful gardens with a gigantic flowerbed clock. In the Casino, a building of curiously mixed styles both inside and out, you can try your luck at the gaming tables (maximum stake five francs), or listen to a constantly changing program of symphony concerts, dance bands and even yodeling.

During the summer Interlaken has a tradition of open-air performances (but the audience sits in a splendid covered grandstand) of Schiller's *William Tell,* a drama with a large cast which perpetuates the memory of the legendary hero and the historic overthrow of the house of Habsburg. The resort also has an outstandingly fine eighteen-hole golf course at Unterseen, close to Lake Thun, but golfers claim that they are put off by the magnificent scenery.

Obviously Interlaken has many restaurants, cafés, bars, dance halls, cinemas and all the trappings that go to make a successful resort but, first and foremost, it is a center for excursions, and as such has few rivals throughout Europe.

Interlaken as an Excursion Center

As we have already mentioned, Interlaken is essentially an excursion center, and a very fine one at that. In the region the Swiss have fully developed their special engineering skill in providing mountain transport. It seems, in fact, as if every peak and crag has been tunneled for trains or elevators, or bound with cables of aerial cabins and chairlifts. Cogwheel trains scurry up and down mountains; motor coaches add a touch of contrasting color to winding roads; cable cars and chairlifts soar silently aloft. Thus sightseers can alight at heights varying from a couple of thousand feet to Jungfraujoch's 11,333 feet. The latter is possibly the finest excursion in Switzerland—some say in Europe—and maybe the most expensive one, too. But first let's take a look at something more modest.

Only five minutes' walk from Interlaken's West station is the lower terminal of the funicular railway up to Heimwehfluh (2,200 ft.), where there are magnificent views of towering Jungfrau, Eiger and Mönch. At the top, too, there's an elaborate scale-model railway which will gladden the heart of any enthusiast. On the other side of the town, not much farther away, is the funicular which will take you on the fifteen-minute ride up to Harder Kulm (4,300 ft.), and to an even finer mountain and lake panorama. There are splendid walks along prepared paths, and you may even see a wild ibex, for they wander freely hereabouts. Just a short distance from the top station is an attractive restaurant with a terrace where you can drink in both the view and something stronger.

Now let's venture farther afield and a trifle higher. From Interlaken East station the Bernese Oberland Railway will take you in six minutes to Wilderswil, a charming little spot; its view of the Jungfrau, according to Ruskin, is one of the three great sights of Europe. At Wilderswil we change to a cogwheel train for the steep, fifty-minute climb to Schynige Platte (6,450 ft.). Even based on Bernese Oberland standards the view from here is remarkably beautiful and fully justifies its fame. Almost as famous is the Alpine Botanical Garden near the summit station, where hundreds of different Alpine plants have been laid out in natural surroundings. Not to be missed, too, if you want a memorable night are the organized moonlight walks along the ridge from Schynige Platte. All you need is to be reasonably fit, well shod, and suitably clothed. Check with the Interlaken tourist office for details.

At this point it is important to emphasize that anyone suffering from heart trouble, weak lungs or high blood pressure should consult his or her doctor before embarking on either of our next two excursions—to Schilthorn and to Jungfraujoch. *Mountain sickness at best is an unpleasant experience, and it can be dangerous.* This only affects very few persons, but you could be one.

The Schilthorn and Mürren

It takes about one and a half hours to get from Interlaken to the top of Schilthorn, starting with a train journey to Lauterbrunnen followed by a ten-minute coach ride to Stechelberg, where you'll see the Mürrenbach, said to be Europe's highest waterfall, tumbling over the cliff. Incidentally, even more impressive and famous are the Staub-bach Falls near Lauterbrunnen, and the Trummelbach Falls some two miles away. At Stechelberg the real trip begins—a four-stage cable-car journey lifting you silently in little more than a half-hour to the summit of Schilthorn, some 9,750 feet above sea level. It was here that scenes were shot for the James Bond film *On Her Majesty's Service*. And if you go into the circular Piz Gloria restaurant above the cable-car terminal, you can sit and watch an Alpine panorama—so grand that it seems faintly unreal—slowly roll past your window, for the whole restaurant revolves continuously. Sit there fifty minutes, and you'll have gone the full circle.

On the way up one of the cable-car stations is Mürren (5,400 ft.), the highest village in the Bernese Oberland. Impressively perched among cliff-top pastures some 2,600 feet above the Lauterbrunnen Valley, Mürren enjoys an incomparable view of Jungfrau and its snow-capped colleagues. It's a first-rate resort, tailor-made for those yearning to escape from the noise and hurly-burly of city life as, in addition to the silent beauty of surrounding peaks and glaciers, it is inaccessible by road so that its streets are blessedly traffic-free. For winter sports, Mürren is world-famous. Especially notable is the funicular to Allmendhubel (6,270 ft.), where a bobsleigh run begins, descending through hairpin bends to the finish over 1,000 feet below.

Instead of going by cable car, a slightly quicker and more interesting way to reach Mürren is by train from Interlaken to Lauterbrunnen, then by funicular up the steep cliff to Grütschalp, and finally by mountain railway along the cliff edge to the resort itself.

The Jungfraujoch

From Interlaken the journey to the Jungfraujoch is in two parts, the first via Lauterbrunnen or Grindelwald to Kleine Scheidegg, and the second from there to the summit station. The usual outward route is from Interlaken East station (1,900 ft.), past Wilderswil and Zweilütschinen to Lauterbrunnen (2,600 ft.) noted for its mountain torrents, beautiful waterfalls and lace. You may not see the last, but you'll certainly see plenty of rushing and falling water. Just before Zweilütschinen, if you look to the right of the train, you'll get a glimpse of the confluence of the rivers Schwarze (Black) Lutschine and Weisse (White) Lutschine, and where the waters join you'll clearly see the difference in color. The "white" is glacier water, and the "black" comes from rocks.

At Lauterbrunnen we join the green cogwheel trains of the Wengernalp Railway, popularly known as W.A.B., and the steep climb to the top really begins. The train twists and turns through tunnels and over viaducts, giving a succession of camera-clicking views of yet more mountain torrents and waterfalls, of the Lauterbrunnen valley down below with the funicular to Mürren up the other side, and of an unending, constantly changing vista of peaks. In early summer the line-side wild flowers are superb.

The first main stop is at Wengen (4,200 ft.), a famous, long-established, well-equipped winter sports and summer resort, but still no more than a mountainside plateau village at the foot of Jungfrau. It's a peaceful one at that, with traffic-free streets, for it cannot be reached by road. The sunset is one of Wengen's claims to fame. You may have admired many sunsets, but here the glow which bathes surrounding peaks and slopes and casts a pink and flame-red light over the entire scene is unique.

Railway to the Heavens

On leaving Wengen you could be excused for wondering where the train is taking you. You know you'll be going higher, although it is difficult to believe that it will be among those wild peaks and distant lands of snow. But you are wrong. For here the Swiss have performed one of their great miracles of engineering. The Jungfrau, this "virgin of mountains," has not only been conquered: it has been tamed by railway tracks, and the steeply climbing train will take you in warmth and comfort to a strange white land between heaven and earth.

Passing through Wengernalp (6,150 ft.), where Byron stayed in 1816 and is said to have gotten the idea for *Manfred,* you soon reach Kleine Scheidegg (6,760 ft.), a small winter sports and quiet summer resort. It doesn't quite belong to the land of eternal snow but is high enough for skiing right up to late spring.

At Kleine Scheidegg we change over to the smart little brown-and-cream train of the Jungfrau Railway which climbs more than 4,500 feet in six miles to the summit station, nearly four and a half miles being in a tunnel through the Eiger and Mönch mountains. The line took sixteen years to build and was opened in 1912. Even today it is still one of the world's railway marvels. Leaving Kleine Scheidegg, where there's a good moderately priced station restaurant, the train passes through pastures with views of Mönch and Grindelwald, as well as the treacherous Eiger North Wall, which we'll see better on the way down. Just before the next station, Eigergletscher (7,610 ft.), which has a small hotel and restaurant, if you look to the right you'll see the kennels of the husky dogs which pull the sleighs at the summit, and next to them is a pen containing a colony of the small, furry marmots which inhabit the high Alps.

Now the train plunges into the long tunnel with leads steeply up to Jungfraujoch—a forty-minute journey. The next station is Eigerwand (9,400 ft.), only a few yards inside the precipitous North Wall. From the station platform short tunnels lead to enormous windows cut into the North Wall, and all trains stop long enough for passengers to walk across to take in the view. Given fine weather, you'll see a magnificent panorama of Grindelwald far below, Lake Thun in the distance, and a multitude of mountains, valleys, fields and forests. At the next station—Eismeer (10,350 ft.)—windows are also cut into the mountain face a few yards from the platform, but here the view is very different and even more impressive. Here for the first time you realize you are in a white world of ice, glaciers and snow.

Atop the Jungfraujoch

From Eismeer it is only about eleven minutes to the Jungfraujoch terminus (11,333 ft.). Remember that from Interlaken you have risen 9,473 feet and that the air, however pure, is also rarefied. Those who move around too quickly before they are adjusted to the altitude may feel giddy, or even become ill. So take it easy; move slowly. Or, as a Swiss friend said to the writers, "For the first fifteen minutes, please forget that you are young."

From the trainside in the underground Jungfraujoch station—the highest in Europe—a rocky corridor used to lead to the *Berghaus,* Europe's highest hotel and restaurant. Alas, this was all burned down in 1972, but it has been replaced with the fine, new *Inn-above-the-Clouds* restaurant and cafeteria seating 290, a feature being the magnificent views from its panoramic windows.

If, when you leave the train, you take the free elevator behind the post office and souvenir shop, it will take you to the corridor leading to the Ice Palace. It's quite a long one, much of it cut through a glacier, its walls, ceiling and floor being of solid ice. On the way you'll pass a full-size car sculptured out of ice, and a replica of a bar complete with tables, chairs, counter and a whiskey barrel. Down a few steps at the end is the great hall, also cut out of ice.

Back at the station, another corridor—the Sphinx tunnel—leads from the lower end of the platform to yet another free elevator, this one whisking you up 367 feet in ninety seconds to the famous Sphinx Terrace. Here there's not only a research institute and astronomical observatory but, from the observation terrace, an incomparable panorama of rock, snow, ice and clouds that is one of the wonders of Europe. Facing south you'll see the primeval, ten-mile-long Aletsch glacier, a tortured ribbon of shattered ice divided into strips by thin traces of black. To the southwest, apparently little more than arm's length away, is the 13,640-foot peak of Jungfrau, and behind you, to the northeast, the peaks of Mönch and Eiger. On a fine day you may see the Jura and Vosges, the Black Forest, and the lakes of central Switzerland.

If you have never been on skis before, but want to try just for fun, you can do so on top of Jungfraujoch at the summer ski school. The school is reached along a path from the Sphinx tunnel exit. The services of an instructor and rental of skis and boots will set you back about ten francs an hour. But although there's a skilift, it's a simple slope and of little interest to serious skiers. Should you want something a little less strenuous, near the ski school for one franc you can have a five-minute sleigh ride, weather permitting, pulled by the husky dogs we saw down at Eigergletscher.

To vary the homeward journey, at Kleine Scheidegg you can get a train which goes via Grindelwald (your ticket is valid both ways), giving you, as it descends steeply around the Eiger, superb views of the North Wall towering above. The North Wall was first climbed in summer in 1938, but it was not until 1961 that the first group of climbers successfully conquered in winter the almost vertical rock face, braving subzero temperatures, and falls of rock, ice and snow. It took them six days to reach the top. As you look up from the comfort of the Jungfrau Railway train, the surprise is not that about forty challengers should have lost their lives on the North Wall, but that anyone, even in summer, should have succeeded. If your eyes are good, from near Alpiglen station you can just see, almost in the center of the North Wall and about halfway up, the windows of Eigerwand station through which we looked on our upward trip.

Grindelwald (3,400 ft.) is a fairly large, year-round resort noted for its glaciers and views. Wetterhorn (12,150 ft.), Finsteraarhorn (14,000 ft.), Eiger (13,000 ft.) and countless other peaks can be seen, not to mention the Lutschine valley, here open and friendly in contrast to the steep, waterfall-bespattered sides you'll see on your way back to Interlaken. Perhaps the greatest attraction is the Firstbahn, Europe's longest chairlift, which in half an hour carries you from Grindelwald up to an altitude of 7,100 feet at First. In summer it's the views which are spectacular; in winter, the skiing, although Grindelwald also has skating, curling and ice hockey.

From Grindelwald it is only about forty minutes back to Interlaken. On our Jungfrau trip we've taken part in many records. We've been on the highest railway in Europe to the world's highest underground station; stood on Europe's highest mountain observation terrace; looked down on the Aletsch glacier, the greatest in the Alps; been on what is almost certainly Europe's finest and most spectacular excursion; and traveled on the world's most expensive railway! But, like some 400,000 people every year, it's a fair bet you'll think it was worth every franc.

Lake Brienz

Returning to our starting point, Interlaken, let us now take a tour around the Lake of Brienz, bordered by steeply rising mountains. Along the wild southern shore, the winding narrow road only goes about halfway. At the end, among green hilly meadows between steeply wooded mountainside and the lake, is Iseltwald. A charming, unsophisticated village resort, it lies partly on a picturesque peninsula jutting out into the quiet waters of the lake, and partly around a small bay formed by the peninsula itself. From Iseltwald, a beautiful forest walk of about an hour and a half brings you to the Giessbach Falls, where fourteen cascades rush down through the rocky cliffs to the lake. Along the northern shore, the road passes through several small resorts before reaching Brienz at the northeastern end. Brienz, the largest place on the lake and a popular resort (but only a very small town), is also the home of Swiss woodcarving, as you will gather from the shop windows. It is also the lower terminal of Switzerland's last steam-driven cogwheel train, which puffs manfully up to the summit of Brienzer Rothorn (7,700 ft.) with its magnificent views. Many artists settled here, and the town's school of woodcarving is subsidized by the government. Brienz again represents the milder beauties of the Oberland. Its climate—though not quite so mild and southern as Lake Thun's Gunten—is much warmer than that of neighboring regions.

About eight miles beyond Brienz, we reach Meiringen, the main town in the Hasli Valley, and the center of the valley's homeweaving industry. It is popular with mountaineers and particularly with tourists, for roads lead north to the Brünig Pass and Lucerne, east over the Susten Pass to Andermatt, and south along the Hasli Valley to the Grimsel, Furka and St. Gotthard passes.

The Hasli Valley, rocky and often gorge-like, is renowned for its dramatic scenery, for the mile long Aareschlucht, an eerie, 600-foot-deep gorge about twenty-five minutes' walk from Meiringen, and for the Reichenbach Falls. Sherlock Holmes enthusiasts won't need reminding that Conan Doyle recounts in "The Final Problem" how the villainous Dr. Moriarty flung the famous detective down these very falls to what was presumed to be his death. And the faithful will remember, too, that it was at nearby Rosenlaui that Holmes spent the night before he was pushed over the falls. Recently, American author Sam Rosenberg, in a book about the death and resurrection of Holmes, put forward a well-reasoned theory that Conan Doyle modeled Moriarty on none other than the famous but somewhat sinister German philosopher Nietzsche. Further evidence is that the hotel register at Rosenlaui proves that Nietzsche had a holiday there in 1877. It is also known that when, at the suggestion of Sir Henry Lunn (the father of winter sports in Switzerland), Conan Doyle visited the falls a few years later to see whether they would be suitable for the denouement of Holmes, he also went to Rosenlaui, where he must have learned of Nietzsche's visit. Elementary, my dear Watson!

If you've time, take the road which climbs up from near the falls to Rosenlaui, some seven miles away. It's steep, rough and narrow, but you'll find yourself among some of the finest Alpine scenery in Switzerland.

The Simmental and Gstaad

From Spiez, on Lake Thun, the highway leads southwest into the Simmental, or Simmen Valley. Weissenburgbad, a short distance north of Weissenburg on the main Simmen Valley road, is hidden in a romantic gorge. Its mineral water, famous since the 15th century, achieves excellent results in curing respiratory troubles. Higher up in the Simmen Valley, we reach Boltigen, just beyond which the Jaun Pass road leads off to the right. This is a most attractive and not unduly difficult side-trip, although there are many hair pin bends up to the 4,950-foot summit and on the descent. You'll be rewarded, too, just before you reach Bulle, by a splendid view of Gruyères, in the middle distance to the left, standing proudly on top of its rocky pinnacle.

Zweisimmen is the main town of the Simmen Valley, and although it is primarily important as a cattle market, it is also a winter sports resort, with a gondola cableway (said to be Europe's longest) to the splendid skiing slopes on Rinderberg (6,600 ft.). Pleasant short walks lead to the Mannenberg ruins and the Simmen Falls.

From Zweisimmen, still following the River Simme, we can reach Lenk by railway or secondary road. Lenk, at 3,600 feet, is surrounded by wild glaciers and thundering waterfalls, and is dominated by the mighty Wildstrübel mountain. From two glaciers, seven torrents rush down to the valley, which is popularly called *Siebental* ("Valley of the Seven"). Lenk is both a spa, founded on one of the strongest sulphurous springs in Europe, and a beautiful and popular winter sports resort. Being in a rather isolated position, it is comparatively cheap.

If, instead of turning at Zweisimmen up to Lenk, we had continued along the main road, passing the resorts of Saananmöser and Schönried, we would have come to Saanen, a winter sports and summer resort. Spare a little time here to turn off the main road into the village, for its streets contain many particularly fine old wooden chalets. Some date from the 16th century and their projecting gables and façades are beautifully carved, ornamented and inscribed. At Saanen, the road forks. One branch goes along the beautiful Sarine Valley, through Château d'Oex and the Pays d'Enhaut, which we have already visited in a previous chapter. The other turns south to go through Gstaad and then over the Col du Pillon to Aigle, in the Rhône Valley.

In recent years, Gstaad has caught up with St. Moritz, Arosa and Davos as a popularity leader and is without doubt the most fashionable of the Bernese Oberland winter resorts. It has an impressive location, surrounded by forests, hills, glaciers and small mountain lakes well stocked with trout. There are golf and tennis tournaments every summer, and during the winter season the annual horse show and ski-joring are among the main attractions. In addition, ice-hockey matches, ski-meetings, curling competitions and toboggan races are also organized. Chalet owners here include Princess Grace and the Aga Khan. Yehudi Menuhin is a frequent visitor here, not least for the famous Menuhin Festival each August.

If we return once again to Spiez, and this time head due south, either by road or by the wonderful Lötschberg Railway, we will pass the ruins of Tellenberg Castle and a mighty stone viaduct before alighting at Blausee-Mitholz, the 3,200-foot-high station for Blausee. Lovely little Blausee, or Blue Lake, has—as its name suggests—a deep blue color, and is a beautiful and impressive sight well worth visiting. Algae and fossilized trees lie at the bottom of the lake and are clearly visible in the crystal-clear water, as are the famous Blausee blue trout. The water is supposed to come underground from the Oschinen Lake, and some scientists maintain that its extraordinary color is due to chemical effects of the minerals as it runs deep in the earth. Others assert that the blue is due to algae.

Leaving Blausee-Mitholz, the train begins to traverse wilder and wilder regions; it goes on climbing and passing across many bridges and through long tunnels. Sometimes, as it twists and turns, you can see the tracks at three different levels. The next stop is Kandersteg, surrounded by massive mountains and scenery as magnificent as you can ever hope to see. Situated at a height of 3,850 feet, it enjoys a rare advantage, being built on a plateau that extends for several miles. In consequence, visitors not keen on Alpine climbing can spend their holiday on high ground and still be able to take pleasant walks on almost flat country. Those who wish to make longer excursions can reach the famous and much-admired Oschinen Lake in about an hour and a half. This is a superb and romantic sight, with an amphitheater of rocks and glaciers in the background. The Kander Falls are also accessible. Kandersteg possesses the usual amenities for winter and summer holidays, including an indoor skating rink, which is now also open in July and August. This small resort, visited in the past by many celebrities, is nearly the most southerly point in the Bernese Oberland. And it ends our tour of this lovely region of Switzerland.

Walking in the Bernese Oberland

The Bernese Oberland is a rambler's paradise. Here are a few suggestions, arranged by districts, both for shorter and longer walks:

Eastern Oberland. Meiringen—Brünig Pass—Lungern. Three and three-quarter hours. On this route you pass the Alpbach gorge, which is a remarkable wonder of nature. The Brünig Pass itself is one of the best-known and lowest passes in Switzerland. *Meiringen—Gross Scheidegg—Grindelwald.* This is for the more ambitious rambler, as the walk takes six and a half hours. You will see the River Aare; you will be impressed by the mighty walls of the Wetterhorn, and have a magnificent view of the mountains encircling Grindelwald. Grindelwald itself is a world-famous glacier village, with mild, green slopes on one side, and terrifying, almost perpendicular mountains on the other.

Center Oberland. Interlaken—Grünenbergpass—Inner Eriz. Six hours. The route takes you amid rich and exotic rocks and wild forests. You pass the Seefeld and Tropfstein caves. Inside, the caves are a maze of crossing passages. At the entrance you will be advised to unroll a ball of string, so that you will be able to find your way out again. In the Eriz region you will see the Zulg stream, which has many other streams and ditches running into it and gives the district a wild appearance. *Spiez—Rengglipass—Wilderswil. Eight hours.* On this route you reach the broad and high Aeschi chain with its widely scattered and picturesque wooden huts and houses. At Aeschi-Allmend there's a particularly beautiful view: to the north the lake and behind it chains of mountains. Between Wilderswil and Interlaken—if you continue—you will see the ruins of Unspunnen, restored.

West Oberland. Gsteig—Pillon Pass—Les Diablerets. Three hours and forty minutes. Parts of this route almost border on canton Vaud. There you find shepherds' huts with dams for protection against avalanches. In the pastures the famous Valais cattle are bred. The Dard is a tumultuous mountain stream that originates from the icicles of the Scex Rouge and throws itself in powerful falls through a narrow gorge and into the open valley of Les Diablerets. The trip from Gsteig is also outstanding. A teleferic now links Reusch and the Glacier des Diablerets. *Kandersteg—Lötschenpass—Goppenstein. Nine and three-quarter hours.* The Gastern valley is easily one of the greatest and finest of the high mountain valleys of the Alps. You see here many steep, high, rocky walls with thundering waterfalls, most particularly the snowy giants of the Valais. The Bietschhorn is the highest among the mountains: its glistening peaks, capped with glaciers, are an impressive and unforgettable sight.

LUCERNE

Heart of Historic Switzerland

To enter Lucerne is to approach the heart of historic Switzerland, for the deeply indented shoreline of the Vierwaldstättersee ("Lake of the Four Forest Cantons")—better known as Lake Lucerne—was the cradle of the Swiss Confederation. To the Swiss, the names of Rütli, Brunnen and Altdorf—all places near the lake—recall the pact signed in 1291 between the clans of Schwyz, Unterwalden and Uri. William Tell and his son walked this countryside; at Altdorf, Tell is said to have defied the Habsburg bailiff, Gessler; and with his crossbow shot an apple from his little boy's head. It hardly matters that the legend has little basis in fact, for it is a charming story which many believe. And its hero, Tell, makes a splendid subject for a play, an opera, memorial chapels and monuments, as well as, of course, for countless souvenirs on sale throughout the district. To the traveler there is special magic in the names of Lucerne, Rigi, Pilatus and Bürgenstock, for their charms have been publicized for at least a century.

Certainly, neither the prehistoric tribes who first established their primitive settlements along these shores nor Bishop Leodegar, the

174

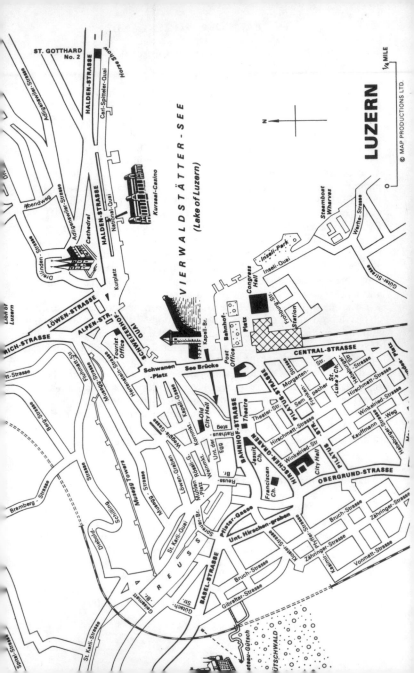

city's patron saint, ever imagined that the scenic beauties of their region would be world-famous.

During the early Middle Ages, Lucerne was a vassal city of the House of Habsburg and, at the outbreak of the conflict between the Swiss and the Austrians, was unwillingly forced to send men and arms against its mountain neighbors. After the defeat of the Habsburg army at Morgarten in 1315, Lucerne felt it necessary to maintain friendly relations with the confederates, for the city then served as a natural marketing and trading center. For economic reasons, as well as to assert their rights as free men, the citizens of Lucerne signed a pact of perpetual alliance with the founder members of the confederation (1332). From that time on, although it did not shake off the final traces of Habsburg rule until after the victory at Sempach in 1386, Lucerne shared the martial fervor of the Swiss, participating in all their conflicts with the outside world. Although a free city and fairly prosperous, Lucerne never achieved the power and wealth of her great allies, Basel, Bern and Zurich. Until the development of modern transport revealed its scenery to enchanted globetrotters, the canton and its capital remained a rather quiet backwater.

Lucerne, with its many 15th- and 16th-century houses, its historic city hall and the delightful covered wooden bridges (which have almost become its trademark), lies where the mountains begin. It has developed essentially as an excursion center, for major industries came relatively late. Until twenty-five years ago, Lucerne marketed mostly the products of domestic crafts, practiced in the neighboring regions: wood and ivory carving, embroidery, wool spinning, and weaving. And yet, despite the many hotels and establishments catering to visitors, the people of Catholic Lucerne have a life of their own. They are laughter-loving, having a lighthearted streak in their temperament—possibly a survival of Austrian influence.

Exploring Lucerne (Luzern)

Like several Swiss cities, Lucerne is built at the end of a lake. To be more accurate, it is at the head of a large bay, for the Lake of Lucerne (or Vierwaldstättersee, as you will usually see it referred to locally) is so tortuous in outline that it is difficult to say where the end is. Through Lucerne—again, like several other cities—a river flows out of the lake, in this case the river Reuss, which is joined just beyond the town by the river Emme. Two 14th- and 15th-century covered wooden bridges and the quaint "old town" with its 17th-century town hall (which lies between them on the northern bank) all help to create an atmosphere of medieval solidity, further enhanced by the picturesque Weinmarkt, the Fritschi fountain and the ancient city walls topped by watch towers. In and around the old quarter is a maze of charming, narrow streets and little squares bordered by lovely old buildings, often with painted façades. And there are plenty of enticing shops, too.

The recently renovated Kapellbrücke (Chapel Bridge), the larger of the two covered bridges, crosses the river diagonally from the old St. Peter's Chapel, past the octagonal Wasserturm (water tower) to the southern bank. The paintings on the timber ceilings of this bridge represent scenes from Lucerne's history. Those on the other bridge, the Spreuerbrücke (or Mill bridge), are typically medieval and illustrate a grim dance of death.

If you cross either of these two bridges, or the busy Seebrücke, you'll come to the "new" town on the south side of the river Reuss. Here, close together, are the lake steamer landing stages, the railroad station (reconstructed after the 1971 fire), and the city's Kunsthaus. Not far away is the theater. And in this part of the town are many hotels, a growing number of good shops and the tourist office.

No visit to Lucerne is complete without a trip to the famous Lion Monument (Löwendenkmal). As much a Lucerne trade-mark as the Kapellbrücke, this is the often-described dying lion designed by Thorwaldsen and carved out of the living rock by Ahorn in 1820–1821. Dedicated to the Swiss Guards of Louis XVI who died after defending the Tuileries during the French Revolution in 1792, the thirty-foot lion, lying in a niche hewn out of the cliffside, forms a unique and surprisingly moving memorial. It is close to the Glacier Gardens, a remarkable natural phenomenon discovered in 1872 by geologists who literally unearthed huge potholes created by glacier water during the Ice Age as well as many prehistoric fossils. There's an Alpine and Ice Age Museum, too.

As a contrast, there are the lively and attractive lakeside gardens and quays, with their magnificent views which give visitors a foretaste of the mountain and lake scenery that lies in store for them. Different again—and a joy to the young of all ages (several hundred thousand visit it each year)—is the city's vast and splendid transport museum with scores of old locomotives, carriages, cars, buses and, in a huge building new in 1972, airplanes and rockets. In the gardens there's even an old lake steamer with a restaurant and cafeteria on board. Incorporated in the transport museum, too, is a fine new planetarium.

As an excursion center Lucerne has few rivals. Among the shorter trips is a two-and-a-half hour conducted coach tour of the town and its surroundings taking in the beautifully situated Richard Wagner Museum at Tribschen. There, souvenirs and relics of the great maestro have been reverently assembled and are on view, together with a fascinating collection of musical instruments, in the house in which he lived. Buses take the holidaymaker to Meggen or Horw; funicular railways to the modest heights of Dietschiberg (with its golf course and outdoor model railway) and Gütsch.

Then there are Lucerne's two neighboring mountains—5,900-foot Rigi to the east of the city and 7,000-foot Pilatus to the south. The summits of both, as we shall learn in the next chapter, can be reached easily and without effort either independently or with a variety of advertised excursions.

Lucerne, indeed, presents the tourist with a problem; which to choose from an almost bewildering selection of day and half-day excursions by train, lake steamer or coach. To pick, almost at random, a mere dozen places, there are—in alphabetical order—Altdorf (capital of Canton Uri and much involved in the William Tell legend); Brunnen (famed for the views from its lakeside promenades); Bürgenstock (where you can look vertically down to the lake); Einsiedeln (pilgrimage center with its notable Abbey Church); the pleasant winter sports and summer resort of Engelberg) little Immensee on Lake Zug; 9,900-foot Kleintitlis (and its glacier); Klewinalp (high above Lake Lucerne); the historic field of Rütli; the little city of Schwyz (which guards Switzerland's priceless archives); Schönbüel (6,600 ft.); and Zurich (Switzerland's largest city). High on your list, too, should be a slow boat journey down the lake, crisscrossing from place to place and presenting you with a panorama of constantly changing beauty. On the other hand, if you want to stay put and steep yourself in cultural activities, what better than Lucerne during its International Music Weeks? Then, each day for three weeks in August and September, there's a different program of music and song by outstanding orchestras, ensembles and artists.

CENTRAL SWITZERLAND

Lakes, Mountains and Legend

Everyone knows the story of William Tell, the apple on his son's head and the well-aimed arrow, and no visitor to central Switzerland will leave without hearing much more about him. But not one in a thousand tourists who gaze respectfully up at his impressive statue in front of Altdorf's gaily painted medieval tower has the vaguest idea whether he ever really existed. They can hardly be blamed, since most Swiss, to whom he is a national hero, don't know, either.

Unfortunately it must be reported that most historians discount the Tell story as mere legend. They point out although much has been written about it through the ages, the story is either contradictory or at variance with historical fact, and there are no valid records to prove the existence of Tell, his son, the apple, or even of the tyrant Gessler. But take heart. Whether there is any truth in the legend or not, all are agreed that, broadly speaking, a situation such as that described in *The Story of William Tell* by Friedrich Schiller did exist in central Switzerland in the 13th century. A proud and independent people were being oppressed by their Austrian overlords. The spirit of rebellion was rife. And all this contributed to the signing in 1291 of the pact of perpetual cooperation and mutual assistance, an event in which Tell is popularly believed to have played a major part.

Thus, although in picturesque detail there may be no more historical truth in the legend of William Tell and the blow he struck for liberty than in a thousand other legends, it is a fair allegory of the times. So the tourists who go to Altdorf each year to pay tribute to his memory are not making an empty gesture. They will find that the spirit of the hardy old archer lives on in the hearts of the people of this region. They're soft-spoken, friendly and tolerant of the views of others, but at the same time carry themselves with a dignity that allows no doubt about their independence. "I am free Swiss" are words that have a solemn meaning in the region.

The William Tell country is the area of central Switzerland surrounding the Lake of Lucerne, or Vierwaldstättersee ("Lake of the Four Forest Cantons"), to give it its Swiss name, and it is certainly one of the most beautiful summer holiday regions Switzerland has to offer. It is also beginning to gain a limited renown as a winter sports region, with the development of such resorts as Andermatt, Einsiedeln and Engelberg (the first-mentioned being in the wild rugged St. Gotthard Pass district). From the top of Gemsstock, approached by cable car from Andermatt, it is said you can see 600 Alpine peaks. But even its friends would not claim that central Switzerland compares for winter sports with the Grisons, Bernese Oberland or Valais.

Smart white steamers—some of them, beautifully kept, picturesque old side-wheelers—ply the Lake of Lucerne and provide an ideal means of transport for exploring the region, assuming that you are not in too much of a hurry. The lake itself is the fifth largest in Switzerland, with a surface area of forty-four square miles and a very long and varied coastline, so that a journey on board one of the slow-moving steamers takes some time. In fact, if you are going to explore all the little towns and resorts that are worth seeing, several days will be required. With this in mind, the transport companies of the region issue a Holiday Season Ticket (valid for fifteen consecutive days) which allows five days of unlimited travel and half-price for ten more days.

Leading off Lake Lucerne in almost every direction are valleys, from most of which branch off yet more valleys, all with a charm of their own and all worth exploring if you have the time. And again and again, you will come across lakes: sometimes tiny ones high in the mountains; sometimes larger ones like Lake Zug. You'll always be in the presence of mountains, often green and gentle, but sometimes spectacularly impressive, like the St. Gotthard group on the region's southern boundary.

Exploring Central Switzerland

As we have already learned, the greater part of Central Switzerland can be explored from Lucerne. One of the most popular excursions is to Mount Pilatus, nearly 7,000 feet and the highest peak in the immediate vicinity. One route is to go by train or lake steamer to Alpnachstad and thence by the electric Pilatus Railway, claimed by its owners to be the steepest cogwheel railway in the world. Sometimes up gradients of nearly 1 in 2, the little red trains take thirty minutes to climb the 5,560 feet to the summit station. Another way of getting to the top is to take a trolley bus from Lucerne to the suburb of Kriens and there join one of the procession of little, four-seat cable cars which take you over mountainside meadows and among trees on an eerily silent, half-hour trip to Fräkmüntegg (4,600 feet). There you change to a forty-passenger cable car for the final, seemingly impossible climb up the near-vertical rock face to the summit.

If you wish, you can go by one route and return by the other, as the terminals of both the cable car and the Pilatus Railway are in the same building, which is perched giddily in a saddle between two of the Pilatus peaks. Above the terminals is the *Bellevue Hotel,* a modern circular structure which many visit to watch, from their bedrooms, the sunrise or sunset. Close by is the older, traditional-style *Pilatus-Kulm Hotel.* It takes little more than ten minutes to climb from the terminals, up steep but well-prepared paths and steps, to the top of the two nearest peaks. From either, and from the various paths and tunnels cut out of the rock, there are magnificent views and it is possible to see (if you've had luck with the weather!) vast distances in all directions. To the north the view extends to the Black Forest in Germany; northeast to the Säntis range and Lake Constance; and southeast to the Grisons. In the southeast, too, are the Alps, and to the west the Jura.

Pilatus owes its name, according to one legend, to Pontius Pilate, whose body, it is said, was brought there after the Crucifixion by the devil, and whose ghost, when disturbed, demonstrates displeasure by bringing storm and destruction to Lucerne. Not unnaturally, to avoid any such happening the town put a ban on anyone climbing the mountain. This lasted until after the Middle Ages. Unfortunately, historians of greater reliability aver that this is nonsense and that the name comes from *pileatus,* or "hair covered," because of the way wisps of cloud often stream from the summit like wind-blown hair.

Certainly Pilatus was the cradle of mountain climbing. Ban or no ban, it has, for centuries, been climbed by a steadily increasing number of mountaineers. The first primitive inn was built at the top in 1856, and Queen Victoria is said to have gone to the summit on muleback some twelve years later. You may not find a mule, but if you want to climb on foot the easiest route is from Hergiswil and it will take you about five hours to get to a well-deserved drink on the *Kulm Hotel* terrace.

After the trip to the top of Pilatus you should plan to go on the next clear day to Mount Rigi. You may ask what you can see from the top of Rigi that you can't from the top of old Hair Covered. In fact you'll find the two mountains have very different personalities. Pilatus is stern, forbidding and grandiose, although with an enigmatic charm, while Rigi (despite its 5,900 feet) seems a friendly, homely little mountain. It has greensward on top, and the slopes are covered with trees and lush pastureland where in summer obviously contented cows graze to a cacophony of cowbells. You may not see as far from its summit, but the views are prettier.

The Top of Rigi

There are two electric rack-and-pinion railways leading up to the top of the Rigi, one from the pretty little resort town of Vitznau, on the northern shore of Lake Lucerne; the other from Arth-Goldau, around the other side of the mountain at the southern tip of Lake Zug. These railways were built by competing companies back in the 1870s, and it was a race to see which outfit would first get its line to the top and capture the lion's share of the lucrative tourist business. The Vitznau line won, but that from Arth-Goldau gets its fair share of trade as its lower terminal, on the main St. Gotthard railway, is more accessible. Vitznau can be reached only by steamer and road. There's now a cable car from Weggis up to Rigi-Kaltbad, where you can join the Vitznau train to the top.

Visitors who want to see everything there can go up one way and down one of the others. Whichever route you take the view is equally impressive. If you're the athletic type and want to try it on foot, start from Küssnacht, which is at the end of the northern flipper protruding from the roughly tadpole-shaped Lake of Lucerne. It will take a good three hours and you will be puffing when you get to the top. But nobody will give you a medal for your pains, as the climb is

The picture-postcard Switzerland is alive and well at Andermatt, the winter resort known also as a starting point for springtime ski tours of the Gotthard area.

*St. Peter's Cathedral in Geneva was Roman Catholic
from 1150 to 1536, Protestant since. Calvin preached here
for nearly thirty years.*

Whether you like crowds or want to be alone, you'll enjoy cross-country skiing in Switzerland. Above, St. Moritz, with about 24 miles of routes; below, the Engadin Ski Marathon, which starts from Maloja and ends at Zuoz.

*Summer in the Alps is bucolic, productive and magnificent,
all at the same time.*

considered strictly child's play in Switzerland. Mark Twain recounts in *A Tramp Abroad* how he labored up the path in the dark so as to be at the top of Rigi for the much-vaunted sunrise, but was so tired when he got there that he fell asleep and didn't wake up until sunset. Not realizing how time had flown, he thought for a moment that the sun had changed direction. Even though he may only have seen the sunset, Twain describes the view in enthusiastic terms.

At the top of Rigi is another *Kulm* hotel, with a restaurant and a terrace where, on summer afternoons, there may be a Swiss boy or girl yodeling and playing the accordion. Even if you don't normally care for yodelers, they make wonderful background music for the lovely view of the lake and distant Alps. Near the Rigi-Kaltbad-First station (4,700 feet) is the *Hostellerie Rigi,* an ultramodern hotel bristling with good and unusual ideas. Not surprisingly, they have a Mark Twain Bar. There is a host of trails winding down through the meadows and woods of the Rigi and its companion hills, and in winter these become ski-runs that are popular with beginners, if not exciting enough for advanced enthusiasts.

The Bürgenstock and Stans

Having taken in the views from the top of Pilatus and Rigi, you may consider you've had your fill of heights. If so, you are going to miss half the fun for we haven't yet been to Bürgenstock, to the Stanserhorn or to Mount Titlis.

The Bürgenstock, a mountain ridge jutting out into Lake Lucerne, isn't particularly high but it rises so steeply from the water that the view of the lake and surrounding area from the top is strikingly beautiful—which probably explains why, for at least part of the year, many famous people, such as Audrey Hepburn, Sophia Loren, Mel Ferrer and conductor Rafael Kubelik, live here. Although you can drive to Bürgenstock up a steep, narrow road from Stansstad, the most interesting and dramatic way is to make the thirty-minute steamer trip from Lucerne to Kehrsiten, where a funicular will take you 1,500 feet above the lake to a group of hotels. This may not surprise you for the Swiss have a habit of crowning their peaks and precipices with a hotel or two.

But here there are five, with a nine-hole golf course thrown in! And even if you are not going to stay there it is worth glancing inside at some of the most luxurious appointments to be found even in a country that invented fine hotel-keeping. Mr. Frey, the owner of the three largest hotels, has combed the world for artistic treasures to furnish his mountain palaces, and a stroll through the various salons and reception halls is much like visiting a fine museum or art gallery, except that the hospitality is better.

Afterwards, unless you've no head for heights, you should walk along the cliff path (about fifteen minutes) to the Hammetschwand electric lift, which, in next to no time, will waft you up the almost vertical cliff face to the summit, some 800 feet higher. From there, if the weather has been kind to you, you'll see most of Lake Lucerne, part of the Jura mountains, and a splendid selection of Alps.

Just to the south of Bürgenstock are Stans and the valley of the Engelberg Aa. Stans is rich in historical memories, and Engelberg is one of the country's outstanding resorts in both winter and summer. And besides there are two more mountains to climb—by funicular, of course. They are the Stanserhorn and Mount Titlis.

From Lucerne, it is an easy journey by the Engelberg railway or by road to Stans, capital of the subcanton of Nidwalden and a pleasant little summer resort with an early baroque church.

The names of three great Swiss heroes are associated with the town of Stans. One is Arnold von Winkelried, who engineered the victory of the Confederates over Leopold II at the battle of Sempach in 1386. The Austrians, armed with long spears, formed a Roman square so that the Swiss, wielding axes and halberds, couldn't get in close enough to do any damage. Shouting "Forward, Confederates, I will open a path!" von Winkelried threw himself on the spears, clasping as many of them as he could to his breast, thus effectively giving his compatriots an opening into the square. Early pictures of this original kamikaze action make him look like a human pincushion.

The next great name in Stans is that of a hermit, Nikolaus von Flüe, who was born in Flüeli-Ranft, some ten miles to the south. It was just a century after Arnold von Winkelried had laid down his life for liberty that Nikolaus also saved the Confederation, although through wise counsel rather than soldierly sacrifice. When the Confederates fell to quarreling over the spoils of the Burgundian wars, he came to the town and mediated in their disputes at the Diet of Stans in 1481. He was canonized in 1947.

The third name to conjure with in Stans is that of Heinrich Pestalozzi, the father of modern education. Although he did not live there, it was in Stans, after nearly 2,000 of its inhabitants had been massacred by the French in 1798, that this great humanist gathered together the homeless children, practicing on them the educational theories that are now world-famous.

From Stans, a funicular and new cable car will take you to the top of Stanserhorn (6,200 feet), where there's a fine view and a new (1973) restaurant.

It is about an hour by train from Lucerne to Engelberg—at first along the lake, then past orchards and meadows, next up the wild canyon of the river Aa, and finally to Engelberg, nestling in a wide, flat valley. Spacious, quiet and surprisingly unspoiled, Engelberg is both a winter sports resort, with a fine selection of slopes served by an unusually good network of funiculars, cable cars, chairlifts and skilifts, and a summer resort for those who want to get away from it all and relax at a reasonable altitude among the mountains. In the village is a Benedictine monastery founded in 1120. Its library contains some rare manuscripts dating back to the 11th century or even earlier.

Towering above is permanently snow-covered Mount Titlis, 10,500 feet and central Switzerland's highest peak. A must for visitors—although not a cheap one—is the sensational ascent to Kleintitlis (9,900 feet) just below the summit. From Engelberg a funicular will take you up to the first of a series of three cable cars, the last stage going directly over the Titlis glacier and its apparently bottomless crevasses to the top station. There, from the sun terrace, the glass-enclosed viewing hall or the restaurant (all new in 1972) you'll see an Alpine panorama (if you have chosen a clear day) which will form a very long-lasting memory. The trip is not recommended, of course, for people with heart trouble; at 10,000 feet the air is pretty thin. But otherwise you need have no worry. The Swiss are a careful people and take their safety precautions very seriously. For example, on the funiculars there are periodic inspections during which huge weights are put in the cars, which are hauled halfway up the incline; then the cable is loosened to see whether the brakes will hold. They have to be able to stop the car within a few feet. All of which is a comforting thought as your little train climbs up a railway as steep as a roof, or as your cable car creeps silently up a seemingly ridiculously thin cable slung between a couple of mountain peaks.

Around and About the Lake

Having climbed some of the more notable peaks in this area comfortably and without effort (there are others, with and without funiculars and cable cars, if you want them), you may now prefer to take a more normal view of things, such as going to Altdorf to see where William Tell is said to have shot his famous arrow, to Schwyz—the cradle of Switzerland, and of course, for a steamer trip down the lake.

There are two routes to Altdorf from Lucerne. One is by steamer all the way to Flüelen at the extreme end of the lake (it takes about three hours) and thence by bus for the couple of miles to Altdorf. The other is via the Gotthard railroad, about an hour's journey. From Lucerne the train follows the lake to the end of the Küssnacht basin, then goes along the southern shore of Lake Zug and next past the smaller Lake Lauerz before coming to Schwyz-Seewen, six minutes by bus from the historic town of Schwyz, to which we shall return in a moment. Less than three miles beyond Schwyz-Seewen the train meets up again with Lake Lucerne at the resort of Brunnen and then follows the lake shore to Flüelen for Altdorf. Between Brunnen and Flüelen, and always close to the railway, is the remarkable Axenstrasse, a road cut out of the cliffs which, at this part of the lake, rise almost sheer from the water. An engineering and scenic wonder, the Axenstrasse, like the railway, dives in and out of one tunnel after another.

Whether you go by train or lake steamer, or out one way and back the other, depends on the time available. But if at all possible try to make at least one trip by steamer between Lucerne and Flüelen. It is a top priority for any tourist in the region, as we shall shortly explain. And try, too, to stop off at the town of Schwyz—fifteen minutes by bus from the steamer landing stage at Brunnen, and much less from Schwyz-Seewen railroad station.

Historic Schwyz

Schwyz, capital of the canton of the same name, should be visited by everyone interested in Swiss history. A quiet, dignified little place (population 11,500), Schwyz seems conscious of the fact that it is the oldest and most historic town in Switzerland, that it gave the country both its name and its flag, and that it is entrusted with Switzerland's most precious archives. It was here that in the 14th century the word Schweiz (German for Switzerland) was first recorded as the name of the mountain confederacy which, over the subsequent centuries, grew to become the Switzerland we know today.

Archeologists say there was a settlement on the site of the present town during the Bronze Age (2500–800 B.C.). By the 13th century the inhabitants of the valley of Schwyz, like much of the rest of what is now central Switzerland, were under the domination of the House of

Habsburg, and were very discontented about it, too. In 1291 they joined with the folk of neighboring Uri and Unterwalden in the famous Oath of Eternal Alliance. You can see the beautifully scripted and sealed original of the documents, battle flags and paintings of the period in Schwyz's Bundesbrief-Archiv (Federal Archives Museum), an impressively simple concrete building completed in 1936 but even today contemporary in every detail.

Schwyz has several notable baroque churches, and a large number of fine old patrician homes dating from the 17th and 18th centuries, not least being the Redinghaus, with its magnificent interior and fine stained glass. Curiously, many of these splendid houses owe their origin to the battlefield. The men of Schwyz had a reputation as fine soldiers and in the 16th and 17th centuries were in considerable demand in other countries as mercenaries. They went abroad, fought in the many battles of the period, collected what in those days was handsome pay, returned home, and with the money built many of the houses you can see today.

From Schwyz it is only a ten-minutes bus ride to Schlattli. There, a funicular (said to be Switzerland's steepest) will take you to a height of 4,300 feet and to the hamlet of Stoos on a cozy mountain plateau. Boasting several skilifts, some going up to nearly 6,000 feet, Stoos in winter is a first-rate, although unsophisticated, winter sports resort. In summer it turns into a hideaway for those seeking peace and quiet (Stoos has no roads, no cars) among Alpine meadows and wildflowers, and with magnificent scenery. Down in the Muotta valley, and not very far from Schlattli, are the ruins of the Suvorov Bridge, over which the French, under Masséna, and the Russians, under Suvorov, fought a major battle in 1799. Farther along the valley you can visit the vast Hölloch Caves. Already over fifty miles of caves and corridors have been explored but they remain strangely unexploited although the public can go in half a mile or so.

Einsiedeln, Sacred and Secular

From Schwyz it is a pleasant eighteen-mile trip northward to Einsiedeln. On the way you can make a side-trip to the small mountain lake of Aegeri, passing, near Sattel, the famous battlefield of Morgarten. There, in 1351, Swiss peasants were victorious against troops of Frederick of Austria, an event which helped pave the way for present-day Switzerland.

Like many another place, Einsiedeln is a winter sports and summer resort, but its real fame lies in other things. Firstly, it is one of Europe's most important pilgrimage centers, the abbey church of the gigantic Benedictine monastery which dominates the town being the home of the Black Madonna of Einsiedeln. Secondly, each year on September 14th it is the scene of the great Festival of the Miraculous Dedication with spectacular torchlight processions. Thirdly, *The Great World Theater,* a religious drama written by Don Pedro Calderón, is performed in front of the abbey church every five years (next performance 1980; if you want to see it, it's essential to book long in advance). Lastly, Paracelsus, the eminent Renaissance physician, was born in the district.

The monastery of Einsiedeln was founded, like the Grossmünster in Zurich, during the time of Charlemagne. Meinrad, a Hohenzollern count and Benedictine monk, seeking to pursue his devotions in solitude, selected the site as being the most remote he could find. He built a little chapel for the image of the Virgin (which had been given to him by the abbess of Zurich), and since food was scarce in the region, two ravens kindly supplied him with the necessities of life. He lived for a while in peace, but some men who thought he possessed hidden treasures murdered him. The ravens followed the slayers to Zurich. Bent on justice being done, the birds attracted so much attention to the men by shrieking round their heads that they were detected and punished. The monastery was built over Meinrad's grave. When it was completed in the year 946 the Bishop of Constance was invited to consecrate it, but as he began the ceremony a voice was heard crying out in the chapel three times, "Brother, desist: God Himself has consecrated this building." A papal bull acknowledged the miracle and promised a special indulgence to pilgrims.

Through the ages the monastery of Einsiedeln has been destroyed by fire on several occasions, each time to be rebuilt, but always the Black Madonna has been saved. When the French Revolutionaries plundered the church, hoping to carry off the sacred image, it had already been taken to the Tyrol for safe keeping. Today the Madonna is housed in a black marble chapel just inside the west entrance to the church. Seen from a distance its color appears to be a rich bronze, not black, and there is something quaint and gentle about the figure, splendidly arrayed in jewels, which lends it a curious grace. The abbey church itself, built by Caspar Moosbrugger in 1735, is considered to be one of the finest examples of baroque architecture in Switzerland, the impressive simplicity and grace of the exterior contrasting vividly with the exuberance of its richly ornate interior. In front of the church is a huge square, the conspicuous centerpiece being a gilded statue of the Virgin surmounted by a large gilded crown. Round the base, water trickles from fourteen spouts, and tradition has it the Christ drank from one of them. To be sure of drinking from the right one, therefore, pilgrims make the round, taking a sip from each in turn.

It is in this square that, as we have already mentioned, every five years Calderón's *The Great World Theater* is presented, with a cast of 700 performers, all amateurs living in Einsiedeln. The play, first performed before the Court of Spain in 1685, is a drama of life and the problems of man. For generations the monks of the monastery have coached these amateur actors for their parts in this and other religious plays.

Exploring the Lake by Steamer

From Lucerne the boat's first call will probably be the popular resort of Weggis, noted for its mild, almost subtropical climate. In 1897 Mark Twain stayed at Weggis for many weeks at the *Hotel Bühlegg* (it's still there!). Behind the resort you'll notice the aerial cableway which goes up to Rigi-Kaltbad, and if you turn round, across the lake you'll see the Hammetschwand elevator going to the top of Bürgenstock. After stopping at Vitznau, lower terminal of the Rigi cogwheel railway, the steamer sails through the giant gateway formed by the promontories of Bürgenstock and Vitznauerstock to call at the resort of Beckenried on the other side of the lake. From here there's a cable car to Klewenalp (5,250 feet), a small winter sports and summer resort in a wonderful position overlooking the lake. The steamer again crosses the lake, this time to the little resort of Gersau, which, from 1332 to 1798, was an independent republic—the world's smallest. Back again the steamer goes to Treib on the Seelisberg peninsula (look for the beautifully decorated chalet, once an inn, beside the jetty) before returning to the northern shore and the resort of Brunnen, famed for the lovely views from its lakeside promenades. At Brunnen the steamer turns south around the Seelisberg peninsula to enter the last basin of Lake Lucerne, the Urnersee, at the end of which is Flüelen. Now in succession come three points of major interest to those who revere the Tell saga and the Oath of Eternal Alliance—the Schillerstein (on the right as you pass the peninsula), the Rütli meadow (a little farther on, just above the Rütli landing stage), and Tellsplatte (on the other—eastern—side of the lake; the boat may not stop there).

The Schillerstein, a natural rock obelisk sticking eighty-five feet up out of the lake, bears the simple dedication "To the author of *Wilhelm Tell,* Friedrich Schiller. 1859." The Rütli meadow is where the Confederates from Schwyz, Unterwald and Uri are said to have met on the night of November 7, 1307, to renew the 1291 Oath of Eternal Alliance. Now it is a national shrine and every year, on August 1st, their Independence Day, Swiss citizens gather in the meadow to swear allegiance to the principles of the alliance—at night the sky glows with the light of hundreds of bonfires on the mountain tops. Tellsplatte, at the foot of the Axen mountain, is the rocky ledge onto which the rebellious archer leaped to escape from the boat in which the bailiff Gessler was taking him to prison, pushing the boat back into the stormy waves as he did so. The Tell Chapel, much rebuilt in 1881, contains four frescoes by Ernst Stückelberg which show the taking of the oath on the Field of Rütli, Tell shooting the apple on his son's head, Tell's escape, and Gessler's death.

From Flüelen it is only a short distance to Altdorf, where in the town's main square Tell is said to have replied to Gessler's challenge and performed his world-famous feat of successfully shooting an apple from his small son's head. With true Swiss caution, he had a second arrow, reserved for the heart of the tyrant should the first miss its mark. The whole drama, as told by Schiller, is enacted every other summer in Altdorf's Wilhelm Tell Theater.

Before leaving Central Switzerland let us return to our starting point, Lucerne, for a quick look at the second largest lake in the region, Lake Zug, little more than a mile from the Küssnacht arm of Lake Lucerne. The Zugersee, to give it its Swiss name, is about fourteen miles long but differs from its neighbors. True, it is typically mountainous at the southern end where the shores slope steeply up to Rigi. But in the north, unlike other lakes in this region, it has no more than gently rising hills, and it is clear that here we are leaving the region of high mountains.

A road hugs the shore round most of the lake. In the northeast is the lakeside town of Zug, capital of its namesake canton (the smallest in the Confederation). Although with much modern development, Zug is an ancient walled city with a distinctly medieval air enhanced by massive towers, and by the delicate spires of the 15th/16th-century church of St. Oswald. In the town hall, an early 16th-century building with Gothic carvings, there is a museum of gold and silver work, embroideries, wood carvings, stained glass, paintings, and with the flag said to have been held aloft to the last by Wolfgang Kolin. He perished in 1422 in the battle of Arbedo, where 3,000 Swiss valiantly tried to hold off 24,000 Milanese soldiers. There's a fountain in his honor in Kolinplatz.

From the Zugerberg (3,200 feet) overlooking the town there is a famous view taking in the peaks of Jungfrau, Eiger, Mönch, Finsteraarhorn and, nearer at hand, Rigi and Pilatus. But if, after your tour, you are tired and have had enough of heights, you need go no farther than Zug's quayside promenades. The view there may not match up to Zugerberg's but it is still a pretty respectable one and you will probably be able to pick out several peaks which, earlier on in our tour of Central Switzerland, appeared before you in wide-screen close-up.

THE GRISONS AND THE ENGADINE

Playground of the World

The canton of Grisons rivals the Bernese Oberland as the Swiss region most familiar to winter sports lovers. Here you will find famous resorts such as Arosa, Davos, Flims, Klosters, Lenzerheide, Pontresina, Scuol-Tarasp-Vulpera, and the vast conglomeration of St. Moritz and its satellite resorts. Here the Engadine, the mountain-bordered valley of the river Inn and its chain of lovely lakes, cuts a 25-mile-long swath across the southern part of the Grisons. A land of contrasts, the Grisons has a rich cultural tradition and a vivid history, as well as scenic wonders that leave the visitor groping for superlatives. It has some of the highest and most rugged mountain chains in Europe, a host of silvery Alpine lakes, trout-filled rivers, and no fewer than 150 valleys sheltering a race of hardy peasant folk who are as independent and proud as they are hospitable.

Covering about 2,800 square miles, the canton of the Grisons is the largest in Switzerland and takes in more then one-sixth of the country. In early days, the people of the Grisons were known as the "gray confederates," from which comes the name of the canton in Swiss-

German—Graubunden. A little more than half the population of 147,000 speak Schwitzerdütsch, a third use Romansch, and the remainder an Italian dialect. The history of the Grisons goes back to 600 B.C., when an Etruscan prince named Rhaetus invaded the area and named it Rhaetia. It became a Roman province, Rhaetia Prima, in 15 B.C., and graves of Rhaetians who fought in the Roman armies have been found as far away as Libya. During the Thirty Years' War, the Grisons were invaded at various times by the armies of Austria, Spain, and France, all of whom sought to control the strategic passes leading to Italy. From the 15th century on, the people of the Grisons allied themselves with the Swiss, but it was not until 1803 that they officially entered the Swiss confederation and became the eighteenth Swiss canton. The principal industries of the Grisons are cattle, wood and tourism, with the last providing the steadiest source of income. Although the Grisons owe their fame to such sparkling winter playgrounds as St. Moritz, Arosa, and Davos, whose luxury hotels attract the élite of four continents, the region, with nearly one hundred holiday resorts, offers many attractions to tourists on modest budgets, too.

Exploring the Grisons

The canton of Grisons is threaded with excellent highways plied by the ubiquitous bright yellow buses of the Swiss postal-coach system. It is also served by a network of railroads, including the Rhaetian narrow-gauge line, which, of course, is completely electrified. This fascinating little railway, the principal artery of the canton, has some 240 miles of track, and passes across 480 bridges and viaducts and through 117 tunnels, many of them spectacular engineering achievements. The tour of the Grisons to be outlined here can be made either by car or by a combination of railroad and bus. It takes the traveler from Chur, the capital city of the Grisons, north to Landquart, then east to Klosters and over to Davos, all via the Rhaetian Railroad. From Davos it leads over the Flüela Pass by bus to Susch, and from there northeast, by either bus or train, to Scuol and by bus to the castle of Tarasp. On returning to Scuol, we head southwest to St. Moritz. After a side trip to Muottas Muragl, we go by bus, via the Julier Pass, northward to Tiefencastel. Here, rejoining the Rhaetain Railway, we loop westward by Thusis and Reichenau back to Chur.

This tour takes a good twelve hours' traveling time, so that with stopovers it should be undertaken only if the traveler can devote at least two full days to it. However, by eliminating the trip from Susch to Scuol and Tarasp, and returning directly to Chur from St. Moritz via the Albula Pass, the tour could at a pinch be shortened to a one-day jaunt. But by rushing hell-bent through the Grisons you will miss much of the region's fascination and get only a superficial glance at its fabulous scenery, something for which you may find it hard to forgive yourself when you return home.

The capital and the principal city of the canton of the Grisons as well as the doorway to the scenic wonders of this mountain area is the town of Chur; in French it is called Coire; in Italian, Coira; and in Romansch, Cuera or Cuoira. Most of its inhabitants speak German, but at least know where they live in any of the other three languages. Romansch, spoken only in the Grisons, is the fourth national language of Switzerland. Spoken, it sounds like Portuguese with a little German mixed in. Chur, which has a population of about 33,000, is medieval in aspect, and beautifully situated at the entrance to the Schanfigg Valley. It is encircled by a corona of wooded mountains, and through the town runs the River Plessur, which joins the Rhine a mile and a half farther downstream.

Chur

Bronze Age relics found in Chur indicate that it was the site of some kind of human settlement in the Celtic epoch. In the year 15 B.C., the Romans established a military outpost here, which they named Curia Raetorum, for the protection of the Alpine routes leading to Lake Constance. This camp was situated on the rocky terrace in the portion of the town south of the river. From about the 9th century, Chur was ruled by the Catholic bishops, who, in 1170, were raised to the status of bishop-princes. But in the 15th century, the irate inhabitants forced the ruling bishop-prince to give up much of his political power over the town. This process continued through the decades until, by 1526, Chur had become a city free from temporal domination of the bishops and subject only to the emperor. Today Chur is a modern, go-ahead city noted for its outstandingly good selection of shops. Although relatively unknown to the tourist, Chur is a good holiday center. A lively spot with plenty to do and lots going on, it is the hub of an excellent road and rail network radiating in all directions. Almost any part of the Grisons can be visited easily from Chur on a day excursion.

Much of the city still retains its medieval character. Narrow streets, cobble-stoned alleys, hidden courtyards, quaint and ancient buildings abound, punctuated by massive structures such as the cathedral with its splendid, 12th-century high altar, the 15th-century St. Martin's church notable for its stained glass, the Rathaus and the Bishop's Palace. Red or green footprints painted on the sidewalks lead the visitor on two itineraries (described in the city's free brochure) which take in most of the sights. Each "walk" lasts about an hour; more if you linger.

From Chur, the route follows the fertile Rhine Valley downstream through vineyards, wheat fields and orchards. At Landquart we leave the Rhine, go through the dramatic Landquart gorge and follow the river Landquart upstream. After a long, winding but gentle ascent past a number of resort villages, including Saas and Mezzaselva (with Serneus down in the valley to the right), we come to Klosters-Dorf and Klosters.

Klosters

Klosters, once a group of hamlets, is now a small town in a valley bordered by mountains. With some 3,000 inhabitants, including film-star Deborah Kerr and author-husband Peter Viertel, it is a typical Grisons village, which has achieved special popularity as a well-equipped winter sports resort. With its neighbor, Davos, it shares access to the long Parsenn slopes that are said to provide some of the best ski-runs in the world. Tobogganing is believed to have originated here. It also has a gigantic swimming pool and a golf course.

Named for the cloisters of a now-extinct monastery, Klosters also has a pretty church with a clock tower. It is decorated with the coat of arms of the Grisons, showing a wild man pulling a fir tree out of the ground on one side, and a complacent apple tree on the other.

Klosters attracts young people who take their winter sports seriously, perhaps because it is smaller and has a more intimate atmosphere than its sister resort, Davos. The excellence of its children's ski school draws many families who rent chalets or flats during the holidays. The starting point for the best of the Klosters-Parsenn ski-runs is the Weissfluhjoch, reached by cable car from the town to the Gotschnagrat and then, after a short ski-run, by another cable car. The run back to Klosters is over six miles long, with a difference in altitude of almost five thousand feet. The variety of runs from the Weissfluhjoch and Gotschnagrat is almost unlimited, but the best-known are the ones that lead north to Küblis or south to

Wolfgang. The new Madrisa ski slopes, reached by the Albeina gondolas, are popular with both skiers (there are several well-placed lifts) and sunbathers.

The railway to Davos crosses the Landquart River by a lofty bridge, climbs through some stately pine forests, and then through Wolfgang, a skiing center, before dropping down again to the Davosersee and the town of Davos itself. Sir Arthur Conan Doyle put in a good deal of time in Davos, and Robert Louis Stevenson finished *Treasure Island* here in 1881.

Probably the most famous name among Swiss winter resorts is still that of St. Moritz, to which we shall come presently, but Davos—like Arosa and Gstaad—is pushing it hard.

Davos

Davos—in reality Davos-Dorf, with its indistinguishable Siamese-twin resort of Davos-Platz—owes its fame to the rise of skiing as the sport *à la mode* among the smart set in all western countries. Fanatic skiers supposedly find in Davos the world's most perfect terrain—the Parsenn run.

Davos lies at one end of the Davos Valley, running parallel to and northwest of the upper Engadine, and separated from it by the Albula chain of mountains, some of which are over 10,000 feet high. On the opposite side of the valley is the Strela chain, dominated by the Weissfluh. The open, sunbathed slopes of this range provide the magnificent skiing that attracts devotees of the sport from all over the world. The Parsenn funicular railway takes skiers from Davos up to Weissfluhjoch, nearly 9,000 feet high, and the upper end of the Parsenn run. From there they can ski down over vast, open snowfields to the town, a drop of 3,500 feet or so. Or, striking off to the northeast, they come to Davos' neighboring resort, which we have already visited—Klosters. Another funicular, combined with a gondola goes to Strela. There's a chair and ski lift to Rinerhorn (7,500 ft.), and a couple of dozen other mountain railways, cable cars and assorted lifts. Nearby is the well-equipped Brämabüel-Jakobshorn ski area, reached by cable car and skilift.

Long before the skiing craze gave Davos international fame the place had a considerable vogue as a health resort. Robert Louis Stevenson stayed at the Hotel Belvédère. Its ideal situation from the standpoint of altitude and climate attracted tuberculosis sufferers as early as 1865, and it still has several of the finest sanatoria in

Switzerland. With 12,000 inhabitants, Davos is even larger than St. Moritz, and it has more hotels and pensions, not counting the rest homes, health clinics and indoor swimming pools.

In addition to its unrivaled ski-runs, Davos also boasts a truly magnificent ice-rink on which hockey matches and exhibitions of international caliber are staged throughout the winter. It is overlooked by a vast and well-appointed terrace. There are two fine ski schools in Davos, either one eminently capable of instilling in the novice sufficient skill to accomplish a fair-sized schuss within a few days. As in some other Swiss resorts, the runs are constantly patrolled by guards who will set him right side up if he happens to do a nose-dive into a snowdrift. Furthermore, the mountainsides are dotted with little inns and taverns, where toes can be thawed out and courage fortified with a jigger of Kirsch. English-speaking visitors who mistrust such foreign concoctions will even find their favorite brands of whisky at most of these places (though at a steep price).

In summer, Davos is pleasant, but no more so than dozens of other Swiss resorts, and it is considerably less picturesque than a great many of them. It offers sailing and swimming in the Lake of Davos, trout fishing in either the lake or the Landwasser River and its tributaries, mountain climbing with experienced guides, golf on an eighteen-hole course, and skating, from June to October, on the open-air ice rink.

The resort is dominated by the steeple of a pretty, late-Gothic church, and the city hall, part of which dates from the 17th century, has some interesting stained-glass windows and coats of armor. There is a medical institute where much effective research has been carried out by Swiss scientists into the problems of tuberculosis, and on top of the Weissfluh another group of scientists has established an institute for the study of snow conditions and avalanches.

From Davos, the road leads over the Flüela Pass to Susch in the Engadine, a distance of eighteen miles. It's a relatively easy drive, as Alpine passes go, with no gradient steeper than 1 in 10, and comparatively few hairpin bends. Although the highway reaches an altitude of 7,800 feet, it is normally open to traffic in winter, but sometimes a toll is charged for snow clearance.

At first the road climbs gently. As it rises dense larch forests give way first to pine trees, then to firs, and finally, above the timber line, to a rocky, desolate waste of boulders and jutting cliffs, much of it snow covered except in summer. It's impressive rather than beautiful scenery. Ahead, on the left, are the rocky slopes of Weisshorn, 10,100 feet, with Schwarzhorn, 10,300 feet, to the right, perennial snow-capped guardians of the pass. Towards the summit, even in August, the traveler may find himself driving through a light snowstorm which muffles the ever present sound of cowbells ringing over the rocky pastures. He will pass between two small lakes known as Schottensee and Schwarzsee.

At the summit itself is the *Flüela Hospiz,* a picturesque wooden chalet with a windmill, offering refreshments and a night's lodging at reasonable rates, though few tourists would care to spend much time in this barren, formidable spot.

The descent takes the motorist through a narrow valley crossing the Susasca, in sight of the 10,600-foot Piz Vadret, to the base of the great Grialetsch Glacier, a spectacular mass of ice and snow that serves as a reminder that this entire country was, long ago, hidden under a vast sheet of ice. The road winds downward, crossing the torrential Fless River, and finally reaches Susch (or Süs) on the River Inn. The Inn, which eventually flows into the Danube, gives its name to this beautiful valley, the Engadine, "The narrow place of the Inn." Because of its chain of popular resorts, to many people the name of the Engadine is more familiar than that of the Grisons, the canton of which it is only a constituent (but important) part.

The Lower Engadine

One need only enter an Engadine house to be acutely conscious of its atmosphere and the almost painful state of cleanliness that exists within. The simple but solid façades, with their wonderful lattices and balconies, always prove attractive to foreigners, and their owners spare nothing to make them more picturesque. The deep windows are rich with flowers—geraniums, begonias and carnations—and flowering vines climb over the latticework. In winter, tiny bags of suet for the birds hang beside the windows.

The people of the Engadine are a proud lot. There is a story about a queen, traveling incognito, who once tried to buy a copper kettle that took her fancy as she was visiting the home of an Engadine peasant. The man didn't want to sell, and an aide drew him aside to tell him that the lady was a ruling queen, not accustomed to having her wishes denied. "Very well," said the peasant, with a haughty gesture even the queen could not match, "I'll *give* her the kettle. But it is not for sale."

Susch, where the Flüela Pass road joins the main highway traversing the Engadine, is a quaint little place. The homes and other buildings here are all modern in construction if not in style, for the part of the village that lies on the left bank of the Inn was destroyed by fire in 1925, only the Evangelical Church being saved. Despite the latter's Roman tower, most of it is comparatively new, dating from 1515. During a restoration in 1742, the late-Gothic style of its windows was changed, but in 1933, on the evidence of recently discovered fragments, they were restored to their original form. Susch is sheltered by the magnificent Piz d'Arpiglias, towering above it like a sentinel.

From Susch, our route follows the River Inn northeast to Scuol (or Schuls), a portion of the trip that can be made by road or rail. It passes through several rocky gorges, through which the Inn tumbles in turbulent fashion, and then emerges into flower-filled plains with a pleasant chain of attractive hamlets: Lavin, Guarda, Ardez, and the quaintly named Ftan.

Guarda, a beautiful village, is under federal protection, to ensure that the peasant dwellings with their two-tone, etched ornamentation, called *sgraffiti,* shall remain unchanged. A narrow lane from Guarda leads through Bos-cha to Ardez. In Ardez, dominated by the ruins of Steinsberg Castle, are more of the graceful *sgraffiti* wall decorations, as well as some fine Italian ironwork, imported from Venice. Ftan, on a secondary road running higher up the hill, but parallel to the main highway, has a colorful old tower with a copper steeple. You'll get a good view, too, of Tarasp Castle, which is on the other side of the River Inn.

Scuol-Tarasp-Vulpera

Scuol (Schuls), Vulpera, and Tarasp, three villages with a combined population of 1,400, form virtually one holiday and health resort complex whose waters are reputed to be highly beneficial to sufferers from liver troubles. Frequented mainly by Swiss and Germans, it is being discovered by British ånd Americans. Beautifully located in the open valley of the river Inn whose grass-covered and wooded sides are backed by mountains, Scuol-Tarasp-Vulpera have hitherto been highly popular summer resorts. Now, thanks to a network of gondola cars and skilifts, and unobstructed south-facing slopes, they are taking on a new role as winter sports resorts as well.

From Scuol and Vulpera, a bus goes up to the historic Tarasp Castle in half an hour, or the trip makes a nice hike of about an hour and a half. It is a real dream castle, pure white, perched on top of a sheer cliff some 500 feet above the valley. Notice the Austrian coats of arms, slit windows, painted shields and double walls. The main tower and chapel date from the 11th century, when it was the stronghold of the knights of Tarasp. Long a source of discord between the powerful Bishop of Chur and the Count of Tyrol, it became the seat of the Austrian governors until the last century, when the Grisons joined the Swiss Confederation. Some years ago, it was sold to a toothpaste manufacturer who spent three million Swiss francs restoring it and then gave it to the Prince of Hesse.

The Swiss National Park

At Tarasp, we have to return along the road to Susch, but instead of turning to go over the Flüela Pass again, we continue up the valley, along the banks of the River Inn, to St. Moritz. Four miles past Susch is the village of Zernez. Close by is the entrance to the Swiss National Park. Patterned after the national parks in the United States, this was created in 1911 by a federal decree stating that "an island of untouched primitive natural existence is to develop here in the midst of the seething waves of civilization." The phraseology seems a bit extreme in view of the tranquility of the surroundings, for here the waves of civilization don't seethe very hard. Within the limits of the seventy-square-mile park there is absolute protection for plants and animals; no shot can be fired, no flower picked, no tree cut down, and it is forbidden to camp or light fires. There is not even the sound of a cowbell since cattle can't be pastured in the park. Herds of chamois roam over the rocks, roebuck feed under the larch trees, deer drink from the transparent, icy streams. The ibex, historic emblem of the Grisons, is also to be seen.

The park lies in a mountainous region, the cleft of the Ofen Pass dividing it in two. But although the highest peak is little more than 10,000 feet, the mountains are extremely rugged, and the valleys, filled with rocky debris, are among the wildest in the Alps. There are numerous hanging glaciers. Nevertheless, walking about the park is a delight, if a hilly one, for there are prepared paths, clearly marked, and visitors must follow them. The season lasts from about the middle of June, after the snow has melted, until it falls again in the autumn.

The park is the richest district in all the Alps for flowers because of its great differences in altitude, its varying rock types and formations, and its position astride the boundary between eastern and western Alpine flora. You'll see many rare plants that are to be found nowhere else in Switzerland as well as alpenroses, edelweiss, dwarf roses, valerian, mountain poppies, primroses, Alpine grasses, shrubs, and almost every variety of meadow flower and Alpine tree. The flowers are normally at their best in the second half of June. Then, although this may vary slightly according to the severity and timing of the preceding winter, the place is a riot of color: gentian, fiery red catchfly, violets of every shade, saxifrage, white Pyrenean and Alpine ranunculus, and a host of other flowers forming a kaleidoscope of bright and varied color in the most superb natural setting.

But the Swiss National Park is not a solitary, floral oasis. Almost wherever you go in the Engadine, you'll find an abundance of wild flowers. Hardly has the last snow of winter melted before the meadows are carpeted with crocuses and soldanella, sometimes even pushing their blossoms through the snow itself. By mid-May, unless it is a late winter, the valleys are covered with millions of white crocuses. Then comes the season of the hairy anemones in pastel shades, found on the hillsides, and before these are faded, the blue gentians start to bloom. Towards the end of June, when the haymaking begins, the beauty of the lower meadows is somewhat spoiled, but the flowers of the high pastures and the mountains remain throughout the summer with a coloring far more intense than anything at lower altitudes. It is worth remembering that many of the wild flowers, almost all except the commonest, are protected by strict cantonal laws. It is forbidden to pick or remove them in large quantities—"large quantities" being officially defined as more than ten specimens.

All the way from Scuol, our road has been closely following the River Inn, as it has done since it crossed the Austrian frontier (fifteen miles the other side of Scuol) to enter the lower Engadine. And it continues to do so through the upper Engadine and past St. Moritz, to the river's source near Maloja. It's a lovely ride, the road climbing and twisting gently but steadily, with peaks, often snow-capped, to either side, and the river gushing in foaming torrents below. The villages are all lovely, and there are many old churches and, not least, some splendid examples of Engadine houses.

The Upper Engadine

After Zernez, the road passes the castle of Rietberg, owned by the Planta family. The Planta crest, a bear's paw, is a familiar sight in the Grisons, and members of the family still live there. They rose to importance subsequent to 1295, when they were named hereditary bailiffs to the bishops of Chur.

Just beyond Zernez, near Brail, you will pass from the lower to the upper Engadine, then through the surprisingly named little resort of S-chanf to Zuoz. Spare a short while here, for Zuoz, a small winter sports and summer resort as well as an education center, is noted for its Engadine houses, many of which were constructed for the Planta family, this village being their home. Indeed, you'll see the Planta family emblem, a bear, on top of the fountain in the main square. The Planta bear's paw is also a frequent decoration in the little church with its tall tower and needle-like spire.

Samedan and Celerina

A few miles farther on, you'll come to Samedan and Celerina, two charming Engadine villages that, if it were not for their vast difference in character, might be called suburbs of St. Moritz. From Samedan you have a magnificent view of the Bernina chain of mountains: Piz Palü, 12,900 feet; Piz Morteratsch, 12,300 feet; Piz Bernina, 13,300 feet; Piz Roseg, 12,900 feet; Piz Tschierva, 11,700 feet; Piz Rosatsch, 10,200 feet; Piz Corvatsch, 11,300 feet; and many others. Samedan also has a golf course and is close to the Upper Engadine airport.

The trip up to Muottas Muragl should not be missed, since it provides a superb view over the lovely valley of the Inn. A funicular goes in fifteen minutes from Punt Muragl, between Samedan and Pontresina, to the summit, reaching an altitude of 8,050 feet, or 2,300 feet above the valley floor. From the top you get an eagle's eye view of St. Moritz far below, and the chain of lakes stretching almost to Maloja, ten miles away, and the nearby watershed of Piz Lunghin. There, within about 500 yards, are the sources of the river Mera, flowing southwest to Lake Como and the Adriatic, the river Inn flowing through the Engadine and eventually to the Danube and Black Sea, and a stream which flows north into the river Julier and thence to the Rhine and North Sea. Understandably, the Engadine is called "the roof of Europe". The mountain panorama forms a full semicircle, with Piz Languard to the southeast and ending with Piz Kesch in the northwest. In the south, near the white peak of the famed Piz Palü, the highest mountains in the Bernina group may be seen, including Piz Bernina itself, above the dark mass of Piz Chalchagn. The wide ridge of Piz Tschierva and the pointed Piz Roseg follow, and then the glacier world of the Sella group, above the cleft of the Roseg Valley. In the foreground, one sees the massive blocks of Piz Rosatsch and Surlej, and farther behind the lovely Piz La Margna, while the peaks of the Bergell mountains loom over the

Maloja Pass. The west side of the valley is bounded by Piz Lagrev, flanked by Piz Julier and Piz Albana, which in turn give way to Piz Nair and the wild and rocky tower of Piz Ot. Deep down on the left, just out of sight, is Pontresina, where the Bernina and Roseg valleys meet, and to the right, in the Inn valley, is Celerina.

Celerina, St. Moritz's little brother, is a first-rate ski resort in its own right with the additional advantage of easy access to all the winter sports facilities of its more celebrated neighbor. The renowned Cresta run, mecca for bobsledders, ends here.

Among the main attractions of the upper Engadine are the many mountain railroads, cableways, etc., some of them built in the last few years. Whether it's for a climbing excursion or just for an afternoon's walk, you can go from St. Moritz to Corviglia by funicular and from there by cableway to Piz Nair, a wonderful 10,000-foot mountaintop viewpoint that has a restaurant and café. On the terrace you can admire the fabulous view while sunbathing in a deckchair with a glass of your favorite potion close at hand. You can go from Celerina by cableway to Val Saluver or, as we have seen, by funicular to Muottas Muragl; from Pontresina by chairlift to Alp Languard; from Bernina by cableway to Diavolezza or to Piz Lagalb; and from Surlej, between Lakes Champfèr and Silvaplana, to Piz Corvatsch (over 10,800 ft.) or from Sils to Furtschellas.

St. Moritz

What eastern Switzerland lacks in large cities is made up for with places bearing world-famous names. Foremost among them is a little village whose natural beauties and health-giving baths have caused it to grow into one of Europe's most famous resorts—St. Moritz. The average visitor thinks of St. Moritz, the site of the 1928 and 1948 Winter Olympics and the setting for a half-dozen films, as something of a world capital. If he goes there, during either the winter or summer season, when the plush hotels are crowded with what remains of European nobility, statesmen, film stars, and Arab oil sheiks, he will not be disappointed. St. Moritz is the playground of the world and a fashionable one, too. But in the summer, it loses some of its glitter, and prices are appreciably less than in winter. Many, indeed, consider that in the time of lowest prices—the latter half of June or early July—St. Moritz is at its best, for then the mountainsides are covered with spring flowers.

It has been fashionable for quite some time. Bronze relics uncovered in 1907 and now on view in the Engadine Museum at St. Moritz indicate that the healing qualities of its waters were known at least 3,000 years ago, long before Rome was founded. The Romans had a settlement there, and later—exactly when is not known—a church was founded on the site and dedicated to Mauritius, one of the early Christian martyrs. The first historical reference to the town was in 1139; and in 1537, Paracelsus, the great Renaissance physician, described the health-giving properties of the St. Moritz springs in detailed treatises. It is said that toward the end of the 17th century, the Duke of Parma led a retinue of twenty-five persons over the mountain passes to take the waters, the first of a still-continuing parade of royal visitors seeking to rejuvenate their jaded livers by drinking from the bubbling fount at the foot of the towering Piz Rosatsch. In 1747, a description of the town speaks of the presence of "cavaliers, marchgraves, and also princes," and in 1793, a German writer said of the taste of the mineral water that "it puckers lips and tongue like the sharpest vinegar, goes to the head and is like champagne in the nose."

St. Moritz grew into a major tourist resort in the last century after the bed of the Inn was altered to prevent the river from destroying the mineral spring. This early engineering feat was carried out by subterfuge. The elders of the village were opposed to the "new-fangled" development, so, when they were all away at a cattle market in Tirano, the younger men voted for the project in a town meeting and had it started by the time they returned. Then the first of the big luxury hotels was built, and by 1859 *Il Fögl Ladin,* the Romansch-language newspaper now published in Samedan, proudly announced that "the unheard-of number of 450 visitors" had come during the year. A half century later, in 1910, the same newspaper more calmly recorded that 10,000 persons had visited St. Moritz.

The elders apparently learned their lesson, for ever since they have devoted themselves to improving the resort and its facilities. After Edison had displayed his electric light at the Paris Exhibition of 1878, it was introduced in St. Moritz by Johannes Badrutt, one of Switzerland's great hoteliers, and a man who did as much as anyone to make St. Moritz into a fashionable winter sports resort. Six years later, St. Moritz pioneered in winter sports with the construction of the first toboggan run—the Cresta—which, as it happened, started on Badrutt's own grounds. Then, in 1895, Philipp Mark, president of the local tourist bureau, gave one of the first ski-jumping exhibitions on a jump he had built himself in St. Moritz. The Olympic jump, with a difference in height of 465 feet from takeoff to landing run, was made for the second-ever Winter Olympics, held here in 1928—an era when winter sports were regarded as a somewhat curious activity indulged in by the eccentric few with time to spare for a winter holiday and purses big enough to pay for it.

Twenty years later—1948—when the Winter Olympics were again held in St. Moritz, the resort became the only one to have staged them twice. Undoubtedly these two events were partially responsible for the superb facilities which have made St. Moritz synonymous with winter sports.

St. Moritz itself is located at an altitude of 6,050 feet in the upper Engadine valley, on the shores of the lovely sky-blue Lake of St. Moritz. The latter is the northernmost of a chain of four lakes around which are scattered a number of resorts that give the upper Engadine much of its charm. The other three are Lakes Champfèr, Silvaplana and Sils. Through all of them flows the Inn, here an infant river which rises nearby. The valley is enclosed by parallel mountain ranges, the Bernina chain on the southeast and the Julier chain to the northwest.

The resort of St. Moritz is in three parts—St. Moritz-Dorf, situated on a mountain terrace 200 feet above the lake, St. Moritz-Bad charmingly located at the end of the lake, and Champfèr-Suvretta. After its heyday as a spa, towards the end of the 19th century, St. Moritz-Bad began to take a back seat to St. Moritz-Dorf, the sparkling winter resort. But in recent years Bad has staged a comeback by laying heavy emphasis on skiing and other winter sports. In 1973 it started a new direct aerial cableway to Signal, feeding the Plateau Nair skilift. In 1976 it opened a splendid spa establishment. Unfortunately, growth has brought Bad ultra-modern buildings, many of which have little architectural merit and blend neither with each other nor with the superb scenery. The charming little lakeside resort is beginning to look like a "Costa Moritza", but its popularity seems assured.

As a town, St. Moritz-Dorf has only minor attractions. There is a leaning tower, all that remains of an old village church built in 1573, and the Segantini Museum, which contains some works by Giovanni Segantini, the versatile 19th-century Italian artist who settled in the Grisons and became a distinguished painter of Alpine life and scenery. Outside is the Olympic Stone listing all the medal winners at the St. Moritz Winter Olympics. The Engadine Museum, in addition to the relics of prehistoric times previously mentioned, has an interesting collection of Engadine furniture. On the modern side, the town has some of the most fashionable shops in Switzerland.

Distractions at St. Moritz are virtually unlimited for the active sportsman, in either winter or summer. It is a skier's paradise, of course, and also offers wonderful ice skating, bobsledding, and riding and horse racing on the frozen lake. In summer, there's swimming, sailing, riding, mountain-climbing, golf, tennis and, in the River Inn, some of the best fishing in Switzerland. Serious connoisseurs of night life and gambling may be a little bored, although in a modest way both are available. The ice rink is open all year.

On Lake Silvaplana, barely four miles from St. Moritz, is the Engadine village of Silvaplana, the first of the unspoiled village resorts outside the St. Moritz complex. Next comes Sils-Baselgia, little more than a couple of excellent hotels, and the tiny village of Sils-Maria, where Nietzsche wrote *Thus Spake Zarathustra.* Peace, quiet and good hotels are keynotes at Maria. Its summer highspots are horse-drawn bus excursions up the beautiful Fex Valley, or gentle mountain hiking amid breathtaking scenery. In winter its attraction is skiing without queueing via the Furtschellas cable car; and always the life and amenities of St. Moritz can be reached easily and quickly.

Pontresina

Half a dozen miles east of St. Moritz, and below our earlier viewpoint on Muottas Muragl, is another famous summer and winter resort, Pontresina, one of whose greatest assets is its altitude—about 6,000 feet above sea level, only a few feet less than St. Moritz itself. Amply provided with fine hotels, Pontresina has everything the holidaymaker could desire. It stands at the center of a network of 124 miles of well-kept paths, some of them passing spectacularly alongside the glaciers that descend from the flanks of the snow-covered mountains above. If walking is too tame for you, there are plenty of guides to take you mountaineering. Or you can sit peacefully under the shaggy pines of the Tais woods and listen to the morning concerts given daily from June through September. There is golf at the nearby eighteen-hole golf course, tennis, swimming in a splendid indoor pool, trout fishing in streams and lakes, two of which are free, and horse riding. The most popular excursion is by horse-drawn bus up the Val Roseg, a really lovely high Alpine valley. It takes about an hour each way, and there's a good restaurant at the terminus.

In winter, Pontresina turns to skiing. Just behind the village is the Alp Languard chairlift, the first level being for beginners, the second recommended only for moderately good skiers. At Bernina, about five miles up the valley by train or bus, are the high rise cable cars to Diavolezza and Lagalb, but the latter's for piste-bashers only. Pontresina is a major ski-touring center with 50 mapped-out tours. It's got a toboggan run, skating, curling and, for those who don't ski, special routes kept open for winter walking. From Pontresina, too, it is easy to get to any of the various cable cars, mountain railways and lifts in the Upper Engadine.

From Pontresina, the Bernina Railway follows the old Bernina post road over the pass to Tirano, Italy, through magnificent scenic country, wild and somewhat grim on the north side of the summit, quickly changing to lush meadows and trees on the southern descent, indicating the warmer, Italian-like climate.

Although our itinerary at the start of this chapter planned a return from St. Moritz to Chur by post bus over the Julier Pass, there is an alternative, and a very attractive one, too. For you can go back by the Rhaetian Railway through the Albula tunnel and down the Albula valley via Filisur, Tiefencastel and Thusis—a fantastic journey in which the gallant little train twists and weaves its way among outstandingly fine mountain scenery well matched by the engineering skill of the railway's constructors. But our planned route is by road over the Julier Pass, which, incidentally, is kept open throughout the winter. From St. Moritz the road goes southwest through Champfèr to Silvaplana, where the Julier road branches northward. If you miss the turning you'll be on the road which goes all the way to Lake Como; very nice, but not what we have in mind.

The Julier Route

The Julier route is one of the three great Alpine passes (the Great St. Bernard and the Splügen are the other two) that are known to have been used by the Romans and, even in those days, the Julier was favored because of its immunity from avalanches. The present road, built between 1820 and 1826, is marked near the top with two pillars about five feet high which, historians say, are the remains of a Roman temple. After the initial steep climb, giving some fine glimpses of the Upper Engadine lakes, the road, dominated by Piz Julier, Piz Albana and Piz Polaschin, climbs more gently, flanked by grim but impressive mountains and tumbling streams. At the 7,500 ft. summit there's a souvenir shop and parking place, and shortly afterwards the Julier Hospice, where refreshments can be obtained.

The first village of any importance after leaving Silvaplana is Bivio, which is about five miles beyond the summit, at an altitude of 5,850 feet. A former Roman settlement named Stabulum Bivio, it is called Bivio in Italian, Stalla in German, and Beiva in Romansch, and those who live here speak all three languages. The village itself is the entrance to the beautiful Val d'Err. From here our road follows the banks of the turbulent Julia River through splendid rocky gorges and over tempestuous cascades to Mulegns and Savognin, passing the artificial Lake of Marmorera, built to store water for hydroelectric power stations. Savognin is an unpretentious winter sports resort with sunny slopes served by a good network of gondola cars, chairlifts and skilifts going up to 8,900 feet. It's got a fine indoor pool and a dozen or more surprisingly good hotels from first class down. In summer there are splendid signposted mountain walks, gondola cars and chairlifts giving easy access to the higher ones. For several years Savognin was the residence of the celebrated painter Segantini. The district and its people are well represented in his works which you'll see everywhere—but only reproductions; originals are very expensive. Six miles farther on we come to Tiefencastel, called Casti in Romansch, which is where the River Julia flows into the Albula. The village was entirely destroyed by fire in 1890, but above the "new" one the tall white church of St. Ambrosius still stands out beautifully against the background of fir trees that cover the encroaching hills. A short distance from Tiefencastel is Vazerol, where there is a monument commemorating the oath of eternal union sworn by the "Free Leagues" in 1471.

At Tiefencastel one can either take the direct road to Chur via Lenzerheide and Churwalden, or go on a more circuitous route by Thusis.

Lenzerheide, which almost adjoins Valbella, is a charming winter and summer resort at an altitude of 5,000 feet, which enjoys long hours of sunshine and is virtually free of fog because of its situation in a high valley open to the south. It has two seasons, June-September (mountain climbers prefer this last month) and December 15 to April.

Although the Lenzerheide-Valbella area is specially good for the intermediate grade skier, one of its principal attractions is the number of practice slopes which nature has thoughtfully provided for beginners. Another is the unusually good assortment of cable cars, chairlifts and skilifts, including, of course, the cable car up to Parpaner Rothorn (9,400 feet).

The organization of pleasures at this resort is thorough. It has an eighteen-hole golf course; there are seven tennis courts with instructors in attendance; horses are available for riding; the Lake of Lenzerheide offers swimming and rowing; you may fish in the Julia and Albula rivers; there is a delightful indoor swimming pool at the Posthotel Valbella; guided mountain excursions are organized every week during July and August; free botanic excursions highlight June, July and August; and if you want to go walking, the resort will hand you a map of the various routes.

At Churwalden, there is the Albert Schweitzer College, its curriculum heavily flavored with the philosophical and religious teachings of the late Sage of Lambaréne. But if you have not made too many stops since leaving St. Moritz, the day will still be young and the longer route by way of Thusis and Reichenau will prove inviting. You can go by train, bus or car.

Tiefencastel to Flims

The rail trip from Tiefencastel to Thusis is particularly interesting from an engineering point of view, since this section of the Rhaetian Railway passes through sixteen tunnels, one of them over three and a half miles long. There are also twenty-seven bridges or viaducts. One of these is the celebrated Solis Viaduct, the center arch being 137 feet across and 293 feet high. The route is wonderfully scenic, threading through spectacular gorges and canyons, interspersed with peaceful valleys and pine forests for contrast.

Thusis, easily the most important town of the Domleschg Valley with about 1,700 inhabitants, is surrounded by high mountains and heavy forests. It has a late-Gothic church dating from 1506 and an open-air lido encircled by forest. The town is the starting point for climbers seeking to conquer the Piz Beverin, the Piz Curver, or the Stätzerhorn. Here the Albula River joins the Hinterrhein (or Upper Rhine). Perched on the rocky heights guarding the entrance to the Via Mala are the ruins of the old Hohenrhaetien Castle. The famous Via Mala, an ancient and dramatic road writhing along the bottom of a deep ravine, has now been replaced by a fine new one, thus cutting out the bottleneck in this important route which leads south, through Andeer, to the Splügen and San Bernardino passes. The latter has now been bypassed by a splendid tunnel cut through the mountain. San Bernadino is a small winter sports resort.

From Thusis, we enter the fertile Domleschg Valley, through which flows the Upper Rhine, to join the Lower Rhine (Vorderrhein) at Reichenau. This valley is one of the most scenic of the area, with numerous old castles, charming villages, and blossoming orchards, with the stately Stätzerhorn towering above it to the east like a sentinel. Houses seen here are typical of the entire Grisons area, high, stuccoed structures with red-tiled roofs and small-paned windows set deep into the thick walls as protection against the cold. There is frequently a wooden balcony-porch running around the house at the second story, with gracefully carved railings invariably bordered with masses of flowers.

Rothenbrunnen, which comes next, is another of the many spas in the Grisons, the mineral waters containing iron. Rothenbrunnen has a children's home, and there are old castles all over the place. In the triangle formed by the junction of the Upper Rhine and the Lower Rhine lies Reichenau Castle, which has a long and fascinating history. Built in the 14th century, it was in 1793 the refuge of the then-exiled future King of France, Louis-Philippe. He lived there under the name of "Professor Chabaud." Later it passed into the hands of the Plantas, the family which owned so many of the castles in the Grisons.

From Reichenau-Tamins—a twin village lying on both banks of the river—it is only six miles to Chur, our starting point, via the attractive village of Ems. However, if you have time, it is well worthwhile making a detour westward to Flims, a summer and winter resort in the Grisons Oberland, the region extending from Reichenau along the Vorderrhein (or Lower Rhine) and as far as Oberalp, near Andermatt.

Located at an altitude of 3,700 feet, on a south-facing terrace overlooking the Rhine Valley, and surrounded by grassy slopes and pine forests beyond which are majestic mountains, Flims is in two sections. Flims-Dorf, mostly villas, is among the meadows. The majority of the hotels are scattered among the pinetrees of adjacent Flims-Waldhaus. Perhaps the greatest summer asset of Flims is the Caumasee, a small lake fed by warm springs that make it possible to swim there as early as June. In winter, aerial cableways to Cassonsgrat (8,650 ft.) and Grauberg (7,300 ft.) as well as several skilifts serve the broad snowfields above the village. A mile or so down the road from Waldhaus is Laax, a nice little village with a couple of small lakes. More important, it's a relatively new but up-and-coming skiing center with some excellent top medium grade and first class hotels. Close to Laax are the cable cars to Crap Sogn Gion (7,250 ft.) and Crap Masegu (8,150 ft.) with a well-planned system of linking skilifts.

Chur to Fashionable Arosa

From Chur one can strike east by rail or road towards the center of the circle we have just completed. It's a dead-end route, both rail and road stopping at the third of the three major resorts of the Grisons—Arosa. It's a long, steep, straggling valley town nearly 6,000 feet above sea level. Aside from the invigorating atmosphere and clean, crystal-clear air that this altitude guarantees, Arosa has gained the reputation of being an unusually friendly resort. The largest of its many hotels is moderately sized so there is none of the chilling formality or impersonal efficiency sometimes found in mammoth establishments.

The accent is on freedom. It's not compulsorily dressy, nor deliberately fashionable, but it can be smart if one wants it that way. In the top hotels a few men may wear dinner jackets, but if they do it's because they want to, not because they have to. It follows that Arosa has fallen heir to some of those who find the winter elegance, ostentation and glitter of St. Moritz just a trifle overbearing.

One of Arosa's specialties is a sport that has always appealed to the upper crust—horseracing. But here it is on snow and ice, and in winter. For although Arosa is an excellent summer resort like St. Moritz, it is more fashionable in the winter, and more popular. And not surprisingly, either, for the ski runs are among the best in Switzerland and are primarily for the average skier. There is always enough snow and, unlike many resorts, one can ski back right down into the village. Arosa has over seventy hotels as well as a number of pensions. These can accommodate about 6,000 visitors, and they need some 2,600 employees, almost the same number as the town's permanent population.

It would be hard to say whether Arosa offers the visitor more in summer or winter. In the former, there is the bathing beach on the little lake, with a swimming instructor at hand, and some of the hotels which open in summer have indoor pools. There are several tennis courts, an artificial ice rink, and a 9-hole golf course, as well as fishing on either of two lakes, and boats for hire. And there are concerts, dances and a seemingly endless program of varied entertainment and sporting events.

In winter, the broad skiing fields above the tree line are made accessible to everyone by a good network of cleverly located skilifts and linking runs, as well as the well-known cable car to Weisshorn (8,700 ft.) and gondola cars to Hörnli (8,200 ft.). Indeed, there are said to be nearly forty miles of prepared runs. The ski school, which has over a hundred instructors, is one of Switzerland's largest. Curling, skating and ice hockey take place on several rinks, the Obersee Ice Stadium having a roofed grandstand for spectators of the events which are held there. For non-skiers (and 50% of Arosa's winter visitors are just that) there are many miles of carefully prepared paths for winter walking, and if you hanker after something different you can take the popular Arlenwald Road sleigh ride. And winter and summer you have a wide selection of entertainment and can enjoy magnificent mountain scenery which is as elegant as the resort itself.

THE VALAIS AND ALPES VAUDOISES

Up the Rhône to the Simplon and Gletsch

Extending along the valley of the upper Rhône from Lake Geneva to the river's source, the scenic canton of Valais (Wallis in German) is one of the most magnificent regions in Europe. The river valley itself is roughly L-shaped, with the angle resting on the town of Martigny, where the Val d'Entremont branches off to lead to the Great St. Bernard Pass. It is the right, or long, leg of the L that is the most characteristic and imposing part of the region.

But the Valais is far more than the riverbed of the Rhône and its cliff-like walls. It is an Alpine network with a score or more of narrow valleys that wind left and right into even more remote areas. Mark Twain wrote in *A Tramp Abroad* of meeting British tourists at Zermatt at the end of one of the side valleys—they had made the journey by mule—but with a few hardy exceptions, such encounters used to be rare. Until quite recent times, only the feet of the mountain folk and their animals could navigate the precipitous hillsides. Even today, some of these more remote districts rarely see a tourist.

As in all Swiss areas, the Valais enjoys the freedom of choice in which language to use. Here, in fact, both German and French are spoken.

Exploring the Valais

From Geneva, the most direct route by road to the Valais leads along the precipitous southern shore of Lake Geneva, which, you will recall, cuts across a corner of France. It is about fifty-five miles to St. Maurice, the real beginning of the Rhône Valley. The usual route, however, goes along the gentler northern shore, entirely in Switzerland, and is about a third longer, although most of this route is covered by fast motorway.

Assuming you have elected to drive along the northern shore, you leave Lake Geneva at Villeneuve, a mile or so beyond Montreux and the Castle of Chillon, and turn inland to drive southeastwards up the Rhône, this side of the river, for the time being, in the Canton of Vaud. At this stage, the valley is broad and alluvial, with distant peaks hinting at more rugged scenery ahead. Seven miles later, at Aigle, the mountains are already beginning to crowd in on each side.

Leysin, in the Canton of Vaud, a popular summer and winter resort, is reached by turning off the main highway to the left and following a winding road for about ten miles up to an altitude of 4,700 feet (or by taking the cogwheel railway from Aigle). The town faces south and enjoys much sun.

Back in the valley, just beyond Aigle, another road thrusts upward to the left, or north. Follow this eight miles and you come to Chesières, and immediately afterwards to Villars (4,200 ft.), one of the region's better-known summer and winter resorts, with splendid views and a nine-hole golf course. From Villars a mountain railway climbs up to Bretaye (6,100 ft.), at the foot of Chamossaire, from which skilifts and chairlifts fan out in all directions to the surrounding heights, where you can find wonderful ski-runs in winter and fine walks in summer. There is also a cable car to Roc d'Orsay (6,600 ft.).

If you have made this detour, instead of returning to Aigle, you can continue beyond Villars. Almost immediately, the road (recently widened) begins its long winding descent, offering a succession of glorious views and passing through several picturesque villages before bringing you back to the main highway at Bex, some six miles beyond Aigle. The whole detour from Aigle to Bex will take rather less than an hour of gentle, if hilly, driving. But try to allow more. It's difficult to resist stopping to admire views, inspect villages, particularly on the downward run, and explore Villars. At Bex, there is complete contrast because, thanks to its sheltered position on the valley floor, this long-established brine spa enjoys a very mild climate—pomegranates, figs and grapes grow here.

Champéry and the Val d'Illiez

Another detour, this time to the southwest, starts from Bex. Don't miss it. You cross the River Rhône, passing out of the Canton of Vaud into that of Valais, go through the industrial center of Monthey, three miles to the west, and then turn, twisting and climbing up the valley that opens before you. After about a mile, a sharp right fork leads up to Morgins, a small mountain and skiing resort at 4,600 feet, practically on the French frontier. Keep left and follow the western flank of the cathedral-like Dents du Midi, the final escarpment of the Mont Blanc range, and you arrive at Champéry, a winter sports and summer resort perched 3,500 feet up in the Val d'Illiez. It has an ideal camping ground a short distance from the village and is an excellent center for walking excursions and skiing. A cable car swings you a good half mile higher to Planachaux (5,800 ft.), where a collection of skilifts gives access to some splendid runs. From Champéry, it's twelve miles downhill to the Rhône again and St. Maurice.

St. Maurice is where the two main roads from Lake Geneva, which have hugged each side of the wide Rhône valley plain, converge. For it is here that both valley and river begin to change character. The mountains have closed in. The Rhône, although still a king-sized river, gradually loses its placidity, giving a foretaste of the mountain torrent it will become as we get nearer its source. St. Maurice owes its name, according to tradition, to Maurice, the leader of the Theban Legion who, with most of his men, was massacred here in A.D. 302 for refusing to acknowledge the pagan gods of Rome. To commemorate the martyrdom, an abbey was built; it rapidly grew in importance and wealth. Recent excavations near the abbey church, mostly 17th-century but partly dating from the 11th, have revealed the foundations of the original building. An outstandingly rich collection of treasures has been discovered, and these are certainly worth a visit.

Just before you reach Martigny, nine miles farther up the Rhône, another mountainous side trip beckons from the valley floor. A right-hand fork will take you west and then south along a narrow military road (dating from World War II) that weaves through the gorges of the Trient River.

Salvan is the first village in this remote valley. Frequented as a

The industry which made Switzerland famous is still based on individual craftsmanship.

In the center of Zurich is its old Urania quarter, with the Observatory as focal point.

The Jura is famous for skiing and cheese-making. When you feel like some après-ski gruyère, you'll be dealing with a small slice, not a 330-lb. mass.

The nation is dotted with examples of local inventions, including this cog-wheel ski train at Rigi, 6,000 feet up in Central Switzerland.

summer resort by Swiss families who rent chalets for the season, it has been so isolated for years that many old traditions survive. On festival days the women have a beautiful and distinctive dress topped by an intricate type of ruching (50 yards per hat) now made only by the older generation. On the evening of August 1, villagers in costume dance to the sound of lively fiddles. The next village, Les Marécottes, is little more than a cluster of chalets and small hotels in the pinewoods. Here the road ends, although a railway continues up the valley and eventually into France and Chamonix.

Martigny in ages past was a Roman camp called Octodorum. Today, as you've doubtless noted, it sits squarely astride a historic crossroads at the sharp angle of the River Rhône, the pivot of the L we were imagining. From the town, roads go over the Great St. Bernard Pass to Italy, the Forclaz Pass to France, along the upper Rhône to the Simplon Pass and beyond, and down the Rhone Valley to Lake Geneva.

The Great St. Bernard Pass

The Great St. Bernard Pass is the oldest and possibly the most famous of the Swiss crossings. Known and used by the Celts and Romans centuries before the birth of Christ, it has watched an endless stream of emperors, knights and simple travelers. In the 11th century, Frederick Barbarossa, the German king and Roman emperor, became almost a commuter over the pass as he went from one country to another to settle the problems which constantly beset him. Napoleon took an army of 40,000 across it en route to Marengo, where he defeated the Austrians in 1800. In somewhat greater comfort than Frederick or Napoleon, you will almost certainly want to explore the pass to the summit, either by car or, better still (because you can watch the scenery while someone else does the driving), by the Swiss postal buses that run to the famous hospice several times a day in summer.

Almost immediately after leaving Martigny, the road to the Grand St. Bernard Pass starts to climb up the valley of the Drance to the village of Sembrancher. Here, a road branches off to the left up the Bagnes Valley, and to the modern, exceptionally well-equipped resort of Verbier (at a height of 4,900 feet). In recent years, it has become very popular with the Swiss and French, thanks largely to the excellent ski-runs served by nearly three dozen assorted skilifts, chairlifts and cable cars, one going up to Mt. Gelé (over 9,900 ft.).

At Sembrancher, the St. Bernard Pass road enters the valley of

Entremont, and four miles farther on, you come to Orsières, where a road to the right leads up the Ferret Valley. It then forks right again to mile-high Champex, a small winter sports resort and a particularly beautiful place in summer due to its lakeside setting. It has a chairlift to La Breya (7,200 ft.). You can also reach Champex from Les Vollettes, near Martigny, but this is by a difficult road.

From Orsières, you begin to appreciate the formidable character of the Great St. Bernard. Rocks and mountains close in on all sides as you reach Bourg-St. Pierre, whose inn was patronized by Napoleon (the chair he is said to have used is on display). Except when the winters are unusually severe, the road is kept open to this point so that postal buses can continue to bring mail and food supplies for the monastery at the top of the pass. From here, whenever the pass is blocked with winter snows, the lay brothers and monks have to carry everything up to the hospice on their backs.

But for travelers today the romantic but formidable old pass, which for centuries has been closed by snow for more than half of each year, has lost much of its fear. For the splendidly engineered new road, which you have seen branching off the old one on which we have traveled, is the approach to the new three-and-one-half-mile-long St. Bernard Tunnel. This burrows through the mountain to emerge in Italy, thus enabling road traffic to use this important international route all the year round.

The hospice itself, bypassed by the new tunnel, is a gaunt block of gray stone standing at the highest point on the old road (8,100 ft.); its founder wanted to make sure that it could be seen from a distance. For centuries the hospice was a stopping-off point for pilgrims and weary travelers who were offered accommodation without charge whether for one night or many. (Now, you are directed to a nearby hotel—the *Grand St. Bernard*).

There is an interesting story about the foundation of the hospice. In the year 1048, Bernard of Menthon, who was Bishop of Aosta, in answer to a request by Hugues of Provence, set out to clear the Mons Jovis—as the St. Bernard was then called—of brigands and highway robbers. It is said that on reaching the summit of the pass the good bishop found a pagan temple, over which he threw his chasuble. The shrine immediately crumbled to dust and, by the same power, the bandits were utterly defeated. Then Bernard, with the help of the canons of his diocese, established the hospice.

The service rendered to travelers by the canons of St. Bernard through the Middle Ages is incalculable. Kings and princes rewarded the hospice by showering estates upon the order. By the 12th century, it owned seventy-nine estates in England and elsewhere, and among these were Priors Inn and the site of the present Savoy Hotel in London, as well as the Hospice of St. Nicholas and St. Bernard at Hornchurch (Essex).

The canons of St. Bernard are splendid athletes. Their training covers a period of seven years and includes not only the study of theology, but also intensive physical preparation, for the priests must pass the official examinations and test for mountain guides, climbers and professional skiers.

The St. Bernard dogs have for centuries been the surefooted helpers of the order. In 1949, after two years' travel on foot in Tibet, Canon Détry, of the St. Bernard Hospice, brought back proof that these dogs originated from Central Asia. The canon believes that in Greek and Roman times, Tibetan dogs were brought to Asia Minor with the silk caravans and used by the Romans as war dogs. When the Romans crossed the Alps, the dogs found their natural climate, and those that escaped from the Roman armies reverted here to their normal state.

From near the hospice there is a chairlift—said to be one of the highest in the world—which will take you to La Chenalette (9,200 ft.), from which, if you are lucky with the weather, you will have a view including no fewer than twenty-seven glaciers.

Beyond the hospice you quickly come to the customs post, the road then winding down into the Great St. Bernard Valley, where it joins up once more with the tunnel route. Before Aosta (Italy) is reached, you will notice that the vegetation is distinctly Mediterrannean in character, and you will find it difficult to imagine that in winter the hospice you have come from so quickly is utterly isolated from the world, snow drifts rising to the second story of the building, some twelve feet high.

Isérables and Sion

After allowing your senses to recover from the remarkable trip and sobering views of the St. Bernard, continue up the Rhône Valley, with terraced vineyards on its northern slopes and apricot trees in the middle. About nine miles from Martigny, you'll come to the village of Riddes, the terminus of a cable car that is the only way to get to Isérables, unless you care to walk up the mountainside.

This is an unforgettable excursion. The cable car rises in a straight line high above the meadows, depositing you on a platform at the entrance to the village, which is built like an eyrie sheer against the rock at a height of 3,400 feet. A single rough street, lined with rustic flower-decked chalets, leads to a venerable Romanesque church. The *mazots,* or barns, are raised on mushroom-shaped blocks to discourage mice from marauding among the winter food supplies and to ensure good air circulation.

The inhabitants of this ancient village have long had the curious nickname "Bedjuids." Some say it is derived from Bedouins and that the people are descended from the Saracen hordes who, after the battle of Poitiers in 732, overran some of the high Alpine valleys. An interesting point for ethnologists! Certainly the people here seem different from many of those in canton Valais, being stocky, swarthy, and dark-eyed.

Back at Riddes on the valley floor, another nine miles takes you to the capital of the Valais, Sion, marked by two rocky hills that materialize in front of you like a fairytale landscape. Crowning the first, Tourbillon, you'll see a ruined castle; on the other, Valére, there is a church. Both indicate the age and ecclesiastical importance of Sion, which has been a bishopric for nearly 1,500 years. Valére's church of Notre Dame, looking more like a fortified castle, dates from the 11th century, or even earlier. The ruins on Tourbillon are those of a bishop's residence built in the 13th century. From either hill, there is a splendid view of the city below. Don't miss Sion's late-Gothic cathedral, notable for its 9th-century Romanesque tower, nor, close by, both the 17th-century town hall, with its gracious carved doors and ancient clock, and the early 16th-century Supersaxo house. The latter is a superb example of deliberately ostentatious luxury carried out with impeccable taste.

Sion's ancient streets once rang with the echoes of pageantry and ecclesiastical pomp. But the town today is a market center, sharing with nearby Sierre the task of collecting the produce of a prosperous agricultural region, where fruit, vegetables and the vine provide a lucrative income. Valais strawberries and asparagus are flown to markets in London and Paris, and the canton produces some of the best wines in Switzerland. In April, the mass of blossoms in Valais orchards is not only a beautiful sight, but gives some indication of the immense amount of fruit to come.

The Valais, however, is not all fertile. It has rocks, mountain torrents and remote high Alpine valleys, so its farmers have to work hard to bring home a harvest. Many of the women wear national workaday costume: a black, long-sleeved dress, with tight bodice and full skirt, white blouse, black shoes and stockings, a colorful apron and a black straw hat trimmed with velvet. But their faces are often tired, and their hands toilworn.

Just north of Sion you can see a resort in the making. At Anzère, on what used to be an almost bare but sunny mountainside plateau, the

Swiss have built a carefully planned, deluxe holiday center with hotels, chalets, apartment blocks, skating rink, shops, large underground car park and all the necessary trappings, including a cable car to Pas-de-Maimbré (7,800 ft.) and seven skilifts. And to the southwest, on the opposite side of the Rhône valley, lies Haute Nendaz, a mountainside hamlet turned smart mini-resort, above it (at 5,200 ft.) being Super-Nendaz.

Up the Val d'Hérens to Evolène

From Sion a good road strikes south up the beautiful Val d'Hérens, past the curious, boulder-capped "pyramides" of Euseigne, to Evoléne and Les Haudères. Before the road was built the people of this valley had to be almost self supporting, and life was frugal. They developed a special homecraft—the spinning and weaving of wool. Nowadays, Evoléne homespun, coarse and warm, is used by many Swiss housewives for knitting into sweaters for their menfolk.

Evoléne's charm lies not only in its scenic beauty, but also in the old brown chalets and in the national costumes the women wear every day. The valley and road continue via Les Haudéres, its picturesque old chalets overshadowed by the heights of the Dents du Veisivi, to tiny Arolla (6,600 ft.), one of the highest resorts in the Valais and popular with mountaineers.

Excursions from Sierre

Ten miles farther up the valley of the Rhône from Sion lies Sierre, a busy market town that has thrived on a great aluminum plant at adjacent Chippis. Much of the town is modern, especially around the station and the terminal of the funicular railway to Montana. And the town boasts of being the sunniest place in the driest region of Switzerland—the Rhône Valley from Martigny to Sierre and beyond. from here, there are three attractive side trips.

The first leads up the northern slope to the adjoining, sophisticated resort complex of Crans-Montana, most attractively perched nearly 5,000 feet up on a spacious sunny plateau among woods, grassland and small lakes. Film stars (including Gina Lollobrigida), tycoons and other celebrities are two-a-penny in the excellent hotels, ultramodern apartment blocks and fashionable shops here. The resorts have a golf course, casino, several cable cars and a whole assortment of chairlifts and skilifts. And among the trees on the surrounding mountain slopes are several large hospitals, where various Swiss cantons and cities send their patients to recuperate—an indication of the health-giving properties of the region. The approach to Montana from Sierre is either by funicular or by an excellent road. But if you prefer it, you can turn left off the main Rhône highway just beyond St. Leonard (five miles downstream from Sierre), visit Montana and Crans, and then drop down into Sierre without any backtracking.

The second side trip leads northeast to Leukerbad (Loèche-les-Bains), an important health spa and winter sports resort set in a huge amphitheater of mountains at an altitude of 4,600 feet. It boasts the hottest springs in Switzerland. From here there are cable cars to Gemmi and Torrent (7,600 feet), where there are wonderful Alpine views and, especially at Gemmi, a famous selection of mountain hikes.

The third excursion is of a very different character. You turn south from Sierre and plunge into the high Alpine valley of Anniviers. Here live perhaps the only remaining nomadic people of Europe, the name of the valley being derived from the Latin "anni viatores" (year-round travelers).

The year of wondering starts in the spring when men, women and children leave their headquarters in the villages, taking with them their priest and schoolmaster. Only one man is left in each hamlet—as the firewatcher. The migrants first descend to the slopes of the valley around Niouc, where they stay a few weeks, living in barns, and *mazots,* to till communal land and plant wheat, maize and potatoes, This done, they move down the valley to Sierre, where they cultivate collectively owned vineyards under an almost feudal statute-labor system: every man resident in the commune is obliged to put in so many days' work. The work in the vineyards is done to the accompaniment of fife and drum (usually six players), which roll out tuneless little airs all day long. In late summer, the nomads move back up the high valley to gather in the crops and then go down again for the grape harvest. When the year's work on the land is over, they return to their mountain villages and remain there, snowed in all the winter.

Things have changed, however, in the picturesquely-sited old village of Zinal, at the head of the valley, once only accessible over a very bad road. Now, with a fine new road kept open throughout the winter it has become a small, carefully planned winter sports and summer resort with a cableway to Sorebois (8,000 feet). But the charming, rustic character of the village, with its ancient barns and chalets, has been retained, all new structures having to blend with the old.

About halfway between Sion and Zinal, at the mountainside village of Vissoie with its strategically placed old tower, a road branches off to Grimentz, a simple little winter sports and summer resort notable for its particularly picturesque old chalets. On the other side of Vissoie a short road climbs steeply up to the ski resort of St.-Luc, now with one of the longest Swiss skilifts.

Zermatt and the Matterhorn

From Sierre, the Rhône road continues eighteen miles up to Visp. At the halfway point, just beyond Turtmann, it passes a left-hand turnoff to the beautiful Lötschen Valley. Visp is the junction for the spectacular railway which, helped by rack-and-pinion, climbs up gradients as steep as 1 in 8 on its one-and-one-half-hour journey to Zermatt. Past picturesque mountain pastures, across rushing torrents, and through steep-sided narrow valleys, it curves and climbs up into the realm of snowy peaks and glaciers. When opened in 1891, it was considered one of the major engineering feats of the time—even today it is a railway marvel. There is no road to Zermatt but from Visp you can drive as far as Täsch (vast car park at the station). There you have to take one of the frequent electric trains for the remaining three miles to Zermatt itself—where no private cars are allowed.

Despite world fame, Zermatt is a pint-sized town with barely 3,200 inhabitants; a little place with a lot of personality and an absolute ban on automobiles. Strolling down Bahnhofstrasse, Zermatt's principal street, the only dangers are the silent, electric mini-trucks which carry baggage between the station and the hotels, a few horse cabs, and a herd of about eighty goats which trot ceremoniously through the town, their bells clanging loudly, at 8:30 each morning.

At an altitude of 5,300 feet, Zermatt is set in a hollow of meadows and trees ringed by mighty mountains, including the unmistakable triangular mass of Matterhorn (14,690 ft.), or Mont Cervin, as the French-speaking Swiss prefer to call it. In winter, skiing is the great attraction, lasting until April on the more accessible runs, and right through the summer in the Theodul Pass area. There are cable cars, chairlifts and skilifts galore, nearly a score of skating and curling rinks, and every possible facility for mountain climbing. Indeed, the name Zermatt is synonymous with mountaineering. Over the last hundred years or more, Zermatt's guides have become world famous and have accompanied expeditions to the Himalayas and other great mountain ranges of the world.

At 5:30 a.m. on Friday, July 13th, 1865, in the tiny hamlet of

Zermatt, a certain Alexander Seiler—we'll meet him again in the next paragraph—stood at the door of his newly acquired hotel waving goodbye to a party of seven men starting off on a dangerous and historic climb. They were Edward Whymper, the Rev. Charles Hudson, Douglas Hadow and Lord Francis Douglas, with three guides, two Swiss—Peter Taugwalder and his son—and one French, Michel Croz. The next day, at 1:40 p.m., Whymper and his party achieved their objective by becoming the first people ever to set foot on the summit of the Matterhorn. But disaster followed: on the way down, Hadow slipped, a rope broke, and all except Whymper and the Taugwalders were killed by falling 4,000 feet down the North Wall.

And what about Alexander Seiler, who waved farewell to the ill-fated party? He was new to Zermatt, having just purchased the tiny village's original hotel—Lauber's Inn—which he renamed *Monte Rosa Hotel*. But he proved to be a born hotelier and the Monte Rosa became merely the first of the famous Seiler group of hotels.

From Zermatt to Gornergrat runs one of the highest cogwheel railways in Europe. Gornergrat has inspired so many grandiloquent descriptions that it is enough to say that among all your memories of Switzerland one of the most vivid will be of standing here at an altitude of nearly 10,200 feet, gazing across glistening glaciers to Monte Rosa (the mountain; not the hotel!), the Matterhorn and anything up to fifty or so almost equally majestic peaks, as well as a grand total of thirty-two glaciers.

Another excellent excursion from Zermatt, this time a three-stage one, is to take the chairlift to Sunnega (7,500 ft.), the gondola car to Blauherd (8,500 ft.), and finally the cable car to Findeln Rothorn (10,200 ft.), where once again—if you're lucky with the weather—the view will make you forget the cost. You can also go to Schwarzee, nearly 8,500 feet, by cableway. From there, the awe-inspiring Matterhorn seems almost near enough to touch. Or you can take the cable car to Trockener Steg (9,700 ft.), where there's the largest summer skiing area in the Alps.

Saas-Fee and Grächen

Zermatt is at the head of one of the two valleys that lead south from Visp. In the other—the road forks at Stalden—is the important winter and summer resort of Saas-Fee at 5,900 feet. Besides a number of skilifts, there are cable cars to Längfluh (9,400 ft.), starting point for skiing and walking tours, at the foot of the Dom, a peak even higher than the Matterhorn, and to Felskinn (9,800 ft.) as well as gondola cars to Hannig (7,800 ft.) and Plattjen (8,300 ft.). From Saas-Fee you can usually ski until mid-July at Felskinn.

A new, up-and-coming holiday resort is Grächen, a sunny village lying on a magnificent mountain-side terrace at an altitude of 5,300 feet. You can reach it by car, or postal bus from St. Niklaus Station. It has all the facilities for a summer and winter resort, with an aerial cableway which brings the tourists up to the splendid skiing fields on the Hannigalp.

Brig and the Simplon Pass

Back at Visp, if you continue up the Rhône Valley, you come quickly to the important rail and road junction of Brig. The small town of Brig has for centuries been a center of trade with Italy, for not only does it guard the Simplon route, but it also lies at the foot of the high valley of the Rhône. The latter leads past the Aletsch Glacier to Gletsch and the Grimsel Pass (for the route north to Meiringen and the Bernese Oberland) or the Furka Pass (towards Andermatt and central Switzerland).

Brig has a curious feature of interest—the Stockalper Castle, Switzerland's largest private residence. It was built between 1658 and 1678 for Gaspard Stockalper, a 17th-century Swiss tycoon who was the first to recognize the importance of the Simplon Pass for trade with Italy, and who amassed immense wealth by exploiting it to the full. But he also made much money from salt and other monopolies, and from a host of shrewd enterprises and deals. Likeable as well as rich, and speaking five languages, Stockalper was apparently quite a character and was welcomed in the courts of kings, the palaces of popes and the salons of international society. Stockalper not only made money—he poured a lot of it into his fabulous new home—the Stockalperschloss. But the people of the Valais gradually came to resent their uncrowned king and his wealth. Eventually, and rather tragically, he had to flee in disguise to Italy over the very pass which had brought him much of his wealth. After six years of exile he returned, only to die shortly afterwards in his palatial home. A huge building, instantly recognizable by its trio of onion-topped towers, and with a gigantic central courtyard surrounded by elegant cloisters, it is certainly worth a visit. Nearby is Brigerbad, where there is a very pleasant open-air thermal bath.

Just above the eastern outskirts of Brig is the entrance to the twin

Simplon Tunnels, through which famous international trains disappear into dank darkness to emerge twelve miles and 500 yards farther on into Italian daylight on the southern side of the Alps. The first of the twin tunnels—the world's longest railway tunnels—was started in 1898 and took six years to complete.

The Simplon Pass road also begins just outside Brig, meandering through deep gorges and over wide, barren, rock-strewn pastures, across the mountains' flanks. As the highway slowly rises, there are glimpses of Brig in the Rhône Valley below, giving an excellent view of these grim historic routes: at one point the Aletsch Glacier can be seen shimmering in the distance.

At the top of the pass stands the *Simplon-Kulm Hotel* (6,600 ft.), and, just beyond it, the Simplon Hospice of the monks of St. Bernard, built 150 years ago at Napoleon's request. A little farther on, cupped in a hollow to the right of the main road, is the Alter Spital. A square, tall building with a church-like bell tower, this hospice was built in the 17th century by our friend, Gaspard Stockalper. Beside it, you can still see parts of the old road of the merchant princes and Napoleon, and it is easy to imagine the hardships which travelers of those times had to bear in crossing the pass. The road drops rapidly from the summit, passing through Simplon village, and then Gondo, the last village in Switzerland.

The recent completion of extensive new tunnels and snow galleries means the Simplon Pass is now open throughout the year, but if exceptional snowfalls temporarily close the road your car can be taken by train through the rail tunnel between Brig and Iselle (the first village on the Italian side).

The Simplon Pass is an impressive gateway to Italy with a succession of splendid views and many stopping places where you can admire them. The road is well surfaced and generally speaking it is one of the easier major Alpine passes.

From Brig up the Rhône to Gletsch

We should not leave the neighborhood of Brig without mentioning one of the most remarkable trains in Europe, the *Glacier Express.* Starting, in fact, from Zermatt, it runs through Brig, up the Rhône Valley, through the Furka Tunnel at an altitude of over 7,000 feet, past Andermatt, over the Oberalp Pass, and then down through Disentis and Chur in the Grisons to terminate in St. Moritz. From Andermatt onwards, it carries a restaurant car. This famous train struggles across the backbone of Europe, running in places where a mountain goat would be hard pressed to find a footing. For miles it toils up gradients so severe that cogwheels are necessary and goes round curves so sharp that it seems in danger of tying a knot in itself. Much of the time, the railway is above the timber line. And just beyond Gletsch passengers have a superb and prolonged view of the gigantic, detergent-blue Rhône glacier, which Nature has kindly placed at exactly the right height and distance to be seen at its best from the carriages of the slow-moving train. Clearly visible, tumbling down the face of the glacier, is the water which forms the river Rhône, here starting ice-cold on its long journey through Switzerland and France to the warmth of the Mediterranean.

From Brig, closely following the route taken by the *Glacier Express,* the main road continues up the valley of the Rhône towards its source near Gletsch, as we have mentioned above. To the north of the turbulent river is the great mass of the Bernese Oberland, with some of the highest mountains in Europe—Aletschhorn, Jungfrau, Mönch, Eiger, Schreckhorn, Finsteraarhorn and many others. Life in this part of the valley is especially hard, the soil poor and the road approach to Gletsch blocked by snow from November until about June. But it is a journey well worth while, one in which grimness, beauty and grandeur combine in a superb and powerful symphony, a fitting farewell to the Valais.

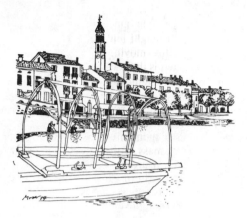

TICINO

Canton of Contrasts

If you go to Ticino, the chances are you'll cross the 10,000 foot St. Gotthard massif, which forms part of the canton's northern boundary. Whether you drive over the famous St. Gotthard pass road (with a fine, new section cutting out the top twenty-five hairpin bends) or take the train through the nine-mile-long tunnel to emerge at Airolo, you'll have the same sensation—that this is Switzerland with a difference.

As the canton slopes southwards from the St. Gotthard heights to the shores of lakes Maggiore and Lugano, you'll notice both climate and scenery gradually become more Mediterranean than Alpine; that chalets give way to cottages of dark, rough-hewn stone and, later, color-washed houses with orange-tiled roofs. You'll see Italianesque churches. At lower levels you'll notice palm trees flourishing happily, and exotic flowers and shrubs of most un-Alpine appearance. You will quickly realize, too, that you have entered an Italian-speaking canton—the only one in Switzerland.

Projecting like a spearhead into Italy, it is hardly surprising that Ticino has a distinctly Italian flavor. This is true not only in its food and wine, but also in its buildings, people, atmosphere and, perhaps above all, its climate. In the lake district December and January can, admittedly, be cold and wet, but the rest of the year is normally blissfully warm and sunny apart from occasional stormy spells—sometimes spectacular although usually shortlived; and summer can be downright hot.

But don't be fooled by Ticino's Italian appearance; you are still very much in Switzerland! Like many another Swiss canton it has winter sports, Alpine scenery, lakes, and plenty of mountain transport as well as typical Swiss efficiency and hospitality. But as an exclusive free offer Ticino throws in an almost Mediterranean climate at lower levels, and three world-famous resorts—Lugano, Locarno and Ascona.

Lugano, on Lake Lugano, deep-set among steep-sided mountains is large, bustling, perhaps a little brash; Locarno, slightly to the north on Lake Maggiore, is quieter, more sophisticated and rather more open; while neighboring Ascona is quaint, colorful and brimming with slightly self-conscious charm.

Just as the three resorts have their distinctive personalities, so do Ticino's many valleys, each vying with the others for scenery and charm; valleys which are almost always quiet and secluded, and occasionally primitive. Like many other unsung attractions in Ticino, these lovely valleys are missed by most tourists although they are nearly all easy to reach, as the canton is endowed with a fine network of public transport. It is also a motorist's paradise, as excellent, if sometimes narrow, roads lead everywhere, in several cases almost to the summit of fair-sized mountains.

The remarkable feature about this canton of contrast, which is fourth in size but tenth in population, and has more than its fair share of attractions, is that it is seen by relatively few British and American tourists, despite prices which, away from the big resorts, are a trifle below normal Swiss standards.

Lugano

Because of its picturesque setting, Lugano is dubbed by some guide books and brochures as "Queen of Ceresio." But although Ceresio is one of the Italian names for Lake Lugano you can forget the word. To most Italians the lake is Lago di Lugano, as it is to the Swiss. But even if you forget Ceresio, Lugano itself will leave an indelible imprint on your memory. Set in a large bay, with the green heights of Monte Brè and Monte San Salvatore standing like sentinels at each end, the Italianesque city fully justifies the superlatives used by writers.

It's a splendid, self-contained resort with a fine assortment of almost everything the visitor could want—hotels, restaurants, cafés, entertainment, culture, sport, and tantalizing shops; beautiful lake and mountain surroundings; and a mild, sunny climate unexpected of a mountainous region. Less well-known is that, like Locarno and Ascona, it is an exceptionally good center for day and half-day excursions by car, coach, train, steamer, mountain railway, or even on foot.

For Lugano lies in the middle of a region called the Sottoceneri (another name you can forget) which extends southwards to the Italian frontier at Chiasso; a region with a wide range of scenery from lakes and lush meadows to mountains; with a multitude of magnificent views; and with a myriad of valleys and villages often so charming, quiet and unspoiled that it is difficult to realize that the bustle, color and gaiety of Lugano is so close.

The region has long been inhabited. It is known that the Liguri were there at least four centuries before Christ. About two centuries later the Romans arrived, bringing with them, as usual, their culture and civilization. By the end of the Middle Ages the region was under the influence of nearby Como. Thereafter, but not always happily, it gradually came under the domination of the Swiss Confederation. But it was not until 1803 that the Lugano region joined with Bellinzona and Locarno to become a fully-fledged Swiss canton—that of Ticino. Half a century later the first trickle of tourists began to arrive.

Exploring Lugano

The hub of Lugano is the lakeside Piazza Riforma with its neo-classical Municipio, or town hall, constructed in 1844. Around and behind the Municipio, and up the hill towards the cathedral, lies the old town, a maze of winding, arcaded streets, sometimes steep and narrow. But outside this central area with its old-world charm and obvious Italian influence, Lugano at once becomes more modern and international with elegant shops, imposing buildings and fine hotels.

It's a short but steep climb to the cathedral of San Lorenzo, which is not the most important of ecclesiastical edifices. But it is worth a visit, firstly for its 16th-century, early Renaissance façade, and secondly for the fine view of the city and lake from its terrace.

Of much greater importance is the Franciscan church of Santa Maria degli Angioli in Piazza Luini, where arcaded Via Nassa—Lugano's principal shopping street—joins the lakeside promenade. Here, facing you as you enter the church, is the gigantic *Crucifixion* fresco painted by Bernardino Luini in 1529, unquestionably his greatest work. The lighting is poor, so to savor the color and detail go there on a bright day. In the church, too, you'll see the *Last Supper* and several other works by Luini.

On a more secular level, and a "must" for art lovers, is the Villa Favorita in Castognola, a trolley-bus ride from the town center. From the entrance gates a ten-minute walk through lovely gardens beside the lake will bring you to the Pinacoteca. Here is the art collection formed by the late Baron Heinrich von Thyssen, generally regarded as being the best private collection in Europe. It is still being added to by the present Baron. In over twenty superbly arranged and cleverly lit salons are displayed masterpieces from the Middle Ages to the 18th century including such treasures as J. van Eyck's *Annunciation* and Dürer's *Jesus among the Scribes.* But it is not open continuously, so check with tourist office or your hotel.

Closer to the town center is Lugano's beautifully cared-for municipal park, the lakeside Parco Civico. Here, weather permitting, you can sit and listen to the daily concerts in a setting of lawns, flower beds and majestic trees. Located in the park is the Villa Ciani, an art gallery which also has important loan exhibitions.

On the Cassarate side of the park is Lugano's vast lido with several swimming pools, lawns for sunbathing, restaurants, etc. But you can no longer bathe from its beach as the Swiss, with more courage than some other nations, have forbidden bathing in the bay until the pollution problem has been solved. Just outside the park on the other side is the Kursaal, a large entertainment center with nightclub, theater, cinema, gaming rooms (boule only), restaurant, and almost always something going on.

One of Lugano's joys is just walking about—along the one-and-one-half-mile, tree-shaded lakeside promenade; around the twisting, narrow streets of the old town; under the arcades of Via Nassa past its opulent shops and beautiful window displays. Another, as we have said earlier, is the excellence of excursions in the surrounding region.

Excursions

Probably the best way of getting your bearings and an idea of the excursion delights in store is to take the funicular trip from Paradiso to Monte San Salvatore (2,995 ft.) or from Cassarate to Monte Brè (3,053 ft.). From either you'll get an eagle's eye view of Lugano and its irregularly shaped lake, and the hills, mountains and valleys of the region. Choose a good day, and go before the clouds have begun to gather around the mountain tops, as they so often do around mid-day.

Even better is the ascent of Monte Generoso (5,590 ft.). Take the steamer to Capolago at the southern end of the lake (about fifty minutes from Lugano) where, beside the landing stage, the little red cogwheel-train will be waiting to take you on its gallant forty-minute climb to the top station. The grassy summit is some 250 feet higher, but you don't need to be a mountaineer or a goat to reach it. There's a prepared path, steep and rough but not too difficult. From the summit, on a clear day you'll see the Po valley and the Apennines in the south, the snow-capped Alps to the north, and much of Ticino in between.

To the Collina d'Oro

Projecting southwards from Lugano is a five-mile-long peninsula with twin parallel ridges. To the west, forming one side of the bay of Agno, is the Collina d'Oro (Golden Hill), the smaller but perhaps the prettier of the two. Longer, higher, more spectacular and with even finer views is the eastern ridge starting at Monte Salvatore and ending at Morcote on the southern tip of the peninsula, the village of Corona being in the center.

The road to the Collina d'Oro leads from Sorengo, on the outskirts of Lugano, past the mini-lake of Muzzano, to Gentilino with its cypress-surrounded church of Sant'Abbondio. In the cemetery are buried Bruno Walter, the conductor, and Nobel prizewinner and poet Hermann Hesse. Hesse lived in Montagnola, the next village, where you will get a fine view of Lugano. The last village along the Collina d'Oro ridge, and almost the end of the road, is Agra. From here, as from other villages, well-marked paths lead over the ridge and also down to the lake shore.

To Carona and the Malcantone

You can reach Carona, and the easternmost ridge, on foot from the top of Monte Salvatore, by cable car from Melide, or—the best way— as part of a car tour of the whole peninsula. From Paradiso the road twists steeply up around Monte Salvatore and then follows the crest of the ridge to go through a narrow archway under part of the old Romanesque church of Carona (it contains the *Death of John the Baptist* by Solari, a villager who was a pupil of Leonardo da Vinci). You need go no farther than the car park just through the arch to enjoy one of the most spectacular of many fine views on the tour. Have a look, too, at the ancient frescoed houses in the village itself.

Beyond Carona the road passes the charming village of Vico Morcote before diving through the woods in a steep, winding descent to the old waterside townlet of Morcote. Spare time here (and pray for parking space) to wander among its lovely old decorated houses and arcades. As you will see from the work prominently displayed in shops, Morcote has a small art colony.

From Morcote you can take the lakeside road round the peninsula, turning right for Lugano, if you are in a hurry, at either Figino or Agnuzzo. Better still, continue round the lake to Ponte Tresa. Don't cross the bridge unless you have a passport: the other side is Italy. Turn right before the bridge and follow the river Tresa—by which Lake Lugano drains into Lake Maggiore—to Madonna del Piano or Molinazzo. At either place, if you bear right you'll head into the Malcantone, a region of wooded hills, green valleys and quiet villages with a choice of some half-dozen different ways of getting back to Lugano.

To the Valleys North of Lugano

North of Lugano, and almost on the city's doorstep, lie several quiet and charming valleys easily reached by car or bus. They offer the visitor any number of memorable walks or drives among beautiful mountains and valleys, sometimes wooded, sometimes with lush pastures colored with wild flowers, and dotted with minuscule, sleepy villages; an area with hundreds of undiscovered picnic spots. The roads are good although usually narrow and often steep, but the traffic is surprisingly light.

Of many drives, one of the best is along Val Colla starting from Tesserete, five miles north of Lugano. Take the road which weaves along the mountainside through Bidogno to Bogno at the head of the valley. There it backtracks to return, often along the valley floor, to Lugano through Sonvico, with its 15th/16th-century church of San Giovanni Battista, and Dino with a church dating from the 12th century.

Or from Tesserete you can go north up Val Capriasca, or west to the village of Ponte Capriasca, where there's a good copy of Leonardo's *Last Supper* as a fresco in the church of Sant'Ambrogio. If you look carefully, you may notice several differences from the original, and also that two scenes—Christ on the Mount of Olives and the Sacrifice of Abraham—have been added by the artist, believed to have been Francesco Melzi.

To Campione and Its Casino

If you want to fritter away your fortune and find you can't do so quickly enough in Lugano's Kursaal with its five-franc limit, Campione d'Italia is a mere twenty minutes away. Almost directly across the lake from Lugano, Campione is a tiny bit of Italy entirely surrounded by Switzerland, and is mainly a large, glamorous, glittering casino where you can play roulette, baccara and what-have-you with almost unlimited stakes.

It was in the 8th century that Campione, then an Imperial fief, was presented to the Monastery of San Ambrogio in Milan. Despite all the political upheavals in the region in the centuries which followed, Campione—except for a brief period—remained Italian and is so today. But if you go there you'll find no frontier post, no customs examination. The money used is Swiss. The postal and telephone services are Swiss, too.

Apart from its casino and anomalous international position, Campione has another claim to fame. In the late Middle Ages many of its citizens became builders, masons and sculptors, emigrating to Milan, where they founded the influential "Campione school" of stonework.

To Lake Como and Italy

Menaggio on Lake Como is only about seventeen miles from Lugano. The trip can be made by road throughout, or by steamer as far as Porlezza, at the Italian end of Lake Lugano, and then by road.

The first village beyond Castagnola in the direction of Menaggio is Gandria. By any standard, Gandria is picturesque with its charming houses rising in tiers from the water's edge; with its flights of steps and its alleys, too steep and narrow for motor vehicles. True, Gandria is "touristy" and is well-equipped with souvenir shops. True, there are equally appealing villages in the region, but there is none so easily and pleasantly reached by the motor vessels which sail frequently from Lugano. If, after exploring the village and fortifying yourself at a café overlooking the lake, you are going back to Lugano it is worth while walking along the lakeside path (it will take about half an hour) to Castagnola, where you can complete your journey in a trolley-bus.

Just beyond Gandria, along the road which runs above the village, you enter Italy, and it is a good mental exercise to observe the many subtle differences which add up to a slight but unmistakable change in character.

It's best to make the trip to Lake Como about the end of April or the beginning of May, for then the azaleas are in bloom, and at the height of the season there is a riot of color along the way. The azaleas are particularly fine in the formal gardens of the beautiful Villa Carlotta (open to the public) about three miles south of Menaggio. Another five miles farther on is Ospedaletto, with the minute, wooded island of Comacina a stone's throw from the shore. Be sure to go over to the island for a meal in the moderately priced restaurant, or even a picnic near the little chapel in the center. A motor launch will soon come to fetch you if you stand on one of the quays.

The open-air markets in most Italian frontier towns during the week offer excellent buys in woolen and leather goods. Local residents loudly defend the advantages of one market over another, but whether you visit Como, Ponte Tresa, Luino or Cannobio on market day (the day varies from town to town) the merchants are nearly always the same—they simply pack their trucks and move on to the next market the next day.

To Mendrisio and Chiasso

Across the Melide causeway, beside the excellent new motorway leading to the frontier town of Chiasso, is the village of Bissone. Here Francesco Borromini, part-architect of the Barberini Palace in Rome, was born, as was Carpoforo Tencalla (1623–1685), who founded a school of painting and architecture in Vienna, later returning to his home town. The Tencalla House in Bissone is now open to the public from April to October. A lovely old Italian Renaissance building acquired by the Ticino Craftsmen and Artists Society, it is furnished in the local style of the 17th century. One can see Tencalla's frescoes in the Church of San Carpoforo in the village.

Ligornetto, the birthplace of Vicenza Vela, now houses the Vela Museum, open daily. Famous in 19th-century Italy, Vela's sculptures are to be found not only in Italian cities but also in Paris, Lisbon and Istanbul. *Spartacus,* in Lugano's Municipio, is also by him. Much of his work has been gathered together in his former villa, now the museum, which has been presented to the Swiss Confederation by his son, a talented painter.

Mendrisio—also the name of the surrounding district—was involved in the great medieval power struggle between the Guelphs and

Ghibellines, roughly representing the Pope and Emperor. Ruled by the Torriani family (Guelph partisans), the town was frequently opposed by the Ghibelline viscounts. The Torrianis finally came out on top, but not until there had been a great deal of violence. Today Mendrisio has a peculiar charm that induces many a traveler to linger. A visit to its historic monuments, like the Chiesa di San Giovanni or the Palazzo Torriani-Fontana, may work its spell on the visitor. Mendrisio is well-known for its elaborate evening processions on Maundy Thursday and Good Friday.

The oldest building in all Ticino stands in Riva San Vitale on the southeastern corner of Lake Lugano. The village, which proclaimed itself a republic in 1798 (and lost its independence after sixteen days!), contains a baptistry dating from about the 5th century, and a large stone baptismal font (for baptism by immersion) from the 5th century.

Locarno

Locarno's magnetism stems from the same sources as that of Lugano, yet its atmosphere is very different. Like Lugano, it enjoys a subtropical climate, romantic lakeside setting, and Ticino's happy fusion of Italian grace with Swiss efficiency, and, naturally enough, has become an international resort. But there the likeness ends. For Locarno, a smaller place on a larger lake, is less townlike and more leisurely and informal.

Locarno has had a disastrous history—particularly in the 16th century, when nearly sixty of her illustrious families, rather than acknowledge the Roman Catholic church, fled to Zurich (where, incidentally, they were largely instrumental in starting the silk industry). Next came a series of devastating floods followed, in 1576, by the Great Plague, of which Saint Carlo wrote in 1584 "only 700 out of the 4,800 who inhabited the town were left."

It was not until 1925 that Locarno came into her own. In that year the little, unknown resort suddenly hit world headlines when Briand, Stresemann, Mussolini and Chamberlain met there to sign the Locarno Pact. The story goes that Lucerne was the favored location, but the French minister's girl-friend, who was fascinated by Locarno, persuaded him to insist upon holding the conference there (ah! l'amour!). A more recent boost to the city's economy has been the establishment of the Locarno Film Festival. Held each year in the autumn, it provides an international film market for Switzerland and has become an event of increasing artistic importance. It brings interesting people from many countries to Locarno and adds another facet to the town's cultural life.

Exploring Locarno

Despite all the attractions of a top-class resort, Locarno has a quiet, rather dignified air. Interesting old streets converge on the delightful Piazza Grande where a fine sweep of Italianesque houses rises above arcaded shops. Locarno's shops, specializing in fashion, antiques, art and local handicrafts, are highly selective and sophisticated, so that even window-shopping is fun. Along the tree-shaded waterfront with its posh hotels, wisteria, orange blossom and magnolias bloom, and in early summer you may see a priest holding services outside the houses of little first communicants.

Locarno has some outstanding Romanesque and baroque churches. Most unusual is the beautiful basilical church, San Vittore, started around the 11th century; the back (the oldest part) and partially restored crypt are particularly fine. A bas-relief of the saint, sculpted in 1462 by Martino Berazone, and now adorning the recently completed tower, was found on the ruined castle of the Muralti close by. Part of this castle was restored in 1926 and is now an important museum. Concerts are held in San Francesco church, reputedly founded by St. Anthony of Padua but rebuilt in 1538 and given an imposing Renaissance façade with emblems depicting Locarno's early class distinctions: an eagle represents noblemen, an ox the citizens, and a lamb the cultivators! For uninhibited baroque extravaganza the 17th-century Chiesa Nuova is hard to beat, with its giant stucco statue of St. Christopher outside and froth of superbly stuccoed angels within. The chancel of Santa Maria in Selva has exquisite frescoes painted in 1400 and extremely moving in their simplicity; and La Collegiate di Sant'Antonio Abate is worth visiting for the trompe l'oeil painting, *The Dead Christ,* by the Orelli brothers.

The Madonna del Sasso sanctuary, crowning a rock—where Brother Bartolomeo da Ivrea saw a vision of the Virgin in 1480—is reached by funicular. The sanctuary, begun in 1487 and enlarged by stages, contains some lovely 15th-century paintings, including two by Bernadino de Conti and Bramantino's *Flight into Egypt.*

Ascona

Only two and one-half miles from Locarno is the small resort town of Ascona. It's on a corner of a bay frequently dotted with trim little yachts, and features an extensive waterside promenade with all sorts of boats for hire. What gives Ascona a character of its own is its gay and relaxed atmosphere—and more particularly its contrast. For almost hidden behind the lively, colorful cafés which line the tree-bordered shore road is Ascona's other face—an intriguing muddle of quaint old streets and twisting alleys surrounding the eye-catching church tower; streets and alleys filled with boutiques, antique shops, bookbinders, art galleries and craft shops. True, some are there to catch the tourist. But the scene is pleasant and unexpected, and the emphasis on art, culture and craftsmanship is an indication of the way Ascona has attracted artists, writers, musicians and composers. Writer Hans Habe and soprano Elizabeth Schwarzkopf live here; Ben Nicolson, the famous British artist, lives not far away at Ronco. And by the lakeside you'll probably see artists displaying their work, although some of it you may consider rather pseudo.

In the surrounding districts also, craftsmanship is highly developed. Baskets, bags, mats and woven cloths come from nearby valleys; ceramics with highly colored fanciful designs of birds and animals, from the Ascona region. Rustic pottery, decorated trays and platters, and wooden *zoccoli* (or clogs) and other quality goods are produced here.

Excursions from Locarno and Ascona

From Locarno and nearby Ascona there are countless contrasting day and half-day trips up valleys, among mountains, and on the lake. One of the best starts in the center of Locarno. By cable railway you can go to Orselina, where an aerial cable car whisks you up to Cardada (4,050 ft.) for the final trip in a chairlift to Cimetta (4,950 ft.). From both grassy summits there are magnificent views of Lake Maggiore and the Alps, as well as wonderful mountain hikes, and if you need sustenance you can get a meal or a snack at either place. In winter there's skiing on the snowy slopes.

A quick and pleasant introduction to the many valley excursions is to the Centovalli, which runs from near Locarno due west toward Italy. To the frontier it's a twenty-four-mile round trip by road, or you can join one of the little tram-like trains which weave their way up the valley from Locarno to Domodossola. Named the Centovalli ("valley of one hundred valleys") because of its many, often gorge-like lateral valleys, it is noted alike for its unspoiled character and beauty, its chestnut trees, and the rustic simplicity of its villages, although Intragna, at the entrance to the valley, is on a rather grand scale and boasts, at the church of San Gottardo, Ticino's highest belltower.

One of the ancient customs still carried out in the Centovalli is the game of *boccia,* which has a slight resemblance to bowling. One day, so the story goes, a bowler's ball struck the painting of the Madonna on the side of a church wall in Rè, a few miles over the border in Italy. A stream of blood appeared on the face of the Madonna and the player was so overcome by his experience that he ended his days as a hermit in the mountains. To this day, on April 30th each year residents of the Centovalli make a pilgrimage to Rè to commemorate the legend.

To Valle Maggia and Val Onsernone

The Valle Maggia has a good highway and is also serviced by postal bus. At Bignasco the valley splits into Val Lavizzera, noted for dairy farming and cheese-making, and Val Bavona, a dramatic gorge with compact stone-built mountain villages and many waterfalls. From San Carlo, where the road ends at the head of Val Bavona, you can now go by cable car up to Robiei (6,500 ft.), where, in the silent beauty of peaks and glaciers, there is a new 40-bed economy-grade hotel.

Through the centuries the Valle Maggia has suffered violent floods, notably in 1747 when Avegno was inundated, and again in 1834 when Peccia was destroyed. This century the mountain waters have been harnessed by the creation of artificial lakes which feed an elaborate system of hydroelectric generators, built inside the mountains.

Typical of the Valle Maggia are the rough-hewn dry-stone *grotti,* often with a solid wall of rock behind them. These are wine vaults for Ticino wines—the red Merlot, which can be excellent, and the white Nostrano, primarily a cooking wine. In Ticino, a restaurant with tree-shaded, granite tables where you can eat, and drink wine from a *boccalino* (small pottery jug), is often known as a grotto. You'll see many of them.

In the town of Maggia, one attraction is the church of Santa Maria delle Grazie di Campagna, a curious blend of the elegant, with its frescoes, and the rustic, with its wood-beamed ceiling. Hanging in the church are many ex-votos, paintings done by country folk in thanksgiving for favors granted through prayer. Painstakingly realistic, and yet naive in their execution, they are a typical expression of the folk art of this area.

The Val Onsernone, sheer and deep, has a winding road passing through several old villages. Connected to Locarno by bus, the region is the center of the straw industry. Since the 16th century, this straw work has found ready markets, but many natives emigrated to Tuscany, Piedmont and Belgium to carry on their craft.

The most beautiful of all the valleys near Locarno, according to many, is the Valle Verzasca. Wild and scenic, waterfalls abound, and the region is largely unspoiled and undeveloped. A well-surfaced though sometimes narrow road goes from Gordola, a few miles east of Locarno, to Sonogno, about fifteen miles up the valley; postal coaches cover the route. Just beyond the village of Sonogno there's a small café where you can enjoy a simple but good meal in the open air. In Brione you can visit a castle, as well as a church with remains of 14th-century frescoes in the style of Giotto, depicting the life of Christ. Primarily, however, this valley is one of natural beauties—campers, hikers and photographers should find their paradise here.

Around Lake Maggiore

A fascinating excursion by car or postal coach from Locarno is to the tiny dry-stone hamlet of Indemini, clinging to the grassy slopes of Mt. Gamborogno. After crossing the river Ticino, you skirt the shore, leaving the highway at Vira-Gamborogno to climb steeply on an excellent road, with the entire northern (Swiss) end of Lake Maggiore spread out below you. Later, on the Passo di Neggia, three miles before Indemini, both Swiss and Italian sections are visible. Indemini has no streets—only steep paths—but it has a café with a balcony looking across stone roofs to the chestnut trees and a valley beyond. Mountain flowers and herbs scent the air, and clusters of stone cottages seem camouflaged against their background. It is worth going on beyond Indemini to enter Italy, rejoining the lakeside at Maccagno for the lovely drive back along the shore (in Switzerland again). The round trip is fifty miles.

On the other side of the lake, the drive from Locarno to Porto Ronco by the upper road takes you through villa-studded wooded hills with occasional views of the lake far below. It then descends dramatically to the picturesque lakeside village of Porto Ronco, from which the two beautiful, little Brissago Islands can be seen. Both are nationally preserved botanical gardens for exotic trees and plants, the larger island being accessible by steamer.

Bellinzona, Crossroads of Ticino

Located in the surprisingly flat and wide valley of the river Ticino, Bellinzona is not only the capital but also the crossroads of the canton. Northwards, highways go to three important and historic passes (the San Bernardino to Chur and the Grisons; the Lukmanier, or Lucomagno, to Disentis; and the St. Gotthard to Andermatt and central Switzerland) as well as to a recently developed one, the Nufenen pass to the Rhône valley. To the west the road goes to Locarno. Southwards there's a fine new motorway to Lugano and Milan.

With a key position astride important trade routes, small wonder that over the centuries Bellinzona has been fought for and bandied about from one overlord to another with almost monotonous regularity. Nearly fifteen hundred years ago there was a settlement where the town is now. Later it came under the sway of the Bishop of Como. In the Middle Ages Bellinzona was the subject of many bitter disputes, and was kicked around like a football by the Bishops and feudal overlords of Como and Milan. The Swiss of Uri bought the town for 2,400 florins in the early 15th century only to lose it in the battle of Arbedo three years later. Finally, in 1503 the town was ceded to the Swiss of Uri, Schwyz and Unterwalden, who brought it three centuries of peace, but only at the expense of harsh rule which lasted until 1803—the year that Bellinzona became part of the newly created canton of Ticino.

With this long and turbulent history in mind, and the town's strategic situation, the visitor will hardly be surprised to find Bellinzona dominated by three fine, 13th/15th-century castles and some formidable walls. One—the Castello Grande or San Michele (often called the castle of Uri)—is on a hillock near the town center. Close by, on a hillside overlooking the station, is the second, the well-restored Castello di Montebello (or Castle of Schwyz), now a museum. Some 500 feet higher up the hill is the last of the trio, the Castello di Sasso Corbaro (or Castle of Unterwalden), from the terrace of which you'll get a fine view of the town and the Ticino valley.

Valle Levantina and Val Bedretto

Busiest of the valleys north of Bellinzona (it carries all the road and rail traffic using the Gotthard route) is the Valle Levantina, down which flows the river Ticino. Despite its heavy traffic the Levantina, between Biasca and Airolo, is a splendid wild Alpine valley, well-wooded and with waterfalls streaking its sides, As you go along it, you will realize that it forms the transition between the subtropical southern Ticino and the truly Alpine north. Stop a while at Giornico to visit the well-restored, 12th-century church of San Nicalao with its unusual carvings of animals and mythical beasts, most particularly in the crypt. Incidentally, it was here that a few hundred Swiss defeated many thousands of Milanese in 1478.

At Airolo the road ahead quickly steepens to climb the St. Gotthard. But if you turn left you'll enter Val Bedretto, where a good but narrow road goes through magnificent Alpine scenery to the recently much improved Nufenen pass, close to the source of the river Ticino.

From Biasca one can also head up Val Blenio and the pretty Valle Santa Maria, which together form the approach to the wild desolation of the Lukmanier pass.

These valleys—even busy Levantino—take the traveler through forests of chestnut at lower levels and conifers higher up; into rustic villages with Romanesque buildings; past milky mountain torrents and waterfalls; and among some of the finest of Alpine scenery. But for the adventurous, prepared to accept roads which may be steep and sometimes rough, there are many more side valleys where the sense of beauty and silence is all but overwhelming.

THE PRINCIPALITY OF LIECHTENSTEIN

LIECHTENSTEIN

Pocket-Sized Principality

Crossing over from the world's oldest living democracy into a monarchy that is the last remnant of the Holy Roman Empire is the easiest thing in the world for anyone driving along the Swiss Rhine valley, between Lake Constance and the Grisons. You turn east at the right moment, cross a bridge, and there you are, smack in the middle of the realm of His Highness, Franz Josef II, Maria Alois Alfred Karl Johann Heinrich Michael George Ignatius Benediktus Gerhardus Majella, Prince von und zu Liechtenstein, Duke of Troppau and Jaegerndorf, and last of the hundreds of reigning kings, princes, dukes, and counts who once populated the map of the Holy Roman Empire.

His Highness rules as a constitutional monarch over only sixty-two square miles and about 24,000 loyal subjects, but don't let appearances fool you. Liechtenstein may look like nothing but an oversized Alpine resort, with its gentle wooded hills in the north, fertile Rhine valley in the west, and craggy mountains in the east. But actually, Liechtenstein is a complete state, with a sound and diversified economy and a prosperous people who can easily afford their friendly smiles and easygoing ways, considering their glowing state of affairs.

Liechtensteiners insist that their case is different from other miniature states. They are not just the product of rivalries between great powers, such as Andorra, a buffer zone between France and Spain, nor are they tolerated only for curiosity's sake, as San Marino is by Italy, neither are they in danger of being swallowed by a bigger power if they lose their ruler, as is Monaco. They could depose their prince any day and continue as a free republic. But they won't because the house of Liechtenstein has proved a lucky charm.

It all started at the end of the 17th century, when a wealthy Austrian prince, Johann Adam von Liechtenstein, bought up two bankrupt counts in the Rhine valley, united their lands, and in 1719 obtained an imperial deed, creating the Principality of Liechtenstein. In January 1969, Liechtenstein celebrated its 250th anniversary.

At that time, the Liechtenstein family was already a power in the Holy Roman Empire. From the time of Hugo of Liechtenstein, a knight in the 12th century with a modest castle near Vienna, their wealth and power had grown consistently. In 1608 they were elevated to Princes of the empire, and when Johann Adam bought his new lands in the Rhine valley, he was already one of the richest men in Europe. The new principality was but a small fraction of the hundreds of square miles all over the Austro-Hungarian Empire that belonged to the Liechtenstein family. Yet it suited his purpose to have a moderate-sized territory and thus qualify for a vote in the Diet of the Princes.

The new principality became the hobby of the wealthy Liechtenstein family. Although they spent most of their time at the glittering imperial court of Vienna or on their estates in Austria, Bohemia, Moravia, and Hungary, they spent most of their money on Liechtenstein. For many decades the rulers played the same role for their principality that the Monte Carlo gambling casino did for Monaco. If something went wrong with the budget, the prince took out his checkbook and asked, "How much?"

The champion spender was probably Prince Johann II, who reigned for a full seventy-one years (almost a record) until his death in 1929. He gave away the equivalent of about 75 million Swiss francs of his private fortune, most of it to make Liechtenstein a better place to live in, and some for sundry charities. None of this huge amount came out of Liechtenstein's taxes.

Speaking of money, contrary to the popular impression, Liechtensteiners do pay taxes, but these are moderate by international standards, and are one of the reasons for Liechtenstein's economic boom in the last three decades. The principality has little difficulty finding capital for investments and has become the seat of numerous international holding and finance corporations. The new income from the economic boom is amply sufficient to make up for the former large subsidies from the private fortune of the princes.

The old saying that the Liechtenstein family may have a principality on the Rhine, but a kingdom in Bohemia, is no longer true. World War I threatened misfortune in view of Liechtenstein's close links with the crumbling Austro-Hungarian empire, but the little country bailed out just in time in 1918 and started the drift towards Switzerland that ended in the complete customs and monetary union of 1924. The Liechtenstein family recovered most of its fortune, then scattered over the new states that succeeded the Austro-Hungarian monarchy. From land, castles, jewelry, and the fabulous Liechtenstein gallery, probably the most valuable private collection of paintings in the world, they diversified their holdings into industry and blue-chip stocks.

The situation looked much gloomier after World War II, when communist Czechoslovakia and Hungary expropriated the land holdings of the prince and offered a "final settlement" of only about 6 or 7 percent of the actual value. Prince Franz Josef II, who had succeeded his childless uncle Franz I in 1938, proudly declined to sell what he regarded as his inalienable rights for some ready cash. But the Liechtenstein family is by no means impoverished. They still own large estates in Austria, the choicest vineyards in Liechtenstein, their art gallery, and good chunks of a dozen or more prosperous industrial enterprises, as well as a bank at their capital, Vaduz, which is doing brisk business with all those foreign corporations in town.

The Prince and His Family

Under these circumstances, nobody will doubt the sincerity of the prayers and congratulations that echoed through Liechtenstein in the summer of 1956, when 15,000 persons, almost as much as the official population at that time, gathered twice at Vaduz. First they celebrated the fiftieth birthday of their ruler (he was born on August 16, 1906, at one of the Austrian castles of the family, Frauenthal in Styria), then the 150th anniversary of Liechtenstein's sovereign independence. For this independence first came in 1806 when Austria's Emperor Franz II gave up his Imperial Crown, thus dissolving the Holy Roman Empire, to which Liechtenstein had previously owed allegiance. In 1815 Liechtenstein joined the German Confederation but once again, in 1866, it regained the full sovereign independence which it still enjoys to this day.

Although the Liechtensteiners could be sure of continuing as an independent state (and a prosperous one) even without a prince, they have no wish to do so and are understandably eager to leave things as nice as they are. Fortunately, they are spared one headache, the question of succession. The Liechtensteins are a prolific stock, and history knows no instance when His Highness' loyal subjects were worried about being left with a vacant throne. In the few cases of childless reigning princes there were always plenty of brothers or nephews around.

One of those nephews is the present ruling prince—Franz Josef II. In the tradition of his house he was the eldest of eight children and is the doting father of four sons and a daughter: Hereditary Prince Johann Adam Pius, Prince Philipp Erasmus, Prince Nikolaus Ferdinand, Prince Franz Josef Wenzel and Princess Nora Elisabeth.

Franz Josef has been careful to educate them in democratic ways proper to the constitutional monarch of a small, freedom-loving country. The children were sent to the public elementary school at Vaduz, together with other Liechtensteiners. The boys then went on to Vienna's Catholic "Schotten Gymnasium," Franz Josef's own prep school, where many generations of Liechtensteiners were educated by the learned padres of the Scottish Brothers order.

Sending the boys to Vienna for schooling was also useful in making them familiar with Austria, where the family still owns large estates and where they have hundreds of relatives by blood and by marriage in the Viennese aristocracy. For, in spite of their democratic ways, the Liechtensteins are bluebloods indeed. The mother of the reigning prince was a Habsburg archduchess, a half-sister of that unfortunate heir to the Austrian throne, Archduke Franz Ferdinand, whose murder in 1914 was one of the things which touched off World War I.

In July, 1967, during a week of nation-wide festivity, Liechtenstein saw a dazzling array of aristocratic Europe, when some eight hundred official guests—and many thousands of unofficial visitors—invaded the little country. On Sunday, July 30th, in Vaduz Church (below the romantic old castle), Crown Prince Johann Adam married Countess Kinsky, member of an old Bohemian family now living in Bavaria.

Objectively speaking, Vaduz castle, although outwardly a jewel of medieval architecture, was at one time anything but an inviting place to live in. Starting in 1905, the gloomy, thick-walled fortress on a cliff overlooking Vaduz was completely done over. Today it really is fit for a prince, lavishly furnished with costly antiques, tapestries, and valuable works of art. The famous Gothic bedroom contains furniture already antique when Columbus sailed for America.

But with all the money and care that went into redecorating the castle, Franz Josef II was the first reigning prince to take up permanent residence there. When Franz Josef succeeded his uncle in 1938, he was thirty-two and still unmarried, but the Liechtensteiners relaxed and rejoiced with him when their new ruler met the Countess Georgina Wilczek in Vienna. The phlegmatic, taciturn prince was properly impressed by vivacious "Gina," one of the reigning belles of Viennese aristocracy. Legend has it that he first met her in a modern version of Andersen's fairytale about the princess and the swineherd, i.e., when she was pressed into the Nazi labor service during the war and had to work on a farm. In any case, they were married on March 3, 1943, and to all appearances have lived happily ever after.

The prince leaves the ruling of his country to a democratically elected diet of fifteen men, but works away at increasing his country's fortune and his own. Friends say he would have made an excellent investment banker, and he knows quite a lot about agriculture and forestry, too, holding a university degree as a forestry engineer.

At the same time Princess Gina has given Liechtenstein a court, an institution that was sorely missed for many decades. The princess completed the new regime that started with the redecoration of the castle, by making it the center of Liechtenstein's life. A continuous stream of guests from Liechtenstein and abroad and frequent return visits of members of the royal family to the homes of local notables have given tiny Vaduz a taste of society and have forged strong bonds between the people and their ruler.

There is still a considerable difference between Vaduz and most other courts, even certain small ones. The prince dislikes pomp. Donning a fancy uniform with gold braid or playing with crown and scepter would seem perfectly ghastly to him. Even the jubilee stamps, issued on the occasion of his fiftieth birthday, show him with only an ermine-collared cape and a heavy gold chain as signs of his office over a simple white tie and tails . . . *no* crown.

The royal family follows an unostentatious style, shunning Cadillacs and Rolls-Royces and preferring cars of medium price. This kind of life strikes just the right note with Liechtenstein's hardworking, solid and sober-minded citizens. They have much of the democratic "no nonsense" attitude of the neighboring Swiss, but they gladly combine it with a little sparkle from the faint imperial glitter that still hangs over their other neighbor, Austria.

The Role of Switzerland

The political marriage of the principality with republican Switzerland has proved advantageous in every way. Except for Swiss economic policy, which extends to Liechtenstein more or less automatically by way of the customs union, there is absolutely no Swiss interference in Liechtenstein's politics. Liechtenstein is perfectly free to dissolve the customs, monetary, and postal union any time. Switzerland also represents Liechtenstein abroad; the only Liechtenstein minister accredited to a foreign government is the one at the Swiss capital, Bern. But the Swiss can act only with Liechtenstein's consent. They cannot enter into any agreement affecting Liechtenstein against that country's will.

Military service was abolished as long ago as 1868. Liechtenstein's present armed might consists of three dozen regular police and some three dozen men in an auxiliary police force. In those dangerous times when Hitler annexed Austria and wanted to unite all German-speaking countries into one Reich, and later during World War II, Swiss diplomacy and influence succeeded in keeping Liechtenstein out of the conflict, but there was no attempt to press Liechtenstein into reintroducing military service.

During the last three decades Liechtenstein has also participated in Switzerland's economic boom. The farm population has shrunk from 60 percent of the total thirty years ago to 3 percent now. Today, the Liechtenstein government is even a little wary of new investments because there are no longer sufficient Liechtensteiners to fill all jobs, and the high percentage of foreign workers employed has created serious problems. Another problem was the protection of the landscape. The government has succeeded there. The factories (their products range from calculating machines to false teeth) are tucked away unobtrusively, and with their clean white-and-glass facades look more like modernistic hotels.

So the Liechtensteiners continue to get the best of two worlds, a democratic freedom, peace, and prosperity like their Swiss neighbors, and a feeling of security from a dignified Prince, a heartening symbol of their independence, who gives much to his country and seeks nothing in return except recognition that he is trying his best to fulfill his office.

Visiting Liechtenstein for its scenery is pleasant, but even more rewarding is the experience of being among people who have found a secure balance in a world of imbalance, a formula for taking the best of old worlds and new alike and making it into a way of life that is today all too rare.

PRACTICAL INFORMATION FOR LIECHTENSTEIN

 WHEN TO COME? Like all Alpine resorts, Liechtenstein has two main seasons, from June to Sept., and (for skiing) from Dec. to Mar. Early May is especially attractive for then it is blossom time in the Rhine valley orchards. All the year round, art lovers will find a look at the fine collections in the *Leichtenstein Gallery,* Vaduz, richly rewarding.

 HOW TO COME? Although several of Europe's international trains, such as the Arlberg Express, cross Liechtenstein (and more pass within a few miles) none stops at the Principality's three small stations. It is best to use the Swiss border stations at Buchs (St. Gallen) or slightly farther-away Sargans, or the Austrian one at Feldkirch. All are well served by long-distance express trains and connected with Vaduz by bus. From Buchs it takes only about fifteen minutes by bus, ten minutes by taxi. Running along Liechtenstein's Rhine frontier is a motorway (E61) going all or part of the way to Lake Constance, Austria and Germany in the north, and southwards past Chur toward the San Bernardino. To the west, motorways go most of the way to Zurich, Bern and Basel, at which last point the German motorway system begins.

 WHAT WILL IT COST? Generally speaking, most prices are on a par with, or sometimes a little lower than, Switzerland. In hotels, full pension with private bathroom (bed, breakfast, two meals, and tips) cost between 40 and 90 frs. a day per person; in about three hotels slightly more; in a few, even less. Lunch or dinner was about 16 to 30 frs. in Vaduz, but less in country inns.

 FORMALITIES. None, if you enter Liechtenstein from Switzerland. There are no checks. All travel documents valid for Switzerland are also valid for Liechtenstein. For entering Liechtenstein from Austria, the formalities are the same as for entering Switzerland. Swiss customs officials and border police do the checking at the Liechtenstein-Austrian border.

MONEY. The Swiss franc is Liechtenstein's legal tender. Swiss currency regulations and rates of exchange also apply to Liechtenstein.

MAIL, TELEPHONE. The Swiss postal system extends to Liechtenstein, with one exception: mail posted in Liechtenstein must bear Liechtenstein stamps. Liechtenstein is famous for finely engraved stamps and frequent new issues. If you have philatelists among your friends, heavy correspondence is indicated. The mail, telegram, and telephone rates are, of course, the same as in Switzerland. Liechtenstein belongs to the automatic Swiss phone system. Any Swiss phone can be reached by simple dialing without the aid of the operator. In the same way you can phone any Liechtenstein number from Switzerland by dialing 075 (the Liechtenstein phone district) and then the listed number.

WHERE TO STAY? There are no deluxe hotels in Liechtenstein, and most of the best ones are in Vaduz and along the Rhine valley. A Liechtenstein specialty are the mountain inns, all at least 4,000 ft. up and all accessible by road. Although, with one or two exceptions, unpretentious, they are recommended to anyone seeking peace, quiet, and fresh air. Prices for full board are applicable for a stay of three days or more. Most of the hotels and mountain inns are modern and have central heating, and also garages. There are camping grounds at Bendern, Triesen and Vaduz.

BALZERS. *Post* (17 beds) and *Römerhof* (32 beds), economy grade. All rooms with bath or shower.

BENDERN. *Deutscher-Rhein* (24 beds), economy; good food.

ESCHEN. *Brühlhof* (20 beds) and *Kreuz* (14 beds), economy grade.

GAFLEI (4,800 ft.). *Tourotel* (70 beds; indoor pool; sauna), top medium grade.

GAMPRIN. *Motel Waldeck* (80 beds), all rooms with bath; economy. Under new management.

MALBUN (5,200 ft.). Best are *Gorfion* (82 beds; all rooms with private bath; recent), *Alpenhotel* (50 beds) and *Turna* (50 beds). Each with indoor pool. All top economy bracket.

NENDELN. *Engel* (40 beds; all rooms private bath) and *Landhaus* (26 beds), country-inn style; both economy grade and modern.

SCHAAN. Top medium grade *Sylva* (24 beds; each room with pri-

vate bath; outdoor pool) and *Schaanerhof* (43 beds; indoor pool). *Dux* (18 beds) and *Linde* (40 beds) are economy.

SILUM (4,920 ft.). *Gasthof Silum* (22 beds), almost rockbottom.

STEG (4,200 ft.). *Alpenhotel Steg* (24 beds), economy.

TRIESEN. Best is medium-grade *Motel Liechtenstein* (70 beds), all rooms with bath; splendid Rhine valley views. *Meierhof* (33 beds), economy.

TRIESENBERG (2,890 ft.). *Samina* (20 beds), simple rooms; good food; economy.

VADUZ. Outstanding in accommodation and situation is rebuilt and enlarged *Sonnenhof* (55 beds), five minutes from town, near Vaduz castle. Lavish comfort and equipment; clever, tasteful decor throughout. Sun balconies and terraces to bedrooms. Indoor pool, sauna. Fine gardens, superb views. Luxury. First class:

Schlössle (55 beds), sauna, and slightly cheaper *Real* (16 beds; all rooms private bath). Medium-grade *Landhaus Vaduzerhof* (47 beds; all rooms private bath; breakfast only), indoor pool. *Engel, Adler, Löwen* and *Hotel Vaduzerhof* are economy.

FOOD AND DRINK. The Liechtenstein cuisine is Swiss with Austrian overtones. There are practically no places to eat in the Principality other than in hotels. The *Sonnenhof* is tops for view and food; the *Hotel Real* is especially known for its cuisine and cellar, and has its own vineyards, but the *Engel* is good, and *Adler* noted for its game. For a nice, reasonably priced meal the *Linde's* the spot.

The *Torkel* restaurant, owned by the Prince and surrounded by his vineyards, barely a five-minute walk from Vaduz center, is a good place to sample Vaduzer, the local red wine, something like a rather light Burgundy. But be wary. It's pleasant but potent. Better stop after a couple of glasses if you're driving. Good country atmosphere.

In most Vaduz hotel restaurants the price of a meal will range from 16 to 30 frs. In the less sophisticated spots and outside town a simple but satisfying meal can be had for about 8 frs.

SHOPPING. Due to the customs union, prices are the same as in Switzerland and you get the same goods. Apart from the usual souvenirs (there are attractive dolls with local costumes) and, of course, the Liechtenstein postage stamps, there is little to tempt you.

ENTERTAINMENT. There are movie houses at Vaduz and Schaan. There is dancing at the *Vaduzerhof* and *Engel* hotels in Vaduz, and at the *Post* at Schaan, *Engel* and *Landhaus,* Nendeln, *Römerhof* at Balzers, and *Waldeck* at Gamprin, as well as at Malbun's *Gorfion, Galina* and *Turna.* Liechtenstein is not the place for nightclubbing.

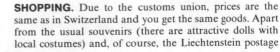

SPORTS. There are *indoor swimming pools* at the *Sonnenhof* and *Landhaus Vaduzerhof* hotels in Vaduz, a sauna-massage at the *Schlössle,* and a pool at the *Schaanerhof* at Schaan, *Krone* at Schellenberg, the *Alpenhotel, Gorfion* and *Turna* hotels in Malbun, and at the *Tourotel,* Gaflei.

Although relatively unknown, Malbun is ideal for *winter sports* and has a near certainty of good snow. An excellent network of reasonably priced chairlifts and skilifts, rarely congested except at high season weekends, serves a wide variety of slopes. The beginners' slopes are unusually good. There are ski schools and experienced guides are available for longer excursions.

Liechtenstein also has some good *fishing* (trout) streams, and the *hunting* (deer, chamois) is excellent, but leases are usually auctioned off for a season or even longer periods. The casual visitor will have to worm his way into the heart of some local lessee to use either rod or gun.

 ART. Largely a a result of the Prince's decision to allow part of his world-famous private collection to be on public display, visitors to Vaduz can always enjoy art exhibitions unmatched by any other community of similar size. Currently occupying the whole top floor of the National Gallery, above the Tourist Office, and beautifully lit and displayed, is a priceless collection of the Prince's painting by Rubens, including the splendid *Toilet of Venus* and the adorable *Little Girl* portrait. The collection is expected to be on display for some time, and is attracting art lovers from many countries. On the floor below are important loan exhibitions. Admission covering both galleries 2.50 frs.

The Historical Museum and Postal Museum are also worth a visit.

USEFUL ADDRESS. *National Tourist Office,* Englandbau, 9490 Vaduz (tel. 21443), for all information and hotel bookings.

Exploring Liechtenstein

Like ancient Gaul, Liechtenstein is divided into three parts: first the so-called lowlands, about ten square miles of wooded hills in the north; next, the flat Rhine valley in the southwest with its eastern slope rising towards the first ridge of mountains; and lastly the mountainous area between the first ridge and the second one which forms a natural border with Austria.

Exploring Liechtenstein, you should start at the capital, Vaduz, about halfway between the northern and southern extremities of the country. Vaduz is the political and natural center of the flat, fertile country along the Rhine. About three-fourths of Liechtenstein's population live in the five communal districts from Schaan, where road and railroad cross the Rhine from Switzerland, to Balzers in the south, where you can cross back into Switzerland via a bridge or via the scenic Luziensteig road on the eastern bank.

The nine miles of road from Schaan to Mäls, the southernmost hamlet, are Liechtenstein's economic showcase. Neat farms, inns and houses, old churches and new schools line the road. Through the gaps on one side you can see the Rhine flats with their rich fields and orchards; on the other, creeping up the wooded slopes, are vineyards and the villas of the wealthy.

The villa quarter of Vaduz is growing steadily. Low taxes make the principality a pleasant dwelling place for people who have or earn good money without being bound to a certain spot by their jobs. Successful novelists and playwrights form a strong group among the "new Liechtensteiners."

The castle of Vaduz completely dominates the town. Perched on a cliff about 300 feet high, it can easily be reached either by car along the road which climbs up from the northern end of Vaduz towards the mountains, or in half an hour by foot. Normally the interior of the castle is out of bounds for tourists, since it is occupied by the royal family and an almost continuous stream of guests.

But even if you cannot enter the castle, a visit is worth the trouble. Originally built in the 13th century, the castle was burned down in the Swabian Wars of 1499 and partly rebuilt in the following centuries, until the complete overhaul that started in 1905 gave it its present form. There is another medieval building about ten minutes on foot from the center of town, the Rotes Haus, once a fortress for bailiffs of a Benedictine monastery in Switzerland.

For pleasant walks off the main road try one of the paths down to the Rhine, about half an hour, and then along the river on one of the two levees. Alternatively, if you go in the opposite direction, a forty-minute climb up the hill will bring you to a romantic ruin, tucked away in the forest, the Wildschloss, once the seat of robber-barons. Cutting across the slope horizontally you reach the village of Schaan via the scenic Fürstenweg (Prince's Path) in less than an hour.

Schaan, about two miles north of Vaduz, offers the same choice of walks down to the Rhine and up the mountains, and so does Triesen, two miles south of Vaduz. Overlooking Triesen is the old St. Mamertus Chapel with quite an extensive view. Between Balzers and Mäls, the two southernmost villages, rises a steep hill bearing Gutenberg Castle, another splendid example of a medieval fortress. Unfortunately, like Vaduz it can be admired only from the outside, being privately owned.

From Vaduz (1,500 ft.) two good but sometimes narrow roads twist and climb steeply up into the mountains past the solidly romantic Vaduz castle (where there's a roadside parking place) and a succession of splendid views across the Rhine valley. At about 2,900 feet you pass the little town of Triesenberg. Beyond the town the road continues to wind upwards and, in about a mile, a side road sheers off to the left towards the mountain hotels of Masescha (4,100 ft.) and Gaflei. Masescha, Gaflei, nearby Silum and Triesenberg, all clinging to the steep side of the Rhine valley, are unpretentious, do-it-yourself skiing centers in winter and lovely centers for walks in summer.

Gaflei, at 4,800 feet, is the starting point of the Fürstensteig, a path along the highest ridge between the Rhine and the Samina valley. Winding among and around several peaks from six to seven thousand feet high, it provides a relatively comfortable way of feeling like Sherpa Tenzing without doing any really dangerous climbing. A pair of good shoes is all you need, but don't try the Fürstensteig if you're apt to feel giddy looking down a sheer drop of a couple of thousand feet or so.

Back at the road junction above Triesenberg, if you now drive on towards the mountains you'll shortly pass through a half-mile tunnel under the first mountain ridge and emerge near the village of Steg (4,200 ft.). Situated in a completely different setting—a high Alpine valley, wild, impressive and with rushing mountain streams—Steg in winter is a simple, no-frills skiing center. In summer it becomes an excellent starting point for a wide choice of not-overstrenuous mountain hikes. One is the hike following the Samina river downstream (northwards) and then turning right up the Valorsch valley to Malbun, a roughly semi-circular excursion. Another is up the Samina valley to the Bettlerjoch pass (6,400 ft.) along a tolerable track, broad enough for jeeps to take provisions up to the Joch Alpine shelter, but forbidden to all other motor vehicles.

At the upper end of the Samina valley experienced climbers can try one of the Liechtenstein's highest peaks, the Grauspitz, Schwarzhorn or Naafkopf, each about 8,400 feet.

If you now take the excellent new road which goes eastwards up easy grades beyond Steg you will find that in little more than a couple of miles it ends abruptly at Malbun (5,200 ft.), a rapidly-expanding, higgledy-piggledy village nestling on the floor of a huge mountain bowl. Hitherto little known outside Liechtenstein, in the last few years Malbun has begun to make a modest impact on the international winter sports scene thanks to the splendid variety of slopes and the generous network of chairlifts and skilifts which serve them. For beginners it is outstanding. Indeed, it was here that the Prince of Wales and Princess Anne learned to ski while they were staying with the princely family at Vaduz castle. Winter finished, Malbun turns into an unpretentious summer resort for those who want complete rest or healthy exercise, plenty of fresh air, and comfortable quarters at a realistic price.

Incidentally, the only way to visit Austria from Liechtenstein via the mountains, without too much climbing, is provided by the path from Malbun to Sareiserjoch (6,100 ft.), the border pass. If you're a glutton for exercise you'll find it takes about two hours on foot.

There's a regular bus service between Vaduz and Malbun but, if possible, go by car—especially in summer. The return journey can take well under two hours including brief viewing stops en route, but leave more time if you can. Provided the weather's good, you'll want to linger.

The part of Liechtenstein least known to tourists is the "lowland" area in the north, which, despite its name, has some fair-sized and very attractive hills. It's worth driving up to the Schellenberg hills (about 3,000 ft.), where you can get fine views of the broad, flat valley of the Rhine with its steep sides, and gaze at an almost uninterrupted panorama of peaks—the mountains of Liechtenstein, Switzerland and Austria. And from your viewpoints you will be able to see most of the little Principality we have just visited.

FACTS AT YOUR FINGERTIPS

Additional practical hints about hotels, restaurants, transportation, etc., of a regional and local character, not contained in this section, will be found throughout the book.

FACTS AT YOUR FINGERTIPS

HOW TO PLAN YOUR TRIP

 WHAT WILL IT COST? Switzerland kept the annual rate of inflation down to 3.4% in 1975 and 1% in 1976, which was the lowest of all industrial countries, and their battle with inflation is unceasing. Swiss prices have certainly risen, but they've done so less rapidly than those of some other countries.

The strength of the Swiss franc means you get precious few of them for your dollar, pound or other currency, but Swiss stability means that most prices, including hotel prices, remain more or less the same from year to year. The table below gives only an *indication* of what you can expect to pay. (For exchange rates, see "Money" later in this chapter.)

For the cash-conscious traveler in Switzerland, the tip is to avoid expensive luxuries: whisky and other imported spirits, taxis, and the fashionable restaurants. You can get an excellent meal (*plat du jour* or tagesplatte), at most restaurants for about 6 frs.

ROOM, BREAKFAST, TIPS AND TAXES
(Price per night in Swiss francs)

Hotel category		Major city	Major resort	Average town	Budget resort
Deluxe	single	60-140	45-190	60-120	75-115
	double	75-240	80-260	85-220	135-250
First class	single	45-100	35-110	52-65	35-75
	double	65-190	75-180	75-120	70-130
Medium	single	35-65	30-80	34-60	27-55
	double	60-110	60-140	60-100	50-96
Economy	single	30-55	22-56	20-45	23-45
	double	48-82	46-110	38-80	45-80

Hotels: You can count on your Swiss hotel room being clean, neat and efficient, even when it is small (often because of the addition of a private bath by an older hotel that has "modernized"). The comprehensive *Swiss Hotel Guide*, issued each year, lists all the members of the Swiss Hotel Association—and that is most of the hotels in Switzerland.

The range is vast—from the elegant and expensive *Baur au Lac* in Zurich and the *Beau Rivage* on the lake at Ouchy, shoreside "suburb" of Lausanne, to the small country inns in farm villages in the Alps, where rooms will be reasonable and food will be excellent.

To ease the confusion of hotel choosing, there are several hotel groups, with properties that have joined together for mutual promotion in hopes of competing with the extensive (and expensive) promotion of the big, modern hotel chains. Look into the properties of *Chic Hotels,* all independently owned hotels in almost 20 resort areas of the country. (Head office at Lavaterstrasse 11, 8027 Zurich.) Another group is the *Ambassador* group, usually smaller, personality properties, but also privately owned and scattered around the country, (Head office at 3037 Stuckishaus, near Bern.) Deluxe properties have grouped as *Groupement des Hôtels de tour premier rang*, with a special magazine. They can be reached through Box 238, 1000 Lausanne. For the small places, around the country, get a copy of *The Inn-Way—Switzerland,* available for $3.95 plus 50¢ postage from Box 605, Southport, CT 06490, U.S.A.

Reductions: A reduction of about 50% for children up to six years old and 30% for those between six and twelve is normal, provided they occupy their parents' bedroom. Prices in winter sports resorts may be 5% to 15% less in summer, and vice versa in summer resorts. Both charge less in spring and autumn, and in the off season. Zermatt hotel rates, for example, are reduced 30% off season.

For further information on hotels, see under "Hotels" in the "Town by Town" section.

Restaurants: Meal prices in Switzerland vary as widely as in any country. If you are welcome in university and student cafeterias, a respectable meal devoid of frills costs as little as 3 frs. In the self-service cafeterias of the Migros supermarket chain and in some department stores, a good meal can be obtained from around 4 frs. But you'll do far better for food and value if you order the *plat du jour,* or the *tagesplatte,* as the menu of the day is called in French- and German-speaking areas respectively. A deluxe restaurant and the table d'hôte menu may be priced at 35 frs. or more. Allow 4 to 8 frs. for Continental breakfast, but most hotels include this in their rates. See also under "Restaurants" in the section "Staying in Switzerland," later in this chapter.

A TYPICAL SWISS DAY

	Approx. cost in francs
Hotel, medium grade *	40.00
Lunch in moderate restaurant **	18.00
Dinner in moderate restaurant **	18.00
Two bus or tram rides	1.60
One taxi ride, 2 kms., including tip	7.00
One theater ticket, good average seat	16.00
One packet (20) Swiss-made cigarettes	1.80
One cup of coffee in popular café, including service	2.00
One bottle Swiss beer in popular café, including service	1.20
English-language newspaper	1.80
	107.40
Add 10 percent contingency allowance	10.80
	118.20

* Bed, breakfast, service and taxes included; per person, per night in double room with bath or shower.
** Three courses and coffee. Includes service but not drinks.

The local cost of living: Although Switzerland is certainly one of the more expensive countries, with fairly high prices, generally speaking incomes are high too, which helps the Swiss to enjoy almost the highest standard of living in Europe.

Some other costs: Good, average seat at opera 15-20 frs., at cinema from 4-7 frs.; museums, art galleries, often free, but maximum charge 4 frs.; parking meters, 20-80 centimes per hour, garage, 24 hours, 15 frs.; bus or tram ride within city limits 60-80 centimes.

Haircut, man's, in average salon 8-10 frs., woman's shampoo and set 15-20 frs.; newspapers, Swiss 70 centimes, British 1.80 frs., U.S. European editions 1.70 frs.; cigarettes, popular American, British, or Swiss, about 1.70 frs. for pack of 20; chocolate, 100 grams (3½ oz.) 1.40 frs. a bar.

Swiss wine per bottle, in a shop, 4 francs up, in a restaurant, 10 frs. up, in a café, 3.50 frs. a carafe (3 dcl., ½ pint); gin and tonic 4.50-6 frs.; American-style cocktail 7-8 frs.; Coke, Pepsi or similar drink in popular café, 1.50-2 frs.; tea, per glass, 1.30-1.60 frs.; ice cream, per cup 2 frs.

PACKAGE TOURS. The price is usually good value when you choose a package tour, but read the small print carefully so that you know exactly what is included. It is the extras (especially if meals are an extra) that add up and make what looks like a reasonable tour expensive. *Swiss Travel Ltd.* is a British-based tour operator specializing in Switzerland, with values that include the airfare and a medium-grade hotel in a known resort area. From the U.S., TWA and Swissair fly directly to Switzerland. Both offer a wide range of tours, including Switzerland with other European countries, and including Switzerland-with-car, Switzerland-with-Holiday Card and all variety of touring possibilities. TWA's *Hotelpass Europe* is a coupon prepaid travel scheme in connection with Hilton Hotels. Swissair's clever *Swiss Travel Invention* has four color-coded price ranges for the coupons you can buy through your travel agent before you leave. Depending on your budget, you can stay at luxury hotels, medium range, low-cost and efficiencies, with a list of the hotels in "your" category and the knowledge that the hotel you stay in will call ahead for reservations at your next destination, if you want that. In addition, half-day sightseeing and other items are offered by many of the local tourist boards in the towns where you stay overnight. *Europacar* is one of several companies with tour arrangements in Switzerland that include either a rental car or perhaps a camper. Your travel agent can give you details and prices, or contact the Swiss National Tourist Office, 608 Fifth Avenue, New York 10020.

VILLA RENTAL. There are thousands of furnished chalets or apartments of all sizes and price levels throughout Switzerland. Off season, a simple but comfortable chalet-apartment sleeping four people could be rented for about 30 frs. per person per week. But during the high season, a deluxe one sleeping five or six costs nearly ten times as much. Many travel agents can make rental arrangements for you, often incorporating reduced-rate travel. You can get an illustrated brochure describing many hundreds of chalets and apartments from *Swiss Chalets* at Elsastrasse 16, 8040 Zurich, Switzerland; or 10 Sheen Road, Richmond, Surrey, TW9 1AE, England. In the U.S., contact At Home Abroad, 136 East 57th St., New York 10022, or the Swiss National Tourist Office at 608 Fifth Ave., New York 10020, for suggestions about firms.

Devaluation—Inflation

Devaluation, revaluation or inflation—although Switzerland has an enviable record in this respect—can alter costs overnight, turning the most carefully worked out budget into grim fiction. Prices mentioned in this book are indicative only of costs at the time of going to press. Check with your travel agent near the time of your trip.

WHEN TO GO? The summer tourist season in Switzerland runs from the month of May to the end of Sept. This is when the weather is best and it is when most British and Americans take their vacations. If you can work yours in before July or after Aug., you will avoid the most crowded period, but even at the busiest times, rooms are available somewhere. Contact the local tourist office, usually at or near the center of town or the railroad station. Many of the best festivals and shows for visitors occur in summer, so if you want to take these in you'll have to accept the crowds and possible accommodation problems. Switzerland's number one attraction is the scenery, and that's just as good in June and Sept. as in July and Aug. Indeed, the Alpine flowers in spring and early summer make it possible to say that it's better then than later on.

Winter Sports. The season starts in Dec. and runs through Apr., sometimes a little later. Feb. and Mar. are the best months. Excellent bargains for ski weeks can be found at most ski resorts in Early December through early January, when the instructors are beginning their season and the heavy crowds have not yet appeared. Instruction-plus-hotel packages are available. There are places in Switzerland where you can ski all year round. It's only a question of getting up high enough. The Swiss National Tourist Office has a special leaflet about it.

Off-season Travel. Transatlantic and some cross-Channel fares are cheaper in the so-called shoulder seasons (spring and fall). So are some hotel rates. Even when hotel prices remain the same, available accommodations are better; the choicest rooms in the hotels and best tables in the restaurants have not been pre-empted, nor are train compartments packed full. If you really want to get under the skin of the country, the time to do it is when its inhabitants are going about their regular daily routines.

Seasonal Events. Twice a year the Swiss National Tourist Office publishes a free booklet—"Events in Switzerland." Here are some you may not want to miss:

January is notable for two sets of celebrations—the *schlittedas* of the Engadine and the Vogel Gryff festival of Basel. The first is informal excursions on fine Sundays when unmarried boys and girls in traditional costume go on gaily decorated sleighs from one Engadine village to another. The Basel celebration, which in English would be the Feast of the Griffin, occurs in the middle of Jan. (not always on the same date, so inquire when it is to take place) and begins with the arrival by boat of the Wild Man of the Woods, who is greeted by the Lion and the Griffin; afterwards a mummers' parade keeps the streets lively for the entire day. Wengen stages the International Lauberhorn ski races.

February is also marked by a folk fete, the burning of Old Man Winter (the Homstrom) at Scuol, in the Lower Engadine, usually on the first Sunday of the month. Carnival is gayest at Basel, where it begins with another mummers' parade on the Monday after Ash Wednesday. Lucerne celebrates the Thursday before Ash Wednesday with its parade of the Fritschi family through the streets, when oranges are distributed to children, the carnival continuing into the following week. At the same time, Schwyz has a mummers' procession of harlequins, called *Blatzli*. In Locarno, Mardi Gras is marked by the Festa del Risotto, when food is given to poor families. International speed skating championships at Davos; horse racing on the frozen lake at St. Moritz.

March is the month for Geneva's auto show and the Engadine Skiing Marathon, Maloja-Zuoz. Davos stages the Parsenn Derby international downhill ski race. Easter is celebrated in a number of Catholic communities by the foot-washing ceremony on Maundy Thursday, and in Fribourg the bishop, in token of humility, kisses the feet of the faithful in the cathedral. Religious processions occur on Good Friday in many southern towns. Mendrisio's is a survival of a medieval Passion Play, and occurs on both Maundy Thursday and Good Friday. Annual Locarno Concerts (through June).

The Landsgemeinde meetings, where you can see Swiss democracy at work in its oldest and most direct form, take place in April in Appenzell, Hundwil or Trogen, Sarnen, Stans and elsewhere. Other events in April are the Festa delle Camelie at Locarno, and the Sechseläuten festival of Zurich, when the centuries-old guilds parade, and the Böögg, a straw scarecrow representing winter, is burned at the side of the lake; the blessing of horses, donkeys and mules at Tourtemagne (Valais) on April 23; and the pilgrimage from the Centovalli across the Italian frontier to the shrine of the Madonna di Rè on the 30th. There is also the Swiss Industries Fair at Basel and the Golden Rose Television Festival at Montreux.

May Day is celebrated with particularly colorful ceremonies at Ragaz (St. Gallen), Romainmotier (Vaud) and Juriens (Vaud). At Cartigny (Geneva) the first Sunday in May is dedicated to the festival of the Feuillu, when the children who have been crowned King and Queen of the May lead a procession from house to house, and on the same day the Landsgemeinde is held at Glarus. Ascension is celebrated elaborately at Beromünster (Lucerne), when priests carrying the sacrament ride on horseback around the district blessing the crops, a ceremony dating from 1509. Corpus Christi is observed at Appenzell by strewing carpets of flowers underfoot; at Kippel (Valais) by a procession headed by the Grenadiers of God, in 19th-century uniforms; and at Bulle, Romont, Fribourg, Châtel St. Denis, Einsiedeln, and Lucerne by colorful rites and pageants. Around mid-May, Neuchâtel has its "Musical Spring" festival, and Lausanne starts its festival of music and ballet.

In June, Geneva makes a considerable to-do about the rose, exhibiting some 100,000 of them, and accompanying Rose Week with concerts, shows, and other amusements. If you want to see cows fight, this is the month when they are pitted against each other in the lower Valais.

It's a month full of music. Lausanne has its "International Festival Weeks" of music and ballet; Zurich, its "International June Festival" (music, opera, drama, etc.); and Montreux its "International Jazz Festival." Bern holds an Art Festival. If you want to look down at it all, go to Mürren for the International High Alpine Ballooning Weeks.

In July Weggis (near Lucerne) has its Rose Festival, and this is the month to see crossbow shooting in the Emmental, and the famous William Tell play which starts at Interlaken and goes on through August. For those who can't get enough skiing in the winter there's the giant slalom on the Diablerets glacier and the summer ski race on Jungfraujoch.

The Geneva festival with a battle of flowers and much jollification is in August. So is Lucerne's music festival and the film festival at Locarno. Folklore is in full swing, Swiss wrestling in the Emmental and elsewhere, folkfests at Interlaken, the National Horse Fair with costumed riders on the strong Jura horses at Saignelégier, and the Menuhin festival at Gstaad. August 1 is a Swiss national holiday, with celebrations and lots of fireworks all over the country, but shops and offices remain open for part of the day. This year Vevey stages its gigantic, five-times-a-century Winegrowers Festival.

In September, Lausanne stages its big industrial and agricultural fair, the Comptoir Suisse, and the Knabenschiessen, or boys' shooting contest, is held at Zurich. Einsiedeln has the Engelweihe, a religious festival marked by spectacular torchlight processions. Montreux and Ascona both have important music festivals.

Throughout September and October, there are vintage festivals everywhere, especially Lugano, Neuchâtel, and Morges. The latter month also holds Geneva's garden show and the picturesque fair of La Chaux-de-Fonds, the Braderie, a tremendous flea market without fleas, and the great "Olma" agricultural and dairy fair at St. Gallen. At Lausanne there's the "Italian Opera Festival."

November is a month of open-air markets, dancing and kermesses, the most quaint being the "Zibelemärit" (Onion Market) of Bern.

The Spengler ice hockey tournament at Davos in December is one of the year's most notable sports events. Christmas merriment begins on St. Nicholas's Day, Dec. 6., with particularly colorful practices in the Goms valley (Valais), Kaltbrunn (St. Gallen), Küssnacht and Arth; goes on through the riotous Escalade festival at Geneva on the 11th and 12th; and ends, after Christmas itself, with the gay, noisy masquerades of St. Sylvester (New Year's Eve).

 WHERE TO GO? The difficulty in Switzerland is not to decide what to see, but what you will have to leave out because of lack of time or money. Among cities demanding to be visited is Lucerne, for its matchless situation on the mountain-rimmed Lake of the Four Forest Cantons. Then, in no special order, are Zurich, Switzerland's largest city, which manages to combine industrialism with both architectural interest and geographical picturesqueness; Geneva and Lausanne with their famous lake; Bern, the capital; Lugano and Locarno in the warm southern lake region, bordering Italy; Basel, "The Gateway to Switzerland," a city too many travelers merely pass through despite its considerable intrinsic interest; St. Gallen, the lace center, with its priceless Abbey Library; Neuchâtel in a beautiful lakeside setting; and Fribourg, tumbling down its valley in medieval splendor.

There are in addition certain towns that tourists have more or less taken over as their own. Lake Geneva's Vevey and Montreux are favorites with vacationists. Interlaken is really more of an international city than a Swiss one. St. Moritz has long been a fashionable winter sports center and is now popular in summer as well. Davos of late years has been rivaling St. Moritz. Arosa is the third of the Grisons trinity. And if you want to get away from your fellow tourists you will be surprised how easy it is, especially in the Valais, parts of the Grisons, Ticino, Jura, and even the Bernese Oberland.

Highlights. Ascent of the Jungfrau by Europe's highest railway probably leads most lists. Other ascents to which tourists flock (mountaineering skill is required for none of them) are up the Bürgenstock on Lake Lucerne, by elevator; up the Rigi or Mount Pilatus, in the same region, by cogwheel railway or cable car; up the Zermatt-Gornergrat cogwheel railway and lofty Stockhorn aerial cableway; by cable railway and three-stage cable car from Engelberg to the top of Kleintitlis; or by cable car from Stechelberg to the top of Schilthorn, and from Schwägalp to the summit of Säntis. Probably the top scenic excursions are those to the falls of the Rhine and the glacier of the Rhône. Then there are the automobile or bus rides over some of the famous passes—the Susten, the Furka, the Julier, the Simplon, the Gotthard (even the scenery from the train, which seems to spend much of its time in tunnels, is spectacular in this region). Of many spectacular train journeys, that on the *Glacier Express* from Zermatt and Brig, past the Rhône glacier to Chur and the Grisons, is among the finest. The lake boats provide always scenically magnificent trips, but perhaps the best is that from Lucerne to Flüelen, which you can make on your train ticket as part of your journey southward, if you are going that way. Finally, the single most visited building in Switzerland is probably the Château of Chillon, on Lake Geneva, near Montreux.

Skiers may prefer Davos to St. Moritz, for the 10-mile ski run there, but *bobsledders* remain faithful to the latter because of the famous Cresta Run. *Mountain climbers* find peaks to tackle almost everywhere, but Zermatt is one of the most popular centers. If you're a beginner, you might do better to go to Rosenlaui and do your climbing under the supervision of the mountaineering school there. *Engineers* and others interested in mechanical processes might well apply for permission to go through the watch factories of La Chaux-de-Fonds. *Naturalists* find a trip through the Swiss National Park in the Grisons worth their while. And the general public will join *geologists* in appreciating that unique spectacle, Lucerne's Glacier Gardens.

The Swiss National Tourist Office publishes two helpful guides: an illustrated *Ancient Castles* and another on the *Historic Inns and Castle Hotels* open to the public.

HOW TO GO? When you have decided where you want to go, your next step is to consult a good travel agent. If you haven't one, the American Society of Travel Agents, 711 Fifth Avenue, New York, N.Y. 10022; and in Canada, A.S.T.A.–Canada, 130 Albert Street, Suite 1207, Ottawa, Ontario; or the Association of British Travel Agents, 53 Newman Street, London W1P 4AH, will advise you. Whether you select *Maupintour Associates, American Express, Thomas Cook* or a smaller organization is a matter of preference and convenience, but there are very good reasons why you should engage a reliable firm.

Travel abroad today, although it is steadily becoming easier and more comfortable, is also growing more complex in its details. As the choice of things to do, places to visit, ways of getting there, increases, so does the problem of *knowing* about all these questions. A reputable, experienced travel agent is a specialist in details, and because of his importance to the success of your trip, you should inquire in your community to find out which organization has the finest reputation.

If you want your agent to book you on a package tour, reserve your transportation and even your first overnight hotel accommodation, his services should cost you nothing. Most carriers and tour operators grant him a fixed commission for saving them the expense of having to open individual offices in every town and city.

If, on the other hand, you want him to plan for you an individual itinerary and make all arrangements down to hotel reservations and transfers to and from rail and air terminals, you are drawing upon his skill and knowledge of travel as well as asking him to shoulder a great mass of detail and correspondence. His commissions from carriers won't come close to covering his expenses, and thus he may make a service charge on the total cost of your planned itinerary. This charge may amount to 10 or 15%, but it will more than likely *save* you money on balance. A good travel agent can help you avoid costly mistakes due to inexperience. He can help you take advantage of special reductions in fares and the like that you would not otherwise know about. Most important, he can save you *time* by making it unnecessary for you to waste precious days abroad trying to get tickets and reservations.

Americans and Britons can arrange with one of the travel credit organizations for a European charge account that enables them to sign for hotel and restaurant bills, car rentals, purchases, and so forth, and pay the resulting total at one time on a monthly bill. This is particularly advantageous for businessmen traveling on an expense account or on business trips whose cost is deductible for income tax. Offering this service are *American Express, Diners Club,* Hilton's *Carte Blanche, Eurocard,* and many others.

There are four principal ways of traveling:

The **group tour,** or package holiday, in which you travel with others, following a prearranged itinerary, and paying a single all-inclusive price that covers almost everything—transportation, meals, lodging, and sometimes sightseeing tours and guides. This will probably cost you much less than if you did the same thing independently.

The **prearranged individual tour,** following a set itinerary planned for you by the travel agent, with all costs paid in advance.

The **individual tour** where you work out the itinerary for yourself, according to your own interests, but have your agent make transportation and hotel reservations, transfers, sightseeing plans.

An elaboration of the above is the **special-interest holiday** designed to pander to your own, maybe peculiar, interests and tastes. The Swiss have hundreds of them from Alphorn blowing courses (yes; a week's half-pension and six one-hour lessons costs around 400 frs.) through painting and sketching classes and horse-riding holidays to Zen meditation. Your travel agent may be able to book you in a group which has the same interest (there are several for railway buffs) or make individual arrangements. The Swiss National Tourist Office has a free booklet about special-interest holidays.

The **freelance tour**, in which you pay as you go, change your mind if you want to, and do your own planning. You'll still find a travel agent handy to make your initial transport reservation and book you for any special event where long advance booking is essential.

Travel for the handicapped person: *Travel Companions Inc.,* P.O. Box 107, Cochranville, Pa. 19330, offers a companion/escort service in Europe to assist the handicapped traveler at any stage. Personnel are mainly multilingual, fully trained ex-airline staff. Other agencies offering this kind of specialized service are: *Handy-Cap Horizons,* 3250 East Loretta Drive, Indianapolis, Ind., 46227; *Rambling Tours,* P.O. Box 1304, Hallandale, Fla. 33009; *Kasheta Travel Inc.,* 139 Main St., East Rockaway, L.I. 11518. The Swiss National Tourist Office publishes a special hotel guide for the handicapped.

For your trip you may be able to use considerably reduced fares by scheduled or supplemental airlines. This is a highly complex and frequently changing matter. Unless you're a travel expert, consult a good travel agent.

Information and advice about travel in Switzerland may also be obtained from these offices of the Swiss National Tourist Office:

New York: Swiss Center, 608 Fifth Avenue, N.Y. 10020.

San Francisco: 661 Market Street, Cal. 94105.

Chicago: 104 South Michigan Avenue, Ill. 60603.

London: Swiss Centre, 1 New Coventry Street, W1V 3HG.

Toronto (Ont. M5L 1E8): Commerce Court West, Suite No. 2015, PO Box 215.

Montreal (Que. PQ H5A 1G5): Place Bonaventure, P.O. Box 1162.

Johannesburg: c/o Swissair, 86 Main Street (POB 3866).

 **CAMPING.** Switzerland is an ideal country for covering a good deal of your route on foot, carrying your luggage on your back, for sleeping under canvas or in youth hostels. It is a paradise for campers, or for trailer camping or taking the gear in your own car. If you stop at random and ask permission of the owner of the land to camp on the spot that has taken your eye, it is rarely refused. There are in addition thousands of camping sites set aside expressly for that purpose. Organized camp sites (usually 1.20 to 4 frs. per person per night) are maintained, among others, by the *Swiss Touring Club* and the *Federation of Swiss Camping Clubs*. Both publish lists of their camps, which

can be obtained from official Swiss tourist offices, or by writing to *Touring-Club Suisse,* 9 Rue Pierre-Fatio, 1200 Geneva, or *Federation of Swiss Camping Clubs,* Habsburgerstrasse 35, 6000 Lucerne. The Swiss National Tourist Office also publishes a free folder, with map, listing over 200 camp sites.

Rent-a-Bike. Cycling in Switzerland can be exhilarating and fun. Much of the country is flatter than you would think, road surfaces are excellent, and Swiss scenery looks best from a bike. Pedal bikes can be hired for about 10 frs. a day at railway stations and elsewhere. What's more, you can hire the like at one station and return it at another. Full details, including suggested bike trips, from Swiss National Tourist Office or Swiss Railways.

The Youth Hostel Way. Youth hostel organizations offer many benefits to tourists under 25, among which are reduced transportation fares. There are youth hostels all over Switzerland for cyclists and hikers, rates ranging from about 2.50 frs. to occasionally 8 frs. a night, the latter in big cities. Linen sleeping bags are compulsory. Youth hostels are called *Jugendherbergen* or *Auberges de la Jeunesse.* Information can be obtained by writing to the *Schweizerischer Bund für Jugendherbergen,* Shopping Center/Hochhaus 9, Postfach 132, 8958 Spreitenbach.

Additional information about this type of travel can be obtained from: *The American Youth Hostels, Inc.,* 132 Spring Street, New York, N.Y. 10012.

In Britain the addresses are: *Camping Club of Great Britain and Ireland,* 11 Lower Grosvenor Place, London SW1W OEY; *Youth Hostels Association,* 29 John Adam Street, London WC2N 6JE (callers only), or Trevelyan House, St. Albans, Herts., or SYHA, 7 Glebe Crescent, Stirling, Scotland; *The Cyclists Touring Club,* Cotterrell House, 69 Meadrow, Godalming, Surrey, or 13 Spring Street, London W.2.

MEET THE SWISS. If you are interested in personal contacts with Swiss families, write or call at the *Zurich Tourist Office,* Bahnhofplatz 15. You will be put in touch with families of similar background and interests to your own and you can the spend a pleasant hour or halfday "getting to know the Swiss." Some other tourist offices in Switzerland make similar arrangements.

 WHAT TO TAKE? Travel light. Airline baggage allowances are now based on size rather than weight. Economy Class passengers may take free two pieces of baggage, provided that the sum of their dimensions—height plus length plus width—is not over 106 inches, and neither one by itself is over 62 inches. For First Class the allowance is two pieces up to 62 inches each, total 124 inches. The penalties for oversize are severe: to Western Europe $40–$50 per piece. In any case, traveling light simplifies going through customs, makes registering and checking baggage unnecessary, lets you take narrow-gauge mountain trains with room for hand baggage only, and is a lifesaver if you go to small places where there are no porters. The principle is not to take more than you can carry yourself (unless you travel by car). It's a good idea to pack the bulk of your things in one bag and put everything you need for overnight, or for two or three nights, in another, to obviate packing and repacking at brief stops.

If you are buying luggage especially for your trip, avoid the heavier and more expensive varieties. Air travelers are well advised to invest in the lightweight luggage designed for their needs. Baggage insurance to cover loss or damage provides valuable protection at trifling cost.

If you wear glasses, take along a spare pair or the prescription, preferably the former. There is no difficulty about getting pharmaceutical products, but if you have to take some particular medicine regularly, especially if it is made up only on prescription, better bring a supply. Its exact equivalent may be difficult for the average pharmacist to identify, though it undoubtedly exists.

Traveler's checks are still the standard and best way to safeguard your travel funds. In the U.S., *Bank of America, Citibank, Republic Bank of Dallas,* and *Perera Co.* issue checks *only* in US dollars; *Thomas Cook* issues checks in US dollars, British pounds and Australian dollars; *Bank of Tokyo* in US dollars and Japanese yen; *Barclays Bank* in dollars and pounds; and *American Express* in US and Canadian dollars, French and Swiss francs, British pounds, German marks, and Japanese yen. Barclays charges no commission at all, Cook and Perera none under certain conditions, and all other firms charge 1% (which actually means that you have to pay for the "privilege" of making the issuing company an interest-free loan which it will then proceed to lend out at interest for itself, a double profit!). Checks already in the currency of the country you visit should there be cashed at face value, which saves you the varying and sometimes excessive "exchange fees" imposed by local banks, hotels, restaurants and shops.

Your choice of brand will depend on several factors. Although Thomas Cook originated the system, in 1874, American Express checks are probably the most widely known, if not always the most readily redeemed or refunded. Bank of America has some 28,000 correspondent banks throughout the world, Thomas Cook about 20,000, Barclays about 8,000. Outside the U.S., Citibank checks are less well known, and their refund policies are cumbersome. The best known and most easily exchanged British checks are those of Thomas Cook, and of Barclays, Lloyds, Midland, and National Westminster banks. Traveler's checks may also be purchased at Swiss banks.

Clothes. Except in the winter season and in the most chic of international rendezvous you won't need formal evening dress. Nonetheless, women visitors staying in first class and better medium grade hotels will be glad to have something smart, but lightweight, for the evenings, and men a lounge suit. That said, elsewhere and on other occasions Switzerland is a country where you can get along most of the year on sports clothes, shifting with the seasons from the summer to the winter variety (and of the latter, in particular, you'll find a tempting selection in Swiss shops, though they are not cheap). In the summer, don't forget a sweater or two; high up in the mountains it grows chilly even on August evenings. Also something to drape over your bathing suit to protect yourself from the sun is advisable if you burn easily; when you go swimming in an Alpine lake there are a thousand or two thousand feet less of atmosphere than at sea level to screen you from the sun's rays.

CUSTOMS. If you propose to take on your holiday any *foreign-made* articles, such as cameras, binoculars, expensive timepieces and the like, it is wise to put with your travel documents the receipt from the retailer or some other evidence that the item was bought in your home country. If you bought the article on a previous holiday abroad and have already paid duty on it, carry with you the receipt for this. Otherwise, on returning home, you may be charged duty (for British subjects, VAT as well).

TRAVEL DOCUMENTS. Generally there is a delay in getting a passport, so apply several months in advance of your expected departure date. **US residents** must apply in person to the US Passport Agency in New York, Boston, Philadelphia, Washington DC, Miami, Chicago, New Orleans, Seattle, San Francisco, Los Angeles or Honolulu, or to their local County Courthouse. In some areas selected post offices are also equipped to handle passport applications. If you still have your latest passport issued within the past eight years you may use this to apply by mail. Otherwise, take with you: 1) a birth certificate or certified copy thereof, or other proof of citizenship; 2) two identical photographs 2½ inches square, full face, black and white or color and taken within the past six months; 3) $13 ($10 if you apply by mail); 4) proof of identity such as a driver's license, previous passport, any governmental ID card. Social Security and credit cards are NOT acceptable. US passports are valid for five years. Switzerland requires no visa from Americans.

If a noncitizen, you need a Treasury Sailing Permit, Form 1040D, certifying that Federal taxes have been paid; apply to your District Director of Internal Revenue for this. You will have to present various documents: (1) blue or green alien registration card; (2) passport; (3) travel tickets; (4) most recently filed Form 1040; (5) W-2 forms for the most recent full year; (6) most recent current payroll stubs or letter; (7) check to be sure this is all! To return to the United States you need a re-entry permit if you plan to stay abroad more than one year. Apply for it at least six weeks before departure in person at the nearest Office of the Immigration and Naturalization Service, or by mail to the Immigration and Naturalization Service, Washington, D.C.

British subjects: Passport application forms with explanatory notes can be obtained from main post offices, banks and travel agents. A British passport is valid for ten years and costs £8. Applicants must complete Form A which should be sent, together with two recent photos, to one of the addresses shown in the explanatory notes. It's best to send the application off not less than three weeks before the passport is required. Switzerland requires no visa from Britons.

British Visitor's Passport. This is a simplified form of passport, obtainable on demand, which costs only £4. But it is not the bargain it seems as it is valid for only one year, and only for most countries in Western Europe and Canada. Applicants must personally take completed application Form VP to a main post office together with two recent photos and one of the specified proofs of identity.

Health Certification. Not required for entry to Switzerland. Neither the United States nor Canada now requires a certificate of vaccination prior to re-entry. Because of frequent changes in law, we suggest you be vaccinated anyway, before you leave. Have your doctor fill in the standard form which comes with your passport, or obtain one from a steamship company, airline, or travel agent.

POLLUTION REPORT

Pollution and clinically clean little Switzerland seem a contradiction in terms. And so they are—or almost. Smog is unknown, a smoking factory chimney a rarity, and except in noisy, fume-filled streets the air is sweet and pure. But river and lake pollution have long been a matter of concern, and strict, new antipollution laws came into effect in 1972. New communal sewage and industrial effluent purification plants are being installed at the rate of about 100 a year, and by the early 1980s all forms of pollution in Switzerland's lakes and rivers will have been eliminated. Already many lakes such as those of Geneva, Zurich, Brienz and Thun are entirely or nearly pollution-free although in a number of them it will be a long and expensive process to restore to normal the oxygen-starved water.

At some others, including the popular lakes of Lucerne, Lugano and Maggiore, pollution is still a major problem. In some places bathing is strictly prohibited, and the signs indicating this are meant to be obeyed. Fortunately, there are many excellent open-air and enclosed pools and lidos, and a growing number of hotels have their own private pools.

 MEDICAL TREATMENT IN SWITZERLAND. The *International Association for Medical Assistance to Travelers Inc.* (I.A.M.A.T.), Suite 5620, 350 Fifth Avenue, New York 10001, or 1268 St. Clair Avenue West, Toronto, furnishes, free of charge, a directory of English-speaking doctors who have trained in the U.S., Canada or Britain. In Switzerland, IAMAT has correspondents in 9 cities. Uniform fees are: office call, $15; house or hotel call, $20; night, Sunday or holiday call, $25. A similar service is furnished by *Intermedic*, 777 Third Avenue, New York, N.Y. 10017. There is a $5 membership charge, but the uniform medical fees are the same as *IAMAT's*. There are 5 correspondents in 3 Swiss cities.

In Switzerland and Liechtenstein there is no free treatment. For surgery consultation expect to pay around 30 frs.; for a doctor's visit, at least twice as much. British visitors, especially those going on winter sports holidays, are therefore strongly recommended to take out a medical expenses insurance policy.

Of many insurance companies, one which specializes in travel and medical insurance is *Europ Assistance Ltd.,* 269 High Street Croydon, CRO 1QH, England. Multilingual staff continuously man a phone service to direct aid from a network of medical and other advisors to those insured. Basic prices: £2.50 per person (higher for winter sports); £9 for cars, £3 for caravans.

HOW TO REACH SWITZERLAND
FROM NORTH AMERICA

 BY AIR. Direct daily flights from New York to Zurich and Geneva are made by *TWA* and *Swissair,* Switzerland's national airline, and also by the latter from Chicago via Boston to Zurich, and from Toronto to Zurich via Montreal. *Air Canada* also flies from Toronto and Montreal to Zurich. There are many other airlines you can use if you make a short stopover at certain cities (see "Stopovers" below).

The best case for first-class travel is that your meals (especially on Swissair) are feasts and your seat is wide. Tourist, when the plane is full, can be too cozy for some, but the price differential is considerable. and for a 7-hour flight, the squeeze of the seat is better than the squeeze on your pocketbook. Travel light, no matter what. A lot of luggage will be a real handicap when you try to maneuver at airports, etc.

 AIR FARES. We are a little tired of writing each year that the North Atlantic fares situation is so complex as to baffle all but hardened air travelers, but it still is, and the subject is made more confusing by fuel surcharges and fickle rates of exchange. It is best to check with your travel agent or airline office on the cheapest fare to suit your particular requirements. Their advice may save you a lot of money.

We might add that as we went to press the "normal" (that is, the highest) round trip air fare by scheduled service airlines between New York and Zurich was $1,364 first class and $922 economy; that the "excursion fare" was only $565. But this is of little use for in between was a gamut of excursion, high season, thrift, student and other fares, each carefully wrapped in its tailor-made conditions. To complicate matters there was talk of further ultra-cheap new fares with—you've guessed?—yet different conditions.

BONUS STOPOVERS TO SWITZERLAND

If you are going to Switzerland on a ticket to Geneva, why not stopover at Paris or Lisbon, Copenhagen or London? These and many other European points may be visited without extra charge when you purchase a ticket from New York to Geneva. (This applies also to Zurich.)

You'll be pleasantly surprised at the way an ordinary roundtrip can be broadened in scope into a very comprehensive circle trip. When you buy a ticket to Geneva, you are entitled to 4,630 miles of transportation in each direction.

Stopovers are of course entirely optional; you can fly on the same aircraft from New York to Geneva direct. However, if you wish to add a number of countries en route, these stopover privileges are certainly useful.

Let's examine some of the available routings to the Swiss city. These are only a sampling of the total number offered and you should discuss the complete range of possibilities with your travel agent.

Leaving New York you can travel first to Lisbon. This is the southern gateway for travelers to Switzerland. After a stopover at the Portuguese city, you are entitled to make additional calls at Madrid and Barcelona.

Paris may be added to the itinerary between Lisbon and Geneva.

Denmark and Germany can be included in trips to Geneva at no extra fare. You fly first to Copenhagen and after a stopover at the Danish city continue to Hamburg. Then come Bremen and Frankfurt. Yet another German city, Stuttgart, may be visited before crossing into Switzerland at Zurich. The trip is completed with a nonstop flight into Geneva. Thus you have broadened your itinerary substantially to include extra countries. Take a look at a map and you will notice that Copenhagen is far off the New York/Geneva direct route, yet it costs no more. This is the advantage of the bonus routing system.

A number of stopover possibilities are also available in Scotland and England, as the next examples show.

You wing across the Atlantic to Glasgow, a fine base for travel to the Western Highlands and islands, as well as Edinburgh.

Leaving Glasgow for London on the next stage of the trip to Geneva, you can fly to Belfast. Continuing to London, you can make intermediate calls at Liverpool, Manchester and Birmingham.

An alternate routing in Britain would take you from Glasgow to London via Edinburgh, noted for its international festival, shopping and sightseeing.

Passengers also can travel to London from New York via Shannon and Dublin, thus giving an opportunity to visit a wide area of Ireland.

Between London and Geneva, additional stopovers can be made in France and Holland. You wing across the English Channel to Paris and then fly to Amsterdam. Finally comes a nonstop Amsterdam/Geneva trip.

What about circle trips for the price of the roundtrip fare? You can widen the scope of your trip by flying to Geneva by one route and returning by another. For instance, on the outward trip you can visit Copenhagen, Hamburg, Bremen, Frankfurt, Stuttgart and Zurich. Homeward-bound stops are in order at Barcelona, Madrid and Lisbon before returning to New York.

But remember, if you are traveling, as so many do, on an *excursion* or *economy* fare there may be certain stopover conditions and restrictions. So check this with your travel agent.

Swissair has arranged a number of specially packaged escorted and unescorted tours from North America at attractive all-inclusive rates. These are available only through selected travel agents. Details from Swissair, North America.

FROM BRITAIN OR IRELAND

 BY AIR. *Swissair, British Airways* and *Dan-Air,* as well as other airlines, connect London with Basel, Bern, Geneva and Zurich. There are also flights from Manchester and Dublin to Geneva and Zurich. At presstime the one-way London-Geneva economy class fare was £55, and the one-month, roundtrip excursion fare London to Geneva or Basel was £68.

But these two examples are of doubtful value as by the time you travel all fares will probably have been altered due to inflation, fickle rates of exchange and modified fares policies. In any event, there are, in addition, a number of sometimes substantially reduced fares with special conditions attached. The best plan, therefore, is to check the whole fares situation with your travel agency or airline office well before departure.

 BY TRAIN. Train service to Switzerland is excellent. In fact, you have an almost infinite variety of routings due to the fact that the country lies at the center of Europe. Practically all the important international trains run through or near Switzerland. Thus you can arrange your itinerary with stopovers at Paris, Strasbourg, Luxembourg, Cologne, Brussels, Rotterdam, or any of a number of other major cities. Your travel agent can advise you on this.

The most direct routes from London to Switzerland are via Dover or Folkestone to Calais. You can sleep on the train, either in couchettes or sleeping cars, or spend the night in Paris.

If you prefer to do your sleeping on a boat, you can leave Liverpool Street Station in the evening, cross via Harwich to the Hook of Holland, and there catch the morning, all first class Trans-Europe-Express *Rheingold* which is fully air-conditioned, has a special observation car for you to enjoy the scenic delights en route, and goes via Basel, Bern and Lausanne to Geneva, where it arrives in the evening.

Swiss railways, both Federal and private, give excellent connections with most international expresses which stop in Switzerland.

Fares. These vary so widely with routing, length of Channel crossing, and type of sleeping accommodation that it would be impracticable to mention them all here. At the time of going to press first class one-way fares from London to Geneva, Lausanne or Zurich were around £39-£42; second class about one-third less. To these figures must be added the cost of sleeping accommodation. The minimum was about £3.50 for a second-class couchette. First-class *Wagons-Lits* sleeping cars are much more expensive.

BY HOVERCRAFT. You can cross from Dover to Boulogne or Calais in 30 to 35 minutes by *British Rail Seaspeed* Hovercraft (adult passenger fare £5.50; cars £6 upwards), or from Ramsgate (Pegwell Bay) to Calais by *Hoverlloyd* (car fares from £17.50, including driver and up to four passengers). Some fares increase slightly during summer peak period. Up to 280 passengers and nearly forty cars are carried on frequent daily services.

BY CAR-FERRY. There are plenty of drive-on-and-off car-ferry routes across the Channel. Shortest sea routes from Dover and Folkestone to Boulogne, Calais and rather longer—Dunkirk, Ostend and Zeebrugge; also Newhaven and Dieppe. Single fares from Dover and Folkestone are about £5.50-£6.60 for adult car occupants and £5 upwards, depending on length and season, for cars; from Newhaven, £7.80-£9.00, and £6.00 respectively. Other longer cross-Channel routes are Portsmouth to Cherbourg and St. Malo; Southampton to Cherbourg and Le Havre; Weymouth to Cherbourg; Plymouth to Cherbourg and Roscoff; Sheerness to Dunkirk and Flushing; Harwich to Hook of Holland; and Felixstowe to Zeebrugge.

Complete tariffs from *Brittany Ferries,* Millbay Docks, Plymouth PL1 7AE (St. Malo and Roscoff routes only), *Normandy Ferries,* Arundel Towers, Portland Terrace, Southampton SO9 4AE (Boulogne and Le Havre routes), *Olau Line,* Sheerness Docks, Sheerness, Kent ME12 1SN (Dunkirk and Flushing routes), *Sealink,* PO Box 303, 52 Grosvenor Gardens, London SW1W OAG (Boulogne, Calais, Cherbourg, Dieppe, Dunkirk, Hook and Ostend routes), *Townsend-Thoresen Ferries,* 127 Regent Street, London W1R 8LB (Calais, Cherbourg, Le Havre and Zeebrugge routes), or AA, AAA, RAC and many travel agents.

Car-sleeper Expresses. If you want to save hours of tedious driving, you can put your car and party aboard the overnight car-sleeper expresses. The most convenient trains are from Calais to Lyss (near Bern) and from Brussels to Brig. As schedules and routes are apt to change year by year, check with AA, AAA, RAC or your travel agent. It is essential to book well in advance.

FROM THE CONTINENT, AUSTRALIA & SOUTH AFRICA

BY AIR. Switzerland can be reached readily by air from all other European countries, the chief airports being at Geneva, Zurich, Basel and Bern.

Australians and South Africans flying to London can break their journey in Switzerland without extra charge. Other stopovers for passengers from Sydney are: Djakarta, Singapore, Hong Kong, Bangkok,

Delhi, Teheran, Istanbul, and Athens in one direction. In the other you call at Rome, Cairo, Bombay and Colombo.

South Africans wishing to stopover en route to Switzerland can visit Luanda (Angola), Las Palmas and Lisbon or Athens, and Tel Aviv *(note:* subject to change).

 BY TRAIN. Switzerland's position in the center of Europe means it is the focal point of main railway routes and enjoys a remarkable service of express trains from almost every European country. Particularly notable are a dozen or so *Trans-Europ-Express* trains (TEE). These are specially built, high-speed, deluxe trains, each with a distinctive name, which bring Swiss cities within a matter of hours of such places as Amsterdam, Barcelona, Brussels, Hamburg, Hook of Holland, Milan, Munich, Paris and Rotterdam—to name but a few. For each, there is a supplementary charge and an advance reservation must be made.

 BY BUS. *Europabus,* the excellent bus service operated internationally by the railroads of Europe, has a service from Amsterdam to Lucerne with overnight stops at Cologne and Frankfurt, and a trip on a Rhine steamer for part of the journey. Other Europabus services are from Turin to Geneva, and Nice to Geneva. You can also go by Europabus on a seven-day Alpine Tour starting at either Geneva or Zurich, a four-day Lake and Mountain Tour from Zurich, or a three-day Swiss Highlights Tour from Geneva taking in Montreux, Bern, Interlaken, Lucerne and Zurich.

 BY SHIP. Going to Switzerland by ship may sound like a joke, but it can be done, and by that we don't mean the short but simple excursion trips from France to Switzerland across Lake Geneva, from Germany to Switzerland across Lake Constance, or from Italy to Switzerland across Lakes Lugano or Maggiore. An unusual way to reach Switzerland through Basel is by the Rhine steamers—miniature cruise liners—which start from Rotterdam and Amsterdam. Including stops and side excursions they take four and a half days for the upstream journey to Basel; rather less the other way.

For Rotterdam and Amsterdam sailings enquire at *KD German Rhine Line,* c/o Paul Mundy Ltd., 11 Quadrant Arcade, Regent Street, London WIR 6EJ; or: *Rhine Cruise Agency,* c/o Dietrich Neuhold Corp., 51 East 42nd Street, New York, N.Y. 10017, and 323 Geary Street, San Francisco, Calif. 94102.

ARRIVING IN SWITZERLAND

CUSTOMS. Except for a restriction to 400 cigarettes or 500 grams of tobacco or 100 cigars and one liter (1¾ pints) of spirits, which should be carried with your hand luggage, (half these quantities for European visitors), nothing in reasonable quantity intended for your personal use is barred—stockings, film, cameras, or whatever else you need during your travels. Switzerland also permits you to bring in and to take out of the country any amount of any currency.

AIRPORT TRANSPORT. Transport by special bus between the airport and the city terminal is very efficient, and costs only a few francs. Those on a tight budget should avoid expensive taxis. The city terminal is always located by the main city railway station, which is also the center of the city's public transport system. Buses from Zurich's Kloten airport go to Winterthur (public bus) as well as other nearby towns; the special airport bus goes only to Zurich's Central *Bahnhof*. From Geneva airport, buses go into Geneva (20 min.) and to Lausanne, around the lake, with a stop at shoreside Ouchy "below" Lausanne.

MONEY. The Swiss monetary unit is the franc, which is divided into 100 centimes (or Rappen). There are "nickel-silver" coins of 5, 10, 20 and 50 centimes (or ½ franc), 1 franc, 2 francs and 5 francs. There are notes of 10, 20, 50, 100, 500, and 1000 francs.

The current rate of exchange is approximately 2.50 frs. to the US dollar, 4.40 frs. to the pound sterling, but due to the unstable worldwide currency situation we emphasize that these rates may change, and before making final plans for your visit you should *check current rates* with your bank or travel agency.

When changing your travelers' checks or foreign currency into Swiss francs, do not do so at "private exchanges" (usually located in tobacconists' or candy shops close to Swiss frontier posts) without first ensuring they will give you the normal rate of exchange. Because such places sometimes offer a low rate you may lose 5% or more on the transaction. It is best always to change checks or money at banks, the larger travel agencies and the bigger stations of the Swiss Federal Railways. The last, which are usually open day and night, appear to give marginally the best rates. Hotels, restaurants and shops invariably give a poor rate of exchange, especially at weekends. Even at banks, avoid changing money on Friday, when the rate tends to sag. The best rate is often obtained on a Tuesday.

LANGUAGE. Of all Europeans, the Swiss are probably the most versatile linguistically. This is partly the result of having French, German, Italian and Romansch as national languages in a country of five million people.

In the better hotels, restaurants, and shops, English will be spoken with fluency and enthusiasm. In more modest establishments, the fluency may be less impressive, but the enthusiasm will be there, as it is even more if you make an effort to speak the local language.

STAYING IN SWITZERLAND

 HOTELS. Swiss hotels have earned the reputation of being second to none. Comfort and frills, of course, decrease with the price, but whether you splash out in a world-famous top-flight hotel or hitch up at a spot charging only 10 or 12 frs. a night for bed, breakfast and service, you can be sure of clean, adequate shelter.

If you intend to visit a great many places in Switzerland it will pay you to get the official "Guide to Swiss Hotels," obtainable free at any Swiss National Tourist Office, or from most local tourist offices in Switzerland. Among other things, it gives each establishment's minimum and maximum prices for rooms and meals under different arrangements and for different seasons; period when the hotel is open; number of beds; and whether there is parking and so on. It also gives a list of resorts and their sports facilities. But it only includes hotels in the Swiss Hotel Association. There are many, particularly in the cheaper categories, which are not members, but these are often shown in regional and local guides. A comprehensive list of Swiss motels is also obtainable free from tourist offices. For suggestions about country inns, get a copy of *The Inn Way—Switzerland* by sending $3.95 plus 50¢ postage to Box 605, Southport, CT 06490.

Living it up: During the winter high season you can pay as much as 350 frs. a day in fashionable Gstaad's *Palace Hotel* for the best accommodation with full board, and several of St. Moritz's top hostelries will set you back nearly as much. So, too, will the *Tschuggen* and the famous *Alexandra Palace* at Arosa, as well as the aptly named *Grand* and *Palace* hotels at Bürgenstock, to mention but a few of the more stylish establishments.

But away from the big name resorts, jet set hotels and palatial homes there are countless spots where dependable charm, cleanliness and highly civilized comfort cost much less than is popularly imagined.

Note: Many hotels at Swiss holiday resorts close for varying periods during the off-season, as do some motels. Summer resort hotels may, for example, close throughout the winter. Even those which cater to both winter sports and summer guests may close for a short period, such as in November. So before you go to a hotel or try to make a reservation, particularly in the off-season, *check that it will be open* when you want to stay.

Except during quiet seasons or in out-of-the-way spots, it is advisable to make reservations in advance. If you have difficulty in getting accommodation in an important town, you will probably find that at the railroad station or airport there is a central room-booking service that will find you a room (even if it's in a private house). There is usually a charge of about a franc.

 RESTAURANTS. The wide price range of meals, even in a single establishment, makes precise classification impossible. Therefore, restaurants in the regional chapters are listed in three grades: *Inexpensive,* often indicated (I), where a meal will cost in the region of 8-12 frs., but may be more, or possibly less; *Moderate* (M), where the price range will mainly be about 12-20 frs.; and *Expensive* (E), where you may pay up to 35 frs. or more for the table d'hôte menu. But because meal prices range so widely many restaurants span more than one grade. An example is the Mövenpick chain, which can be (I), (M) or even nearly (E). The tip is to study the menus usually displayed outside. If prices match your purse, go in. Swiss restaurants are dependably clean and, barring a few tourist traps with lots of yodeling for coach loads of jolly excursionists, provide both good food and good value.

 WEATHER. The Swiss climate varies considerably. As in most mountain countries, it is changeable, with much rain, but also with a lot of sunshine in between. In north and central Switzerland, count on drizzle and cold, and when the sun shines you will be pleasantly surprised. With recent seasons of "unusual" weather, the best advice is to always travel with at least one lightweight wool outfit. and at least one sweater, to layer them all on in an "unusual" cold spell in midsummer. Count on rain. The *Knirps* folding umbrellas were invented in Switzerland for very good reason, and having one with you always is a good idea.

Temperatures.

Average maximum daily temperatures in degrees Fahrenheit and centigrade:

Geneva	Jan.	Feb.	Mar.	Apr.	May	June	July	Aug.	Sept.	Oct.	Nov.	Dec.
F°	39	43	50	59	66	73	77	75	70	57	46	39
C°	4	6	10	15	19	23	25	24	21	14	8	4

Not so in the Alps. There, apart from low-lying valleys and lakes, winter is very cold with much snow, although often with blissfully warm, sunny intervals. The Alpine summer can be delightful and, in some of the valleys, very hot.

In the Ticino, south of the Alps, the climate is very different, being more Mediterranean in character: mild winters, hot sunny days in summer.

READING MATTER. You'll seldom have to look far for your favorite reading although some of the bulkier magazines may cost twice as much (or more) than their newsstand price at home. International editions of various news periodicals are available within hours of their publication.

TAXIS. Taxis are expensive in Switzerland. Avoid them if you're counting every franc. Fares vary but you should count on around 3 francs on the meter when you get in plus between 1 and 2 frs. for each kilometer traveled. And don't forget the tip—15% for short trips, 10% for long ones. In Basel and some other cities there are minicabs costing 1.50 frs. plus 1.20 frs. per kilometer. Our advice is to master the effective, efficient public transportation system.

 MAIL. The rate for letters up to 20 grams weight (about three-quarters of an ounce) mailed from Switzerland to western European countries is 80 centimes; for normal-sized postcards, 70 centimes. No airmail surcharge to most European countries: they go airmail anyway. Surface mail letters to the U.S. costs 70 centimes up to 20 grams. Airmail letters to U.S.: up to 5 grams, 1.10 frs.; 10 grams, 1.30 frs. Aerogram (stamped letter form) costs 1 fr.

TELEGRAMS. As in most European countries, telegrams are sent in Switzerland from post offices. Telegrams to nearly all European countries including Britain can also be given to most train conductors. But telegrams to the United States *must* be sent via post offices.

 ELECTRIC CURRENT. As in the case with most Continental countries, electric current in Switzerland is of the 220-volt, 50-cycle alternating variety. The 220 volts will burn out any American appliance not equipped with a transformer, and the 50 cycles will make all American 60-cycle clocks and appliances with built-in timers run too slow, even with a transformer. Swiss electric outlets require a Continental-type plug. Adaptors on sale at most electrical shops.

 TIPPING. By law, all Swiss hotels, restaurants, cafés and bars must include tips in the bill. This normally takes care of everything. Nothing further is required except that some people give the hotel baggage porter one franc; two for much baggage. Naturally, if anyone is especially helpful—e.g., the hotel desk porter in saving you money, or giving you advice on tours or nightlife—an appropriate reward would be appreciated.

In Switzerland tipping has not become the vice it is in so many countries. Hands are rarely thrust out, threateningly, palm upwards. Although, even with the Swiss, tipping is not always an exact science, here more than in most countries, what the tipper believes he ought to give is usually about the same as what the tippee expects to receive. Generally speaking, the rules and customs of the game are as follows:

Although in an average restaurant you won't need to pay anything if they hang up your hat and coat, if you deposit them in a cloakroom where no charge is made it is customary to give about 50 centimes per person to the attendant. Neither washroom attendants nor usherettes in theaters and cinemas expect tips.

Tip taxi drivers about 10% to 15%, the larger percentage for shorter rides. There's a standard tariff for railroad porters—at present 1.50 frs. per article.

With men's barbers as well as women's beauty parlors and hairdressers give a good 10%; for a shampoo and set about 2 frs. or 15%, whichever is higher.

TELEPHONES. The excellent Swiss telephone service is entirely automatic—not only for local calls, but for intercity service as well. Booths with operators are in attendance in all post offices and the railway stations of the large cities. With new type automatic coin boxes the cost of a call depends on time and distance. As long as you feed the machine with the coins indicated, you will remain connected. Frequently the machines bear instructions in English. To call one large city from another, you usually have only to dial first the call numbers of the other city, and then follow it with the number of the subscriber you are calling. In a number written thus: (083) 35135, the numbers in parentheses call the town, the rest is the local number.

For information and inquiries, dial 111. If you have difficulty getting through or want to make a complaint, dial 112. For police dial 117, and fire 118. These numbers apply almost throughout Switzerland.

PUBLIC TOILETS. Lavatories in Switzerland, even in the simplest spots, are usually modern, and invariably clean. Look for a W. C. sign, or (in French, German and Italian speaking areas respectively) *Toilettes, Toiletten* or *Gabinetti.* Ladies: *Dames* or *Femmes; Damen* or *Frauen; Signore* or *Donne.* Gentlemen: *Hommes* or *Messieurs; Herren* or *Männer; Signori* or *Uomini.* Public lavatories are at stations, cable car termini and similar, and near major tourist attractions and features. Otherwise not very common. Use those in cafés, gas stations, department stores, etc. Normally free, but any slot locks usually take a 20 centimes coin.

CLOSING DAYS AND HOURS. Swiss holidays are as follows: New Year's Day; Good Friday; Easter Monday; Ascension; Whit Monday (Pentecost); Christmas; and Boxing Day (the day after Christmas). There are also many local holidays. Trams and buses in the big cities usually start at 5:30 a.m., and run until midnight.

Normal business hours for shops are from 8 a.m. to 12:15 p.m. and from 1:30 p.m. to 6:30 p.m., but there are many local and individual variations. The standard hours are observed most closely in the cities; in purely resort towns, the hours are apt to be longer, and the noontime break omitted. It is customary for shops to close for a half day sometime during the week, and the day chosen by a particular shop is often announced by a sign in the window. The ordinary office hours are 8-12 and 2-6, and Saturday afternoon is a holiday.

Opening hours for banks vary from city to city: usually 8 a.m.-4.30 or 5 p.m.; closed for lunch and on Saturdays. Best check with your hotel. Travel agency banking services normally operate the same hours. When banks are closed and at other times, you can change money at the principal railroad stations.

Post offices are usually open in the cities from 7:30 a.m. until noon, and 1:45 p.m. to 6 p.m.; on Saturdays, close about 12:30 p.m.

Pharmacies are open from 8 a.m. to 6:30 p.m. Notices on their doors when closed give the address of other pharmacies remaining open for night or Sunday service.

CASINOS. Some Swiss resorts have a casino but it's a far cry from Las Vegas or Monte Carlo. *Boule,* a modest version of roulette, is the favored form of gambling. The minimum bet is usually 1 fr. and the maximum only 5 frs. While this modest 4-to-1 ratio of lowest to highest wagers frustrates most "systems," it also makes losing a fortune a major undertaking. The Swiss don't want you throwing yourself off the Jungfrau or Matterhorn because of bad luck at the gaming tables. They're also opposed to big-scale gambling on moral grounds, preferring to give you more material value for your money. If you *must* try your luck, go to Lugano in southern Switzerland, cross the lake to the Italian enclave of Campione (many visitors do), and you'll find an eminently respectable but high-stakes casino—or you might try Konstanz (Germany) just over the northern border. The popular French casinos at Divonne, only a few miles from Geneva, and at Evian, a pleasant boat trip across the lake from Lausanne, attract a cosmopolitan crowd.

STUDYING IN SWITZERLAND. Switzerland is justly noted for its fine schools, and many English-speaking students from Great Britain and the United States go there, both for the thoroughness of Swiss education in general and to perfect themselves in either French or German. From the point of view of acquiring perfect control of a foreign language, the schools of French Switzerland rather hold the advantage over those of German Switzerland, for while written German is the same in Switzerland as in Germany, the spoken language differs considerably, and though High German is taught in the schools, the student does not have the help of hearing this form of the language spoken all about him. Swiss French, however, is excellent—in Geneva, and especially Neuchâtel, French probably is spoken as well as in any place in the world except Tours, certainly better, on the average, than Paris, though perhaps with less gusto. Also Americans in particular may find the methods of the German schools somewhat strict and rigid in comparison with the schools they are used to. The French schools are more relaxed.

If you are looking for a school at the preparatory or finishing school level, write to *Fédération Suisse des Ecoles Privées,* 40 Rue des Vollandes, 1211 Geneva, giving all pertinent details—age of the prospective student, whether you prefer a one-sex or mixed school, type of course desired, whether to complete the pupil's education or prepare him or her for the university, and so forth. They will save you the trouble of plowing through catalogs by sending you the names of four or five schools which meet your requirements, thus narrowing the field. At the same time, however, ask them to send you the booklet "Federation of Swiss Private Schools," which not only lists but describes and illustrates the more important ones. The Swiss National Tourist Office publishes a useful booklet, "Private Schools in Switzerland."

At university level, plenty of opportunities exist for study. For information, apply to any Swiss tourist office.

There are special summer schools from early July to late August for 10- to 18-year-old youngsters. Details in booklet "Holiday Language Courses and Centers," free from Swiss National Tourist Office. Languages (chiefly French), sports, physical culture, excursions and hiking are part of the course. American parents can take advantage of special rates which include economy class jet transportation by *Swissair* and cover also living accommodation, 3 meals daily, any necessary medical services, and the tuition for the 8-week course. Brochures from travel agents and Swissair offices.

Student tours are organized by a number of tour operators in the United States, incorporating short courses at European universities that include Switzerland. Write to: *Educational Travel Assn.,* 535 Fifth Avenue, New York 10036; or *University Travel,* 44 Brattle Street, Cambridge, Mass. 02138.

 WINTER SPORTS. Switzerland is generally considered an expensive country, but when it comes to winter sports vacations, it offers some of the best bargains in the Alpine area. For one thing, the Swiss, with their long experience of tourists, have standardized prices. The bills do not shock you with unexpected extras. Resorts are categorized according to A, B and C, and lessons and rental of equipment are priced accordingly, with the A resorts being the top cost-and-facility places. (The C places offer the best values; they are often "next year's" top spot.)

At such fashionable resorts as Arosa, all-inclusive terms for a stay of at least three days can run as high as 230 frs. per person per day, or as low as 30 frs. if staying at a pension. Similar terms at smaller resorts, such as Splügen, range from a maximum of 80 frs. to a minimum charge of around 30 frs. per day.

Ski school charges vary considerably from place to place. Roughly, however, you will pay for a week's ticket (six half-day lessons) about 55 frs. in the big-name resorts, and around 50 frs. in the rest.

Money Savers. Inquire about "all-in" weeks, which are all-inclusive-priced holidays, for promotion at other than high season. To get the best value buy your ski school tickets for as long a period as possible. You may save on the basic costs by joining a ski club or ski school, and sometimes the choice of hotel makes a difference. There are all sorts of reduced-price tickets for cable cars, ski lifts, etc., such as 5-ride, 10-ride, group, weekly, monthly. Ask what the possibilities are in a place where you expect to stay a few days. Many resorts offer reductions on ski lifts as well as at hotels and ski schools from mid-Jan. to early Feb. and from mid-Mar. onward.

There's no need to bring equipment with you. All the more popular resorts can fit you out from top to toe, and at many places you can hire boots, skis, and often skibobs. Many places sell secondhand equipment, which is in excellent condition.

You'll almost certainly save considerably by going on one of the many winter sports package holidays which are organized by a number of specialist firms. The all-inclusive price—covering travel, hotel accommodation and meals—will be much cheaper than anything similar you can arrange yourself. In addition, you'll probably be able to hire boots and skis, use skilifts and have ski instruction at reduced rates. Inquire at your travel agency.

Ski Areas. Among the best places for real beginners are *Adelboden, Château d'Oex, Grindelwald, Kandersteg, Lenk, Leysin, Saas-Fee* and *Wengen.* For those with a little experience *Davos* and *Klosters* can be recommended because of the wide Parsenn snow slopes and the variety of runs. At Klosters the slope from Schwendi to Klosters is a good one for those with at least moderate experience, while the Casanna Alp-Klosters run is perhaps one of the most interesting in the Swiss Alps for skiers not quite ready for the more difficult *pistes.* Davos has something special for novices in its former bobsled run, whose track provides unpracticed skiers with an easy safe descent, two and a half miles long, which is entered after an easy run from the Weissfluhjoch.

For experts, the Parsenn area is hard to beat. In addition to the Parsenn Derby course, there is the challenging fast run from Gotschnagrat by way of Gotschnawang and Gotschnaboden to *Klosters,* of which the first two stages are very steep, and the Gotschnagrat-Drostobel-Klosters Dorf run, with its 3,600-foot drop, known as "La Fameuse." The Kandahar run at *Mürren* is one of Switzerland's most famous. *Davos, St. Moritz, Wengen, Gstaad, Zermatt, Andermatt* all offer particularly good terrain for the skier who likes to pit his skill against difficult problems.

Long-season resorts providing fairly dependable snow conditions to Easter and beyond are plentiful. *St. Moritz* can guarantee skiing this late, at altitudes reached by overhead cable railway. *Kleine Scheidegg* will give you some snow in May; *Engelberg, Pontresina, Säntis, Schilthorn* and *Verbier* in June; *Andermatt* and *Saas Fee* into July. And there are many places where you can ski throughout the summer, details of which are given in the leaflet "Summer Skiing in Switzerland," obtainable free from any Swiss National Tourist Office.

Davos, Gstaad, St. Moritz, and *Flims* are tops in skating centers. Ski jumping, skibobbing, ice hockey, curling, bobsledding, and sleighing are other attractions offered at most of the well-known resorts. For a more detailed description of facilities, consult the regional chapters.

Membership of the Swiss Ski Club (through any of the local groups affiliated with the central organization) gives discounts, insurance against sports accidents, admissions to competitions, and other benefits. For a list of clubs, write to Schweizerischer Skiverband, Luisenstrasse 20, 3000 Bern 6.

SPAS. Switzerland is a country rich in natural mineral springs, of which there are said to be nearly 300. Around the health-giving waters of many of these springs, medicinal spas have grown up. Some, like Bad Ragaz-Pfäfers, for example, have been known for centuries, are world-famous, and offer all of the expected trappings of an international watering place. Others are small, unsophisticated, and known to few apart from the Swiss and their immediate neighbors.

Often the spas are fine, modern establishments; sometimes they are a little dated in their appearance. But all are spotlessly clean, and whether you are there for a thorough-going cure, for rest and relaxation, or for something in between, you will find they offer skilled and sympathetic attention at surprisingly reasonable prices.

The hotels at most of the spas have special all-in rates which include room, all meals, tips, and resort and other taxes. These special terms (called *Prix à forfait* or *Pauschalpreis)* are, however, only when you stay at least three days.

A booklet describing many of the Swiss spas, and another listing hotels with their all-inclusive terms, can be obtained from the *Swiss National Tourist Offices,* as well as from most local tourist offices in Switzerland.

The following table shows some of the many Swiss spas, with their heights above sea level, and a broad indication of the principal disorders in which they specialize as well as some of the main treatments available.

Treatments	Place	Medical indications
Baden (1,300 ft.)	Rheumatism; paralysis; gynecological disorders	Thermal, steam and carbonic acid baths, inhalations, douches, underwater massage, mechanotherapy, electrotherapy, spa water drinks.
Bad Ragaz (1,700–2,300 ft.)	Rheumatism; paralysis; heart, circulation and urinary disorders.	Baths, underwater massage, inhalations, mud packs, electrotherapy.
Bad Vals (4,100 ft.)	Circulatory, liver and respiratory disorders.	Inhalations, massage, Kneipp, etc.

Treatments	*Place*	*Medical indications*
Bex-les-Bains (1,500 ft.)	Rheumatism; circulatory, gynecological, nervous and respiratory disorders; obesity.	Brine baths and compresses, carbonic acid baths, inhalations, electrotherapy, spa water drinks.
Lavey-Les-Bains (1,400 ft.)	Rheumatism; circulatory, gynecological, respiratory and skin disorders.	Baths, douches, inhalations, irrigations, hot sand baths.
Lenk-im-Simmental (3,600 ft.)	Rheumatism; respiratory and skin disorders.	Baths, inhalations, carbonic acid baths, underwater massage.
Leukerbad (4,600 ft.)	Rheumatism; paralysis; circulatory, gynecological and skin disorders.	Carbonic acid baths, mud packs, hydrotherapy, underwater massage, spa water drinks.
Passugg (2,700 ft.)	Stomach, intestinal, urinary and circulatory disorders.	Baths, underwater massage, mud packs, electrotherapy, spa water drinks.
Rheinfelden (900 ft.)	Arthritis; circulatory, gynecological, respiratory and urinary disorders; debility.	Brine baths, brine/mud packs, inhalations, underwater massage, electrotherapy, spa water drinks.
Rietbad (3,000 ft.)	Rheumatism; circulatory, intestinal, respiratory, skin and stomach disorders.	Sulphur and carbonic acid baths, inhalations, douches, mud packs, underwater massage, spa water drinks.
St. Moritz-Bad (5,800 ft.)	Rheumatism; circulatory, gynecological and urinary disorders.	Carbonic acid and peat baths, underwater massage, electrotherapy, colonic lavage, spa water drinks.

Treatments	Place	Medical indications
Schinznach-Bad (1,200 ft.)	Rheumatism; paralysis; circulatory, liver, respiratory and skin disorders.	Sulphur baths, inhalations, mud packs, underwater massage, spa water drinks.
Schwefelberg-Bad (4,600 ft.)	Rheumatism; respiratory and skin disorders.	Sulphur and carbonic acid baths, mud packs, inhalations.
Scuol-Tarasp-Vulpera (4,100 ft.)	Circulatory, intestinal, liver, stomach and urinary disorders.	Carbonic acid baths, inhalations, colonic lavage, hydro-electro-therapy, spa water drinks.
Stabio (1,100 ft.)	Rheumatism; respiratory and skin disorders.	Sulphur baths, mud packs, inhalations, spa water drinks.
Zurzach (1,150 ft.)	Rheumatism; circulatory and nervous disorders.	Electrotherapy, underwater massage, fango packs, traction.

Swiss spas are invariably under medical supervision, and for all but the simpler treatments a doctor's consultation is advisable if not obligatory. But you won't find the spas to be depressing concentrations of the seriously ill. Many who go there do so solely to escape for a short while from the rat race of modern life; to obtain rest and relaxation that come from the spa and its surroundings; and to benefit from the health-giving qualities of both the waters and the less drastic of the treatments available.

TRAVELING IN SWITZERLAND

 TRAINS AND BUSES. Switzerland boasts an entirely electrified railway system. The cars are spotlessly clean. Round trip tickets, good for ten days, are sold for 15-25% less than the price of two single tickets. Children under six are carried free and up to sixteen pay half-fare. Swiss railway tickets are valid on lake steamers where the latter operate between points also served by the railway.

A practical cheap ticket is the *Half-Fare Travel Card*. For $16, you can travel at half-fare as much as you like during fifteen days; for $22, one month.

MONEY SAVER

One of the most economical ways of traveling about is to use the *Swiss Holiday Card,* introduced for the first time in 1972. This gives holders unlimited travel without any further payment on most Swiss trains, postal coaches and lake steamers. In addition, holders can buy tickets at 25% to 50% reduction on a large number of mountain railways and aerial cableways.

A real bargain, the *Card* costs for 8 days $45 for 2nd class, $63.50 for 1st class; 15 days $63.50 and $88 respectively; one month $88.50 and $122.50. Remember, this includes fares; no further payment is needed. The *Holiday Card* is only on sale in foreign countries. Remember that Swiss 2nd class is excellent; certainly good enough for most needs.

For a man aged sixty-five years or over (women, sixty-two years) there is another type of special pass. This allows purchase of rail tickets at half-fare but does *not* include such purchases. It is only a permit to buy. The cost of this bargain is $31.50 (about £20) for a year, but it must be purchased abroad. Holders of this pass are also given specially reduced rates at more than 500 Swiss hotels, though not during Feb., Mar., July and Aug., or over the Christmas, Easter and Whitsun holidays. Further information may be obtained from any Swiss National Tourist Office.

In some of the popular holiday districts *Regional Holiday Season Tickets,* valid for seven or fifteen days, can be obtained that allow at least five days unlimited travel by train, mountain railways, lake steamers and Alpine postal coaches, with half-fare for the rest of the time. These are only sold in Switzerland.

On many of the Alpine bus routes and excursions the buses have panoramic windows specially designed to allow passengers a good view. These buses are useful even to visitors with their own cars, for motoring over the Alps requires the driver's full concentration on the road and doesn't allow him much opportunity to enjoy the almost constant succession of varied and magnificent scenery. Tickets can be obtained from any of the offices of the transport undertakings concerned, and seats on postal buses can be reserved at post offices.

Trams and buses usually operate from about 5:30 a.m. until midnight. In many towns, tickets must be bought from an automatic machine at the bus or tram stop before boarding the vehicle. Fares around 60-80 centimes.

STEAM RAILWAYS PRESERVATION. Although the Swiss were the first (or among the first) country in the world to dispense with steam traction on the railways in favor of electrification, they were also one of the first to recognize the appeal of steam for railbuffs and tourists. They have seen to it that there is now a wide selection of steam-hauled trains the length and breadth of Switzerland. Swissair run up to sixteen special tours every year from the

United States, called "The Railroader," providing steam trips on at least seven lines. Steam weekends are programmed by the Swiss National Tourist Office in Britain in association with Swiss Federal Railways and the private lines. A leaflet with details of lines where there is some steam operation, with fares, steam supplements, etc., is free from Swiss National Tourist Office.

Berner Oberland Bahnen. A climb from Wilderswil to Schynige Platte by rack-and-pinion steam engine. The train operates for special parties with a minimum of thirty passengers.

Blonay-Chamby. Near Vevey, this is a museum line run by Swiss enthusiasts on Saturdays and Sundays throughout the summer. Usually, seven steam trips are run each way on operational days, and specials may be chartered by groups. It owns no fewer than eleven fascinating and varied steam engines. It is meter gauge and sometimes its engines venture on specials onto neighboring lines such as the Montreux-Oberland. The route is hilly and scenic, over about five miles.

Bodensee-Toggenburgbahn. Standard-gauge private railway in northeast Switzerland which hires out a steam engine and vintage train for groups. It is especially popular for wedding parties and is called "Amor Express" accordingly. The run is normally between Herisau and Nesslau, twelve miles.

Brienz Rothornbahn. Climbs the Rothorn from Brienz on the lake of that name. It is Switzerland's last surviving mountain railway with regular steam operation (summer only). The five-mile trip takes an hour.

Brig-Visp-Zermattbahn. Runs special trips with steam engines between St. Niklaus and Täsch during May and early June, also mid-Sept. and all Oct., but no Sun. The distance is twelve miles.

Mittelthurgaubahn. Standard-gauge private railway which hires out a steam engine and vintage train for private groups from Wil to Konstanz and return (eleven miles each way).

Rhaetian Railways. A very large privately owned meter-gauge system serving the Grisons. Owns two steam engines, sometimes hauling public excursions but usually hired out for special trips. Landquart to Davos, thirty-one miles, is most popular run.

Sensetalbahn. Steam runs in the Sense Valley every first and third Sunday afternoon from in May, June, Sept. and Oct. (two round trips between Flamatt and Guemmenen).

Sihltalbahn. Narrow-gauge railway from Zurich (Selnau) to Sihlwald, running the famous *Schnaaggi-Schaaggi* steam train with a delightful little 1899 0.6.0 tank. Public runs as advertised, giving a long stop at terminus,

Sihlwald, to view the giant French "Mountain" engine *Le Boeuf,* preserved there as a contrast. Groups can charter the *Schnaaggi-Schaaggi* any day.

Solothurn-Zollikofen-Bern-Bahn. Two steam runs, Worblaufen to Solothurn (every second Sun. May to Oct.) and Worblaufohn to Worb Dorf (every fourth Sun. May to Oct.).

Vitznau-Rigibahn. Historic rack-and-pinion climb to summit of Mt. Rigi overlooking Lake Lucerne. Was opened in 1869, second mountain railway in the world (first was Mt. Washington in New Hampshire). Steam provided with two quite modern rack tank engines on periodic excursions, May to the end of Sept., over the 4 miles up to Rigi Kaltbad (a 43-minute run).

Waldenburgerbahn. Historic steam train from Liestal to Waldenburg runs third Sunday every month, May to October.

A *Eurailpass* is a convenient, all-inclusive ticket that can save you money on over 100,000 miles of railroads, and railroad-operated buses, ferries, river and lake steamers, hydrofoils, and some Mediterranean crossings in 13 countries of Western Europe. It provides the holder with unlimited travel at rates of: 15 days for $170, 21 days for $210; 1 month for $260; 2 months for $350; 3 months for $420; and 2nd class student (up to age 25) fare of 2 months for $230. Children under 12 go for half-fare, under 4 go free. These prices cover first-class passage, reservation fees, and surcharges for the Trans Europe Express services. Available to US, Canadian and South American residents only, the pass must be bought from an authorized agent in the Western Hemisphere or Japan *before* you leave for Europe. Apply through your travel agent or the *Swiss National Tourist Office,* 608 Fifth Ave., New York 10020, N.Y. and 661 Market St., San Francisco, Calif. 94105.

MOTORING. Switzerland has two automobile associations, the Automobile Club de Suisse, Laupenstrasse 2, Bern, and the Touring Club Suisse, 9 Rue Pierre-Fatio, Geneva. Your auto club is almost surely affiliated with one of these two. Ask the *Swiss Tourist Office,* before you leave, to give you their official road map, a marvel of condensation, which on a single sheet gives you not only a route map for the entire country, but drive-through maps for the chief cities.

Swiss roads are usually well-surfaced but, except for the increasing number of motorways, they are often winding and hilly—and frequently, of course, mountainous. High average speeds are out of the question.

If you take your own car to Switzerland the only documents you need are the car's registration papers and a valid driving license, but it is wise to have an insurance Green Card. Caravans require the usual Customs documents (obtainable through your motoring organization).

You drive on the right. In built-up areas the speed limit is 60 km.p.h. (37 m.p.h.). On all other roads, except where clearly marked to the contrary (e.g., motorways), there is a strictly enforced speed limit of 100 km.p.h. (62 m.p.h.). It is compulsory to wear seat belts if the car is fitted with them.

In Switzerland, as in most European countries, vehicles coming from the right normally have priority, and will expect it. In other words, you must give way to vehicles approaching from your right-hand side. The exceptions are on main roads marked by a yellow diamond sign, or by a blue road sign. In such cases *you* have priority over traffic coming from the right.

On mountain roads which are marked with a road sign showing a yellow posthorn on a blue background, the yellow postal buses have priority over all other vehicles. Such buses have a distinctive three-note horn that is liberally used to announce their approach around blind corners and narrow turns: when you hear it, allow as much passing room as the size of your car permits. If the road is too narrow for you and the bus to pass, you must follow the instructions of the driver as to backing up, pulling to one side, etc.

Traffic going *up* a mountain road has priority over all traffic, except postal buses, going *down*.

Along mountain roads, where snow chains are frequently needed (and sometimes compulsory) in the winter, there is an established service to equip cars with them. Snow Chain Service Posts are identified by signs bearing the words *Service de Châne à Neige.* Chains can be hired throughout Switzerland.

If an automobile breaks down, assistance can be obtained through the local telephone exchange (ask operator for "Autohilfe"). Roadside repairs or towage to the nearest garage are free to motorists with international touring documents issued by the motoring organizations.

Gasoline (petrol) costs around 1 fr. a liter for super, and 98 centimes for regular grade.

Car Hire. Several airlines have plans whereby you may arrange when purchasing your plane ticket to have a self-drive or chauffeur-driven car awaiting you at the airport or your hotel. The Swiss railroads have a similar arrangement, available at most big stations.

There are dozens of car rental firms in the country; some of the larger ones are: *Avis,* main office at Flughofstr. 61, Glattbrugg and 14 other offices. *Hertz,* Lagerstrasse 33, Zurich and 12 other offices. *Europcar,* Badenerstrasse 812, Zurich and 11 other offices. *Budget,* Scheideggstrasse 73, Zurich and 8 other offices throughout the country. (See also *Practical Information* section in following chapters for local addresses.) Most important car-rental companies have offices at Basel, Geneva and Zurich airports.

MAJOR ALPINE PASSES

Except in midsummer, it is advisable to check road and weather conditions ahead before starting across any of the major passes. The sun may be shining down where you are, but that's no guarantee that snow and ice aren't turning the pass itself into a nightmare of poor visibility and slick surfaces. Or highway repairs may necessitate one-way traffic along certain stretches that will delay you for hours. Both of the Swiss automobile clubs issue daily bulletins, and you can telephone the nearest office if your hotel or local Swiss tourist bureau can't advise you on the spot. With most of the important passes, somewhere on the approach road there is a prominent notice stating whether the pass is open or closed.

Swiss Touring Club mechanics in black-and-yellow cars patrol the most frequented mountain passes: St. Gotthard, Susten, Furka, Grimsel, Julier, Simplon, Flüela, Mosses, Pillon, etc.

Bernina. This pass, connecting St. Moritz with Tirano, across the Italian border, among the most scenic of Switzerland, is traversed by rail as well as highway. The principal attraction is the exquisite Piz Palü, with its sensational glacier, which is seen just beyond the 7,700-foot summit of the pass. From Poschiavo onward, the atmosphere is distinctly Italian. Tirano is the home of two of Italy's most illustrious families, the Viscontis and the Pallavicinis.

The pass is open most of the winter. Maximum gradient 10%. The narrow-gauge Bernina Railway takes three hours for the trip.

Great St. Bernard. The granddaddy of all Swiss passes. Although best known for the legendary lifesaving dogs kept by the monks from the famous hospice, the Great St. Bernard connecting Martigny with Aosta (Italy) is historically one of the most important passes in Europe. It was known and used by the Celts, and later, but long before the birth of Christ, by the Romans. The old pass road, which reaches a height of 8,100 feet, is relatively easy driving for an Alpine pass, having a maximum gradient of about 10%, but is narrow in parts. The summit section is usually closed about mid-Oct. to mid-June, but a fine 3¾-miles-long tunnel, which burrows some 2,000 feet under the summit, now enables the crossing to be made throughout the year although chains may be necessary in winter.

There is a Swiss postal bus service from Martigny to the hospice, June-September, two and a half hours; an Italian one from the hospice to Aosta, two hours.

Julier, Maloja. The approach roads for both of these passes connect at Silvaplana, near St. Moritz. Open the year round, they provide an excellent connection between the Grisons and Italy, starting at Chur and passing through Lenzerheide and Silvaplana. On both, the highway is excellent and kept relatively free of snow in winter, although in January and February chains are recommended. The scenery is less rugged than along the western passes but no less pleasing. The countryside is heavily wooded even though the summits of both passes rise above 6,000 feet. *Julier:* modern, well engineered; maximum gradient 12%. *Maloja:* modern road; gentle, easy ascent from Silvaplana; much steeper—9%—with hairpins coming from Italy.

Postal buses run from St. Moritz to Lugano, an all-day excursion and one of the most rewarding trips you can make in Switzerland.

Oberalp, Furka, Grimsel. These three connecting passes constitute the primary east-west Alpine traverse, crossing the northern approach to the St. Gotthard at Andermatt. The Oberalp (6,700 ft.) begins at Disentis near the source of the Rhine and is the boundary between the cantons of Grisons and Uri. The Furka (8,000 ft.), between Andermatt and Gletsch, affords a sensational view of the 8-mile-long Rhône Glacier, and at the western end connects with the Grimsel Pass road leading to the Bernese Oberland. The Grimsel (7,100 ft.) was known to be in use as early as the 13th century. The principal attraction now is the 1,200-foot-long, 375-foot-high Spitallam Dam, one of Europe's outstanding engineering feats. The whole Oberalp-Furka-Grimsel area is noted for the beauty of its wildflowers in summer.

Furka open mid-June to mid-Oct.; hairpin bends but mostly good road; heavy weekend traffic; maximum gradient 10%. *Grimsel:* open mid-June to mid-Oct.; modern surface, comparatively easy, heavy weekend traffic; maximum gradient 10%. *Oberalp:* open mid-June to end Oct.; narrow road, mostly good surface; numerous hairpins; max. gradient 10%.

St. Gotthard. A pass of considerable historic importance, the 6,900-foot St. Gotthard, leading from the northern cantons to the Ticino, was traversed by carriage as early as 1775 by an Englishman named Greville. Until the railroad tunnel was completed in 1880 the pass was the principal route between central Europe and Italy. Today it is a good road and, since the completion of a new by-pass avoiding the top twenty-five hairpins, a moderately easy drive. Weekend and holiday congestion, however, can make the crossing both slow and tedious. So, as the approach to the St. Gotthard is more scenic than the pass itself, you need not feel guilty about putting your car on a train (see page 58) between Göschensen and Airolo for the 9-mile ride through the tunnel. Pass usually open mid-May to mid-Oct. Max. gradient 10%.

San Bernardino. The completion (1968) of the new tunnel, almost four miles long, under the old San Bernardino pass has given this route added importance. The old road, although fairly easy, maximum gradient 10%, was usually closed mid-Oct. to June over its 6,800-foot summit. With the new tunnel, this route connecting the central Grisons with Bellinzona and Lakes Lugano and Maggiore is now open throughout the year.

Simplon. This major route between Switzerland and Italy was completed at the beginning of the 19th century at the order of Napoleon Bonaparte. When the railway tunnel—the longest in the world—was opened in 1905 Napoleon's road over the pass lost much of its importance. Recently, the road—which reaches 6,500 feet—has been much improved. As a result of new tunnels and snow galleries it is now open throughout the year and, as Alpine passes go, is a relatively easy drive. Cars can also be carried on trains through the rail tunnel between Brig and Iselle.

Swiss postal coaches run between Brig and Gondo on the Italian border, a two-and-a-half-hour trip.

Susten. An alternative to the Furka/Grimsel pass route is the Susten, which connects Wassen, north of the St. Gotthard, and Andermatt with Meiringen. This is a first-class highway, the pride of all the Swiss Alpine passes. The Susten region is a favorite of mountain climbers, the two chief attractions being the 12,000-foot Dammastock and Sustenhorn; both climbs begin at Gadmen—guides are available. Less experienced climbers will find the 10,000-foot Susten-Limmi not too difficult. A quarter-mile tunnel underpasses the summit of the Susten.

Open mid-June to late Oct.; magnificently engineered; easy to drive; heavy weekend traffic; maximum gradient 9%.

There are several buses a day from Meiringen to Susten, a 3½-hour trip.

OTHER ALPINE PASSES

BRUNIG. 3,300 ft. Usually open all year. Good surface, not too many hairpins. Maximum gradient 8%.

FLUELA. 7,800 ft. Usually open during the winter, sometimes with a toll. Not too difficult. Maximum gradient 10%.

FORCLAZ. 5,000 ft. Usually open throughout year. Good surface most of way. Maximum gradient 8%.

JAUN. 4,900 ft. Except for brief interruptions, usually open most of year. Good surface, but narrow. Maximum gradient 10%.

KLAUSEN. 6,400 ft. Open from June through end of Oct. Some sharp turns, gravel over summit. Maximum gradient 9%.

LUKMANIER. 6,300 ft. Open early June to early Nov. Good surface. Maximum gradient 9%.

MOSSES. 4,700 ft. Usually open all year. Relatively easy, modern road. Maximum gradient 8%.

NUFENEN. 8,100 ft. Fairly narrow approach roads lead to new construction over summit. Maximum gradient 10%. Open June-Sept.

OFEN (or **FUORN**). 7,100 ft. Usually open throughout year. Good surface, relatively easy. Maximum gradient 10%.

PILLON. 5,000 ft. Usually open throughout year. Fairly easy. Maximum gradient 9%.

SPLUGEN. 6,900 ft. Open June to mid-Oct. Good surface but many hairpins and tunnels. Maximum gradient 9%.

UMBRAIL. 8,200 ft. Open late June to mid-Oct. Switzerland's highest pass, narrow and well-supplied with hairpin turns. Gravel surface otherwise not overly challenging. Maximum gradient 9%.

ALPINE TUNNELS

Alpine rail tunnels, through which cars and their occupants are carried by train, make possible year-round transit of the St. Gotthard, Simplon, Lötschberg, and Albula passes; detailed information on timetables, charges, and fares obtainable from Swiss National Tourist Office branches. In addition, there are three splendid road tunnels—the Great St. Bernard, Mont-Blanc and San Bernardino.

Albula. Rail tunnel Tiefencastel to Samedan. Automobiles about 60 frs. one way, including driver.

Trains run about four times a day the year round.

Great St. Bernard. Road tunnel. Martigny (Switzerland) to Aosta (Italy). Almost 4 miles long. The first Alpine road tunnel to be built. Tolls levied according to size; from 12 to 27 frs. for car. Drivers are requested to carry either Swiss or Italian money for the payment of tolls.

Lötschberg. Rail tunnel. Automobiles 40 frs. irrespective of length. Charges are for the journey Kandersteg to Brig, and include vehicle and up to eight passengers remaining in it during journey. (See below for the Brig-Iselle section through the Simplon.)

Trains run about a dozen times daily, summer and winter.

Mont Blanc. Road tunnel opened in 1965. Connects France (Chamonix, near Geneva), with Italy (Courmayeur). For cars, tolls are based on engine size, and range from 27 to 45 French francs. Payment must be made in French, Swiss or Italian currency.

St. Gotthard. Rail tunnel. Göschenen to Airolo. Automobiles 28 frs. irrespective of length. Charges include vehicle and up to eight passengers remaining in it during journey.

Trains run at frequent intervals from about 5 a.m. until midnight. Extra trains are put into service when traffic is unusually heavy.

San Bernardino. From Hinterrhein to San Bernardino. A 4-mile-long road tunnel beneath the old pass. Connects the Grisons with Ticino, Lakes Lugano and Maggiore. No toll charges.

Simplon. Rail tunnel. Brig to Iselle (Italy). Automobiles 35 frs. irrespective of length. Charges include vehicle and up to eight passengers remaining in it during journey.

Trains run at approximately hourly intervals (every half-hour in July and Aug.) from about 7 a.m. to 8 p.m.

ON THE ROAD. One of the most confusing experiences for many motorists is their first encounter with the metric system. The following quick conversion tables may help to speed you on your way.

1 kilometer is 0.623 of a mile; or roughly, 8 kilometers equals 5 miles.

Kms.	Miles	Kms.	Miles
1	⅝	16	10
2	1¼	30	18½
3	1⅞	50	31
4	2½	100	62⅛
5	3⅛	500	310½
10	6¼	1,000	621⅜

Motor fuel. An Imperial gallon is approximately 4½ liters; a U.S. gallon about 3¾ liters.

Liters	Imp. gals.	U.S. gals
1	0.22	0.26
5	1.10	1.32
10	2.20	2.64
20	4.40	5.28
40	8.80	10.56
100	22.00	26.42

Tire pressure: measured in kilograms per square centimeter instead of pounds per square inch; the ratio is approximately 14.2 pounds to 1 kilogram.

Lbs. per sq. in.	Kgs. per sq. cm.	Lbs. per sq. in.	Kgs. per sq. cm.
20	1.406	26	1.828
22	1.547	28	1.969
24	1.687	30	2.109

USEFUL ADDRESSES. The *American, British, Canadian,* and *Indian Embassies* and the *Irish Legation* are located in Bern; *American* and *British Consulates* as well as offices of the *American Express* and *Wagons-Lits/Cook,* are located in most of the major cities (for addresses, see regional chapters).

Swiss Tourist Office. The Swiss National Tourist office maintains an English-language information service in Zurich at Talacker 42, but the local tourist office for the city (where they also speak English) is situated in the main railroad station. In almost every town and resort there is a local tourist office—"Verkehrsverein," "Office du Tourisme," or, in Ticino, "Ente Turistico"—where you are sure to find someone who speaks English. In Geneva it is located at 2 Rue des Moulins; in Basel at Blumenrain 2; Lausanne, d'Ouchy 60; Lucerne, Pilatusstrasse 14; Lugano, Riva Albertolli 5. Regardless of size, tourist offices are invariably helpful.

LEAVING SWITZERLAND

DUTY-FREE SHOPS at Swiss airports are good but the price advantage is not considerable because Swiss taxes, generally, are lower than in some other countries. Count on finding high-quality clothes, with a limited selection, plus plenty of chocolates, watches, clocks, and some high-quality tourist items such as cowbells, dolls in country dress, etc.

CUSTOMS RETURNING HOME. Americans who are out of the United States at least forty-eight hours and have claimed no exemption during the previous thirty days are entitled to bring in duty-free up to $100 worth of articles for bona fide gifts or for their own personal use. The value of each item is determined by the price actually paid (so save your receipts). Every member of a family is entitled to this same exemption, regardless of age, and their exemption can be pooled.

Not more than 100 cigars may be imported duty-free per person, nor more than a quart of wine or liquor (none at all if your passport indicates you are from a "dry" state or under twenty-one years of age). Only one bottle of perfume that is trademarked in the United States may be brought in, plus a reasonable quantity of other brands.

Do not bring home foreign meats, fruits, soil, or other agricultural items when you return to the United States. To do so will delay you at the port of entry. It is illegal to bring in foreign agricultural items without permission, because they can spread destructive plant or animal pests and diseases. For more information, read the pamphlet "Customs Hints," or write to: "Quarantines," U.S. Department of Agriculture, Federal Buildings, Hyattsville, Md. 20782, for pamphlet No. 1083, *Traveler's Tips on Bringing Food, Plant and Animal Products into the United States.*

All purchases must now be taken into the U.S. with you, and may no longer be packed in unaccompanied baggage.

Antiques are defined, for customs purposes, as articles manufactured over 100 years ago, and are admitted duty-free. If there's any question of age, you may be asked to supply proof.

Gift items may be mailed to friends, but not more than one package to any one address on any same day ("day" of customs processing, that is), and none to your own address. Notation on the package should read "Gift, value less than $10." Liquor, tobacco or cigarettes, and perfume must not be mailed.

If your purchases exceed your exemption, list the items that are subject to the highest rates of duty under your exemption and pay duty on the items with the lowest rates. Any article you fail to declare cannot later be claimed under your exemption. To facilitate the actual customs examination, it's convenient to pack all your purchases in one suitcase.

British subjects. There is now a two-tier allowance for duty-free goods brought into the U.K., due to Britain's Common Market membership. *Note: The Customs and Excise Board warns that it is not advisable to mix the two allowances.*

If you return from an EEC country (Belgium, Denmark, France, W. Germany, Holland, Eire, Italy, Luxembourg) and goods were bought in one of those countries, duty-free allowances are: 300 cigarettes (or 150 cigarillos, or 75 cigars, or 400 gr. tobacco); 1.5 liters of strong spirits (or 3 liters of spirits not over 38.8 proof, or fortified or sparkling wine) plus 3 liters of still table wine; 75 gr. (90 cc or 3 fl.oz) perfume and 375 cc (13 fl.oz) toilet water; gifts to a value of £50.

If you return from a country outside the EEC—such as Switzerland or Liechtenstein—*or if the goods were bought in a duty-free shop on ship, plane or airport* the allowances are less: 200 cigarettes (or 100 cigarillos, or 50 cigars, or 250 gr. tobacco); 1 liter of strong spirits (or 2 liters of other spirits, or sparkling or fortified wine) plus 2 liters of still table wine; 50 gr. (60 cc or 2 fl. ounces) perfume and .25 liter (250 cc or 9 fl. ounces) toilet water; gifts to a value of £10.

Canada. In addition to personal effects, the following articles may be brought into Canada duty-free: a maximum of 50 cigars, 200 cigarettes, or 2 pounds of tobacco and 40 ounces of liquor, provided these are declared to customs on arrival. The exemption is $150, and gifts mailed to friends should be marked "Unsolicited Gift—value under $15".

**SWITZERLAND
TOWN
BY
TOWN**

SWITZERLAND—TOWN BY TOWN

A Guide to Hotels, Restaurants and other Practical Information

The listing that follows presents hotels and other facilities in the key vacation towns of Switzerland. In addition to the full coverage given to Geneva, Lausanne, Lucerne, Bern, Basel and Zurich, pertinent information is given for many of the small towns and villages mentioned in the preceding text.

AARAU. Hotels: *Aarauerhof* (89 beds), top medium grade. *Anker Garni* (36 beds), economy grade.

ADELBODEN. Best is top first-class *Nevada;* indoor pool, sauna. Medium grade are *Bristol, Huldi Waldhaus, Parkhotel* (pool, sauna), *Adler, Beau-Site. Edelweiss-Schweizerhof* is economy.

AESCHI. *Baumgarten,* economy.

AIROLO. Both the *Motta-Poste* and *Delle Alpi* are economy grade.

ALTDORF. Hotel: *Goldener Schlüssel* (50 beds), economy.

ANDERMATT. Hotels: Best are the medium-grade *Kröne* (85 beds), *Helvetia* and *Monopol-Metropol* (both 60 beds), and *Kristall* (44 beds); *Alpina,* ¼ mile from village center is owner-managed; superb views. *Alpenhof, Badus, Bergidyll, Drei Könige, Schweizerhof, Schlüssel* and *Sonne* are economy.

ANZERE. Hotels: *Des Masques* (93 beds) and *Zodiaque* (250 beds), top first class; both new.

APPENZELL. Hotels: *Hecht* and *Säntis,* both medium grade.

ARBON. Hotel: The *Metropol* (60 beds), beside Lake Constance; modern, with roof garden, outdoor pool, sailing school. Top medium.

AROSA. Luxury leaders are the *Tschuggen* (230) beds and *Alexandra-Palace* (200 beds), both ultra-modern, and the slightly cheaper *Arosa Kulm* (140 beds) and *Park Hotel* (190 beds), each with indoor pool and sauna.

Top first class are *Eden* (170 beds), *Hof Maran* (100 beds), *Savoy* (160 beds) and *Prätschli* (160 beds) in quiet situation above village), followed by *Bellavista* (160 beds; indoor pool), *Bellevue* (120 beds), *Excelsior* (120 beds; indoor pool), *Raetia* (90 beds), *Seehof* (120 beds), and *Valsana* and *Waldhotel* (each 160 beds; indoor pool).

Slightly cheaper are *Des Alpes* and much renovated *Post*.

Medium-grade hotels include *Alpensonne, Belvédère, Brüggli, Carmenna, Central, Cristallo, Isla* (new), *Streiff* and *Suvretta;* also slightly cheaper *Beau Rivage, Touring, Belmont* and *Hubelsee;* last two, breakfast only.

In the economy bracket are *Alpina, Erzhorn, Hold* and *Vetter*.

ASCONA. Deluxe leaders are *Eden Roc* (80 beds) and slightly cheaper *Delta, Sonnenhof* (each 100 beds), and *Casa Berno* (110 beds). First-class hotels include *Acapulco* (1½ miles from town), *Albergo Ascona, Europe au Lac* (all three, 80 beds), and *Monte Verita* (48 beds).

Among medium-grade hotels are the *Arancio, Bellaria, Moro, Riposo, Seeschloss,* and *Schweizerhof.* All the above hotels have indoor or heated outdoor pools. *Mulino* and *Pergola,* economy.

BADEN. Hotels: The deluxe *Staadhof,* first class *Verenahof* and *Ochsen,* all under same management, have spa waters piped into hotel. *Limmathof* and *Bären,* also first class. All except *Bären* with indoor pool. The *Parc* and rather cheaper *Adler* and *Hirschen* are economy bracket.

Restaurants: *Kursaal* (E). Boule is played at the Kursaal-Casino, where there is dancing.

BAD RAGAZ. Hotels: The *Quellenhof,* (200 beds) located in a park, is luxurious and has direct access to baths. So has adjacent *Hof Ragaz* (180 beds), slightly cheaper and less elaborate. Near the station is the smart, first-class *Cristal* (100 beds), with indoor pool and sauna.

PRACTICAL INFORMATION FOR BASEL

WHERE TO STAY? There is an accommodation bureau in the main station if you arrive without reservations. Basel has seven hotels in the deluxe or near luxurious range. Pride of place goes to one of Europe's legendary hostelries, the 120-bed **THREE KINGS** (*Drei Könige* or *Trois Rois,* in German or French). Cleverly modernized throughout while retaining a traditional atmosphere, today's hotel stands where inns have stood since the 11th century. Kings and emperors have stayed there. Its terrace overlooking the Rhine is as famous as its cuisine.

The other six are:

ALBAN-AMBASSADOR, 165 beds. In Jakob Burckhardtstrasse, a residential area, ten mins. walk from center. Modern, garage.

BASEL, 105 beds. By the town hall. Ultramodern but neither cramped nor clinical. Excellent food, snack bar.

EULER, 100 beds. In the station square. Modernized but still elegant. Outstanding cuisine, terrace, garage.

HILTON, 370 beds. Faces gardens near station square. Air conditioned, indoor pool, sauna, and all usual amenities.

INTERNATIONAL, 300 beds. Between station and city center. Contemporary decor, two good restaurants, indoor pool, sauna, garage.

SCHWEIZERHOF, 110 beds. In the station square. A family-owned hotel with pleasant terrace. Nondescript exterior belies traditional luxury inside.

Other hotels close to the station include the first class *Victoria Bahnhof* (150 beds; breakfast only), as well as the medium grade, *Bernina* (75 beds; breakfast only), *Greub* (70 beds) and *Jura* (100 beds). Among economy class hotels are *Bristol* (55 beds) and *St. Gotthard-Terminus* (60 beds). Cheaper still and a real find is the small *Flugelrad* (40 beds) in a quiet lane just by the station. Delightful restaurant.

Not far away are the first-class *City* (130 beds), *Drachen* (62 beds) and *Excelsior* (80 beds; breakfast only).

Facing the Rhine, beside Mittlere bridge in Klein Basel, is first class *Merian* (80 beds) and close by on the river promenade the popular, medium grade *Krafft-am-Rhein* (80 beds). Also medium is *Admiral* (200 beds), heated rooftop pool.

The modern *Alfa* (70 beds), medium grade, is on the southern fringe of the city at Birsfelden.

 RESTAURANTS. The finest food in Basel is probably at the Hotel Euler's *Fine Bouche* restaurant or at the *Bruderholz*. For Italian food at its best (not just pasta or pizza) go to *Donati*. Top class, too, are *Schützenhaus*, Hilton's *Wettstein Grill*, International Hotel's *Charolaise,* and The Three Kings' *Rôtisserie des Rois*. All the above are (E).

Among more interesting brasseries are *Fischerstube* (just across the river in Rheingasse) where the doctor-owner brews beer on the premises, and *Braunen Mutz* in busy Barfüsserplatz, both (M).

Possibly Basel's best fondue is at the cosy *Elizabethenstubli* or the rather more expensive *Taverne Valaisanne.* For typical Basel restaurants with local specialties try the *Basler Keller* (in the Hotel Basel), *Goldener Sternen, Safranzunft,* or *Schlüsselzunft* restaurants; all (M) or slightly more.

Good spots in a cash crisis are *Schumachernzunft,* Hutgasse (try their "leberli mit rösti", a delicious meal), *Gifthüttli,* Scheidergasse, or the cheaper *Hasenburg,* also Scheidergasse (crammed with students and atmosphere, but devoid of frills). Other cash savers are the department store restaurants and the somewhat Spartan *Migros* self-service cafeterias.

For quaintness try the tiny, highly popular *Teufel,* in Andreasplatz (off Scheidergasse)—16 different teas, 16 ice creams, numerous filled pancakes and little else but walls filled with pictures of the devil (teufel).

ENTERTAINMENT. The fine *Stadttheater* produces opera, operetta, musical comedy, ballet and drama; the *Komödie,* plays (in German). Cabaret at the *Théâtre Fauteuil.* The many nightspots range from dance bars and nightclubs with and without floorshows to striptease. Some stay open to 2 a.m. or later. You can check all entertainment in *This Week in Basel,* free from hotels, banks, etc.

MUSEUMS. Kunstmuseum, St. Albangraben. Weekdays 10 a.m.–5 p.m.; also 8–10 p.m. on Weds. (closes noon to 2 p.m., Oct.–May). Entrance 2 frs., but Wed. p.m., Sat. and Sun. free. One of the most interesting and enjoyable art museums, it has an impressive collection of important works beautifully displayed, from 13th century triptychs to today's abstract and minimal art.

Antiken-Museum, St. Albangraben 5, 10–noon, 2–5; Weds., 2–5, 8–10 p.m. Entrance 2 frs. (Wed., Sat., and Sun., free). Opened in 1966, it is the only one of its kind in Switzerland, with Greek art 2500–100 B.C., Italian art 1000 B.C.–A.D. 300.

Kirschgarten, Elizabethenstrasse 27. 10–noon, 2–5. Entrance 2 frs., but Wed. p.m., Sat. and Sun. free. Museum of 18th-century Basel life contained in an old house. Furniture, costume, clocks, porcelain, silver, toys, etc.

There are also the *City and Cathedral Museum; Gewerbe Museum; Historical Museum* (temporarily closed); *Ethnological and Natural History Museum;* the *Jewish Museum; Kunsthalle;* the *Swiss Pharmacy Museum;* a musical instruments collection; the *Swiss Gymnastic and Sports Museum;* and the largest zoo in Switzerland, complete with aquarium. At Riehen, on the outskirts of the city (tram No. 6), is the *Dorf- und Spielzeugmuseum,* Baselstrasse 34, featuring European toys, and life in a village.

It is advisable to check opening times, and current exhibitions, in *This Week in Basel.* Most museums close on Mondays.

SHOPPING, or certainly window-shopping, in Basel is inclined to center on elegant Freiestrasse. But don't miss the less famous streets (and their sometimes tiny side streets) which wind most of the way from the Fischmarkt area to the station.

CAMERAS. *E. Balzer Sohn,* Steinenvorstadt 20. *Fotohaus Kierks,* Weissegasse 5. *Wolf Foto Kino,* Freiestrasse 4. *C. Hoffmann,* Clarastrasse 36.

FOOD SPECIALTIES. *Centralhallen,* Streitgasse 20. *Frey Sohn,* Centralbahnstrasse 9. *Schiesser,* Marktplatz 19. *Heinrich Spillmann,* St. Johann Vorstadt 47.

HANDCRAFTS. *Heimatwerk Basel,* Freiestrasse 39.

JEWELRY. *Bijouterie Lonville,* Freiestrasse 1. *Ch. Gobat,* Gerbergasse 25. *E. Gut Co.,* Marktplatz 21. *Henzi,* Barfüsserplatz 22. *Emil Linn,* Streitgasse. *U. Sauter,* Freiestrasse 27.

LEATHER. *W. Langmesser Alligator,* Gerbergasse 66.

SOUVENIRS. *Franz Carl Weber* (also toys), Freiestrasse 17. *"Au Souvenir,"* Centralbahnstrasse 15. *Füglistaller,* Freiestrasse 23.

SPORTS EQUIPMENT. *Leonhard Kost Co.,* Freiestrasse 51.

TYPEWRITERS. *Hermes Schreibmaschinen,* Aeschenvorstadt 24.

WATCHES. *Bijouterie Lonville,* Freiestrasse 1. *H. Boesch,* Spalenberg 37. *Greoges Bourquenez,* Centralbahnstrasse 5. *Bucherer,* Steinen-vorstadt 53. *R. Erbe,* Freiestrasse 15. *Ch. Gobat,* Gerbergasse 25. *Grquwiler,* Freiestrasse 53. *E. Gut Co.,* Marktplatz 21. *Henzi,* Barfüsserplatz 22. *Hummel,* Aeschenvorstadt 24. *Emil Linn,* Streitgasse 5. *U. Sauter,* Freiestrasse 27. *Hermann Schudel,* Steinenvorstadt 1 (off Barfüsserplatz). *F. Schweizer,* Gerbergasse 67. *E. Weber,* Greifengasse 9.

CAR HIRE. *Avis,* Steinengraben 42; *Hertz,* Gartenstrasse 120; *Budget Rent-a-Car,* Turkheimstrasse 17; *Self-Drive,* Sempacherstrasse 10; *Europcar,* Gempenstrasse 25.

HOW TO GET TO TOWN FROM THE AIRPORT. Basel (St. Louis) airport to city center, 6 miles. Airport coach to air terminal (railroad station) 4.50 frs., taxi about 16 frs.

CITY TOURS. By bus, with multilingual guide; daily throughout the year, 1¾ hours for 10 frs.

USEFUL ADDRESSES. *Basel Tourist Office,* Blumenrain 2, tel. 25.38.11. *American Express,* Aeschengraben 10. *Cook's,* Freiestrasse 109 (P.O. Box 41).

BEATENBERG. *Blümlisalp-Beatrice.* Top economy grade.

BECKENRIED. Hotel: *Edelweis* (50 beds), economy. Restaurant and tearoom: *Rössli am See,* terrace.

BELLINZONA. Best hotels are the *Croce Federale* (27 beds), *Internazionale* (53 beds, breakfast only), and *Unione* (75 beds), all economy.

PRACTICAL INFORMATION FOR BERN

HOTELS. There is a 24-hour accommodation office in the station if you need help in finding a place to stay. Bern has many good hotels; the two deluxe ones are: **Bellevue Palace** (220 beds), situated high above the river with superb views of the Alps, next to the Swiss Parliament building. Modernized but definitely a hotel in the grand tradition. Excellent restaurants. **Schweizerhof** (180 beds), opposite the new station is another hotel in the grand manner noted for its furnishings of antiques and fine paintings. Memorable cuisine.

First class and convenient for the shops and station are *Bären* (80 beds), *Bristol* (110 beds), *Metropole* (100 beds, attractive modern decor, good restaurants); *Savoy* (100 beds), and *Stadthof* (50 beds). A few minutes west of the station is the *City* (73 beds) and *Alfa* (60 beds, garage beneath the hotel).

Among many medium grade hotels are *Krebs* (60 beds; breakfast only; much modernized) and *Wächter* (80 beds), both within a few paces of the station, as well as *Continental* (65 beds), near the Kornhausplatz.

Also near Kornhausplatz is the economy bracket *Volkshaus* (110 beds, breakfast only), an old hotel but recently renovated rooms are

good. Next door, under same ownership, is a group of seven attractive new restaurants and snack bars. Other economy hotels include the *Glocke* (40 beds), near the Clock Tower, and *Goldener Adler* (50 beds), not far from the Nydegg Bridge.

On the city's southern fringe, atop Gurten Hill (2,800 ft.) is the medium grade *Gurtenkulm* (62 beds), the place to stop for magnificent Alpine views if you don't mind going into town by funicular and streetcar.

MOTELS. At **Muri,** 2 miles southeast of city, *Motel Krone* (26 beds). At **Munchenbuchsee,** 5 miles north, *Motel Bern-Biel* (80 beds). Both open year round.

RESTAURANTS. The standard of Bern's cooking is high, there are many good eating places, and the city has a reputation for giving better than average value for money. The listing (E), (M) or (I) signifies expensive, moderate or inexpensive.

The *Bellevue* and *Schweizerhof* hotels both have justly famous grill rooms (E). Slightly cheaper, with notable French cuisine, are the *Ermitage,* Marktgasse 15, *Mistral,* Kramgasse 42, and *Du Théâtre,* Theaterplatz 7. The *Della Casa,* Schauplatzgasse 16, *Räblus,* Zeughausgasse 3, and *Ratskeller,* Gerechtigkeitsgasse 81, are also good and (M-E).

The *Kornhauskeller,* Kornhausplatz, once a large wine store and granary, has a popular cellar-restaurant where one can sit down in front of a 10,000 gallon wine barrel. It accompanies local atmosphere with Swiss and local specialities such as Bernerplatte. Another typical cellar-restaurant, said to be the oldest in Bern, is the restored, 17th-century *Klötzlikeller,* Gerechtigkeitsgasse 62. Both about (M). If you want to watch a rather noisy but well-presented

folklore show while you dine you can do so at the Hotel Glocke's *Swiss Chalet* (M-E), Rathausgasse 75.

The Bernese call their huge new railway station the biggest restaurant in town, for inside its glass walls are no less than thirteen remarkably good restaurants, buffets, snackbars and assorted eateries where you can get anything from an expensive meal to a simple snack at a rock bottom price.

A good spot for *fondue, raclette* and *viande séchée* (mountan dried beef or pork, sliced wafer thin) is the *Taverne Valaisanne* (M), Neuengasse 40. *Le Mazot* (M), Bärenplatz 5, is one of several other restaurants specializing in Swiss cheese dishes. One of the best places for *rösti* in its many varieties is the *Zytglogge* (M), Theaterplatz 8.

Pinocchio, Aarbergasse 6, a small

restaurant with an attractive decor, has excellent Italian food. For a paella and other Spanish dishes try the *Commerce*, Gerechtigkeitsgasse 74. Both (M-E). Succulent salads and other vegetarian dishes are at *Vegetaris* (I), Neuengasse 15, a first floor restaurant where, surprisingly, you can eat outside in a quiet first floor garden.

Among the many inexpensive spots in Bern are *Spatz*, Bärenplatz 7, *Börse*, at the other end of Bärenplatz, and the new *Siebe Stube* group of restaurant-snackbars at Zeughausgasse 9.

The *Mövenpick* restaurant-snack-bar chain has four branches in Bern with prices mostly in the moderate bracket. When the order of the day is a good fill-up at a rock bottom price, and comfort and charm are of secondary importance, try the *Migros* supermarket chain's self-service cafeteria in Marktgasse.

Many of the so-called tearooms, which are often mouth-watering confectioners as well, serve reasonably priced light meals, among these being *Abberglen*, Spitalgasse 36, *Bäreck*, Bärenplatz 2, *Colibri*, Amthausgasse 18, *Meyer*, Marktgasse 31, and *Tschirren*, Kramgasse 73.

 ENTERTAINMENT. Unless you understand German, the theater in Bern will be pretty well lost on you, except for the *Municipal Theater*, which stages opera, operetta, ballet and plays. Bern is noted for its "cellar theaters", which are inclined to be ephemeral. The more hardy are *Zähringer-Refugium* (experimental plays, songs, jazz), *Atelier-Theater* (modern plays and avant-garde shows), *Theater-am-Käfigturm* (comedies, musicals, pantomime), *Katakömbli, Kleintheater* (plays), *Die Rampe* (guest performances, chanson singers), and *Theater am Zytglogge* (guest performances and shows by Bern university students). Every June Bern has a theater festival with artists from many countries participating.

You may be able to see moving pictures in the original English, with their Swiss audience reading subtitles instead of listening to a dubbed soundtrack.

Concerts are customarily given in the 1,400-seat *Casino* or in the *Konservatorium*. A summer feature of the musical life of Bern is the *Abendmusik*, religious vocal and organ music given on Tues. in the cathedral, with its fine 5,000-pipe organ. For information on current entertainment, get a copy of the *Berner Wochenbulletin* from your hotel or the tourist office.

Nightclubs in Bern are far from spectacular, but they allow you to while away an evening agreeably and get in some dancing. In Switzerland, incidentally, except in the more elegant international-type places, it is not incorrect to ask a stranger to dance. The *Mocambo* has two floorshows at Genfergasse 10, most elegant spot in town. *Chikito*, Neuengasse 28, has also the *Frisco-Bar. The Swiss Chalet*, Rathausgasse 75, has a Swiss folk music show every evening. Some of the hotels and restaurants also get into the evening entertainment field. The *Schweizerhof* has subdued music during dinner in its Schultheiss Grill, but there is no music in its pleasant *Arcady-Bar*. Neither is there at *Bärentatze-Bar,* Speichergasse, or *Scotch-Bar,* Genfergasse. You can dance at the *Kursaal* (or, if you wish, fritter away your money at boule), and in the *Kornhauskeller* orchestra and yodelers create a certain amount of pandemonium. Dance bars include the vast *Babalu*, Gurtengasse 3, and *Happy Light* (mainly for young people), Casinoplatz.

MUSEUMS. Current visiting hours and entrance fees (if any) can be checked in the museum leaflet free from the tourist office, or in the booklet *This Week in Bern* free from hotels, banks, etc.

Kunstmuseum, Hodlerstrasse 12. Bernese and Swiss art from the 15th century; European art, 19th and 20th centuries. Houses Paul Klee foundation (world's largest Klee collection) and Rupf foundation (cubist art).

Swiss Postal Museum, Helvetiaplatz. Development of the Swiss postal system. Includes one of the world's largest stamp collections.

Historical Museum, Helvetiaplatz. Various historical collections. Its highlight is the booty captured from Charles the Bold of Burgundy after his defeat by the Confederacy in 1476.

Natural History Museum, Bernastrasse 15. Notable for the Von Wattenwyl collction of African animals, mounted in natural settings and looking as if they were alive.

Kunsthalle, Helvetiaplatz. Loan exhibitions, usually of contemporary art.

Swiss Alpine Museum, Helvetiaplatz. Mainly about mountaineering and mountain rescue.

The **Botanical Institute and Gardens** (which include a fine collection of Alpines) are across the Lorraine bridge. The **Rose Gardens,** just up the hill beyond the Nydegg bridge, contain every type of rose grown in Switzerland, and a good collection of shrubs, as well as the best view of the old city. There is a small **zoo** at *Dählhölzli*.

SPORTS. *Riding* at the Riding School Eldorado at Gurtentali (5 miles from city). *Golf* at Blumisberg (18 miles west of Bern), 18 holes, 6,636 yards. *Curling*—6 covered rinks. *Ice skating:* 3 rinks, open end of Sept. through Feb. *Swimming:* Indoor and outdoor pools (latter always free). *Tennis. Trap-shooting.*

SHOPPING in Bern can mean a leisurely investigation of the shops in the city's fabled arcades, but it doesn't have to be limited to them. Go as far afield as you like, and you may find that most priceless of acquisitions, a bargain! As for the arcades, look for them in the old town, on the Marktgasse, Kramgasse, Gerechtigkeitsgasse, Metzgergasse and other streets.

ANTIQUE CLOCKS. *J. Otto Scherer*, Kramgasse 26.

CAMERAS. *Christener*, Marktgass-Passage 1.

HANDCRAFTS. *Oberländer Heimatwerk*, Kramgasse 61.

JEWELRY. *Rösch Co.*, Marktgasse 50. *Gübelin*, Schweizerhoflaube.

SOUVENIRS. *M. Steiger Cie.*, Aarberggasse 21. *Franz Carl Weber* (also toys), Marktgasse 52. *Christen Cie.*, Marktgasse 28. *Theodor Meyer,*

Marktgasse 32. *Oberländer Heimatwerk,* Kramgasse 61.

SPORTS EQUIPMENT. *Sportgeschäft Vaucher,* Theaterplatz 3 and Marktgasse 2.

TYPEWRITERS. *A. W. Muggli,* Hirschengraben 10.

WATCHES. *R. Hugentobler,* Waisenhausplatz 11. *Kellerman S.A.,*

Marktgass-Passage. *Gebr. Pochon,* Marktgasse 55. *W. Rösch Co.,* Marktgasse 50. *Th. Sonderegger,* Spitalgasse 36. *A. Türler Co.,* Marktgasse 27. *F. Zaugg,* Bollwerk 15. *Zigerli Iff AG.,* Spitalgasse 14. *Gübelin,* Schweizerhoflaube. *P. Trachsel,* Theaterplatz 13.

CITY GUIDES. Official guides to help you tour Bern are available at the Tourist Office. Rates: up to 2 hrs. about 35 frs. Daily city tours by coach with polyglot guides start from near the main station: price about 11 frs.

CAR HIRE. *Avis,* Effingerstrasse 20. *Hertz,* Casinoplatz/Kochergasse 1. *Europcar,* Zieglerstrasse 30. *Budget,* Laupenstrasse 15.

 **USEFUL ADDRESSES.** *Official Tourist Office,* in the main railroad station, open Mon.-Sat., 8 a.m.-6:30 p.m.; Sun. 10 a.m.-5 p.m. *American Express,* Spitalgasse 33. *Cook's,* Bubenbergplatz 8. *American Embassy,* Jubiläumstrasse 93. *British Embassy,* Thunstrasse 50. *Canadian Embassy,* Kirchenfeldstrasse 88. *Indian Embassy,* Kalcheggweg 20. *Irish Legation,* Dufourstrasse 9. *English-Swiss Association,* Amthausgasse 1, meets Thurs. 8:30 p.m. *Rotary Club,* Hotel Bellevue Palace. *Lions Club,* Hotel Schweizerhof. *St. Ursula's Anglican Church,* Jubiläumsplatz, Kirchenfeld. *Christian Science Church,* Helvetiaplatz 6.

PRACTICAL INFORMATION FOR THE BERNESE OBERLAND

 WHEN TO COME? The "seasons" in the Bernese Oberland are June–Sept. and Dec.–Mar. Despite the many admitted advantages of "off-season" travel, it must be faced: "off-season" in this part of the world can be pretty dull, even if the weather is good, which it isn't likely to be. However, to avoid the crowds, which are getting bigger annually, better plan "early" or "late" season; avoid "mid-season" if possible, unless you can afford luxury accommodations and travel.

 WHAT TO SEE? This question is easy to answer. In the Bernese Oberland you'll see what you came to Switzerland to see: the Alps. You'll see them wherever you turn, either until you can't stand the sight of them any more, or until your friends have to tear you away, depending upon how you are affected by mountain scenery. The city of Bern (described in the previous chapter) is delightful, and it is recommended that you spend some time exploring it on foot, but otherwise, just choose an alp and let yourself go!

HOW TO GET ABOUT? Travel comes high in the Bernese Oberland, in terms of both altitude and money: the *Jungfraubahn,* for example, is probably the most expensive stretch of track in the world. But you'll understand why after you reach the highest railway station in Europe, its terminus. Consult your travel agent early to determine what the best Swiss Federal Railways holiday ticket buy is for you, depending on the length of your stay and the number of people in your party. A car is handy to get you around the Bernese Oberland, but on many trips the last leg will have to be by cable car or mountain railway.

SPORTS. Any sport enthusiast will find his heart's delight in the Oberland. Those who are interested in native games will find ample opportunity for wrestling— but be cautious because you may find your Swiss opponents a trifle fierce for your taste. You may watch *Hornussen,* the "hornet game," a kind of Swiss cricket chiefly practiced in the Emmental. Sixty teams take part in the annual tournaments and about 1,300 players assemble on such occasions. The "hornet" is a flat disc, and the visitors find the game as difficult to understand as cricket or baseball is for foreigners.

Angling is one of the most popular sports in the district and trout are abundant. But you'll need a license, which may be obtained at the local tourist offices.

BOATING. Rowboats may be hired at most villages on Lakes Thun and Brienz. Rowing is a pleasant pastime and usually very easy on the lakes, but if you take your rowing more seriously than the average vacationist, you will find clubs at Interlaken and on Lake Thun, with first-rate outrigger boats and skiffs. The Bernese Yacht Club—the seat of which is in Thun-Hilterfingen—organizes two races each summer, with about twenty boats competing. Sailing schools at Hilterfinger, Spiez, and Interlaken-Neuhaus.

SKIING. The Bernese Oberland is, of course, one of the world's most celebrated winter sports areas. A separate book would be required to do full justice to the winter activities of the resorts of the Oberland, but here is a brief rundown on the principal centers, an attempt to highlight the individual character of each. Remember, every one of these resorts has its own tourist office; a postcard will bring you detailed information concerning any of them.

ADELBODEN (4,450 ft.), by bus from Frutigen. Sunny and picturesque. Hahnenmoos cableway. Fine selection of skilifts; skibob run; ice rinks; indoor pool.

BEATENBERG (3,800 ft.), by bus

from Interlaken or from Thun. The sunniest of the Bernese Oberland winter resorts. Chairlift (20 mins.) to Niederhorn (6,300 ft.). Open slopes fully exposed to sun. Ice rink, curling, indoor pool.

GRINDELWALD (3,400 ft.), by mountain railway from Interlaken, 40 mins.; by road, 30 mins. Sunny ski fields, wide open. Much mountain transport including chairlift to First (7,100 ft.) and cable car to Pfingstegg (4,500 ft.). Unlimited variety of ski runs from easy to difficult. Ice rinks. Indoor pool.

GSTAAD (3,450 ft.), on the Montreux-Oberland railway. Fashionable, and best-known winter sports and summer holiday center of Bernese Oberland. Three cable cars, many skilifts; much to do. Year-round glacier skiing made possible by Reusch-Diablerets cable car; also year-round ski school.

JUNGFRAUJOCH (11,300 ft.) by mountain railway from Interlaken. Almost year-round skiing, unlimited tours, guides available (and advisable). Sphinx terrace, 11,720 ft. "Ice Palace" cut into glacier. New 280-seat *Inn-Above-the-Clouds* restaurant with panoramic viewing gallery.

KANDERSTEG (3,850 ft.), by Lötschberg line direct from Bern. Famous ski jump; ice rink, curling. Aerial cable car to Stock, 8 mins. to 6,000 ft.; chairlifts to Sunnbühl, 6,350 ft., and Oschinen, 5,600 ft. Five skilifts. Excellent spring skiing. Road open year round.

KLEINE SCHEIDEGG (6,750 ft.), by mountain railway from Lauterbrunnen or Grindelwald. Outstanding for early Dec. and late spring skiing. Good mountain transport center. Magnificent runs to Wengen and Grindelwald, returning by train.

LENK (3,600 ft.), by rail or road via Zweisimmen. Unpretentious and relatively inexpensive winter sports and summer resort. Good connecting cableways, ski and chair lifts to Betelberg (5,400 ft.) and Metschberg (5,800 ft.) and Metschstand (6,800 ft.) skiing areas. Excellent touring. Skibob runs. Skating, curling. Indoor pool. Modernized Kurhaus opened 1975.

MEIRINGEN (1,950 ft.). Cable cars, chairlift to excellent Plan Platten skiing area. Skibob run.

MURREN (5,400 ft.), main access by mountain railway from Lauterbrunnen. No motor traffic. Highest winter resort of Bernese Oberland. Funicular to Allmendhubel, chairlift to Maulerhubel, many other lifts serving wide variety of runs. Skibob run. Skating, curling. Cableway to Schilthorn (9,750 ft.) with revolving restaurant at summit and spectacular mountain panorama.

SAANENMOSER (4,200 ft.). Fairly small, but with good slopes and runs. Skibob run. Funisleigh, skilifts, toboggan run, ice rink, curling.

WENGEN (4,200 ft.), reached from Lauterbrunnen by Wengernalp railway; no road access. Very popular, long-established winter sports resort with superb selection of slopes, unlimited downhill runs, and all winter sports facilities. Mountain railways to Kleine Scheidegg, Eigergletscher, Jungfraujoch, Grindelwald, etc. Cable car to Männlichen. About a dozen ski and chairlifts. Skibob and toboggan runs. Skating, curling, and ice hockey rinks.

ZWEISIMMEN (3,150 ft.), by rail from Montreux or Bern. Specially good for children and beginners. 6 cableways and lifts. Varied runs. Ice rink. Indoor tennis.

MOTELS. At **Einigen**, *Motel Hirschen* (63 beds) and at **Faulensee**, *Marti-Motel* (closed Nov. to Apr.; 44 beds), both near Spiez. At **Grindelwald**, *Motel Grindelwald* (closed mid.-Oct. to mid.-Dec., 40 beds). At **Gstaad**, *Motel Rütti* (50 beds). **Interlaken**, *Marti Motel* (closed Nov. to Mid-Mar., 50 beds). *Golf-Motel* (40 beds) and *Golfhotel Neuhaus* (closed Nov. to Feb.; 100 beds). At **Kandersteg**, *Motel Kandersteg* (65 beds). At **Meiringen**, *Motel Sherlock Holmes* (24 beds). At **Merligen**, *Motel Mon Abri* (60 beds). At **Münsingen**, Motel *Münsingen* (70 beds). At **Wilderswil**, 3 miles from Interlaken, *Motel Luna* (32 beds). At **Zweisimmen**, Motel Zweisimmen (50 beds). All open year round except where stated to the contrary.

BIEL (BIENNE). Hotels: *Elite* (80 beds), first class, and *Continental* (100 beds), medium grade, are both centrally situated and modern.

Restaurants: *Seefels,* fish specialties, auto park; *Buffet de la Gare,* moderate prices.

BONINGEN. Medium grade is *Seiler-au-Lac* with lakeside garden.

BRAUNWALD. Hotels: *Alpenblick, Bellevue, Niederschlacht* are medium grade. *Alpina,* economy.

BRIENZ. *Bären* is about the best, but it is single, small. Fair restaurant.

BRIG. Hotels: *Couronne* and *Victoria* (both 80 beds), medium grade. *Sporting* and breakfast-only *Europe* (both 50 beds), economy.

BRISSAGO. The *Mirto* (46 beds) and *Mirafiore* (40 beds), outdoor pool, and *Camelia* (40 beds) are medium grade.

BRUGG. Hotels: *Bahnhof* and *Rotes Haus,* both economy; latter with good restaurant (I).

BRUNNEN. Hotels: *Waldstätterhof* (180 beds), orchestra, open-air restaurant, pool; *Bellevue au Lac* (90 beds); *Parkhotel Hellerbad* (100 beds); and *Schmid am See* (44 beds); all top medium grade.

Economy: *Elite* (110 beds) and *Hirschen* (50 beds), both with dining terraces; *Metropol au Lac* (25 beds). All above, on or near lake shore.

Restaurants: *Bellevue au Lac* (M) has open-air dining on lake front, *Bahnhof* has garden restaurant. The *Casino* presents concerts, dances and boule.

BULLE. Hotels: *Alpes Terminus* (66 beds) and cheaper *Du Tonnelier* (35 beds) are both economy grade.

BUOCHS. Hotel: *Krone,* economy.

BURGDORF. *Stadthaus,* 18th-cent. town hall now economy hotel.

BURGENSTOCK. Hotels: *Grand* and *Palace* (both 130 beds), luxurious. *Park* (120 beds), first class: all three under same management and overlooking lake. *Honegg* and *Waldheim,* (both 70 beds), economy.

CAMPIONE. Though part of Italy, this enclave uses Swiss money and Swiss postal service. *The Grand Hotel* (73 beds), outdoor pool, is first class.

CELERINA. The 160-bed top first-class *Cresta-Palace* is the leader and has an indoor pool. *Kulm* is also first class. Medium grade are *Misani* and *Murail.* In the economy bracket are *Posthaus* and *Secchi.*

PRACTICAL INFORMATION FOR CENTRAL SWITZERLAND

WHEN TO COME? April through Oct. is the season in central Switzerland, although you can usually count upon a few weeks of warm sunshine after the first frost in late fall, and what glorious colors! Most of this region is heavily wooded and autumn here with its fleeting Indian summer is incredibly spectacular. But don't try to stretch your luck too far, because it can be cold, foggy, and wholly unpleasant in the off-season. The Aug./Sept. music festival in Lucerne is one of the outstanding events of its kind held in Europe: it is wise to plan hotel accommodation and ticket reservations at least six months in advance. In June, Weggis celebrates its "Rose and Children's Festival.'

WHAT TO SEE? Lake of Lucerne, or the Vierwaldstättersee (Four Forest Cantons' Lake), as the Swiss call it, is the heart and soul of the country, as Swiss as Valley Forge is American or Hastings is British. It is no exaggeration to say that this region is idyllically beautiful. No matter how many feet of Kodachrome you take here, nothing will ever match your first view of this region in its full splendor. One must first see the overall view from one of the vantage points: the Rigi, Pilatus, Bürgenstock or Dietschiberg, and then, if possible, take the classical boat excursion from Lucerne to Flüelen (this excursion can be made at no additional cost as a part of the regular train trip from Basel or Bern to Lugano via the St. Gotthard line).

HOW TO GET ABOUT? The most rewarding way of getting around Lake Lucerne is on one of the comfortable white steamers which glide silently and smoothly hither and yon. If you can't or don't want to go by boat, the whole of central Switzerland is served by a first-rate network of trains, buses, cable cars, and funiculars. On most of these you can use the Swiss Holiday Pass or fifteen-day Regional Holiday Season Ticket. If you've got a car, you'll find the highways of the region are excellent and it is easy to get about, but the main routes can become somewhat congested during the summer holiday months.

SPORTS. Central Switzerland is more a sightseer's than a sportsman's paradise, but there are good lidos and swimming pools, boating and watersports everywhere, and tennis as well as golf at Dietschiberg and Bürgenstock. Winter sports, however, deserve a special note. With the exception of Andermatt, Engelberg and Stoos, the ski resorts of central Switzerland attract few foreigners. They are primarily nonfashionable, inexpensive resorts jammed at the weekend with Swiss from nearby Lucerne and Zurich. But during the week foreign visitors, not being tied to a city desk, can enjoy unbelievable freedom on the slopes and skilifts. However, beware Saturdays, Sundays and holidays unless skiing means so much that you are prepared to wait an hour or more for a cable car or skilift. Because of relative lack of elevation some resorts (Andermatt, Engelberg and, possibly, Stoos excepted) have a fairly short winter season.

Here are the highlights of the major winter sports centers in this scenic corner of Switzerland:

ANDERMATT. A family-type ski resort on the road to the St. Gotthard Pass (the road over the pass is closed in winter), easily reached from Göschenen, on the main Gotthard line, by the Schöllenen railway direct to the resort. Plenty of snow until late spring. Cable car to Gemsstock (9,800 ft.). Summer skiing; 6 skilifts; the runs tend toward the difficult. Sledding, skating, curling, ski-jumping, etc.

ENGELBERG. This is the largest and most popular winter sports resort that central Switzerland can boast. Engelberg is an hour or so by train or car (the road is clear the year round) from Lucerne. The village itself is only 3,500 feet above sea level, but after you have taken the cable car to Trübsee and the skilift (chairlift in summer) to the Jochpass you are at 7,000 feet. If this isn't high enough, from Trübsee cable cars will take you to Kleintitlis (9,900 ft.; panoramic restaurant); excellent ski runs. Skating, bobsledding, curling and indoor, heated pools.

HOCH-YBRIG. Rapidly developing new skiing area (6,500 ft.). Seven chairlifts and skilifts, prepared *pistes,* restaurants, etc., already available. Best access by cable car from Weglosen (with large, multi-story car parks).

HOSPENTAL. A small village-resort about one mile from Andermatt. Skilift to the Winterhorn.

KLEWENALP. Small winter and summer resort on mountain terrace high above Beckenried, to which it is connected by cable car, on Lake Lucerne. Three skilifts.

LUNGERN AM SEE. Small resort near the Brünig Pass reached by rail or road from Lucerne. Several skilifts, cableway to Schönbüel, ice rink.

MELCHSEE-FRUTT. Small secluded resort on Lake Melch, with road access from Sarnen. Two skilifts; motor sleigh to Tannalp.

OBERIBERG. Attractive mountain village resort served by postal coach from Einsiedeln. Three skilifts.

RIGI. One and a half hours from Lucerne; is one of the finest, if least known, skiing grounds in Europe. Unfortunately, there is sufficient snow only for a few weeks, usually in late Jan. or early Feb., so rather difficult to plan much in advance. But if you hit it right, the sunny, open slopes from the Rigi-Staffel to Goldau, Vitznau and Lauerz are excellent.

SORENBERG. Small, secluded resort in Marienthal. Postal coach from Schüpfheim on the Lucern-Bern railway. Seven skilifts, cable way Sörenberg-Brienzer Rothorn.

STOOS. An hour from Zurich or Lucerne to Schwyz and then 8 mins. by cable railway. A tiny, charming, secluded resort with no road traffic. Altitude over 4,200 feet ensures almost certain good snow throughout winter. Skilifts to Fronalpstock (6,300 ft.) and Klingenstock (6,000 ft.) with interesting variety of runs back to Stoos. Ski school, ice rink, ski jump. Heated pool (summer).

MOTELS. At **Giswil,** *Motel Landhaus* (90 beds), 20 miles south of Lucerne. At **Kriens,** on southern fringe of Lucerne, *Motel Luzern-Süd* (62 beds). At **Kussnacht** 8 miles northeast of Lucerne, *Pic-Nic Motel* (28 beds). At **Merlischachen,** near Kussnachts, *Motel Swiss Chalet* (45 beds). At **Sachseln,** 17 miles south of Lucerne, *Motel-Hotel Kreuz* (105 beds). At **Seewen,** *Motel Barcarola* (90 beds). At **Stans,** 10 miles southeast of Lucerne, *Motel Rex* (50 beds). Some close Nov.-Mar.

CHAMPERY. Hotels: *De Champéry* (100 beds, sauna) and *Beau Séjour* (45 beds; nightclub), medium grade. *Des Alpes* (notable food), economy.

CHAMPEX. Nearest to chairlift terminal and close to lake are *Crettex* (120 beds), first class, and *Glacier* (65 beds), economy. At quiet end of lake overlooking water are *Des Alpes et Lac* (100 beds), first class, and *Grand Combin* (60 beds), medium grade.

CHATEAU-D'OEX. *Beau-Séjour* (70 beds) and recently renovated *Chalet Bon Accueil* (30 beds) are both medium grade.

CHATEL-ST.-DENIS/LES PACOTS. Hotels: *Ermitage* (50 beds, indoor pool) and *Treize Cantons* (15 beds), economy grade. Restaurants: *Café Tivoli* (noted for its fondue) and *Corbetta.*

CHEXBRES. Hotels: *Du Signal,* 130 beds, indoor pool, medium grade. *Bellevue,* 42 beds, and *Victoria,* 45 beds, are economy bracket.

CHUR. Hotels: Best in town is top medium grade *Rohan* (60 beds; elegant restaurant; indoor pool), closely followed by *ABC* (66 beds; breakfast only), both near station, as well as *Post* (85 beds) and modernized *Stern* (70 beds, marvelous Grisons atmosphere, excellent food and wines. Last two near town center.

In the economy bracket are *City* (110 beds; clinical but comfortable), *Freieck* (60 beds; renovated throughout; all rooms with W.C.), and

cheaper *Obertor* (110 beds).

Restaurants: *Du Nord, Stern* (excellent regional specialties), *Zollhaus* (atmospheric), *Rebleuten Zunfthaus* all (I to M).

CRANS. Hotels: *Du Golf* (165 beds), *De l'Etrier* (250 beds), both deluxe, and first-class *Beau Séjour* (100 beds) have indoor pools. Also first class, each with 100 beds, *Alpina Savoy, Excelsior* and *Royal. Alpha* (50 beds), medium grade, has indoor pool. *Elite,* outdoor pool, and cheaper *Beau Site,* both 50 beds, economy.

Restaurants: *Au Robinson,* near funicular station, Valais specialties; *Le Prado,* light lunches, auto-park.

CRESUZ. Hotel: *Le Vieux Chalet* (15 beds; no private baths), typical Fribourg, chalet-type; inexpensive.

DARLIGEN. *Du Lac,* economy.

DAVOS. Hotels in Davos Platz are headed by the deluxe 220-bed *Belvédère,* followed by the *Central* and *Morosani's Post* (each 120 beds), *Europe* (130 beds), *Schweizerhof* (150 beds)and *Sunster-Park* (220 beds), all with indoor pools, and *Waldhotel-Bellevue* (90 beds).

Among first-class hotels are *Du Midi* (180 beds), *Sunstar* (140 beds; indoor pool) and *Victoria* (100 beds). Medium grade are *Angleterre, Bellavista, Bernina* (breakfast only), *Rinaldi,* and *Terminus.*

At Davos Dorf: *Derby, Fluela* and *Seehof* (each about 130 beds) are in the deluxe bracket. First class are

Meierhof and *Montana* (each 80 beds). *Bristol* (100 beds) and *Parsenn* (60 beds) are medium grade.

In the mountains above Davos, reached by funicular, is the deluxe *Berghôtel Schatzalp* (170 beds).

Belvédère, Central, Derby, Des Alpes, Europe, Fluela, Morosani's and *Montana* hotels have nightclubs. Lively pastry and coffee shops during winter include *Schneider's* and the *Fäh.*

DIABLERETS, LES. Hotels: *Grand Hôtel* (140 beds), and *Eurotel* (248 beds), recent; both first class and with indoor pools. *Mon Abri* (50 beds) is medium grade.

EINSIEDELN. *Pfauen* (55 beds), *Bären* (60 beds); both economy.

ENGELBERG. Hotels: The *Belle-vue-Terminus* and *Ring* (both 120 beds) are elegant and first class.

Medium grade are the *Alpina, Crystal, Central, Edelweiss, Engel, Hess, Maro, Spannort* and *Sch-weizerhof. Alpenklub* and *Marguerite* are economy.

ESTAVAYER-LE-LAC. Hotels: *Du Lac* (32 beds), pleasant lakeside terrace; economy.

EVOLENE. *Hermitage* and *Dent Blanche,* both economy.

FAIDO. *Milano* (70 beds) and *Faido* (38 beds), both economy grade.

FLIMS. Leader is top first class *Parkhotel* (340 beds); beautiful grounds but reports suggest disappointing food. Cheaper are delightful *Adula* (135 beds), always full, long advance booking essential, and *Des Alpes* (180 beds).

Medium grade include *Crap Ner, Schweizerhof, Segnes Post.* All except last with indoor pool.

FLUELEN. Hotels: *Urnerhof* (65 beds) and *Sternen* (35 beds) are economy.

FLUMSERBERGE. Hotels: *Alpina* and *Gamperdon,* both economy.

FRIBOURG. Hotels: *Berthold* (56 beds), *Elite* (40 beds), *Fribourg* (60 beds), and *Rose* (80 beds) are medium grade. *City* (45 beds) and *Ter-minus* (55 beds) are both economy grade and breakfast only.

Restaurants: The *Café Romand* for cheese specialties, especially fondue. The *Buffet de la Gare, Gambrinus, de la Grenette, Rex,* and *Vieux-Chêne* are (I-M).

FURIGEN. Hotels: *Fürigen-Belle-vue* (130 beds), medium grade.

GANDRIA. The *Moosman* (40 beds) is economy grade.

PRACTICAL INFORMATION FOR GENEVA

WHEN TO COME? From the visitor's standpoint, Geneva is a summer city, best visited in the usual holiday season, when, of course, it is inevitably crowded. The four-day "Fêtes of Geneva," with fireworks, street dancing, parades of flower-covered floats, etc., occurs in the middle of Aug., and naturally Geneva, like all Swiss communities, celebrates the national holiday, August 1. There is also much merrymaking during the festival of Escalade, Dec. 11–12. To check what's on, get a copy of *La Semaine à Genève (This Week in Geneva),* from your hotel. Information of all types can be obtained from the Geneva Tourist Office, 2 Rue des Moulins.

WHERE TO STAY? To the casual observer, Geneva sometimes seems to consist mainly of hotels, but in reality these are barely enough for visitors during the peak season, and accommodation is a problem during the big international conferences. With the opening of new hotels in the last few years things are a little easier. If you arrive without a reservation, you will find an office in the Cornavin Station that will place you somewhere, but it may be in only a modest although comfortable hotel.

To visitors staying at least three full days, many hotels offer pension rates that include room and board (rates supplied by hotels upon request).

NORTH SHORE

Deluxe hotels on this side are:

BEAU RIVAGE, 13 Quai du Mont-Blanc, 180 beds; air conditioned; fine grill room; renowned restaurant.

DES BERGUES, 33 Quai des Bergues, facing the river opposite Rousseau Island; air conditioned; 190 beds; distinguished atmosphere.

BRISTOL, 10 Rue du Mont-Blanc. Now a deluxe spot with matching prices.

INTERCONTINENTAL, 7 Petit Saconnex, near the Palais des Nations. An 18-story hotel with 785 beds; several restaurants; heated swimming pool; dinner-dances.

MEDITERRANEE, 14 Rue de Lausanne. Cheapest in this category. Ultra-modern; 210 beds; opposite rail station.

DE LA PAIX, 11 Quai du Mont-Blanc, 180 beds; modernized and very attractively furnished.

PRESIDENT, 47 Quai Wilson, 450 beds; air conditioned; tastefully furnished in antique style; expensive.

RAMADA, 38 Rue de Berne, 432 beds, air conditioned. New 1975. Own large garage.

LA RESERVE, 301 Route de Lausanne; 110 beds. In pleasant park; lakeside terrace; expensive.

DU RHONE, Quai Turrettini, overlooking river; 440 beds.

RICHEMOND, Jardin Brunswick; famous, family-owned and -run hotel; 200 beds; lake view; dinner-dances nightly in bar-grill.

ANGLETERRE, 17 Quai du Mont-Blanc, 110 beds; facing lake; air-conditioned restaurant. Run down, poor service.

Among first class hotels near the lake are *Amat,* 22 Rue Amat (200 beds), *Ambassador,* 21 Quai des Bergues (air-conditioned; 132 beds), *California,* (100 beds, breakfast only), and fine modern *Du Midi,* Pl. Chevelu (140 beds).

The *Royal,* 41 rue de Lousanne (210 beds, good snack bar and restaurant), *De Berne,* 26 Rue de Berne (air-conditioned; 130 beds) and *Cornavin,* 33 Blvd. James Fazy (175 beds) are handy for the station. So are medium grade *Alba,* 19 Rue du Mont-Blanc, *Astoria* and *Suisse,* both Pl. Cornavin, and *Rivoli,* 6 Rue des Pâquis. On the west side of the station are medium grade *Ariana,* 7 Rue J-R.Chouet, and *Epoque,* 10 Rue Voltaire. All except *De Berne, Astoria* and *Epoque* breakfast only.

In a residential area northwest of the station is the first class *Grand-Pré,* 35 Rue du Grand-Pré (130 beds; breakfast only). Near the Palais des Nations are the first class *Eden,* 135 Rue de Lausanne (70 beds) and the slightly cheaper *Mon Repos* at No. 131 (130 beds).

SOUTH SHORE

Near the Jardin Anglais, at 3 Rue de la Tour-Maîtresse, is the recent deluxe, 70-bed *L'Arbalete* with a restaurant noted for its typical Swiss dishes; air conditioned.

In a residential area at 11 Route de Florissant is *La Résidence,* 160 beds, first class; highly recommended by readers; easy parking; tennis. Under same management is the rather cheaper, 90-bed *Parc-Hotel,* 42 Avenue Krieg. Indoor pool.

MOTELS. At **COLLONGE-BELLERIVE,** *Motel Riviera* (100 beds), about 5 miles northeast of Geneva. At **COMMUGNY,** *Motel le Léman* (25 beds); at **FOUNEX,** *Motel de Founex* (240 beds); at **MIES,** *Motel de la Buna* (15 beds); at **PERLY,** *Motel Perly* (32 beds); at **VESENAZ,** *Motel la Tourelle* (45 beds). All within about 20 miles of Geneva. Except at Perly (closed Jan.) and Collonge-Bellerive (closed Nov.-Feb.) all open throughout year.

RESTAURANTS. Geneva is full of good restaurants, with French cooking dominant, though here there are plenty of places that provide the mixed Swiss cuisine, as well as many specializing in the dishes of other countries. There are few pleasanter places to lunch or dine on a fine day than *La Perle du Lac,* 128 Rue de Lausanne (closed November-March). You can be served out of doors in a park right on the lakeside, facing a wonderful panorama. Like the view, the food—lake-fish dishes and other specialties—is tops. You can reach it by car along the lake-front or by bus No. 5. There is also a motor-boat service from the Pâquis embankment. The counterpart on the other bank is the restaurant in the *Parc des Eaux-Vives,* elegant, in the former mansion of Louis Favre, with excellent food. Both (E), closed Mon.

The tourist office has a helpful free leaflet listing many Geneva restaurants. The listings (E), (M), or (I), indicate expensive, moderate or inexpensive.

One of Geneva's best restaurants, with excellent cuisine and service, is *Le Gentilhomme* (E), grill of the Hotel Richemond. It is pleasantly situated on the Jardin Brunswick, the little park facing the lake. The wine list carries some rare Swiss wines. There is music at apéritif time and dancing at night.

The Hotel Du Rhône also has a topflight restaurant, *Le Neptune* (E); outstanding menus and good wine list. The terrace is a fashionable rendezvous in summer for cocktails.

Notable, too, for their elegance as well as their food, are the *Rôtisserie du Chat Botté* of the Hotel Beau Rivage, the *Amphitryon* of the Hotel des Bergues, and the restaurant of the Hotel de la Paix. All (E).

At the *Intercontinental,* if you've a head for heights, you can dine by candlelight in their 18th-floor restaurant with a superb lake view.

Leading restaurants are *Le Duc,* 7 Quai du Mont Blanc (for excellent fish); *Le Senat,* 1 rue Emile Yung; *Le Marignac,* 32 ave. Eugene-Lance, Grand Lancy; *Le Curling,* Chemin Fief-du-Chapitre, Petit-Lancy; and *Le Boeuf Rouge,* 10 rue des Paquis.

First-rate restaurants are *Or du Rhône,* now at 19 Blvd. Georges Favon, whose specialties are steaks and chicken grilled over an open fire, and *Au Fin Bec,* 55 Rue de Berne;

closed Sun., both (E).

L'Aéroport (E) at Cointrin is worth visiting for its hors d'oeuvres and airport view, and the *Buffet Cornavin* (M) in Geneva's main railroad station has a good grill room and French restaurant.

For atmosphere try *Le Mazot,* 16 Rue du Cendrier, the décor being that of Valais, the canton through which the Rhône flows on its way to Lake Geneva, *Au Pied du Cochon* (M), just off Place Bourg-de-Four (specialties: pigs' feet, onion soup, steaks), or *Les Armures* (M), 1 Rue Puits-St. Pierre (close to town hall).

For a nautical touch, dine at *Le Bateau* (closed Tues. in winter), an old paddle steamer converted to a restaurant and moored at the south end of the Pont du Mont-Blanc; for Provençal cuisine go to *L'Aïoli* (I–M), Pl. du Port; and for lake fish try *Creux-de-Genthod* (M–E), closed Jan./Feb., by the lakeside 4 miles north of the city.

In the (I–M) price bracket are: *Chez Bouby,* 1 Rue Grenus (reader recommended), *du Centre* in Place du Molard, and *Plat d'Argent,* 7 Rue Cherbuliez, said to be Geneva's oldest restaurant.

There are several Chinese restaurants, including the *Chinois,* 7 Rue Tour-Maîtresse, *Fleur de Ming,* 8 Rue du Prince, *Le Mandarin,* 1 Rue Chantepoulet, *Trois Bonheurs,* 29 Rue Cité, and *Au Dragon d'Or,* 3 Rue Chaponnière. The first is closed in July. Most are fairly expensive.

The best Italian restaurant in Geneva is *Roberto* (E), 13 Rue Madeleine (closed Sat. evening and Sun.). Good for French specialties and wine from the barrel is *Kléber* (M to E), 14 Rue Kléberg. *Le Coqenpate,* 10 Rue Voltaire, under same management as Hotel Epoque, is best known for dishes featuring chicken.

You can get excellent Spanish food, and also see Flamenco dancing, at *Don Quijote,* 1 Rue de Berne. Spanish cuisine, too, and fish specialties, at *Le Catalan* (closed Sun.), 171 Route de Florissant at Conches, just outside the town. Both (M–E).

For everything from a snack to moderately expensive grills and seafood try *Mövenpick,* 40 Rue du Rhône and 17 Rue du Cendrier.

Budget troubles? Try the self-service *La Rochelle,* 5 Rue du Commerce (6th floor), the self-service restaurants of the *Migros* chain, or the department stores—all in the inexpensive bracket.

About 4 miles southwest of city center is *L'Auberge Communale de Confignon* (M–E), an old inn with splendid food and magnificent views. The *Lion d'Or* (E), at Cologny, northeast of the city, also has fine food. Nearby (15 minutes from Geneva), the restaurant of the *Casino de Divonne,* noted for its excellence.

SHOPPING. The best of French luxury products and haute couture boutiques complement the magnificent Swiss watches, winter sports equipment, cine cameras, and the gorgeous embroidery and laces from St. Gallen.

BOOKS. *Payot,* 2 Rue Vallin. *Naville Cie.* (also stationery and artists' supplies), 5 Rue Lévrier and thirty other local branches.

CAMERAS. *Amrein-Graf,* 27 Quai des Bergues. *Photo Mont-Blanc,* 17 Rue du Mont-Blanc. *Photo des Nations,* Place Longemalle. *Photo et*

Ciné, 1 Rue du Mont-Blanc. *Photo Pour Tous,* 5 Boulevard Georges Favon. *Photo-Centre,* 3 Rue du Marché.

CANDY, SWEETS. *Chocolaterie du Rhône,* 2 Rue du Rhône, *Rohr,* 3 Place du Molard, *A la Bonbonnière,* 11 Rue de Rive.

CLOTHING. *Carnaval de Venise,* 12 Rue du Mont-Blanc. *Chemiserie Centrale,* 19 Croix d'Or. *Reginald Rolls,* 7 Corraterie.

DEPARTMENT STORES. *Au Grand Passage* and *Bon Génie Nouveautés,* both Rue du Marché, and, rather cheaper, *La Placette,* Rue Grenus.

DRUGSTORES. *Pharmacie Principale,* 11 Rue du Maché. *Finck,* Rue du Mont-Blanc.

FURNITURE. *La Botique Danoise,* 100 Rue du Rhône, Danish furniture and arts.

FURS. *Sistovaris,* at 40 Rue du Rhône, and *Tigre Royale,* at no. 60.

HAUTE COUTURE. Boutiques include *Courrèges* at 78; *Dior,* 60; *Lanvin,* 62; *Lapidus,* 114; *St. Laurent,* 51; *Smaga/Ungaro,* 51; all Rue du Rhône. *Weyeneth-Givenchy,* 5 Rue des Alpes, and *Cardin,* 15 Rue du Cendrier.

JEWELRY. *Boujon Frères* (silver and pewter), 3 bis Rue de Rive. *Bucherer,* 26 Général Guisan and 22 Rue du Mont-Blanc. *Van Cleef et Arpels,* 12 Quai Général Guisan. *Golay Fils Stahl, S.A.,* 1, Place des Bergues. *Gübelin,* 60 Rue du Rhône. *Imhof,* 4 Passage des Lions. *Lombard* (rare custom-made designs), 5 Rue de la Corraterie. *Piaget,* 40 Rue du Rhône.

LEATHER. *Au Faubourg St. Honoré,* at 43, and *Favre* at 60 Rue du Rhône. *La Marjolaine,* 19 Rue de la Croix d'Or.

MUSIC. *Sautier Jaeger,* 12 Place

de la Fusterie. *Champion,* 8 Rue Versonnex.

OPTICAL GOODS. *Lindegger Co.,* 104 Rue du Rhône. *Wiegandt,* 10 Quai Général Guisan.

PORCELAIN, GLASSWARE. *Kuhn,* 17 Rue du Marché. *Rosenthal,* 84 Rue du Rhône.

SHOES. *Aeschbach,* 4 Rue du Rhône. *Lôw Prothos,* 35 Rue due Rhône. *Rivoli-Bally,* 18 Rue du Marché.

SOUVENIRS. *Jouets Weber* (also toys,) 12 Croix-d'Or. *A l'Ours de Berne* (also woodcarvings), 28 Quai Général Guisan.

SPORTS EQUIPMENT. *Charles,* 27 Quai des Bergues. *Hofstetter,* 12 Corraterie.

TOILETRIES. *Francine,* 5 Rue de la Fontaine. *Nouvelles Galeries,* 9 Corraterie, perfumes only. *Geiser et Neuhaus,* 2 Rue Bonivard, are also hairdressers.

WATCHES. *Baszanger,* 6, Corraterie. *Au Rubis,* 21 Rue du Mont-Blanc. *Bucherer,* 26 Quai Général Guisan and 22 Rue du Mont-Blanc. *Pierre Bergerioux,* 4 Rue de Rive. *Böhni,* 30 Rue du Rhône. *Châtelain,* 4 Tour de l'Ile. *Chronométrie du Molard,* 40 rue du Marché. *Chronos,* 1 Chantepoulet. *Clarence,* 3 Rue du Marché and 3 Quai du Mont-Blanc. *A. Collet,* 8 Place du Molard. *Au Diamant,* 7 Rue du Mont-Blanc.

F. Fatio, 21 Quai des Bergues. *Gil,* 9 Rue du Mont-Blanc. *E. E. Golay,* 1 Rue du Mont-Blanc. *Golay Fils Stahl, S.A.,* 1, Place des Bergues. *Gübelin,* 60 Rue du Rhône. *Th. Horovitz,* 15 Blvd. Georges-Favon. *Imhof,* 4 Passage des Lions. *A la Montre Suisse,* 17 Rue du Mont-Blanc. *Nicolet,* 7 Rue du Mont-Blanc. *Piaget,* 40 Rue du Rhône. *Horlogerie de la Paix,* 21 Quai des Bergues. *Patek Philippe Co.,* 22 Quai Général Guisan. *Port Royal,*

Place du Rhône. *Rive-Bijoux,* 116 Rue du Rhône. *Léon Scherrer Co.,* 29 Rue du Rhône. *Schussel Cie.,* 1 Place du Port. *J. P. Steiner,* 19 Place Montbrillant. *Vacheron Constantin,* 1 Rue des Moulins. *Horlogerie du Rhône,* 78 Rue du Rhône. *Diamant-art,* 19 Rue du Rhône. *Big Ben,* 14 Rue du Rhône.

ENTERTAINMENT. Geneva is not Paris, but it comes closer to it than any other city in Switzerland, and can be fairly lively in the evening. There are two theaters, the *Grand Théâtre* and the *Comédie,* for opera, operetta, or plays. You may have a chance to see experimental productions at the *Théâtre de Poche,* and there is a marionette theater at 4 Rue Constantin. American and British films are shown in English in certain cinemas. In others they are dubbed into French, but usually there are one or more showings a day with the original English soundtrack.

In summer, there are free band concerts and other musical entertainment in bandstands in the parks all over the city, and there are plays and concerts in the lovely courtyard of the *Hôtel de Ville.*

Concert halls are *Victoria Hall,* Rue Général Dufour, where the fine Orchestre Suisse Romande gives its symphonic concerts; *Conservatorie de Musique,* Place Neuve; *Radio Geneva,* 66 Boulevard Carl-Vogt. There are folk dances Tuesday and Thursday at the *American Community House,* 3 Rue de Monthoux; for those who are interested these include square dances. Theater and concert tickets can be had at *Au Grand Passage,* 50 Rue du Rhône, fourth floor, or *Sautier Faeger,* 12 Place de la Fusterie.

Nightclubs are a few cuts below the standards of the larger international capitals, but are reasonably priced. With a good floor show, average entrance will cost around 10 frs.; a Scotch somewhat more. If a "hostess" joins you at your table or at the bar and suggests you buy her a drink, she means champagne (she gets a percentage from the house). Don't be afraid to say no— you won't be the first. The liveliest places are possibly the *Ba-Ta-Clan,* 15 Rue de la Fontaine, which has heard about striptease, and the *Moulin Rouge,* Place de Cirque. The *Pussy Cat Saloon,* 15 Rue Glacis-de-Rive, puts on two first-class international shows and striptease, at 10:30 p.m. and 1 a.m. *Club 58,* with the same entrance, is a more casual drinking/entertainment spot. Probably the best spot in town, and the place to go if you want to avoid striptease, is *Maxim's,* Place des Alpes. There's neither striptease nor floorshow at *La Tour,* 6 Rue Tour-de-Boël, but it always has two bands.

There's dancing at *Le Grillon,* 5 Place de la Fusterie (also tea-dances at 3:30 p.m.); at *Club 58,* 15 Rue Glacis-de-Rive; and *Hit Club* (disco), 3 Rue du Marché.

MUSEUMS. All Geneva's permanent museums are closed on Good Friday, Easter Sunday, Ascension, Whit Sunday, third Sunday in September, Christmas, December 31, and New Year's Day. The most important collections are listed below. There are in addition over thirty art galleries that have interesting temporary shows from time to time. To check on them, see *La Semaine à Genève (This Week in Geneva),* the information bulletin.

Ariana, Avenue de la Paix, Headquarters of International Ceramics Academy. Collection of European and Oriental china and earthenware. The collection of old Nyon and Geneva chinaware is particularly notable. Open Apr.–Oct., 10–12, 1–5, except Mon. Entrance free.

Art and History, Rue Charles-Galland. Open all year, 10–12, 2–6, closed Mon. morning. Entrance free. Fine permanent collection of archeological objects, paintings, and sculpture, particularly strong in decorative art, with emphasis on Genevese enamels.

Athénée Museum, 2 Rue de l'Athénée, permanent exhibitions of French and Swiss paintings (also on sale). Admission, 2 or 3 frs., adults.

Baur Collection, Rue Munier-Romilly 8, not far from the Art and History Museum. In a former private house, a fine collection of Chinese and Japanese ceramics, jades, prints, etc. Open daily except Mon., 2–6.

Petit Palais, 2 Terrasse Saint-Victor, has modern art from 19th century onwards, and also loans exhibitions. Open daily except Mon.; admission 5 frs.

Ethnographic, 65-67 Boulevard Carl-Vogt. 10–12, 2–5, closed Mon.

Museum of Old Musical Instruments, 23 Rue Lefort. Opening times vary.

Horological Museum, 15 Route de Malagnou (beside Natural History Museum). Fine collection of timepieces.

Natural History, 11 Route de Malagnou. 10–12, 2–5, entrance free. Splendidly arranged collection in new building. There is also a Botanical Museum and Conservatory near the United Nations buildings.

History of Science Museum, 128 Rue de Lausanne; good display of scientific instruments. Open 2–6; also Sun., 10–12.

Palais des Nations, Parc d l'Ariana; European Office of the United Nations. Guided tours of the building at least twice daily throughout year except Dec. 21–Jan. 2. Admission 2.50 frs.

Palais Wilson, 51 Quai Wilson. 9–12, 2–6, free. Educational exhibition of the International Education Bureau.

Rath, Place Neuve. For temporary shows, frequently extremely good, often with exhibits from other countries. Notable for watch and jewelry exhibition in Sept. 10–12, 2–6; closed Mon. Admission, 2 frs., adults.

Voltaire, 25 Rue des Délices. 2–5 Mon. to Fri. Entrance free. Relics of Voltaire and his times—portraits, busts, furniture, etc.

CHURCHES. Worth a visit is the picturesque *Russian Orthodox Church,* Rue Toepffer, service 10 a.m. For services in French, the leading Protestant church is *St. Peter's Cathedral,* service at 10 a.m.; the leading Catholic church is *Notre-Dame,* 6 Place Cornavin, masses at 7:30, 9, 10, 11:30 a.m., 5 and 8:30 p.m.

The *Synagogue* is at Place de la Synagogue; times vary. *American Church,* 2 Rue Alfred-Vincent: Holy Communion 8 a.m., Family Worship 9:15, Morning Prayer 11.

English Church, 14 Rue de Mont-Blanc; Holy Communion 8 a.m., Matins and sermon 10:30, Evensong 8:30 p.m. Wed., Holy Communion 7:45 a.m. *Church of Scotland,* in the Auditoire, Place de la Toconnerie, Sundays at 11 a.m. *Lutheran Church,* Place du Bourg-de-Four. Service at 11 a.m.

All times given above refer to Sun. unless otherwise specified. Because times are apt to vary, it is best to check in Sat. newspapers or with your hotel.

SPORTS. You can go *swimming* in the heart of the city at the Pâquis jetty, an artificial swimming take-off point built out from the Quai du Mont-Blanc, but you'll probably enjoy it more if you go out a little way by No. 2 or 9 bus to Geneva Plage, near the yacht harbor, on the eastern fringe of the city, or on the other side of the free Reposoir beach, a little more than a mile from the center on the Lausanne road. If you want a heated, undercover pool of Olympic dimensions, try the new municipal swimming bath at Quai des Vernets. You can hire *boats* at either the Quai du Mont-Blanc or the Quai Gustave-Ador, on the other bank. At Geneva Plage you can make arrangements for *water skiing. The Geneva Golf Club* (18 holes; 6,835 yards) is at Château Bessinge, Route de la Capite, Cologny (Bus A from Rive to Chemin de Fraidieux); also at *Casino de Divonne,* 15 minutes from Geneva. *Tennis* can be played at the Eaux-Vives park, No. 2 bus; at the Drizia Tennis Club, Stade de Champel; the International Tennis Club, Chemin Rigot; and several other places. For *horseback riding,* mounts may be hired at the Geneva Riding School, 17 Chemin de Grange-Falquet, or Manège de Meyrin, 31 Chemin Golette. *Fencing,* Geneva Fencing Society, 17 Rue Dancet. *Trap shooting,* Ball Trap Club, Plan-les-Ouates, information from the Armourer, E. Mayor, 30 Rue du Rhône. *Chess,* Geneva Chess Club, Brasserie Eaux-Vivienne, 3 Rue Eaux Vives. *Bridge-Club des Bergues,* Rue Michel Roset. *Bowling,* Bowling AMF, 67 Chemin de l'Etang, which also has a restaurant serving American meals, or at 11 Rue des Maraîchers.

TRANSPORTATION. *Taxis* start at about 3 francs, then cost about 1.40 frs. per kilometer (⅝ of a mile). You pick them up at ranks, or call them by phone (dial 165). *Drive-yourself cars* may be hired from *Avis Rent-a-Car,* 44 Rue de Lausanne; *Europcar,* 28 Rue du Pâquis; *Hertz,* 60 Rue de Berne; and *Budget,* 36 Rue de Zurich. All have offices at Geneva airport. If you wish to engage a chauffeur, it is best to make arrangements through your hotel porter. *Horse carriages* are pleasant, but expensive; make a deal with the driver. *Bus* and *trolley bus* services cover the city, fares starting at 80 centimes. Tickets must be obtained at bus-stop slot machines before boarding vehicles. *Motorboat* services take you from one bank to the other; fares from 1 fr. upwards. For longer trips on the *lake steamers,* inquire at the departure point at the Jardin Anglais.

HOW TO GET TO TOWN FROM THE AIRPORT. Geneva (Cointrin) airport to city center, 2 miles. Airport coach to railroad station (air terminal) 3.50 frs.; taxi around 12 frs.

USEFUL ADDRESSES. Local information and advice: *Office du Tourisme,* 2 Rue des Moulins. *British Consulate,* 37/39 Rue de Vermont. *American Express,* 7 Rue du Mont-Blanc; 12 Chemin Rien; 41 Ave. Giuseppe Motta. *Cook's,* 4 Rue du Mont-Blanc. *Money exchange* outside banking hours, Cornavin railway station 6:30 A.M. to 11 P.M.; Cointrin airport, 24-hour service. *American Community House,* 3 Rue de Monthoux. *English Genevese Society,* 2 Rue Athénée. *American Club of Geneva,* Intercontinental Hotel.

GERSAU. Hotels: *Müller* (130 beds), medium grade, and *Seehof* (40 beds), economy; both on lake.

GLARUS. Hotel: *Glarnerhof,* 55 beds, economy grade.

GLETSCH. Hotel-restaurant: *Glacier Du Rhône* (110 beds), medium grade. Here you dine (M) at carved rustic tables.

GLION. Hotels: *Victoria* (80 beds), first class; *Des Alpes Vaudoises* (100 beds) medium; each with outdoor pool. *Mont Fleuri* (60 beds), economy.

GOLDIWIL. *Jungfrau,* economy.

GRACHEN. Hotels: The *Beau-Site, Bellevue* (both with indoor pool), *Elite, Grächerhof,* and *Walliserhof,* all with 50 to 70 beds, are economy grade. So is the comfortable *Hotel zum See* (40 beds), situated

above the village beside a lovely little lake.

GRENCHEN. Hotel: *Krebs,* economy grade.

GRIMENTZ. *Marenda* (65 beds) and much cheaper *De Moiry* (80 beds), good food, are economy.

GRIMSEL. *Grimsel-Hospiz* (50 beds), *Grimsel-Passhöhe* (30 beds) at summit; both economy grade.

GRINDELWALD. *Grand Hotel Regina,* deluxe, 180 beds, air conditioned and soundproofed, indoor pool, sauna. First class are *Sunstar, Weisses Kreuz, Belvédère, Parkhotel Schönegg* and *Schweizerhof* (each with indoor pool) and *Silberhorn* (kosher). *Derby-Bahnhof* and *Alpina* (newly refurbished), *Spinne* and *Résidence,* all medium grade.

PRACTICAL INFORMATION FOR THE GRISONS

WHEN TO COME? The resort season for the Grisons is June to Sept., and Dec. to Apr., but in each resort there is always at least one hotel open in the off-season. Mar. and Apr. are generally too messy with slush and melting snow to be pleasant in the towns. May and June are lovely months for wild flowers, and Oct. and Nov., while often rainy, generally allow a few crisp, cold weeks to enjoy the brilliant color of the foliage. Nights in the Grisons are cool enough for a topcoat even in mid-summer, especially above 2,000 feet, which most of it is.

WHAT TO SEE? The smart resorts of the Grisons—St. Moritz, Arosa, Klosters, Davos—are at their sparkling best in winter sports high season and in themselves something to experience: mink coats over ski clothes, the international rich at play. But the real charm of this region has nothing to do with worldly wealth. It is found in the National Park, a nature lover's delight, abounding in wildlife with everything left in its natural state; in the beautiful Engadine valley with, at the upper end, its chain of quiet blue lakes reflecting towering snowcapped peaks; and in picturesque old mountain villages, peopled by unspoiled peasants, often still speaking their Latinate language, Romansch.

HOW TO GET ABOUT? Special holiday tickets issued by the Swiss federal railways are valid on the privately owned railway networks of the Grisons and the post office bus lines as well. Highways in the Grisons are excellent and most are kept open the year round. Here your own car will be appreciated perhaps as much as anywhere else in Switzerland. Drive (or go by postal bus) through the Julier and Maloja pass—Chur, Lenzerheide, St. Moritz, Maloja, and on down into the Italian lake district—scenically this is one of the most rewarding trips you can take in Europe. But many other less famous roads will take you through almost as splendid and equally varied scenery.

SPORTS. Winter and summer, the Grisons resorts are planned for sportsmen: golf, tennis, swimming, riding, mountaineering in summer, and even skiing, such as at Corvatsch near St. Moritz. Skiing, sledding, skating, curling, ice-hockey and horseracing (on snow) are the outstanding winter sports.

MOTELS. At **Chur**, *Mot-Hotel Sommerau* (106 beds). At **Savognin**, *Bergmotel* (96 beds; closed Oct., Nov., May).

SHOPPING IN THE GRISONS. AROSA: Cameras. *Carl Brandt, Rolf Koradi* "Foto Willy"; *Foto Homberger.* **Food Specialties.** *Reformhaus* (health foods), Poststrasse; *Emil Simmen* (chocolate and pastries), Bahnhofplatz, Obersee.

Souvenirs. *Belmont* and *Benker.* **Sports Equipment.** *Koller Knechtle; Skihalle und Sportgeschäft Kulm; Sprecher-Sport; Carmenna-Sport.* **Watches.** *Joos,* Poststrasse; *Hans Jäggi.*

CHUR. Souvenirs. *Bündner Heimatwerk* (also handcrafts), Mühleplatz.

Sports Equipment. *A. Hochholdinger Sporthaus,* Poststrasse.

Watches, Optics. *Joh. Disam Söhne,* Bahnhofstrasse. *H. Jäggi,* Bahnhofstrasse 42. *E. Joos Co.,* Poststrasse 32.

DAVOS. Cameras. *Holliger,* Promenade. *Paul Weber,* Promenade 51.

Souvenirs. *H. Trauffer,* Davosplatz.

Sports Equipment. *Jack Ettinger Sport,* Davosplatz.

Watches. *E. Barth,* Promenade. *Leicht,* Promenade 40. *Chronometrie Stäuble,* Promenade 33.

KLOSTERS. Cameras. *Jacob Compeer.* **Watches.** *Leo Maissen, Schauerte.*

LENZERHEIDE. Souvenirs,

Sports and Travel Goods, *Sporthaus Alpina. Franz Peskö Sport- und Schuhhaus.* **Watches and Jewelry.** J. Disam *Söhne.*

PONTRESINA. Candy and Pastry. *Confiserie-Tea Room "Engiadina" C. Gianotti. Tea Room "Piz Süss."* **Souvenirs.** *Flück. Rominger. Unica.* **Watches.** *Bott.*

ST. MORITZ. Cameras. *Rutz Co.,* Hotel Crystal. *"Foto Max,"* Galerie du Palace. *Götte,* House Monopol.

Embroidery, Linen, Lace. *Ebneter Biel,* Hauptstrasse. *Ed. Sturzenegger,* Dorfstrasse.

Optical Goods. *Götte,* Dorfstrasse. **Souvenirs, Handcrafts.** *E.*

Branger, Postplatz. *Franz Carl Weber* (also toys), Postplatz. At St. Moritz-Bad: *Huber-Aeschimann; K. R. Holinger* (wall clocks).

Sports Equipment. *Othmar Ender. Max Lamm,* Dorfstrasse. *Albert Sheuing, Testa-Sport.*

Watches. *E. K. Bittmann. Bucherer. Gübelin. Willy Muntwyler. Arth. Scherbel.*

SAMEDAN. Handcrafts. Engadiner Heimatwerk.

SCUOL - TARASP - VULPERA. Cameras. *W. Rauch.*

SILS. Handcrafts. *Engadiner Heimatwerk.*

CAR HIRE. *Avis,* at Grabenstrasse 5, Chur; Fluelastrasse 2, Davos; and Parkhaus, St. Moritz. *Hertz* at Kasernstrasse 92, Chur; Guggerbachstrasse 5, Davos; Garage Central, Klosters; Kulm Garage, St. Moritz. *Europcar,* Talstrasse 30, Davos.

USEFUL ADDRESS. *Cook's,* St. Moritz, Hauptstrasse 65.

GRUYERES. Hotels: *St. Georges* (25 beds; good restaurant), *Gruyerotel* (70 beds; breakfast only), and cheaper *De Ville* (21 beds).

GSTAAD. *Gstaad Palace,* deluxe, center of society life in Gstaad, with indoor pool, sauna, tennis, golf, riding. First class are *Alpina, Bellevue, Reuteler* (each with outdoor pool). *Alphorn, Olden, Rossli* and *Victoria* (each with indoor pool), medium grade. *Chalet Christiania* (breakfast only), *Neueret,* both indoor pool, and *Bernerhof* are economy.

GUNTEN. First class; *Hirschen am See. Du Lac,* top medium grade.

HAUTE-NENDAZ. *Mont-Calme* (35 beds) and *Sourire* (58 beds), both economy.

HEIDEN. Hotels: *Krone-Schweizerhof,* 60 beds, pool. *Heiden,* 100 beds, indoor pool, sauna; both first class.

HERGISWIL. Hotels: *Belvédère* (outdoor pool); *Pilatus* (indoor pool). Both 100 beds; top medium grade.

HILTERFINGEN. *Marbach* and *Bellevue au Lac,* both medium grade.

HORN. Hotel: *Bad Horn,* recently reconstructed. Medium grade.

HOSPENTAL. *Meyerhof* (50 beds), economy.

PRACTICAL INFORMATION FOR INTERLAKEN

WHERE TO STAY? Small though it is, Interlaken has nearly ninety hotels and can put up 5,000 visitors without difficulty.

The three leading hotels, all in the near-deluxe bracket, are the famous *Victoria-Jungfrau* (360 beds), fine indoor pool; the marginally cheaper *Beau-Rivage* (170 beds), recently modernized, new indoor pool, sauna, beauty farm; and eighteen-story *Metropole* (180 beds), indoor pool, sauna; pleasingly ultramodern; superb views from upper floors and rooftop cocktail bar.

First class are the *Belvédere* (100 beds), *Bernerhof* (70 beds), near the West Station, ultramodern but colorfully cozy; and *Royal St. Georges* (150 beds), nice rooms in new wing. First class but slightly cheaper is the *Du Lac* in a quiet spot near Lake Brienz steamer landing stage and East Station, the terminal of Jungfrau region mountain railways, owned and run by the Hofmann family since 1888; pleasant dining room overlooking river; much praised by readers; used and recommended by the writers. Also first class are *Goldey* near the river, *Krebs* and *National* in the town center, and *Regina* near the Tell theater.

In the medium grade near the West station and town center are *Merkur, Weisses Kreuz, Bristol-Terminus* and *Eurotel* (last one, breakfast only); out near the Tell theater, the *Parkhotel Mattenhof,* outdoor pool; and in a quiet, open area but less than 5 mins. from the shops and station is the exceptionally pleasant *Stella,* probably one of the best in its class (recently modernized throughout; new wing 1971; fine indoor pool; satisfying American breakfast included in rates).

Among a very wide selection of economy-bracket hotels, the cheaper ones include *Anker, Helvetia, Rugenpark* and (breakfast only) *Beyeler,* all without private baths.

MOTELS. See under Bernese Oberland.

RESTAURANTS. Most of the good eating in Interlaken takes place in hotel restaurants. The *Jungfrau-Grill-Stube* (E) of the Victoria-Jungfrau Hotel, which has an attractive Oberland atmosphere, is noted for charcoal grills and all Swiss dishes, including fondue. The *Krebs Hotel* has a terrace with a view of Jungfrau, and its open-air restaurant (M) specializes in grills and Bernese dishes. Excellent materials, impeccably prepared and served, rather than lengthy menus, are keynotes of the *Du Lac* (M). The Metropole boasts several restaurants—all attractive—including the *Charolais* (E), *Raclette Taverne* (M) for Swiss dishes, and *Metrosnack* (I). The enormous *Schuh,* a traditional rendezvous in Interlaken, is both a restaurant (M-E) and a tearoom with memorable *pâtisseries.* All the above are in Höheweg. Among other tearooms are *Siegenthaler* and *Deuschle.* For large, outstandingly good pizzas try *Piz-Paz* (I) in Jungfraustrasse. If cash is a problem, aim for the huge, first-floor cafeteria (I) of *Migros,* opposite the West station, where the food is good and cheap, but don't expect any charm.

SHOPPING. Souvenirs. *Oberländer Heimarbeit,* Höheweg 115. *Oberländer Webstube,* Höheweg 78. *Michel,* Höheweg 72. *"Magasins des Alpes,"* Höheweg. *"Bazar Tivoli,"* Höheweg. *Albert Schild,* Bahnhofstrasse 19. *Shop "Diana"* (wood carvings), Höheweg 197.

Sports Equipment. *Karl Molitor Sporthaus,* Höheweg. **Textiles.** *Ed. Sturzenegger,* Höheweg. *Oberländer Webstube,* Höheweg 78.

Watches. *Bucherer,* Banhofstrasse and Höheweg. *F. W. Eisenhart,* Höheweg 54. *E. W. Fiechter,* Höheweg 2. *F. Kirchhofer,* Höheweg 9. *L. Luyten,* Höheweg. *A. Mersmann,* Höheweg 101. *H. Schertenleib,* Bahnhofstrasse.

USEFUL ADDRESSES. *Official Tourist Office,* Höheweg 37 (Hotel Metropole building). *Cook's,* Höheweg 29. *Saddle horses,* Ernest Vögeli, Scheidgasse, Unterseen. *Church of England* and *Church of Scotland* services in the *Schlosskirche* during the season.

THE JURA

MOTELS. At **Bevaix,** 8 miles southwest of Neuchâtel, *Motel du Cheval d'Eau* (40 beds). At **Chavannes-Sous-Romont,** *Motel la Poularde* (18 beds). At **Chez-Le-Bart,** 10 miles southwest of Neuchâtel, *Motel Bellerive* (90 beds). At **Estavayer-Le-Lac,** *Motel du Cerf* (20 beds). At **Gempenach,** 4 miles east of Murten, *Motel Gempenach* (20 beds). At **Gruyeres-Epagny,** *Motel Gruyères* (40 beds). At **La Chaux-De-Fonds,** *Motel du Jura* (22 beds). At **La Neuveville,** *Motel La Neuveville* (56 beds). At **Sonceboz,** 9 miles northwest of Biel, *Motel Heimelig* (10 beds) and *Motel Le Grillon* (21 beds). At **Thielle,** 6 miles east of Neuchâtel, *Novotel Neuchâtel Est* (120 beds). All open year around except *Gempenach* and *La Neuveville* (both closed Jan.).

SHOPPING. Biel (Bienne). *Handcrafts.* Oberländer Heimatwerk, Kanalgasse 9. *Souvenirs, toys.* Franz Carl Weber, Nidaugasse 1. *Watches.* Chatelain Dubois, Nidaugasse 14. **La Chaux-De-Fonds.** *Watches and Chronometers.* H. Sandoz Co., 50 Avenue L. Robert. **Fribourg.** *Handcrafts.* La Clef du Pays, Rue des Epouses. *Watches.* Grauwiller, 36 Place de la Gare.

KANDERSTEG. *Royal-Bellevue,* first class, indoor pool. *Victoria, Schweizerhof* and *Parkhotel Gemmi,* indoor pool, top medium grade. *Adler, Alpenhof* (indoor pool) and *Bernerhof* are economy.

KLEINE SCHEIDEGG. *Scheidegg,* medium grade.

KLEWENALP. *Hotel Klewenalp* (60 beds), very pleasant; fine location above lake; dancing; medium grade.

KLOSTERS. In the deluxe category are the *Silvretta* (180 beds), *Vereina* (170 beds), and *Pardenn* (130 beds), last two with indoor pool. Top first class is the delightful *Chesa Grischuna* (50 beds), noted for its food (E); nightclub.

Medium grade are the *Alpina,* excellent restaurant (E), and *Weisskreuz-Belvédère* (50 beds each). *Sporthof* and *Bundnerhof* are economy.

KREUZLINGEN. Hotel: *Plaza,* economy grade.

KUSSNACHT AM RIGI. *Engel* (20 beds), economy, was the 15th-century town hall, once the meeting place for local "parliaments."

LAAX. *Happy Rancho* (450 beds), top first class, exceptionally well equipped. Slightly cheaper, *Riva* (80 beds), beside lake. Both with indoor pool, new.

LA CHAUX-DE-FONDS. Hotels: *Club* (newest; 80 beds), *Fleur-de-Lys* (56 beds), and *Moreau* (66 beds); all good economy grade.

LAKE GENEVA COUNTRY

MOTELS. At **Bex,** *Motel St. Christophe* (32 beds). At **Bussigny,** about 5 miles northwest of Lausanne, *Novotel Lausanne Ouest* (300 beds). At **Chalet-a-Gobet,** *Motel Vert-Bois* (60 beds). At **Cully,** Motel Intereurop (140 beds). At **Etoy,** between Rolle and Morges, *Motel Lunika* (40 beds) and *Motel des Pêchers* (42 beds). At **Grens-Sur-Nyon,** *Motel du Pressoir* (50 beds). At **Montreux-Clarens,** *Motel de la Baye* (80 beds). At **Prangins,** near Nyon, *Motel de l'Aerodrome* (28 beds). At **Rennaz,** near Villeneuve, *Motel de Rennaz* (60 beds). At **Servion,** 10 miles north of Vevey, *Motel des Fleurs* (70 beds). At **St. Prex,** near Morges, *Motel du Bourg* (36 beds). At **St. Sulpice,** between Lausanne and Morges, *Motel des Pierettes* (46 beds). At **Vallorbe,** near French frontier, *Motel Les Jurats* (40 beds). At **Vevey,** *Motel des 4 Vents* (32 beds). At **Villars-Le-Terroir,** near Echallens, *Motel Beauregard* (46 beds). All open year round except Prangins closed Jan. and Feb., and Rennaz, closed Jan.

LANGENBRUCK. *Bären,* renowned family-run restaurant where Napoleon stopped. A few simple rooms, but worth a visit at mealtime (M).

PRACTICAL INFORMATION FOR LAUSANNE

HOTELS. The hotels of Lausanne are renowned for their quiet elegance, inimitable air of luxury (even in the moderately priced establishments, comparatively speaking), and, above all, for their courteous service. Be sure to book well ahead of coming, particularly if you plan to be here in summer. All the year round the Lausanne Tourist Office offers package holidays which include hotel rooms (deluxe downwards), meals, city transport, entertainment and sightseeing. Details from Lausanne Tourist Office or travel agents.

The three deluxe hotels are:

BEAU-RIVAGE, 300 beds. Stands in its own gardens facing the lake at Chemin de Beau-Rivage, Ouchy.

LAUSANNE-PALACE, 300 beds. In the city center, yet beside some pleasant gardens. Superb view from the terrace restaurant.

ROYAL SAVOY, 190 beds. In a large private garden, with swimming pool, about five-minute walk from the lake and only slightly more from the town center.

First-class hotels near the town center include the near-luxurious *Terminus,* 52 Ave. de la Gare (100 beds) and the slightly cheaper *Alpha-Palmiers,* 34 Rue du Petit-Chêne (270 beds), on a steep hill; *Continental,* 2 Place de la Gare (180 beds); *Jan,* 8 Avenue de Beaulieu (100 beds); *Mirabeau,* 31 Avenue de la Gare (100 beds; garden); *De la Paix,* 5 Avenue Benjamin-Constant (recommended by readers; 230 beds); *Parking Hotel Motor Inn,* 9 Avenue Rond Point (210 beds; centrally situated, but with adequate private parking); and *Victoria,* 46 Avenue de la Gare (100 beds).

Medium grade, centrally situated, are the *City,* 5 Rue Caroline (120 beds); *De Lausanne,* 1 Avenue Ruchonnet (80 beds); *Elite,* 1 Avenue Ste. Luce (56 beds); and *Regina,* 18 Rue Grand St. Jean; last two, breakfast only.

Situated in a quiet residential area, down the hill between the city center and Ouchy, and with few parking problems, are the first-class *Carlton,* 4 Avenue de la Cour (90 beds), and the recently re-opened *Orient,* 10 Avenue d'Ouchy (35 beds).

Close to the lake at Ouchy, both first class, are *Château d'Ouchy* (70 beds), dating from the 12th century and once the residence of the Bishops of Lausanne, noted for 800-years-old Hall of Knights, and *La Résidence* (90 beds), behind and owned by Beau Rivage. Also at Ouchy, with café terrace overlooking the lake, is the medium-grade *Angleterre* (50 beds).

On the eastern fringe of the city at Pully is the medium-grade *Montillier,* 35 Avenue Lavaux (90 beds).

RESTAURANTS. For fine cuisine and wines in an elegant setting, try the grillrooms of the Hotel Lausanne-Palace or Beau-Rivage, the Hotel Continental's *Rôtisserie le Beaujolais,* or *La Grappe d'Or,* all expensive. In the Alpha-Palmiers Hotel is the steak house *La Calèche,* expensive, and the typical Swiss cellar *Carnotzet du Petit-Chêne,* noted for its cheese specialties and fondue bourguignonne. *La Mandarin,* Avenue du Thèâtre, offers Chinese cuisine. Both latter (M).

The local *Mövenpick,* mostly (M), is in Place de Riponne (seafood, grills, ice creams; air conditioned). *La Chaumière* (M), 23 Rue Centrale, has a rustic setting; American specialties. Unpretentious but with excellent food, especially cheese fondue, is reader-recommended *Café de Jorat* (M), Place de l'Ours. Also moderately priced is *Chez Godio,* 2 Place Pépinet. Place St. François has two big, relatively inexpensive restaurants: *Nyffenegger* and *Grand Chêne.* In the center of the city are many pizzerie serving good Italian food.

At the lakeside restaurant, *La Voile d'Or,* you can dine with a marvelous view in the excellent, fairly expensive French restaurant, eat at the moderately priced snack bar, or spend the whole day sunbathing, swimming, or dancing in the open. *Chez Pitch* (M), Port de Pully, with a nice outdoor terrace, has steak and fish specialties.

At Signal de Sauvabelin, amid wonderful lake and Alpine views, are the *Swiss Chalet Restaurant* and the nearby *Restaurant du Lac*.

SHOPPING. As a shopping center, Lausanne is first-rate. Luxury stores are to be found in the Rue de Bourg and Rue St. François, also on the north side of the Place St.-François. A cheaper shopping quarter is around the west (Geneva) side of the Grand Pont.

CAMERAS. *Schnell Fils*, 4 Place St.-François.

DEPARTMENT STORES. *Innovation*, 5 Rue du Pont. *Bonnard*, Place St.-François. *La Placette*, Rue St.-Laurent.

FOOD SPECIALTIES. *A la Fermière*, 8 Rue St.-François.

JEWELRY. (See also Watches.) *A l'Emeraude*, 5 Place St.-François.

LEATHER. *Au Départ*, 10 Rue de Bourg.

OPTICAL GOODS. *Durring*, 30 Petit-Chêne.

SOUVENIRS. *Jouets Weber* (also toys), 23 Rue de Bourg.

SPORTS EQUIPMENT. *Sports-Ausoni*, 5 Place St.-François, *Schaefer-Sports*, 18 Rue St.-François.

TYPEWRITERS. *Hermes S.A.*, 3 Rue Pépinet.

WATCHES. *A la Belle Montre*, 11 Rue de Bourg. *Au Diadème*, 3 Rue de Bourg. *Bijoux-Windsor*, 34 Ave. de la Gare. *Golay Fils Stahl*, 12 Place St.-François. *Grumser*, 11 Rue St. François. *Bernard Mathez*, 1 Avenue du Théâtre. *Pro Bijoux*, 20 Place St.-François. *A l'Emeraude*, 5 Place St.-François. *Guillard S.A.*, 1 Palud. *E. Châtelain*, 10 Rue du Pont.

ENTERTAINMENT. The *Beaulieu* and the *Municipal* theaters present opera, operetta, concerts, plays, etc., all year round. International festival of music and ballet in May and June. The *Théâtre des Fauz-Nez* (120 seats only) gives avant-garde plays in French.

The *Tabaris* is one of the most modern nightclubs in Switzerland and also about the most expensive. The *Brummell* in the Palace Hotel's building is also a first-class nightclub. The *Métropole* is more moderately priced. Good places to dance are the *Scotch-Bar, Johnnie's,* the *Paddock* in Victoria Hotel, the *Château d'Ouchy,* and the *Voile d'Or* down by the lakeside.

MUSEUMS. Three are clustered in the Palais de Rumine—the *Cantonal Fine Arts, Natural History* and *Botanical Museums.* The *Museum of Decorative Art* is at 4 Rue Villamont. There is a *Roman Museum* at Vidy, a museum of old Lausanne situated in the old bishopric, and an *Olympic Museum.* All are free.

SPORTS. There is an 18-hole *golf* links at En Marin, 4 miles out of town, and mini-golf at 18 Petit-Chêne. *Tennis* at Stade-Lausanne, Lausanne-Sports, or Montchoisi. *Horse racing,* flat, steeplechase, and trotting, at nearby Morges, beginning of June. *Horseback riding,* Centre Equestre Lausannois at Chalet-à-Gobet, 4 miles out of town. *Swimming* at Bellerive-Plage (75,000 square meters), at the new Mon Repos indoor pool in the city center, and the Vert Bois and Montchoisi pools. All watersports available.

CHURCHES. *Church of England,* Christ Church, Avenue d'Ouchy, communion at 8 a.m., service at 10:30. *Church of Scotland,* 24 Avenue de Rumine, service, 10:30 a.m. *Christian Science,* 9 Avenue Ste.-Luce, English service, 11 a.m., *Synagogue,* corner of Avenue Florimont and Avenue Juste-Olivier. Several other Catholic and Protestant churches.

USEFUL ADDRESSES. Local, regional information and hotel booking office: *Lausanne Tourist Office,* 60 Avenue d'Ouchy, tel. 27.73.21. *American Express,* 14 Avenue Mon Repos, and 5 Chemin de Roseneck, Ouchy. *Wagons-Lits/Cook,* 7 Grand Chêne. *British and American Club,* 27 Avenue de Rumine, open daily 3:30–7 p.m.

CAR HIRE. *Avis,* 50 Avenue de la Gare; *Europcar,* Parking Mon Repos; *Hertz,* Parking de Montbenon.

LENK. *Kurhaus* (modernized), Bellevue, Kreuz and *Wildstrubel,* all top medium grade; *Sternen,* economy.

LENZERHEIDE. Top first class are *Kurhaus* (100 beds), *Schweizerhof* (150 beds) and modern, cheaper *Sunstar* (170 beds), latter two with indoor pool. Remarkable *Guarda Val* (63 beds), is a group of old Grisons farmhouses a mile from town in its own small village of Sporz, skilfully converted to charming, luxurious hotel.

In the top economy bracket are *Lenzerhorn* (50 beds), *Post* (45 beds), the well-run friendly *Parkhotel* (60 beds), and recent *Central* (100 beds).

At Valbella, on the Chur side of Lenzerheide, the 160-bed *Posthôtel Valbella,* first class, has indoor pool, fine cuisine (M). *Kulm* and *Waldhaus* (each 50 beds), economy.

LIESTAL. Hotel: *Engel* (30 beds), comfortable family hotel, easy train to Basel, pleasant surroundings here. (M).

Restaurants: *Bahnhof* (M), with terrace; *Kanone* has live trout.

LE LOCLE. Hotel: *Des Trois Rois* (40 beds), economy grade; excellent restaurant.

Restaurants: *Chez Remo* and *Buffet de la Gare.*

LES MARECOTTES. *Mille Etoiles,* and cheaper *Joli-Mont,* both economy and about 50 beds.

LES RASSES. Hotel: *Grand Hotel* (100 beds), medium grade, pool (indoor), sauna.

LEUKERBAD (LOECHE-LES-BAINS). Leaders are the 90-bed *Des*

Alpes and the 200-bed *Bristol,* with new medical-treatment wing, both first class. Medium grade are *Grand Bain* and *Maison Blanche* (indoor pool), two of many hotels in this and economy grade. In many, prices include thermal baths.

LEYSIN (Canton of Vaud). *Grand* (250 beds), *Résidence* (200 beds), each with indoor pool, *Relais* (100 beds) and *Eden* (85 beds) are all first class. Smaller are economy *Mont Riant* and *Les Orchidées.*

PRACTICAL INFORMATION FOR LOCARNO

HOTELS

LA PALMA AU LAC, overlooking Lake Maggiore, is luxurious and the best in Locarno. Indoor swimming pool, sauna. 200 beds. Everything you could want in a deluxe hostelry. Excellent restaurant (E).

The top first-class hotels, roughly in price order, are **REBER AU LAC** (130 beds), on delightful lakeside promenade, heated outdoor pool, tennis; **PARK HOTEL** (125 beds), lovely gardens, heated outdoor pool; **MURALTO** (144 beds), near-luxurious hotel with unusual attention to detail and quality, excellent food, cheerful service, fine view of lake, highly recommended; **ESPLANADE** (120 beds), very comfortable, spacious, traditional-style hotel with huge, well-tended gardens in quiet residential area, large heated outdoor pool.

Top medium-grade hotels include *Beau Rivage* (90 beds), *Grand* (150 beds, heated outdoor pool), *Quissiana* (90 beds; indoor pool), and *Schlosshotel* (60 beds; heated outdoor pool).

Among economy-bracket hotels are *Camelia* (55 beds), *Carmine* (44 beds), *Du Lac* (50 beds), and *Montaldi* (75 beds). Also the exceptionally well designed and run *Remorino* (44 beds, outdoor pool), quietly situated in Minusio, a few minutes from the city center; near-first-class comfort at economy prices; highly recommended by the writers; no restaurant but close to *Grotto Campagna* restaurant (see below).

In a fine situation some 800 feet above the town is the *Orselina* (120 beds). Also about the same height, at Brione is the 70-bed *Dellavalle.* Both medium grade and with private, outdoor, heated pools.

MOTELS. See Ticino Practical Information.

 RESTAURANTS. Though a small town, Locarno has a number of excellent restaurants. *Da Emilio,* on the lake front, *Chez Alfredo,* in the Muralto hotel, *Ristorante Oldrati,* and *Ristorante du Lac* are all first-rate, in the higher price bracket. *Gambrinus* and *Montaldi* have good food at moderate prices, as does *Caverna degli Dei,* which features Italian specialties. If you want to dine on a tree-shaded terrace with granite tables, try the *Grotto Campagna* at Locarno-Minusio; fine food, including fish, at moderate prices. *Verbania au Lac* and *Dell'Angelo* are both good and inexpensive. In Brione, *Los Gatos*

(Spanish specialties), *Grotto Ca Nostra* (dine in the open on granite tables), and *Da Stefano* are excellent although fairly expensive.

SHOPPING IN LOCARNO. Souvenirs. *Franz Carl Weber,* Via Stazione 3. **Watches**. *Bucherer,* Piazza Grande. *Ch. Zenger,* Via Stanzione Muralto.

LOSONE. About two miles north of Ascona: *Albergo Losone* (100 beds), outdoor pool, first class.

PRACTICAL INFORMATION FOR LUCERNE (LUZERN)

HOTELS. Lucerne has three internationally famous, luxury hotels:

GRAND HOTEL NATIONAL (300 beds) has a magnificent situation facing the lake. One of Switzerland's top hotels, its suites are fit for a king, its ordinary rooms for a crown prince—the hotel's doorman has touched his cap to both. Service and cuisine are of the same high standard as the appointments.

THE PALACE (300 beds) is aptly named. A spacious establishment and the most modern of the three, it faces the lake across a tree-lined promenade. It has a grill, a famous bar, and nightclub.

THE SCHWEIZERHOF (300 beds), slightly nearer the town center, looks across busy Schweizerhofquai to the lake. Oldest of the top three and with traditional elegance in its public rooms, although reader-comment suggests that some bedrooms are below par.

The 180-bed, top first-class *Carlton-Hotel Tivoli* has a view of the water, as does the slightly cheaper, recently improved, first-class 300-bed *Europe Grand.* In the same price bracket as the *Europe* are two recently built establishments, the 150-bed *Astoria,* panoramic rooftop terrace and bar, and 100-bed *Luzernerhof,* as well as the *Montana* (120 beds), which has a hillside location with magnificent mountain and lake views, and its own private funicular. Other hillside hotels with splendid views are the top medium-grade, historic *Château Gütsch* (outdoor pool), where Queen Victoria stayed, and the cheaper *Royal,* both 75 beds.

Visitors like hotels beside or close to the river Reuss, and there are many, including the first-class, old-world *Balances Bellevue* (110 beds), as well as the medium-grade *Des Alpes* (75 beds; reader recommended; excellent food). Also the economy-class *Raben-am-See* (70 beds) and *Schiff* (30 beds).

On the south (railroad station) side of the river is the long-established, top medium-grade *Wilden Mann* (80 beds), modernized but still retaining its old-world atmosphere and charm, several rooms being furnished with antiques; notable restaurant.

Within easy reach of the railroad station are the first-class *Monopol* (175 beds) as well as the medium-grade *Bernerhof* (135 beds), *Continental* (70 beds), *Diana* (50 beds), *Park* (60 beds), and *Schiller* (110 beds); also economy-bracket *Central* (50 beds).

On the Haldenstrasse, close to the

lakeside promenade, are the medium-grade *Eden au Lac* (70 beds), and economy *Beau Séjour au Lac* (50 beds).

The medium-grade *De la Paix* (70 beds; indoor pool), which some of our readers recommend, is on Museggstrasse, by the Alpenstrasse, which leads from the lake. A few

steps behind it, in Löwenstrasse, is the 200-bed *Union,* top medium grade; well-known restaurant (M).

At Lucerne-Seeburg, just outside the town, are the *Hermitage* (45 beds), lakeside location, garden restaurant with lovely views, and the *New Hotel Seeburg* (75 beds); both first class and with outdoor pool.

MOTELS. See Central Switzerland Practical Information.

 RESTAURANTS. Lucerne's most famous restaurant is undoubtedly that of the *Wilden Mann,* mentioned above, which comes fairly by its medieval atmosphere, since it has been operating since 1517. The *Old Swiss House,* near the Lion of Lucerne, is not so titled in coy spirit but is an old patrician home converted with considerable gastronomic success into a restaurant. Both (M). Another gourmet favorite is *Zur Gerbern,* with bar, built in 1334, at 7 Sternenplatz, in the old city near Kapellplatz. The *Astoria* hotel has a pleasant roof-garden restaurant for cold dishes only. *Li Tai Pe* (E) is a notable Chinese restaurant, highly popular with the discerning citizenry. If you want a fine view of the town from a smart restaurant, take the funicular up to the *Château Gütsch* (M).

In a lazy mood chose the *Stadt München,* where you may relax at a table on the terrace over the river Reuss and watch the water rush by while enjoying good, moderately priced food.

For a more elegant mood, there is the *Schwanen,* smack in front of the lake, but here you must have a reservation or arrive early to get a table on the small balcony with its view of lake and mountains, the chief reason for coming here. This is no reflection on the food, which is first-rate, and of wide variety.

For Swiss specialties such as fondue and raclette, with appropriate Swiss wines, at reasonable prices, try *Le Mazot,* Eisengasse, or *Walliser*

Kanne, Münzgasse. Both (M).

For meals and snacks, American style, there is a branch of the *Mövenpick* chain in Grendelstrasse. Prices are moderate unless you are unable to resist the seafood specialties. If you enjoy your swimming at the Strandbad in late morning, you can eat at the nearby open-air *Lido* restaurant.

The *Kunsthaus* (E), near the boat landing stage, has a pleasant garden terrace. Moored the other side of the bridge at Schweizerhofquai is the old paddle steamer *Wilhelm Tell,* now a collection of bars and restaurants ranging from moderately economical to fairly expensive.

ENTERTAINMENT. Behind the uninspiring exterior of the Kursaal/Casino is a large entertainment center putting on variety shows, concerts, dancing, and folklore evenings with yodeling, flag tossing and blowing of the Alphorn. You can play *boule* there, take tea on the lakeside terrace, or have a meal in the restaurant. Dancing also, sometimes with a floorshow or specialty acts, at the Palace Hotel's *Intimo* nightclub, at *Hazyland, Du Pont* and elsewhere. For hearty Swiss fun try the *Floragarten* beer garden. From the landing stage near the station, every evening during the summer there's a special lake boat trip with music, dancing and Swiss folklore on board.

For tennis, go to Brüelmoos beside the Lido, to the Spittelerquai, or to Allemand; for golf (18 holes) to Dietschiberg; for swimming to the lido or to the indoor pool at Allemand.

See "The Week in Lucerne," free from the Tourist Office or your hotel, for full details of entertainment and sport.

MUSEUMS. The **Glacier Gardens,** unique in the world, with many Ice Age glacier mills, some enormous; 8 a.m.-6 p.m.; entrance 3 frs. **Swiss Transport Museum,** 9-6, Sun. 10-6; admission 4.50 frs. Outstandingly fine collection of rail locomotives and carriages, airplanes, cars, ships; many working models; now also has Switzerland's first planetarium and a building for aerospace exhibits.

Art Museum, near railway station, 10-12, 2-5, closed Mon. Admission 2.50 frs.

Costume Museum, at Utenberg, 9-12, 2-5:30. Admission 1 fr.

Wagner Museum, at Tribschen, once his home, 9-12, 2-6, Sun. 10:30-12, 2-5; entrance 2 frs.

Panorama, 8 (Sun. 9)-12, 1:30-6. Admission 1.50 frs.

For something different, go to the **National Museum of Bread and Pastry.**

Outside main holiday season opening and closing times may alter. Some entrance fees may rise. Children usually half price or less.

SHOPPING IN LUCERNE. There's an awful lot of souvenir junk in this town, somewhat obscuring the fact that Lucerne is a good shopping center.

CAMERAS. *Hans Blättler,* Pilatusstrasse 17. *Ecker A. G.,* Kapellplatz 10. *Jean Grau,* Alpenstrasse 4. *Jos. Koch,* Zum Theilinghus, Weggisgasse 3. *Paul Weber,* Pilatusstrasse 1.

EMBROIDERY, LINEN, LACE. *Mühlebach Birrer,* Kapellplatz 1. *Ed. Sturzenegger,* Schwanenplatz 7 and Haldenstrasse 5. *Margrit Raebsamen,* Alpenstrasse 2. *Au Trianon* (Elisabeth Kaeslin), St. Leodegar 2.

FOOD SPECIALTIES. *Jules Bachman,* Pfistergasse 23. *Seinet,* Weggisgasse 28.

HANDCRAFT.   *Innerschweizer Heimatwerk,* Stiftstrasse 4.

JEWELRY. *Werner Bossard,* Schwanenplatz 7. *Bucherer,* Schwanenplatz 5. *Albert Burger,* Kapellgasse 10. *Gübelin,* Schweizerhofquai 1. *F. Koller,* Bundesplatz 10. *Kurz,* Weggisgasse 25. *E. Leicht-Mayer Cie.,* Haldenstrasse 3. *W. Manser,* Weinmarkt 14. *W. Ruckli*, Bahnhofstrasse 22. *G. Schaub*, Grendelstrasse 2.

SOUVENIRS. *Innerschweizer Heimatwerk*, Stiftstrasse 4. *Funaro's Art Gallery*, Schweizerhofquai 6. *Franz Carl Weber* (also toys), Grendelstrasse 10, *Schnarrwyler*, on the Chapel Bridge. *A. Schmid-Linder*, Denkmalstrasse 9. *Ernst Schmocker*, Löwenstrasse 12. *Aux Arts du Feu*, Kapellplatz 7. *C. Casagrande*, Kapellgasse 24.

SPORTS · EQUIPMENT. *Rieser Sport*, Winkelriedstrasse 14. *Fritz Genhart*, Löwenstrasse 14.

WATCHES. *Paul Bäurer*, Kapellgasse 21. *Bader*, Pilatusstrasse 3A and. Weggisgasse 8. *Max Birnbaum*, Pilatusstrasse 34. *H. J. Boeckmann*, Hertensteinstrasse 62. *Bucherer*, Schwanenplatz 5. *Albert Burger*, Kapellgasse 10. *Gübelin*, Schweizerjofquai 1. *Kost Brechbühl*, Pilatusstrasse 19. *Kurz*, Weggisgasse 25. *E. Leicht-Mayer Cie.*, Haldenstrasse 3. *Max Michel*, Hertensteinstrasse 8. *H. Prêtre*, Weinmarkt 11 and Pilatusstrasse 8. *Walter Ruckli*, Bahnhofstrasse 22. *Louis Spöring*, Kornmarkt 8. *Isely Inc.*, Schweizerhofquai 6.

CAR HIRE. *Avis*, Zurichstrasse 35; *Europcar*, Löwenstrasse 20; *Hertz*, Horwerstrasse 81.

USEFUL ADDRESSES. *Local Tourist Office*, Pilatusstrasse 14. *American Express*, Schweizerhofquai 4. *Cook's*, Haldenstrasse 1. *English Church*, Haldenstrasse. *Anglo-Swiss Club*, Hotel Union, Löwenstrasse 16.

PRACTICAL INFORMATION FOR LUGANO

HOTELS. Over eighty hotels line the lake from Paradiso, on the western edge of the city, to Castagnola, at the eastern end, but at many hotels around the town center or along the lake shore motorists will find parking is a problem in the season. If you have a car, check beforehand if your chosen hotel has parking arrangements or a garage. If not, you may prefer to select one away from the town center and lake shore.

Deluxe

ADMIRAL, 150 beds. Near lower terminal of San Salvatore funicular and not far from the lake in Paradiso. Air conditioned. Indoor and outdoor pools. Garage.

COMMODORE, 130 beds, is on the lakeside boulevard between Lugano and Paradiso. A modern hotel with interior decor based on a "ship" theme, it features traditional elegance and quality. Air conditioned. Attractive restaurant. Outdoor pool. Garage.

EDEN AU LAC, 140 beds, is on the water's edge at Paradiso. Outstanding, elegant, except when crowded with groups. Contemporary decor and furnishing. Brimful of careful thought and efficient design. Air conditioned. Indoor pool. Sauna, massage. Garage.

EUROPA GRAND, 170 beds, faces

lake at Paradiso. Completely renovated 1973. Incorporates complex of shops, beauty parlor, snack bar, nightclub. Fine indoor heated pool.

EXCELSIOR, 190 beds. Faces lake near boat landing stages and town center. Cheapest of top six.

SPLENDID-ROYAL, 125 beds, close to Commodore, has an old-world elegance in its furnishings, but is modern in all other respects. Indoor pool; sauna.

First Class

Hotels with private outdoor heated swimming pool include: *Bellevue au Lac,* Paradiso (125 beds; recently modernized), *Du LacSeehof,* on lakeside at Paradiso (90 beds; all rooms with balcony; sauna; massage), *Meister,* Paradiso (130 beds; indoor pool), *Villa Castagnola,* facing lake across road at Castagnola (120 beds; fine indoor pool; tennis), as well as slightly cheaper *Arizona,* on hill by rail station (110 beds), *Belmonte,* Castagnola (80 beds), and *De la Paix,* Paradiso (116 beds).

Other first-class hotels include *Beau-Rivage au Lac* (140 beds, every room with balcony) and marginally cheaper *Dan* (60 beds; kosher food), both at Paradiso.

Medium Grade

Numerous hotels in this category include *Nassa* (54 beds; breakfast only), in a street of smart shops only a few paces from the lake; and *Nizza* (60 beds), heated outdoor pool, at Paradiso.

Economy Grade

Among many economy-grade hotels is Lugano's largest, the *Calypso,* Paradiso (320 beds, indoor and outdoor pools, sauna); *Ticino,* in town near the foot of railway station funicular (45 beds), good food; and *Derby,* above the lake at Sorengo (78 beds).

MOTELS. See *Ticino Practical Information.*

 RESTAURANTS. Italian cooking prevails in Lugano, with Ticinese specialties added, though French and German dishes may also make their appearance. *Bianchi's,* Via Pessina 3, is justly singled out by knowledgeable residents as one of the best and most elegant, but *Orologio,* Via G. Nizzola 2; *Galleria,* Via G. Vegezzi 4; and *Huguenin,* Riva Albertolli 1, are also fine but a bit expensive.

The *Eden Grill* (E), in the Eden Hotel, Paradiso, has a number of grilled specialties, including scampi, and in Loreto, the *Piccolo Grill* features Florentine steak. The *Hotel Ticino* (M) has good international food, and *Cyrano's,* Corso Pestalozzi 27, and *Firenze,* Castagnola, are also first-rate but reasonably priced.

For a filling meal at around 4 or 5 frs. try *Innovazione* department store's self-service. Among tearooms are *Saipa,* Via Nassa, and *Cafe Vanini* in Piazza Riforma, the latter a lively spot.

At Sorengo, the *Grotto del Renzo,* moderate in price, serves tempting frogs' legs among other specialties, and the garden restaurant *San Grato,* in Carona, near Monte San Salvatore, is excellent. The *San Marco,* near the train station in Agno, is first-rate, and moderate in price. At Vezia, the *Villa Recreatio,* now open all year, is an elegant but expensive restaurant. *La Romantica,* on the waterfront at Melide, features nightclub acts. It's expensive. So, too, is Campione's *Casino,* where the smart set congregates.

MUSEUMS. *Villa Favorita,* at Castagnola, is one of the finest private art collections in Europe. In over twenty beautifully appointed rooms is displayed the collection of the Baron von Thyssen—including works by Van Eyck, Carpaccio, Ghirlandaio, Dürer, Franz Hals, Holbein, Titian, Tintoretto, Caravaggio, Velazquez, El Greco, Van Dyck, Rubens and Rembrandt. Opening times and dates vary so check with the tourist office or your hotel.

The *Villa Ciani,* in the City Park, is an art gallery specializing in loan exhibitions. The *Vincenzo Vela Museum* at Ligornetto contains many sculptures by the 19th-century artist, who became popular in Italy. Open 9–12, 2–5 daily. Feb.–Nov.

After seeing Switzerland, you'll particularly enjoy *Swissminiatur* at Melide, 3 miles from Lugano, with many fine models (1/25th size) of typical or famous Swiss buildings, steamers, trains, etc. Open 8–6 daily, except June–Sept., when it's open till 11 p.m.

SPORTS. *Golf,* 18-hole course, open all year, Lugano Golf Club, Magliaso. There are many *tennis courts* about the town, two lighted at night, and a covered court, Lido Tennis Club (6 frs. an hour, extra for night lighting). *Fishing,* lake and river, Mar.–Oct.; licenses at the Municipio, Piazza Riforma. *Boats* for hire. *Saddle horses,* Mario Roggiani, Crespera 7; S. Pedretti and Hubertus, both at Origlio; Scuderia Bijoux, Camilo Quadri, Bedano. *Bathing* at Lugano's huge lido with heated pools, lawns, buffet/restaurant: entrance about 2 frs., with cabin 4.50 frs., for whole day. Bathing is banned in parts of Bay of Lugano.

SHOPPING IN LUGANO. Primarily a resort town, Lugano has elegant and expensive shops where you can find a Pucci dress or an ancient Persian vase at a high price. Ticino specialties and handcraft can be found in the *Ticino Shop,* Via Canova 16.

CAMERAS. *Foto Brunel,* Via Nassa. *Foto Max,* Riva Vincenzo Vela. *Photohaus H. Ruedi,* Portici Via Nassa 1. *Vincenzo Vicari,* Via Magatti 1.

JEWELRY. *A Croci,* Via Fr. Soave 2. *A Mersmann,* Via Nassa 5. *Fratelli Sautter,* Via della Posta 3. *Federico Kistner* (silverware), Via Nassa 3. *Bucherer,* Via Nassa 56–7. *Golay Fils Stahl,* Via Nassa 11. *Gübelin,* Via Nassa 7.

OPTICAL GOODS. *Götte,* Via Pessina 8.

SOUVENIRS. *Franz Carl Weber,* Via Nassa 5. *Gusberti,* Via Canova 7. *Weber and Bläuer,* Via Nassa.

SPORTS EQUIPMENT. *Greco*

Sport di Luciano Caravati, Via Magatti 3. *Balmelli Sport,* Via della Posta. *Prosperi-Sport,* Via Peri.

WATCHES. *Anghinoni,* Via Petrarcha. *A Croci,* Via Fr. Soave 2. *E. Brugnoli,* Via Cattedrale 8. *Bucherer,* Via Nassa, 56–7. *Caldenoni Gisielli,* Via Nassa 1. *B. H. Glasson,* Via Nassa 68. *Golay Fils Stahl,* Via Nassa 11. *Gübelin,* Via Nassa 7. *Kistner,* Via Nassa 3. *A. Mersmann,* Via Nassa 5. *Fratelli Sautter,* Via della Posta 3. *Steffen,* Via Nassa 13.

CAR HIRE. *Avis,* Riva Paradiso 38; *Hertz,* Via Ciani 5; *Europcar,* Via Bagutti 3; *Budget,* Via Beltramina 7a.

USEFUL ADDRESSES. *Ente Turistico,* Tourist Office, next to the Kursaal, Riva Albertolli 5, tel. 3.21.21. *American Express,* c/o Danzas, Piazza Manzoni 8; *Cook's,* Riva Vincenzo Vela 12; *English Church,* Via Clemente Maraini; *Christian Science Church,* Via Marconi 2 (near Kursaal); *Synagogue,* Via Maderno 11. *British Vice-Consulate,* Via Maraini 14a, Loreto.

LUNGERN AM SEE. *Alpenhof* (60 beds) and *Derby-Bären* (46 beds), both economy.

MALOJA. At summit of pass, *Kulm,* 40 beds, economy.

MARTIGNY. *Du Rhône* (90 beds; breakfast only), and *Post* (55 beds); *Kluser* (70 beds), restaurant specializes in trout and dried meats; all economy grade.

MEIRINGEN. *Sauvage,* and cheaper *Hirschen* and *Weisses Kreuz,* economy; last two no private baths.

MELCHSEE-FRUTT. *Reinhard am See* (140 beds), medium grade. *Sporthotel Kurhaus* (100 beds), economy.

MELIDE. *La Romantica,* built in the 18th century as a stopover for Kings of Savoy en route to Italy, is now a small, luxurious restaurant and nightclub; fine gardens and private beach.

MERLIGEN. *Beatus,* deluxe; indoor swimming pool, sauna.

MONTANA. First class are *Supercrans* (50 beds) and *Ambassador* (100 beds); each with indoor pool, sauna. *Parc* (135 beds), *Mirabeau* (90 beds), *Curling* (70 beds); and cheaper *De la Forêt, Valaisia* (both 100 beds) and *St. Georges* (75 beds) are medium grade. *Beau Regard, Forest* and *Du Lac* are economy.

MONTE GENEROSO. At 5,500 feet, beside the summit station of the mountain railway, is the new *Monte Generoso Vetta* (18 beds); economy bracket; no private baths.

PRACTICAL INFORMATION FOR MONTREUX

HOTELS. In the deluxe category are the vast *Montreux-Palace* (350 beds) and its smaller stable mate *du Cygne* (50 beds), both under the same management, and with outdoor pool, tennis. In top first class category are *Eden* (210 beds; outdoor pool), *Eurotel* (270 beds; each room with kitchenette; indoor pool, sauna; underground garage; on lakeside), *Excelsior* (140 beds; indoor pool; beside lake), and *National* (100 beds; in town but with elevated, quiet gardens with fine view and pool). Both latter furnished with much character. Also first class are *Golf* (100 beds) and *Suisse-Majestic* (270 beds). Among many top medium-grade establishments in the town are *Bonivard, Bon Accueil,* and *Parc et Lac;* at Territet, *Bristol.*

Special, free, hotel booking phone available day and night at the town tourist information office.

MOTELS. See Practical Information for Elsewhere in the Region.

 **RESTAURANTS.** *Taverne du Château de Chillon* (M), with noisy, open-air terrace facing the lake; *Excelsior* (E) is outstanding among hotel restaurants; *Bavaria,* café-type, good beer, excellent for snacks and light meals; *Vieux-Montreux,* typical cellar restaurant, good food.

 ENTERTAINMENT. Opened in 1975 near the Eden Hotel, *Montreux Casino* has restaurant, nightclub, bar, swimming pool, gaming rooms (boule). The *Hungaria* has dancing and a floor show. The *Museum Club* is a typical Swiss restaurant with dancing. Wednesday evenings, lake steamers make trips from Territet, Montreux and Clarens, dancing on board.

 SPORTS. There is an eighteen-hole *golf* course at Aigle; *tennis* courts at the Montreux Tennis Club, which recently constructed an inflatable roof for use over the courts in winter; *horses* for hire at the Nouvelle Ecole Montreusienne d'Equitation at Villeneuve; *swimming* at Montreux-Plage, which now has a new Olympic-sized pool; *boats* for hire (rowboats and sailboats) and *water skiing* at Montreux-Plage and Casino de Montreux.

 SHOPPING. Cameras. *Photo-House Ch. Hosennen,* 14 Rue Chillon, Territet. **Embroidery, Linen, Lace.** *Ed. Sturzenegger,* 54 Grand-Rue. **Jewelry.** *Bornand Cie.,* 64 Grand-Rue. *Roman Mayer,* 39 Avenue du Casino. **Watches.** *Bornand Cie.,* 64 Grand-Rue. *Roman Mayer,* 39 Avenue du Casino. *R. Seiler,* 88 Grand-Rue. *F. Sollberger,* 90 Avenue des Alpes. *R. Benoit,* 42 Grand-Rue. *J. Boechat,* 30 Grand-Rue.

MUSEUMS. Château de Chillon; Old Montreux Museum; the Krüger Villa in Clarens.

USEFUL ADDRESSES. *The Tourist Office,* 42 Grand-Rue, tel. 61.33.84; *American Express,* 43 Avenue des Alpes; *Cook's,* 32 Avenue du Casino. Anglican *churches* at Territet and Clarens. Christian Science in Montreux. *British Vice-Consul,* 19 Avenue Bon-Port.

CAR HIRE. *Avis,* Garage Imperia, 14 Avenue Du Théâtre; *Hertz,* 126 Avenue des Alpes; *Joseph Gailland,* 8 Avenue des Alpes.

MORCOTE. The top first-class, 250-bed *Olivella* has two heated pools, one enclosed. The medium-grade, 35-bed *Carina-Carlton* has an outdoor pool. *Rivabella* (35 beds) is economy.

Reasonably priced lakeside restaurants with excellent food are the *Ristorante della Posta* and the *Svizzero.*

MORGES. Hotels: *Du Lac* (52 beds), good food; first class. *Mont-Blanc* (60 beds), medium grade. Both by the lake. *De la Couronne* and (breakfast only) *De la Gare* are economy.

MORGINS. *Bellevue* (140 beds; indoor pool, sauna), first class.

MURREN. *Mürren Palace,* top first class, is center of winter social life. Rather cheaper are *Eiger* and *Jungfrau-Lodge. Alpina, Bellevue, Edelweiss* and *Jungfrau* are top medium grade. *Belmont,* economy.

MURTEN (MORAT). Hotels: *The Weisses Kreuz* (55 beds) and *Du Bateau* (30 beds; attractive lakeside situation) are first class.

MURTEN-MEYRIEZ, on the lake, has *Le Vieux Manoir* (40 beds), top first class old house in charming setting, park, private harbor. Excellent but expensive grill room—reserve at weekends and holidays.

Restaurant: *Couronne,* specialty: lake perch and trout.

PRACTICAL INFORMATION FOR NEUCHÂTEL

HOTELS. Between the port and the station is the new, first class *Eurotel* (200 beds; indoor pool; sauna). On the lake shore are the slightly cheaper, splendidly situated *Beaulac* (100 beds) and the economy *Touring* (80 beds). *Central* (52 beds) and *City* (60 beds), both in the lower town; *Beaux Arts* (46 beds) near the university; all three economy. Also economy is spacious, friendly, chalet-style *Chaumont et Golf* (60 beds) among pine trees and meadows on mountain slope 3,600 feet up with magnificent views across lake to Alps; funicular from town, or fifteen minutes by car.

RESTAURANTS. The new Eurotel has gained a reputation for excellent French cuisine in its *Pinot Noir* restaurant (M—E) and value for money in its *Carrefour* (I—M). *Café du Théâtre* (renovated and under new management; local specialties), *St. Honoré* (French cooking), and *Banneret* (Swiss and South American specialties) are all about (M). Possibly the best in the district is *Boccalino* (E), three miles away at St. Blaise; renowned Italian specialties.

ENTERTAINMENT. *Municipal Theater* produces plays. *Théâtre de Poche* is minute, somewhat avant-garde and experimental. Dancing and floorshows at the *A.B.C., L'Escale* and the *Rotonde.* Evening sail on the lake, 8:15 p.m. daily June–Sept., in good weather; on Saturday night, with dancing on the boat.

MUSEUMS. The most interesting are the *Fine Arts and History* museum and the imaginative, secluded *Ethnology* museum; both open 10–12 and 2–5. Also the museum of *Archeology,* open 2–5. All closed Mon. Don't miss the famous automatic dolls in the History museum. Constructed between 1719 and 1773 by Swiss watchmakers, they have toured Europe in their time, and will still write, draw and play for you. Demonstrations the first Sunday of each month at 2:30 p.m. For other performances, check with the Official Information Office.

SPORTS. There is a 9-hole *golf* course at Pierre-à-Bot. *Tennis* at Les Cadolles, Le Mail, and Chaumont. *Swimming* at the Neuchâtel lido (swimming pool), open 9 a.m. to 8 p.m. First-rate *skindiving* center with dormitory accommodation; write Maison du Plongeur, Case Postale, Neuchâtel. *Ski slopes* in Jura, reached by coach (30 mins. from town).

CAR HIRE. *Hertz* at Mobil Station Roccarino, 14 Quai Perrier.

USEFUL ADDRESSES. *Official Information Office,* 1 Place Numa-Droz, tel. 25.42.42. *Cook's,* 1 Place Pury. *Rotary, Lions, Kiwanis* clubs, inquire at Hôtel du Peyrou.

NEUHAUSEN. Hotel: *Bellevue,* medium grade; overlooks Rhine Falls.

NYON. Hotels: *Clos de Sadex,* elegant first class (30 beds), lakeside garden, notable restaurant. App. 10 min. from town. In town: *Beau Rivage* medium; *Des Alpes* economy.

OLTEN. Hotels: *Schweizerhof* and *Emmental,* economy grade.

Restaurants: *Walliser Kanne,* terrace overlooking the Aare, Valais specialties; *Ratskeller,* in a building dating from 1673, weapons collection, French cooking, Munich beer.

OBERIBERG. *Posthotel* (50 beds) and *Roggenstock* (36 beds); both economy.

PILATUS. Ultramodern, circular *Bellevue* (50 beds), *Pilatus Kulm* (30 beds), traditional decor. Both economy and near summit.

PONTRESINA. The 180-bed *Schloss* and the 230-bed *Kronenhof* are deluxe. First class is the *Walther* (120 beds). Medium grade hotels include *Park* (120 beds), *Schweizerhof* (140 beds), *Sporthotel* (160 beds), and slightly cheaper *Collina* (70 beds) and *Engadinerhof* (150 beds).

In the economy price bracket are *Albris, Steinbock* (each 40 beds) and *Weisses Kreuz* (80 beds)

PORRENTRUY. Hotel: *du Cheval Blanc,* 50 beds, a few rooms with private bath; economy grade. Excellent food. Specialties: champignons bourguignonne; wood fire grills. Under the same owner-management: large stables, riding, horse trekking.

RAPPERSWIL. Hotels: *Schwanen,* medium. *Du Lac, Speer,* economy.

RHEINFELDEN. Hotels: *Eden* (indoor pool) is first class. Top medium grade are *Schützen* (indoor pool), *Schwanen* and slightly cheaper *Schiff*. *Ochsen* is economy.

Restaurants: *Feldschlösschen-*

Stadt, Rhine terrace, fish and regional specialties; *Wiedmer,* tearoom, with terrace on the Rhine.

SWITZERLAND'S RHINELAND

MOTELS. At **Egerkingen,** junction of N1 and N2 motorways, *Motel Agip* (110 beds). At **Hauenstein,** 3 miles northeast of Olten, *Motel Nord-Süd* (60 beds). At **Itingen,** 13 miles southeast of Basel, *Motel Ochsen* (55 beds). At **Solothurn,** *Motel Touring* (30 beds). All open year round.

 SHOPPING. Brugg. *Handcrafts.* Heimatwerk and Webschule. Belart Appenzeller, Törlirain 1. **Schaffhausen.** *Candy and Pastry.* Café-Tea Room Reber ("Schaffhauserzungen" a specialty), Vordergasse 21. **Solothurn.** *Music.* Hug Co., Stalden 4. **Stein-Am-Rhein.** *Handcrafts.* Heimatwerk.

RIGI. At summit: *Rigi-Kulm* (100 beds), economy. At Rigi-Kaltbad: first-class *Hostellerie-Rigi* (110 beds), outstanding contemporary decor, indoor pool, sauna; and *Bellevue* (80 beds) medium grade.

ROCHERS-DE-NAYE. Hotel: *Rochers-de-Naye* (32 beds). Simple, inexpensive, beside summit station at 6,700 feet. Fine views.

ROLLE. Hotel: *Domino Lac* (30 beds), economy grade.

ROMANSHORN. Hotels: *Seehotel* (old-fashioned, lakeside inn) is medium grade. *Boden* (fish specialties) is economy.

RORSCHACH. Hotels: *Anker* (terrace, overlooking lake) and *Waldau* (swimming pool); both economy.

Restaurants: *Mariaberg,* Bavarian cooking, Munich beer; *Bahnhofbuffet,* terrace on lake, grows its own wines, fish specialties.

SAANENMOSER. *Sporthotel,* first class.

SAAS-FEE. Leaders are medium grade *Grand* and recently reconstructed *Walliserhof* (both about 100 beds). Many economy-bracket hotels include *Allalin, Bristol, Christiania, Derby, Elite* and *Park,* all in 40-60-bed range; also *Beau-Site* (120 beds), nightclub, *Dom* (110 beds), Kellerbar nightclub. Slightly cheaper still *Des Alpes* (breakfast only), *Alphubel, Gletschergarten* and *Touring.*

ST. GALLEN (ST. GALL), Hotels: *Walhalla* (82 beds, indoor pool, sauna), near station, and *Hecht* (100 beds), excellent restaurant (M), in town center, are first class. Medium grade are *Metropol* (50 beds), and *Montana* (25 beds). *Ekkehard* (50 beds) and *Continental* (57 beds) are economy. So are the delightful *Dom* (65 beds), a very comfortable, friendly place quietly situated near the cathedral, and the *Touring* (44 beds); last two, breakfast only.

Restaurants: Besides the hotels, the *Bahnhof Buffet* (I-M), the *Schützengarten* (M), and the *Gaststube* Schlössli are good. *The Baratella* for chicken and Italian food.

SHOPPING: Embroidery, Linen, Lace. *Ed. Sturzenegger,* St. Leonhardstrasse 12. Handcrafts. *Heimatwerk,* Hinterlauben 6. Watches. *A. Engler,* Multergasse 31. *Ernst Frischknecht,* Marktplatz 20. *Labhart,* Marktgasse 23.

ST.-LUC. *Bella Tola St.-Luc* (65 beds), medium grade. *Du Cervin* (100 beds), economy bracket.

ST. MORITZ. Hotels: Has long had four of the best, most famous and expensive deluxe hotels in Switzerland.

Palace (350 beds). Still owned by the Badrutt family who pioneered winter holidays in Switzerland. At the back it's only a few paces from the town center; at the front, in unbelievable contrast, is peace, quiet, and a superb unobstructed view of lake and mountain. Suites, service flats, night club, indoor pool—it's got the lot.

Engadiner Kulm (300 beds). Slightly further from the town center; slightly higher. Backed by a road but with extensive grounds and similar wonderful, unobstructed views in front. Every amenity including indoor pool.

Suvretta House (380 beds). About a mile southwest of the town in a quiet, secluded situation among woods and mountainside meadows. Splendid views of upper end of Inn valley. An elegant, exclusive establishment with every conceivable luxury including indoor pool. Good enough for the Shah of Iran to have a villa in the grounds.

Carlton (200 beds). Built in 1913 as the winter home of the Russian czar, it became a hotel in 1919 and built up a reputation for elegance and service. Two recent changes of ownership and policy.

Larger establishments in the first class bracket: *Crystal* (180 beds; indoor pool), *Monopol* (120 beds; indoor pool), and *Schweizerhof* (150 beds), all in the town; *Eurotel* (200 beds; indoor pool), at Champfèr; and *Park-Kurhaus* (250 beds) at St. Moritz-Bad.

Among good medium grade hotels in the town are *Albana* (130 beds), *Bären* (90 beds; indoor pool), *Belvédère* (120 beds; indoor pool), *Calonder* (70 beds), *Eden* (50 beds; breakfast only), *Hauser* (70 beds), *La Margna* (100 beds), *Languard* (40 beds; breakfast only), *Neues Post* (120 beds), *Steffani* (100 beds; much enlarged and renovated), *Steinbock* (34 beds), and *Waldhaus* (60 beds). *Aurora* (25 beds; breakfast only), *Bernasconi* (60 beds) and *Grünenberg* (30 beds) are economy.

At St. Moritz-Bad, newest medium grade hotel is excellent *San Gian* (96 beds), one of the best in its category. Also medium are *Bellevue* (90 beds), *Chesa-sur-En* (30 beds), *Edelweiss* (100 beds; kosher) and *Nolda* (50 beds). *Bernina* and *National* (40 beds each) are economy.

Restaurants: These include the famous *Chesa Veglia,* the *Suvretta House Supper Club,* Hotel Bernasconi's *Cascade,* the *Corviglia restaurant* at the top of the funicular, and the *Monopol's Grischuna;* all expensive. Cheaper are those of the *Schweizerhof* and *Steinbock* hotels. One of the best inexpensive eateries in town is the self-service cafeteria of the *Hotel Steffani* which also has its much more expensive *Engadine* restaurant and *Stuva Grill.* For tea, try *Calèche, Hanselmann, Hauser* and *Olympic.*

Many hotels have dancing. The *Hotel Crystal* is a popular spot. For young folk it's the Steffani's recently renovated *Malibu Club.*

SAMEDAN. First class are *Bernina* (120 beds) and *Quadratscha* (50 beds; indoor pool). *Des Alpes* (70 beds) and *Sporthotel* (50 beds) are top economy.

SAVOGNIN. *Cresta* (140 beds; indoor pool) and cheaper *Danilo* (80 beds; good food) are first class. Economy is charming *Tgesa Romana* (26 beds); off main road near chairlift; modern chalet style; all furniture made by hotel carpenter; excellent small restaurant.

SCHAFFHAUSEN. Hotels: *Bahnhof, Kronenhof,* and *Park-Villa,* all medium grade.

Restaurants: *Fischerzunft,* near the Rhine boat dock, specializing in *Felchen* and *Aschen,* two varieties of Rhine trout; *Brauerei Falken,* beer cellar operated by the Falken brewery, bowling alley; Frieden, antique décor.

SCHWYZ. *Hirschen* (32 beds) is economy bracket.

SCUÓL-TARASP-VULPERA. At Scuol best is recently renovated, first class *Belvédère* (90 beds), lovely views of valley and mountains at back. *Engadinerhof* (130 beds) and slightly cheaper *Guardaval* (80 beds) and *Post* (50 beds) are medium grade. The *Grand-Kurhaus* (170 beds) at Bad Tarasp is first class. At Vulpera, in well laid-out, spacious gardens with swimming pool and tennis courts, are the near deluxe *Waldhaus* (180 beds), first class *Schweizerhof* (160 beds) and economy *Silvana* (45 beds).

SEELISBERG. Hotel: *Bellevue* (75 beds), medium grade.

SEENGEN. Hotel: *Schloss Brestenberg,* 17th-century manor house converted into small hotel (40 beds), medium grade; overlooking lake.

SIERRE. *Atlantic, Arnold* and *Terminus,* all economy, last with garden restaurant and Valais specialties.

SILS-MARIA-BASELGIA. At Maria, best is deluxe *Waldhaus* (220 beds; indoor pool), above village, among trees, wonderful views. *Schweizerhof* (130 beds) is medium grade. Good value is top economy *Pensiun Privata* (40 beds), full of comfort, character and charm; owned and run by international ski champion Giovanoli; recommended. Best at Baselgia is near-deluxe *Margna* (110 beds). Medium grade *Chesa Randolina* (62 beds) is farmhouse modernized and enlarged with remarkable good taste.

SILVAPLANA. The *Albana* (40 beds, sauna) is top first class. *Sonne* (100 beds) is medium grade.

SIMPLON. *Fletschhorn,* no private baths; at Simplon-Kulm, 1,700 feet higher, *Bellevue;* both economy.

SION. *Du Rhône* (80 beds), medium grade. In the economy bracket, all in 40-60-bed range, are *Continental, Cerf, Touring* (good restaurant) and *Treize Etoiles,* latter with small but excellent restaurant (M) adjoining.

Restaurants: *Au Vieux Valais* and *Coup de Fusil* for Valais specialties.

SOLOTHURN. Hotels: *Krone* (30 beds), modern rooms with bath, at the steps to the cathedral, excellent food; medium grade; one of the oldest inns in Switzerland, with a great tradition. *Roter Turm,* new and bright, and *Astoria;* both economy grade.

Restaurants: *Zunfthaus zu Wirthen* (M), in old guildhall; *Misteli-Gasche,* operated by same family for forty years; *Bahnhofbuffet* (I).

SPIEZ. *Belvédère* and *Eden,* first class. *Bahnhof, Alpes* and breakfast-only *Erica* are medium.

SPLUGEN. *Posthôtel Bodenhaus* (80 beds), noted 250-year-old building, where Queen Victoria, Napoleon, Tolstoi and other famous persons are said to have stayed. Medium grade.

STANS. Hotels: *Engel* and *Stanserhof* (both about 45 beds), economy.

Restaurants: *Krone; Cafe-Tearoom Frei,* garden, fine pastries.

STANSSTAD. Hotels: *Schützenhaus* (90 beds), medium grade. *Standhotel Winkelried* (80 beds), economy; beside lake, sailing, dancing, good food. Both with garden.

Tearoom: *Hermann.*

STEIN-AM-RHEIN. Hotel: *Grenzstein,* economy. Restaurants: *Sonne; Cafe Krone,* in Rheinfels hotel, has terrace over the Rhine.

STOOS. Hotels: *Klingenstock* (45 beds), outdoor pool, economy.

SUSTEN PASS. *Steingletscher,* inexpensive.

THUN. *Holiday, Beau Rivage* (indoor pool), *Bellevue* (outdoor pool) are medium grade. *Elite* and *Freienhof* (modernized 14th-century hotel in old town) are economy.

PRACTICAL INFORMATION FOR THE TICINO

WHEN TO COME? With mild climate the year round, Ticino is one of the sunnier spots in Europe. In midsummer, the temperature can be nearly tropical, but there are always cool breezes and plenty of shade. Spring and fall are delightfully pleasant, and though even winter is relatively mild, Dec. and Jan. can be risky—it may be cold and rainy then.

WHERE TO GO? One can divide the Ticino into three areas for exploration—Lugano and the Sottoceneri Valley, Bellinzona and the northern valleys, and Locarno and its neighboring valleys. Using these towns as a home base, from each you can make countless delightful excursions into the areas surrounding them. The simple, sometimes primitive, villages in remote valleys are one of the more fascinating aspects of the Ticino, and to visit them, you'll frequently want to go on foot, though the postal coach goes nearly everywhere. But whether your taste is for this, or the more comfortable resort towns of Locarno, Ascona, or Lugano, there are delights for everyone.

HOW TO GET ABOUT? The network of highways, railways, postal coaches, funiculars, and lake steamers is extensive in the Ticino, and there's no problem in getting from one place to another. Most people quickly discover that a leisurely pace is best—there's great delight in just wandering about and seeing the countryside and the people. If you are visiting the region for any length of time, you can save money by purchasing either a Swiss Railways Holiday Pass, which is also good for postal coaches, some lake steamers and gives up to 50% reduction on mountain railways and cable cars, or one of the seven-day Regional Holiday Season Tickets.

SPORTS. Because of pollution, bathing is banned in parts of the Bay of Lugano and at certain places around Locarno (details from local Tourist Offices). There are splendid public pools; also many hotels with private ones. Boats can be hired reasonably at the quays in any of the three towns. There are two golf courses—one at Magliaso, near Lugano, and another between Locarno and Ascona, both 18-hole. Riding, mountain climbing, and tennis are available, too. And in the Airolo/Faido region there are excellent winter sports facilities. You can ski, too, at Cimetta overlooking Locarno.

MOTELS. At **Castione**, 3 miles north of Bellinzona, *Motel Castione* (70 beds). At **Claro**, 5 miles north of Bellinzona, *Motel San Gottardo* (70 beds) and *Motel Riviera* (55 beds). At **Coldrerio**, between Lugano and Chiasso, *Motel Mobil* (123 beds). At **Lumino**, 3 miles northeast of Bellinzona, *Motel Lumino* (60 beds). At **Melano**, 6 miles south of Lugano, *Motel Lido* (60 beds). At **Mezzovico**, *Motel Mezzovico* (180 beds). At **Ponte Tresa**, *Motel Ponte Tresa* (60 beds). At **Riazzino**, between Locarno and Bellinzona, *Motel Riazzino* (70 beds), and *Motel Lago Maggiore* (70 beds). At **Vezia,** 2 miles north of Lugano, *Motel Vezia* (140 beds). At **Vira-Gambarogno**, on Lake Maggiore opposite Locarno, *Touring Motel Bellavista* (96 beds). Check in advance as some close in winter.

TROGEN. Hotel: *Krone,* pleasant chalet-type; moderate.

UNTERWASSER. Hotels: *Sternen,* medium grade. *Säntis,* economy.

PRACTICAL INFORMATION FOR THE VALAIS

 WHEN TO COME? Except for those interested in winter sports, for whom there is every variety of resort and facility, the Valais is strictly summertime country, with a few weeks' margin for late spring and early autumn. Although the summer can be quite hot along the Rhône valley with a surprising amount of sunshine, the evenings are invariably refreshingly cool. The Valais is easy to reach by train. By road, the Grimsel pass route is closed Oct. to June, but tunnels give a near certainty of traversing the St. Bernard and Simplon passes throughout the year. Road access from the Lake Geneva direction, via Martigny, is always easy.

 WHERE TO GO? Seen from a train descending from the Lötschberg heights (part of the rail trip from Bern to Brig via Spiez) the valley of the Rhône is one of the most impressive spectacles that Switzerland can offer. Almost as awe-inspiring is the view from the valley floor as one follows the rushing river Rhône by train or automobile from Sion to Brig. The visual attractions of the Valais are many and diverse: the region between St. Maurice and Sion is rich in Roman and medieval historical interest; the Grande Dixence, straddling the formidable Val des Dix, is the world's highest concrete dam and one of its engineering marvels; Zermatt, in the shadow of the Matterhorn, a sparkling resort in both winter and summer; Sion, with its towering church and castle, representing ancient struggles between church and State; Brig, the crossroads of international trade in another era, with its fascinating Stockalper Castle and remnants of Byzantine architecture; the 16th-century church at Raron, between Sierre and Brig, where poet Rainer Maria Rilke is buried; and a host of resorts varying from the fashionable, expensive Crans-Montana-Vermala group to small, secluded villages.

HOW TO GET ABOUT? Again the special holiday ticket offered by the Swiss Federal Railways is your best bet, even if you have your own car. The narrow mountain roads of the Valais are in good condition, but it is recommended that you leave them to the skill, experience, and confidence of the superbly trained driver of the flashing yellow sightseeing buses operated by the Swiss Post Office (your special holiday ticket is good for postal bus travel, too). If you're traveling from Switzerland to Italy through the Valais, be sure this part of your journey is during the day: the Valais is a spectacle which it would be a pity to miss through night travel. From Sion airport there is an air sightseeing service to anywhere in the Alps.

SPORTS. Zermatt, of course, is the winter-sports capital of the Valais, as well as the summertime departure-point for the classical Matterhorn climb. Here's news: *you* can climb the Matterhorn! If you can walk, are strong in wind and limb, have a few days to spare to get in condition, and can afford to hire one of Zermatt's expert guides, he'll get you to the top of that formidable lump of rock and bring you down again in one piece. The expedition will take a couple of days and on the way, at 12,000 feet, you'll find, wonder of wonders, the highest lavatories in the Alps.

Saas-Fee and Grächen are also excellent for skiing and mountaineering, less crowded than Zermatt. Not far from Sierre is Crans-Montana, a lovely if expensive resort area in both winter and summer. Its golf course is claimed to be one of the first ever installed on the Continent, and it is still one of the best. Farther west in the Valais, you'll find Verbier magnificent for skiing. So too is Champéry, a bit more accessible if not as much developed.

Completely different is the rustic, village resort of Zinal, with a cable car going up to 8,000 feet. And newest of all is Anzère, a purpose-built, deluxe resort to the north of the Sion.

MOTELS. At **Bex**, canton of Vaud, *Motel Saint-Christophe* (45 beds), excellent restaurant. At **Bourg-Saint-Pierre**, *Motel au Bivouac Napoleon* (40 beds). At **Charrat**, 3 miles northeast of Martigny, *Motel Mon-Moulin* (30 beds; closed Jan.). At **Gampel**, 11 miles east of Sierre, *Motel Vallesia* (30 beds). At **Lavey**, *Motel Idéal* (45 beds). At **Martigny**, *Motel La Croisée* (48 beds), *Motel des Sports* (42 beds) and *Motel Transalpin* (40 beds; closed Dec.-Feb.). At

Raron, 12 miles west of Brig, *Motel Simplonblick* (40 beds). At **St. Leonard**, 3 miles east of Sion, *Auto-Grill du Soleil* (28 beds) and *Motel 13 Etoiles* (36 beds). At **St. Maurice**, *Motel Inter-Alps* (80 beds). At **Saxon**, 7 miles northeast of Martigny, *Motel de la Tour-d'Anselme* (24 beds). At **Sembrancher**, *Motel la Prairie* (15 beds).

SHOPPING. Crans. *Watches.* A Aeschlimann. G. Saucy. **Martigny Ville.** *Watches.* F. Rhoner, Avenue de la Gare. **Montana.** *Jewelry and Watches.* Montana Bijoux, S. A. **Saas-Fee.** *Handcrafts.* Walliser Handgewebe. Gebr. Lomatter. Peter M. Zurbriggen. **Sierre.** *Watches.* W. Boillat. **Sion.** *Watches.* Horlogerie des Galeries. **Verbier.** *Watches.* Ernest Vouilloz (Artor). **Villars.** *Watches.* Grosjean-Victoria Bijoux. Art Boutique. **Zermatt.** *Cameras.* A. Perren-Barberini. *Souvenirs.* Isidor Perren-Biner. *Sports Equipment.* Sporthaus "Glacier-Sports," "Perren Sport." *Watches.* Chronométrie Stäuble. Kellerman S.A.

VERBIER. First class are *Parc, Rhodania* (both 80 beds) and *Farinet* (50 beds). Medium grade includes *Belair* (80 beds), *Grand Combin* (52 beds) and *Post* (60 beds), indoor pool. *Rosa Blanche* is economy.

PRACTICAL INFORMATION FOR VEVEY

HOTELS. The leading hotel in Vevey is the top first-class *Trois Couronnes* (120 beds), with a somewhat Victorian interior but also with a lot of comfort and character; terrace; open-air restaurant overlooking the lake. Next come the first-class *Du Lac* (90 beds), overlooking the lake, and the medium-grade *Comte* (70 beds). *Vieux-Vevey* (48 beds; sauna), *Pavillon & Buffet* (25 beds), *Suisse* (50 beds), and *Touring Gare* (52 beds) are economy grade.

On Mont Pèlerin with splendid Alpine views are the deluxe *Mirador* (90 beds; indoor pool) and top medium-grade *Parc* (150 beds; outdoor pool).

RESTAURANTS. One of the pleasantest places to eat is on top of Mount Pèlerin (take funicular from Vevey). There are several restaurants there and wonderful views across the lake to the Alps beyond. Down in the town are the *Restaurant-Tearoom Livet,* the best-known spot, and in the market-place *Chez Pierre Restaurant au Raisin,* an excellent gastronomic rendezvous. The *Buffet de la Gare* is good. By the lakeside are the *Restaurant du Casino* (lakeside terrace and park), *Restaurant du Château* (cheese specialties), and *Voile au Vent* (fish specialties). Vevey is a quiet place with little night life.

At Les Pléiades (take the mountain train from Vevey), with its panoramic view of the whole Lake Geneva region, is the simple but cozy restaurant and pension *Les Pléiades.*

About 7 miles north of Vevey, in the village square of Châtel-St.-Denis, is the atmospheric *Café Tivoli*. Noted for fondue.

SHOPPING. *BOOKS. Payot,* 51 Rue d'Italie. *PERFUMES. Parfumerie Jacinthe,* Rue du Simplon.

VILLARS (Canton of Vaud). *Parc* (150 beds), indoor pool, is deluxe. *Eurotel* (250 beds), indoor pool, and cheaper *Renardière* (60 beds) are first class. *Montesano* and *Marie Louise* are medium.

VILLENEUVE. Hotels: *Bryon,* (60 beds), first class. *Au Vieux Pêcheur,* (40 beds) medium. Economy: *de l'Aigle* (28 beds), restaurant specialty *Entrecôte Cafe de Paris; Le Château* (20 beds), excellent restaurant; *du Port* (36 beds), restaurant noted for *Fondue Bourguignonne.*

VISPERTERMINEN. *Rothorn, Gerbieden* (both 30 beds), charming chalet-style, are economy.

VITZNAU. Hotels: *Park* (145 beds), deluxe, on lake shore, lido, park, tennis, indoor pool, sauna; *Vitznauerhof* (100 beds), medium grade. *Alpenrose, Kreuz* and *Rigi* are all economy.

WEGGIS. Hotels: *Albana,* fine view, excellent cuisine (100 beds), *Alexander,* near lido (80 beds); *Beau Rivage,* lake shore (70 beds); *Park,* lakeside garden (110 beds); *Schweizerhof* (55 beds); all medium grade. In the economy bracket are *Central, National* and *Post-Terminus* and slightly cheaper *Bühlegg, Paradies, Rigi,* and *Rössli.*

WEGGIS-HERTENSTEIN. Nicely situated hotel, *Hertenstein* (100 beds), top medium grade, large park on lake, indoor and outdoor pools.

WEGGIS-LUTZELAU, located between Weggis and Vitznau: *Strandhotel* (80 beds), is economy.

WENGEN. Deluxe are *Métropole,* *Park-Beausite* (each with indoor pool, sauna) and *Palace* (with dancing). *Lauberhorn* and *Regina* (dancing) are first class. *Alpenrose, Brunner, Falken, Belvédère* and *Silberhorn* (last two with dancing) are medium grade. *Eiger,* economy.

WESSEN. Hotel: *Strandhotel du Lac,* 70 beds, economy grade.

WIL. Hotel: *Derby,* medium grade, excellent terrace-restaurant.

WILDHAUS. Hotels: *Acker* (200 beds), first class, and *Hirschen* (130 beds), medium grade; each have indoor pool. *Alpenblick, Alpenrose* and *Toggenberg,* economy.

WILGEN-SARNEN. Hotel: *Wilerbad* (130 beds); quietly situated overlooking lake; highly recommended by readers. Economy grade.

WINTERTHUR. Hotels: The family-owned *Wartmann* (70 beds), convenientin town, modern rooms with traditional feelings; *Garten Hotel* (80 beds), all rooms with bath, air conditioning, situated in park. *Krone,* with a tradition going back over 500 years. Both medium grade.

ZERMATT. One of the newest and best but not most expensive of hotels is the top first-class *Nicoletta* (110 beds; indoor pool); used and recommended by the writers. Leader of the famous Seiler group is the deluxe *Mont Cervin* (220 beds; indoor pool). Others are first-class *Monte Rosa* (100 beds) and, at 8,475 feet, the medium-grade *Schwarzsee* (16 beds).

Four well-known hotels are owned by Zermatt's burghers. Best is deluxe *Grand Hotel Zermatterhof* (170 beds).

Above Zermatt at 8,480 feet is the *Riffelberg* (60 beds); at 10,190 feet the *Kulmhotel Gornergrat* (50 beds), both medium grade, and at 11,150 feet the economy *Belvédère* (25 beds), the highest hotel in this part of the world.

Reader-recommended are the old Valais-style *Tenne* (60 beds) and cheaper *Couronne* (50 beds), both first class, the recently modernized, medium-grade *Dom*, and economy *Albana* (breakfast only).

Also excellent: first-class *Beau-Site*, and *Christiania* (both with indoor pools), *National-Bellevue*, and *Schweizerhof.* First class is the traditional-style, atmospheric *Walliserhof.* Medium-grade, *Derby.* Economy bracket (all breakfast only) *Alfa, Chesa Valese, Eden* (indoor pool) and *Europe.*

For good steaks, try *Chez Gaby*, a small intimate restaurant run by a ski instructor.

ZINAL. *Flatotel les Erables* (220 beds; indoor pool) economy.

ZUG. Hotels: *Ochsen, Rosenberg* and *Guggithal* (each about 60 beds), medium grade. *Löwen*, economy.

ZUOZ. *Castell* is medium grade. *Alva* and *Engiadina* economy.

PRACTICAL INFORMATION FOR ZURICH

WHEN TO COME? Zurich's climate is erratic the year round, though you are not likely to run into extreme heat or cold at any time. If you are lucky and arrive on a crystal clear day, and are thrilled by the sight of snowcapped mountains rising above the lake, enjoy it while you can: the very appearance of those mountains presages rain. In recent years, March has been a magnificent month, summery and clear, but there's no promise that this will continue. April and May are almost certain to be rainy and relatively cold, although you may get some blissfully warm, sunny days. Early summer through fall: the odds are with you. Winter is mostly cold, although the temperature only rarely drops below zero in the city.

All the explosive forces that are bottled inside the staid, reserved Zurichers are released during the *Sechseläuten,* a continuous program of processions, bands, fireworks and general jollification on the third or fourth Sunday and Monday in Apr. The merrymaking culminates on Monday evening in the burning of *Böögg,* a huge cotton-wool snowman symbolizing winter.

During the International June Festival, Zurich consecrates itself to the arts: music, theater, the fine arts; magnificent concerts featuring great orchestras and soloists; operas and plays performed in various languages; folk music; outstanding exhibits of painting and sculpture.

Zurich is an active city, and it's safe to say that whenever you happen to be there, something will be going on. Be sure to ask your hotel porter for a copy of the *Official Weekly Bulletin* (in English). It lists current events and sundry handy information such as restaurants, cinemas, shows, shopping. Other useful brochures are available from the Zurich tourist office (in main station), including a booklet describing excellent year-round program of excursions in and around the city.

HOTELS. If you want the best—and can afford it—the super-deluxe department alone has five in the city itself. These are:

ATLANTIS, Döltschiweg 234. On the southern fringe of the city near the 2,800-ft. Uetliberg. 330 beds; indoor pool, sauna. Has 100-bed annex in medium price bracket.

BAUR AU LAC, Talstrasse 1. Stands in its own lakeside minipark near the end of Bahnhofstrasse. An elegant, 230-bed establishment.

DOLDER GRAND, Kurhausstrasse 65. Has a long and distinguished career; 300 beds. Perched up among pine-woods on the eastern side of the city but only about ten minutes from the center. Outdoor pool.

EDEN AU LAC, Utoquai 45. A charming, popular, 75-bed hotel with a very pleasant outlook across the lake.

ZURICH, Neumuhlquai 42. A 400-bed hotel in the heart of the city beside the river Limmat. Only a few minutes' walk from the main station. Indoor pool, sauna.

Close runners-up in the deluxe category are the **ASCOT** (110 beds) **CARLTON-ELITE** (115 beds), **CONTINENTAL** (250 beds), **GLARNISCHHOF** (130 beds), **NOVA-PARK** (1,000 beds, indoor pool), **ST. GOTTHARD** (200 beds), **STORCHEN** (110 beds), and new **WALDHAUS DOLDER** (114 beds); all near center except Ascot, on southwestern fringe, and Waldhaus, near Dolder Grand. In the same category is the **INTERNATIONAL** (700 beds; indoor pool) at Oerliken, an easily reached district 3 miles from the city center. About a mile from the airport is the **ZURICH-AIRPORT HILTON** (550 beds; indoor pool) with all expected Hilton amenities and its own bus to the city.

Good value are the two first-class *Holiday Inns,* both about 7 miles from the city. The bigger (340 beds) is beside the airport; the other (270 beds, slightly cheaper), at Regensdorf; each with indoor pool. Of many first-class hotels in the city, those handy for the station and Bahnhofstrasse area include the very comfortable little *Kindli,* as well as the *Franziskaner, Glockenhof, Schweizerhof* (only hotel in Bahnhofplatz), and *Simplon.* Quietly situated near the Kunsthaus is the *Florhof* (56 beds), an elegant old mansion skillfully turned into a modern, near-luxury hotel; used and recommended by the writers. Near the Opera House is the charming *Europe,* much praised by readers and a favorite of opera stars; in the Enge district to the south, the *Engamatthof* and, nearer to the lake, *Im Park,* once a mansion where Mussolini stayed; and on the Dolder heights, the *Sonnenberg.*

Among numerous medium-grade establishments are *Ballaria, Du Théâtre,* the recently refurbished *Rigihof,* the *Helmhaus Garni* (reader-recommended), *Waldorf,* and *Zürcherhof.*

Outside the city, the *Seehotel Meierhof* (indoor pool) at Horgen, halfway along the lake, can be recommended, and at Glattbrugg there's the *Airport Hotel* (not to be confused with the *Airport Hilton);* both first class.

MOTELS. At **Adliswil,** 4 miles south of Zurich, *Motor-Inn Jolie Ville* (145 beds). At **Brutten,** 10 miles northeast of the city, *Motel Steighof* (20 beds). At

Rudolfstetten, 10 miles east, *Motel Rudolfstetten* (24 beds). At **Sihlbrugg,** 13 miles south, *Motel Sihlbrugg* (40 beds). At **Winterthur,** *Motel Wölflingen* (45 beds). All open year round.

RESTAURANTS. If cost is no object, the *Veltliner Keller* in the old part of the city (Schlüsselgasse 8, you'll have to ask a half-dozen times before you find it!) is a *must.* Here you have regional specialties (fully described in English on the menu) and wines, superbly prepared and served by colorfully costumed waitresses. Even if the food weren't magnificent, it would be worth a visit just to see the splendid carved-wood décor of the dining rooms. But it is most definitely in the expensive category.

Next (but no less important) on the luxury-gourmet list is the *Baur au Lac Grill* (E), not to be confused with the main dining room of that hotel. Here the cuisine is French at its best, with an excellent selection of regional dishes, and practically anything you want prepared to order.

Definitely a place to go to, and highly recommended is *Kronenhalle* (M–E), at the foot of Rämistrasse. The works of Matisse, Braque, Picasso, Bonnard and other famous artists which adorn its walls are all originals, and match the restaurant's friendly atmosphere and memorable food. It was James Joyce's favorite restaurant. Maybe you'll sit at the author's table in the corner below his portrait, fondly inscribed to the proprietor.

The *Rôtisserie Côte d'Or* (M–E) in the Goldenes Schwert hotel is excellent and is reader-recommended.

After you have been to the above places, you'll want to continue your gastronomical tour by trying the *Kranzler-Huguenin,* a distinctive tea-room/restaurant and a well-known confectionary shop, the *Franziskaner,* and the St. Gotthard Hotel's seafood restaurant and grill. If you insist on killing yourself, make a tour of the guildhall restaurants; the *Zunfthaus zur Zimmerleuten* (carpenters), *Rüden* (the attractive Gothic restaurant of the Society of Noblemen with the *Rüden*—the dog—in the coat of arms), *Saffran* (spice merchants), *Königstuhl, Zunfthaus zur Schneidern* (tailors), or the *Schmiden* (blacksmiths; try their Zunftwein). Good food. Swiss and Zurich specialties. Most are (M–E).

For well-prepared food from a not overelaborate menu, try the quietly elegant small restaurant (M–E) of the *Florhof Hotel* near Kunsthaus and Schauspielhaus.

On a warm evening, if the weather is good, try the *Bauschänzli* on its own little island in the Limmat River near the Quai Bridge (with concerts) or go to *Fischstube Zurichhorn* (E), built over the lake. You get there by watertaxi from the Bürkliplatz or the Utoquai. Food is excellent, but rather expensive. Very close is the recently opened *Kasino Zürichhorn.* Another good spot is the restaurant of the *Bellerive au Lac* (E), with excellent French cooking and a terrace overlooking the lake.

About 6 miles from the city center on the west shore of the lake at Thalwil is the small deluxe *Hotel Alexander am See,* and a bit farther along at Horgen the *Seehotel Meierhof,* both having restaurants (M–E) noted for their excellent cuisine.

There are few cities in Europe that

offer as many good moderately priced restaurants as Zurich: one is *Zeughauskeller*, the old Zurich arsenal at Parade-Platz, where you can dine from about 10 frs. upwards. It has an English language menu. The *Bahnhofbuffet* (main railroad station restaurant) is in the same category for price and quality, but apt to be a bit noisy. *Kropf* (I), Gassenstrasse 16, is also good value.

Zurich's equivalent to Paris' existentialist *Deux Magots* is called the *Cafe Select*, Limmatquai 16. Here you'll see bearded young poets and painters treating their blue-jeaned girl friends to Coca-Cola or milk (nothing stronger is served). Although Select in name, the spot doesn't exactly major in elegance, but for about 5 frs. you can have a good *plat du jour*.

For atmosphere, entertainment and good food try *Töndury's Widder* in a 16th-century building at Widdergasse 6, or *Kindli*, Oberer Rennweg. Dinner at the latter, with an outstanding folklore show, is expensive, but lunch is economical.

The outstanding exotic restaurants of Zurich are the *Hongkong*,

Seefeldstrasse 60 (Oriental), *Bodega Española*, Münstergasse 15, and *Emilio's*, Müllestrasse 5 (Spanish). *Chiantiquelle*, Stampfenbachstrasse 38, *Piccoli-Accademia*, Rotwandstrasse 48, *Ciro's* Militarstrasse, and *Pizzeria Napoli*, Sandstrasse 7, near Manesseplatz, all Italian.

The *Chässtube* (M), Löwenstrasse 66, specializes in Swiss cheese dishes. On the vegetarian front, the two *Gleich* restaurants, the first at Seefeldstrasse 9 and the other at Gubelstrasse 2, and *Hiltl*, Sihlstrasse 26, are all superb of their kind and inexpensive.

Deserving of special mention is a chain of restaurants called *Mövenpick* (the Swiss-German name for the seagulls around Zurich). Check addresses in the phone book. Service and décor give the Mövenpick an American look, but the cuisine is Continental and includes everything from a snack to moderately expensive grills and seafood specialties, always impeccably fresh. Also run by the Mövenpick people is a growing number of *Silber Kugel* snack bars, ideal for the budget-conscious.

 ENTERTAINMENT. Zurich's nightspots can be described as undistinguished. Without wasting too much time we can classify them as follows: Striptease/hostess—*Maxim*, *La Puce* (in the small bar), *Terrasse*, and *Red House*. Dancing—*Mascotte* (usually fine jazz), *La Ferme* (rustic decor), *Bellerive*, *Diagonal* of the Baur au Lac hotel (chic), *Hazyland* (good music; Western saloon decor), and numerous excellent discotheques. And at *Kindli* (see "Restaurants," above) there's Swiss folklore and a first-rate musical show. But as nightspots are anything but permanent institutions and can change their character, it is best to check beforehand with your hotel porter.

The Zurich *Schauspielhaus* is one of the most progressive serious theaters of Europe. If you have a special interest in the stage, you'll probably enjoy their classical and modern drama and comedy even without understanding German. The *Opernhaus* (grand opera, light opera, operetta), although not quite up to Paris or Milan standards, produces top-notch performances for the annual June festival. The *Bernhard* theater plays broad farce, the small *Theater am*

Hechtplatz is an experimental stage for all sorts of acted entertainment from musical comedy in Swiss-German patois to existentialist drama, and there are many other interesting theaters and concert halls.

Many British films are shown in Zurich soon after their London releases. Chances are, though, you will already have seen the American films. English and Italian films have their original soundtracks with German and French subtitles; French films have German subtitles. It is best to book in advance.

In July and August, the *Helvetia*, a showboat, leaves Bürkli-Platz for Rapperswil every Friday evening at around 8:15. Dancing to an orchestra. Return about midnight. Fare about 25 frs. Inquiries: Zurich Tourist Office.

MUSEUMS. The **Swiss National Museum** (Landesmuseum) is just behind the main railway station. Worth a visit, particularly if you have an interest in Swiss history (usually open 10–12 and 2–5; closed Mon. mornings; free).

The **Zurich Art Museum** (Kunsthaus), Heimplatz. Small but outstanding permanent collection, strong in French moderns. Special exhibits and loan shows are often superb.

The **Museum of Applied Arts** (Kunstgewerbemuseum), Ausstellungstrasse 60. Graphic and applied arts, outstanding in its class, fine library.

The **Rietberg Museum** has an admirable collection of primitive and Oriental sculptures.

Centre Le Corbusier (Bellerivestrasse/Höschgasse near lake) is the last building designed by the famous, Swiss-born architect, and devoted largely to his art.

Consult the complete list of museums, etc., in the *Zurich Weekly Bulletin* or museum leaflet free from the tourist office.

INVESTMENT. Unique in Switzerland, probably the world, is the luxurious *Investors' Club* recently opened by the Union Bank of Switzerland just off Bahnhofstrasse. Inside, while munching a snack or drinking coffee, you can watch world stock quotations on giant TV screens, or discuss banking or investment problems with Swiss hostesses, as expert as they are pretty. And you can go in without charge.

SHOPPING IN ZURICH. Leading south from the main railroad station and busy Bahnhofplatz (under which lies "Shop-Ville," Zurich's new subterranean shopping center) is the fashionable and elegant Bahnhofstrasse, which the Zurichers call "the Fifth Avenue of Switzerland." In this street and in those leading off to the right and left you'll find some of the handsomest shops and department stores in Europe. Opening hours 8 or 9 a.m. until 6:30 p.m. (Sats. 4 p.m.).

CAMERAS. *Foto-Bachmann*, Dreikönigstrasse 8. *Foto-Hänssler*, Münsterhof 17. *Ganz Co.*, Bahnhofstrasse 40. *Hausmann Co.*, Bahnhofstrasse 91.

W. Koch Optik, Bahnhofstrasse 11. *Eschenmoser,* Birmensdorferstrasse 20. **HANDCRAFTS AND SOUVENIRS.** *Schweizer Heimatwerk,* Rudolf-Brun-Brücke, Bahnhofstrasse 2, Rennweg 14 and Zurich Airport. *"La Ticinella,"* Fraumünsterstrasse 13. *"Spindel,"* Bahnhofstrasse 31. *Seiler Teddy's Souvenir Shop,* Limmatquai 34. *Franz Carl Weber,* Bahnhofstrasse 62.

HAUTE COUTURE. *Maison Bouchette,* Genferstrasse 6.

JEWELRY. *Allemann,* Bahnhofstrasse 26. *Pierre Baltensperger,* Bahnhofstrasse 40. *Bucherer,* Bahnhofstrasse 50. *M. Burch-Korrodi,* Bahnhofstrasse 44. *Gübelin,* Bahnhofstrasse 36. *E. Meister,* Paradeplatz and Bahnhofstrasse 28. *Solvil,* Bahnhofstrasse 37 and Bahnhofplatz Shop-Ville. *Emil Kofmehl,* Bahnhofstrasse 61.

LEATHER. *Leder-Locher Cie.,* Münsterhof 18.

OPTICAL GOODS. *Götte,* Bahnhofstrasse 98 and Löwenstrasse 29.

SPORTS EQUIPMENT. *Fritsch Co.,* Rennweg 42. *Och Co.,* Bahnhofstrasse 56. *Sträuli-Sport,* Rennweg 30.

TYPEWRITERS. *August Baggenstos,* Waisenhausstrasse 2 and Uraniastrasse 7.

WATCHES. *Ernst Albrecht,* Limmatquai 104. *W. Allemann,* Bahnhofstrasse 26. *Ed. Barth Cie.,* Bahnhofstrasse 94. *Chronometrie Beyer,* Bahnhofstrasse 31. *Horlogerie S. Brunati,* Bahnhofstrasse 24. *Bucherer,* Bahnhofstrasse 50. *E. Demuth,* Bahnhofstrasse 86. *M. Galli,* Theaterstrasse 16. *Gübelin,* Bahnhofstrasse 36. *Heinicke,* Limmatquai 32. *Eugen Hugentobler,* Limmatquai 108. *Emil Kofmehl,* Bahnhofstrasse 61. *Kurt Meier Uhren,* Bahnhofstrasse 47. *Meister Uhren AG,* Bahnhofstrasse 33. *Solvil,* Bahnhofstrasse 37 and Bahnhofplatz Shop-Ville. *Oscar Stahel,* Sihlstrasse 3. *J. Tobler,* Limmatquai 24. *A Türler Co.,* Paradeplatz and Zurich Airport. *Waldburger,* Bleicherweg 10.

CAR HIRE: *Avis,* Stampfenbachstrasse 62, also Airport-Hilton hotel; *Hertz,* Lagerstrasse 33 and Hotels International, Nova-Park and Zurich; *Europcar,* Josefstrasse 53; *Budget Rent-a-Car,* Tödistrasse 9; *Tilden International,* Lindenstrasse 33, and *Winterhalder,* Gerbergasse 4. All also at Zurich airport.

HOW TO GET TO TOWN FROM THE AIRPORT. Zurich (Kloten) airport to city center, 7½ miles. Airport coach to main railroad station 5 frs.: taxi about 38 frs. plus tip.

USEFUL ADDRESSES. *Zurich Tourist Office,* situated in main railway station. *American Consulate,* Talacker 35. *British Consulate,* Dufourstrasse 56. *Swiss National Tourist Office,* Talacker 42. *American Express,* Bahnhofstrasse 20. *Cook's,* Talacker 42. *Swiss Friends of U.S.A.,* Zunfthaus zur Simmerleuten, Limmatquai 40. *Swiss British Society,* Mythenquai 60. *Golf,* Zumikon Links (18 holes), 30 mins. by Forch tram from Stadelhofen station; Dodler Hotel, 9 holes. *Swimming,* Lido Beach on lake; Waidberg Woods pool; Dolder Hotel pool; Hallenschwimmbad, Sihlstrasse 71.

ZURZACH. Hotels: *Zurzacherhof* (100 beds, all rooms with bath) is first class. *Turmhotel,* with restaurant and terrace on top of tower (spa waters piped into hotel for baths), outdoor pool, top medium grade, and *Ochsen,* economy.

ZWEISIMMEN. *Rawyl-zum-Stern-en, Krone* and *Simmenthal* are top economy grade. Try the *Forellensee,* near Juan Pass, for delicious trout dishes.

ENGLISH-FRENCH-
GERMAN-ITALIAN VOCABULARY

ENGLISH	FRENCH	GERMAN	ITALIAN
Come in!	Entrez! (on'tray)	Herein!	Avanti!
Can anyone here speak English?	Y a-t-il ici quelqu'un qui parle anglais?	Spricht jemand hier englisch?	C'è qualcuno che parla inglese?
Do you speak English?	Parlez-vouz anglais?	Sprechen Sie englisch?	Parla inglese?
Do you understand?	Comprenez-vous?	Verstehen Sie?	Capisce?
I don't understand	Je ne comprends pas	Ich verstehe nicht	Non capisco
Don't mention it	Pas de quoi	Bitte sehr	Niente
I beg your pardon	Pardon	Verzeihung	Mi scusi
Good morning	Bonjour	Guten Morgen	Buon giorno
Good day	Bonjour	Guten Tag	Buon giorno
Good evening	Bonsoir	Guten Abend	Buona sera
Good night	Bonne nuit	Gute Nacht	Buona notte
Good-bye	Au revoir	Auf Wiedersehen	Arriveder La, Arrivederci
How are you?	Comment allez-vous?	Wie geht es Ihnen?	Come sta?
How much … many?	Combien?	Wieviel?	Quanto … quanti?
I don't know	Je ne sais pas	Ich weiss nicht	Non so
No	Non	Nein	No
Yes	Oui	Ja	Si
Please speak more slowly	Parlez plus lentement, s'il vous plaît	Bitte, sprechen Sie langsam	Parli più lentamente, per favore
Sit down	Asseyez-vous	Setzen Sie sich	S'accomodi
Thank you very much	Merci bien	Danke sehr	Grazie mille

ENGLISH-FRENCH-GERMAN-ITALIAN VOCABULARY

There is, there are	Il y a	Es gibt	C'è, ci sono
Very good ... well	Très bien	Sehr gut	Molto bene
What is this?	Qu'est-ce que c'est?	Was ist das?	Che cosa è questo?
What do you want?	Que voulez-vous?	Was wünschen Sie?	Cosa desidera?
Please	S'il vous plaît (sillvooplay)	Bitte (bi'teh)	Per piacere, per favore
What is your name?	Comment vous appelez-vous?	Wie heissen Sie?	Como si chiama?
With pleasure	Avec plaisir	Mit Vergnügen	con piacere
You are very kind	Vous êtes bien aimable	Sehr freundlich	Lei è molto gentile
Sunday	Dimanche	Sonntag	domenica
Monday	Lundi	Montag	lunedi
Tuesday	Mardi	Dienstag	martedi
Wednesday	Mercredi	Mittwoch	mercoledi
Thursday	Jeudi	Donnerstag	giovedi
Friday	Vendredi	Freitag	venerdi
Saturday	Samedi	Samstag	sabato
Is there ...	Y-a-t'il ...	Gibt es ...	C'è ...
– a bus for ... ?	– un autobus pour ... ?	– einen Autobus nach ... ?	– un autobus per ... ?
– a dining car?	– un wagon-restaurant?	– einen Speisewagen?	– una carrozza ristorante?
– an English interpreter?	– un interprète anglais?	– einen englischen Dolmetscher?	– un interprete inglese?
– a guide?	– un guide?	– einen Führer?	– una guida?
– a good hotel at ... ?	– un bon hôtel à ... ?	– ein gutes Hotel in ... ?	– un buon albergo a ... ?
– a good restaurant here?	– un bon restaurant ici?	– ein gutes Restaurant hier?	– un buon ristorante qui?
– a sleeper?	– une place dans le wagon-lits?	– einen Schlafwagen?	– una cuccetta nel vagone letto?
– a train for ... ?	– un train pour ... ?	– einen Zug nach ... ?	– un treno per ... ?

362

ENGLISH-FRENCH-GERMAN-ITALIAN VOCABULARY

— time to get out?	— le temps de descendre?	Hat man — Zeit auszusteigen?	— E ora ... di scendere
Thank you	Merci	Danke	Grazie
Where is ...	Où est ...	Wo ist ...	Dov'è ...
— the airport	— l'aéroport?	— der Flugplatz?	— l'aeroporto?
— a bank? (money exchange?)	— une banque? (change?)	— eine Bank? (Wechselstube?)	— una banca (un ufficio di cambio)?
— the bar?	— le bar?	— das Buffet?	— un bar?
— the barbershop?	— le coiffeur?	— ein Coiffeur/Friseur?	— un barbiere?
— the bathroom?	— la salle de bain?	— das Badezimmer?	— la sala di bagno
— the ticket (booking) office?	— le guichet?	— der Schalter?	— lo sportello?
— a chemist's shop (drug store)?	— une pharmacie?	— eine Apotheke?	— la farmacia?
— the movies (cinema)?	— le cinéma?	— das Kino?	— il cinematografo?
— the checkroom?	— la consigne?	— die Gepäckauf-bewahrung?	— il deposito bagali?
— the British (American) Consulate?	— le consulat d'Angleterre? (américain)	— das englische (amerikanische) Konsulat?	— il consolato d'Inghilterra? (d'America)
— the Customs office?	— la douane?	— das Zollamt?	— la dogana?
— a garage?	— un garage?	— eine Garage?	— un autorimessa
— a hairdresser?	— un coiffeur?	— ein Coiffeur?	— un parrucchiere?
— the lavatory?	— la toilette	— die Toilette?	— il lavabo?
— the luggage?	— les bagages?	— das Gepäck?	— i bagagli?
— the museum?	— le musée?	— das Museum?	— il museo?
— the police station?	— le poste de police?	— die Polizei?	— la polizia?
— the post office?	— le bureau de poste?	— das Postamt?	— l'ufficio postale?
— the theater?	— le théâtre?	— das Theater?	— il teatro?
— the railway station?	— la gare?	— der Bahnhof?	— la stazione?
— a tobacconist?	— un tabac?	— ein Tabakladen?	— una tabaccheria?

ENGLISH-FRENCH-GERMAN-ITALIAN VOCABULARY

When ... (At what time ...)	Quand ... (A quelle heure est)	Wann ...	Quando ... (a che ora)
– is lunch?	– le déjeuner est-il servi?	– ist das Mittagessen?	– A che ora è il pranzo?
– is dinner?	– le dîner est-il servi?	– ist das Abendessen?	– si cena?
– is the first (last) bus?	– le premier (dernier) autobus?	– geht der erste (letzte) Autobus?	– parte il primo (l'ultima) autobus?
– is the first (last) train?	– le premier (dernier) train?	– geht der erste (letzte) Zug?	– è il primo (l'ultimo) treno?
– does the train leave (arrive)?	– le train part-il (arrive-t-il)?	– geht der Zug ab (kommt der Zug an)?	– parte (arriva) il treno?
– does the theater open?	– ouvre-t-on le théâtre?	– wird das Theater geöffnet?	– si apre il teatro?
– will it be ready?	– sera-t-il-(elle) prêt (prête)?	– wird es fertig sein?	– sarà pronto?
– does the performance begin (end)?	– la séance commence-t-elle (finit-elle)?	– beginnt (endet) die Aufführung?	– comincia (finisce) la rappresentazione?
– can I have a bath?	– pourrai-je prendre un bain?	– kann ich ein Bad nehmen?	– poso fare il bagno?
Which is ...	Quel est ...	Welches ist ...	Qual'è ...
– the way to ... street?	– le chemin pour la rue ...?	– der Weg nach ... Strasse?	– la strada per ...?
– the best hotel at ...?	– le meilleur hôtel de ...?	– das beste Hotel in ...?	– il migliore albergo di ...?
– the train (bus) for ...?	– le train (autobus) pour ...?	– der Zug (Autobus) nach ...?	– il treno (l'autobus) per ...?
What is ...	Quel est ...	Was ist ...	Qual'è
– the fare to ...?	– le prix du voyage à ...?	– der Fahrpreis nach ...?	– il prezzo per ...?
– the single fare?	– le prix d'aller?	– der einfache Fahrpreis?	– il prezzo per l'andata?
– the round trip (return) fare?	– le prix d'aller et retour?	– der Preis der Rückfahrkarte?	– il prezzo per andata e ritorno?

ENGLISH-FRENCH-GERMAN-ITALIAN VOCABULARY

the price?	le prix?	der Preis?	il prezzo?
the price per day?	le prix par jour?	der Preis pro Tag	il prezzo per giorno?
per week?	par semaine?	pro Woche?	settimana?
the price per kilo?	le prix du kilo?	der Preis pro kilo?	il prezzo al kilo?
the price per meter?	le prix du mètre?	der Preis pro Meter?	il prezzo al metro?
the matter?	Qu'est-ce qu'il y a?	los?	Che c'è?
this?	Qu'est-ce que c'est?	das?	Che è questo?
the French (etc.) for?	Comment dit-on ... en français?	Wie sagt man auf deutsch?	Come si dice in Italiano?
Have you ...	Avez-vous ...	Haben Sie	Ha Lei ...
any American (English) cigarettes?	des cigarettes américaines (anglaises)?	amerikanische (englische) Zigaretten?	delle sigarette americane (inglesi)?
a timetable?	un horaire?	einen Fahrplan?	un orario?
a room to let?	une chambre à louer?	ein Zimmer zu vermieten?	una camera libera?
anything ready? (food)	quelque chose de prêt?	etwas fertig?	qualcosa di pronto?
any fruit?	des fruits?	etwas Obst?	della frutta?
How long?	Combien de temps?	Wie lange?	Quanto tempo?
How often?	Combien de fois?	Wie oft?	Quante volte?
I want ... would like ...	Je désire ... je voudrais	Ich brauche ... Ich möchte ...	Vorrei ...
my bill	mon compte	meine Rechnung	il conto
the chambermaid	parler avec la femme de chambre	mit dem Zimmermädchen sprechen	parlare con la cameriera
a dentist	consulter un dentiste	einen Zahnarzt	consultare un dentista
a dictionary	un dictionnaire	ein Wörterbuch	un dizionario
a doctor	consulter un médecin	einen Arzt	consultare un medico
to buy	acheter	kaufen	comprare
something to drink	quelque chose à boire	etwas trinken	qualcosa da bere

INDEX

(The letter R indicates a restaurant listing, H is a hotel or motel.)
(For an index to the Practical information section, please consult page 259.)

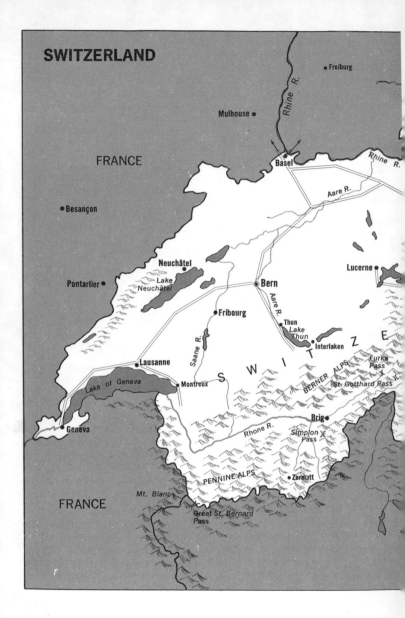

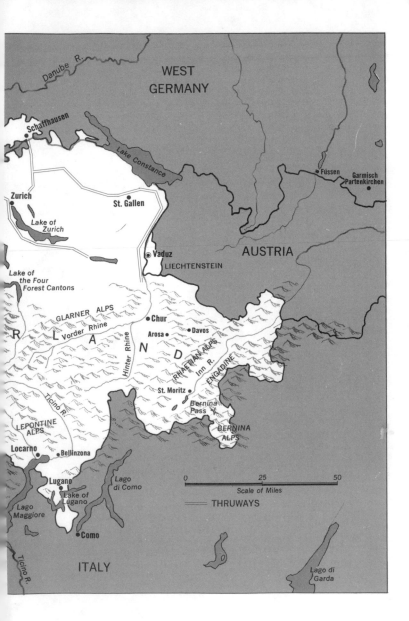